WHEN FREEDOM WOULD TRIUMPH

THE CIVIL RIGHTS STRUGGLE IN CONGRESS, 1954–1968

LOUISIANA STATE UNIVERSITY PRESS
BATON ROUGE

Published by Louisiana State University Press
Copyright © 2007 by Robert Mann
All rights reserved
Manufactured in the United States of America
An LSU Press Paperback Original
First printing

This is an abridged and revised edition of *The Walls of Jericho: Lyndon Johnson, Hubert Humphrey, Richard Russell, and the Struggle for Civil Rights*, published in 1996.

Designer: Michelle A. Neustrom
Typeface: Whitman
Typesetter: Newgen
Printer and binder: Edwards Brothers, Inc.

Library of Congress Cataloging-in-Publication Data

Mann, Robert, 1958–
    When freedom would triumph : the civil rights struggle in Congress, 1954–1968 / Robert Mann.
        p.   cm.
    "An LSU Press paperback original"—T.p. verso.
    "Abridged and revised editon of The walls of Jericho: Lyndon Johnson, Hubert Humphrey, Richard Russell, and the struggle for civil rights, published in 1996"—T.p. verso.
    Includes bibliographical references and index.
    ISBN-13: 978-0-8071-3250-0 (pbk. : alk. paper)   1. Civil rights movements—United States—History—20th century.   2. African Americans—Civil rights—History—20th century.   3. Johnson, Lyndon B. (Lyndon Baines), 1908–1973.   4. Humphrey, Hubert H. (Hubert Horatio), 1911–1978.   5. Russell, Richard B. (Richard Brevard), 1897–1971.   6. Legislators—United States—Biography.   7. United States. Congress. Senate—Biography.   8. United States—Race relations—Political aspects—History—20th century.   I. Mann, Robert, 1958–   Walls of Jericho.   II. Title.
    E185.61.M296   2007
    323.0973—dc22
                                                                2006035984

The paper in this book meets the guidelines for permanence and durability of the Committee on Production Guidelines for Book Longevity of the Council on Library Resources. ⊗

In memory of Clyde Taylor

Before the Civil War, days were dark,
And nobody knew for sure
When freedom would triumph
"Or if it would," thought some.
But others knew it had to triumph.
In those dark days of slavery,
Guarding in their hearts the seed of freedom,
The slaves made up a song:
    Keep Your Hand On The Plow! Hold On!
That song meant just what it said: Hold On!
Freedom will come!

    —From "Freedom's Plow," by Langston Hughes

Contents

Photographs follow page 98.

Acknowledgments

Originally published by Harcourt Brace in 1996 under the title *The Walls of Jericho: Lyndon Johnson, Hubert Humphrey, Richard Russell, and the Struggle for Civil Rights,* this volume is an abridged and revised version of the original text that incorporates scholarship and archival material not available in 1996. The original text and this version could not have been written without the support and assistance of others. Many people deserve my wholehearted gratitude:

My then-literary agent, the late Clyde Taylor, for his friendship, his wise counsel, and his aggressive advocacy. Clyde's sudden death several years ago was an enormous blow to his friends and family. Even now, not many days pass that I don't think of Clyde and regret that he is not on the other end of the phone line for an idle chat or a vigorous discussion of politics or history. It is to Clyde and his memory that this book is dedicated with lasting affection.

Rand Dotson, my editor at LSU Press, for his enthusiasm for the book, his counsel, and his patience while my professional responsibilities delayed the project for several years.

My original editor at Harcourt Brace, John Radziewicz, for his encouragement, his help in improving the first manuscript, and his commitment to the project; and Dan Hammer, who copyedited the original manuscript with great skill and who remains a true and valued friend.

The staff of the Lyndon Baines Johnson Library in Austin, Texas, including Allen Fisher, Linda Hanson, and E. Philip Scott; the staff of the Richard B. Russell Library for Political Research and Studies in Athens, Georgia, particularly Pam Hackbart-Dean and Sheryl B. Vogt; the staff of the Moorland-Spingarn Research Center at Howard University in Washington, D.C.; the staff at the Minnesota Historical Society in Saint Paul; and the staff of the U.S. Senate Library.

For research assistance, Sue Kerr and Marci Lichtl, who were graduate students in the political science department at Louisiana State University. For their cheerful help and guidance, I wish to give special recognition to many librarians and students at the Middleton Library at Louisiana State University and to the staff of the East Baton Rouge Parish Library.

Several people helped me immensely with their honest and insightful scrutiny of the original manuscript, in whole or in part. They are Dave Norris, George Reedy, Max Kampelman, Wayne Parent, Paul Mann, Vincent Marsala, George Brazier, Clyde Taylor, and Raymond Wolfinger. While these people improved the manuscript with their thoughtful and careful critiques, any errors of fact or any flawed conclusions are the fault of no one but the author. Those wishing to inform me of errors may write to me in care of my publisher.

I must pay tribute to the many journalists and historians whose works proved helpful to my research. In chronicling the broader civil rights movement, I benefited from several excellent sources, including Taylor Branch's well-researched trilogy of the King years: *Parting the Waters, Pillar of Fire,* and *At Canaan's Edge;* David Garrow's exhaustive biography of King, *Bearing the Cross: Martin Luther King, Jr., and the Southern Christian Leadership Conference;* Adam Fairclough's *To Redeem the Soul of America: The Southern Christian Leadership Conference and Martin Luther King, Jr.;* and *The Civil Rights Era: Origins and Development of National Policy, 1960–1972,* by Hugh Davis Graham.

I also owe debts of gratitude to Gilbert Fite for his biography *Richard B. Russell, Jr., Senator from Georgia;* Robert A. Caro for his monumental biography of Lyndon Johnson, *The Path to Power* (Vol. 1), *Means of Ascent* (Vol. 2), and *Master of the Senate* (Vol. 3); the late Merle Miller for the invaluable oral history interviews contained in his biography, *Lyndon;* the late Hubert H. Humphrey for his refreshingly candid autobiography, *The Education of a Public Man: My Life and Politics;* and Denton L. Watson, for his exhaustive biography of Clarence Mitchell, *Lion in the Lobby: Clarence Mitchell, Jr.'s Struggle for the Passage of Civil Rights Laws.*

Four books in particular helped me understand the culture of the Senate in the 1950s: *U.S. Senators and Their World,* by Donald R. Matthews; *Citadel: The Story of the U.S. Senate,* by William S. White; *Deadlock or Decision: The U.S. Senate and the Rise of National Politics,* by Fred R. Harris; and *The U.S. Senate: Paralysis or a Search for Consensus?* by George E. Reedy.

The best examination of John F. Kennedy's civil rights record is *The Bystander: John F. Kennedy and the Struggle for Black Equality*, by Nick Bryant. For those who wish to delve more deeply into the history of the Civil Rights Act of 1964, I highly recommend the fine work by Charles and Barbara Whalen, *The Longest Debate: A Legislative History of the 1964 Civil Rights Act*. David J. Garrow provides an excellent chronicle of the origins of the Voting Rights Act of 1965 in his book *Protest at Selma: Martin Luther King, Jr., and the Voting Rights Act of 1965*.

For insight into Lyndon Johnson's personality and presidency, three books that contain annotated transcripts of many of his telephone conversations were particularly useful: *Taking Charge: The Johnson White House Tapes, 1963–1964*, by Michael R. Beschloss; *Reaching for Glory: Lyndon Johnson's Secret White House Tapes, 1964–1965*, also by Beschloss; and *Kennedy, Johnson and the Quest for Justice: The Civil Rights Tapes*, by Jonathan Rosenberg and Zachary Karabell. Nick Kotz's book *Judgment Days: Lyndon Baines Johnson, Martin Luther King, Jr., and the Laws That Changed America* is perhaps the best study of the relationship between these two fascinating leaders.

I wish to thank the firsthand witnesses to many of the events described in this book for generously sharing their experiences and insight: Ellen Brown, Clark Clifford, the late J. William Fulbright, Theodore Hesburgh, Hubert Humphrey III, Proctor Jones, Max Kampelman, Nicholas Katzenbach, Anthony Lewis, Russell B. Long, Harry McPherson, Burke Marshall, George Reedy, Herman Talmadge, Strom Thurmond, Ted Van Dyk, Harris Wofford, and Raymond Wolfinger. In addition, I relied on hundreds of oral history interviews compiled by the John F. Kennedy Library, the Lyndon B. Johnson Library, the Library of Congress, Columbia University, the Minnesota Historical Society, the U.S. Senate Historical Office, the Richard B. Russell Library for Political Research and Studies, and the Moorland-Spingarn Research Center.

I must also acknowledge that some people declined or did not respond to requests for interviews in the early and mid-1990s. They include Russell Baker, Herbert Brownell, Robert Byrd, Joseph Califano, Ramsey Clark, Muriel Humphrey Brown, Edward Kennedy, Eugene McCarthy, Mike Mansfield, William Proxmire, George Smathers, Theodore Sorensen, and Jack Valenti. Although I did obtain recollections by some of these people from other sources—including oral histories—their firsthand accounts were greatly desired and would have been valuable.

In describing legislation, I relied heavily on *Congressional Quarterly's* yearly almanacs and weekly reports. Since 1945 *Congressional Quarterly* has covered the day-to-day activities of Congress with unsurpassed skill, insight, and accuracy. Its various publications are vital tools for anyone writing about Congress in the post–World War II era. For my description of debates, I primarily used the *Congressional Record,* but often the *Congressional Quarterly* or *Congressional Almanac.* As the most accurate record of the minute-by-minute proceedings of both houses, the *Congressional Record* has its shortcomings. Members routinely edited and sometimes expunged their remarks at the conclusion of a debate. While I have no reason to doubt that the notations in this book were actually spoken in debate, it is impossible to assure the reader of the *Record*'s absolute accuracy.

For their friendship and support, I also wish to thank my new colleagues at the Manship School of Mass Communication at Louisiana State University in Baton Rouge, particularly Dean John Maxwell Hamilton, Dr. Kirby Goidel, and Adrienne Moore, director of the school's Reilly Center for Media & Public Affairs. For wise counsel and friendship, I am indebted to Dr. Wayne Parent, chair of LSU's political science department and a renowned authority on southern politics.

Finally, for their support, friendship, and love, I thank my wife, Cindy, whose love and encouragement sustain me; my children, Robert and Avery; my parents, Robert and Charlene Mann; my father-in-law and mother-in-law, Alfred and Gerry Horaist; my brother, Paul Mann, and his wife, Marlo Meuli; and my sister, Sarah Luker, and her husband, Gary Luker.

WHEN FREEDOM WOULD TRIUMPH

INTRODUCTION

On November 27, 1963, Lyndon Johnson—only president for five days—stood before the U.S. House of Representatives and embraced the legacy of the nation's fallen president, John F. Kennedy. "Let us continue" the work Kennedy began, he forcefully declared to a still-grieving nation. "This is our challenge—not to hesitate, not to pause, not to turn about and linger over this evil moment, but to continue on our course so that we may fulfill the destiny that history has set for us."

The voice of the new president had a slow drawl—perhaps more Southwest than Deep South, but a drawl nonetheless. For many Americans, it was the first time they had ever heard this man, their new president, speak at any length. And what they heard from the lips of the first truly southern president in a century was unexpected and, for some southerners, distressing. Civil rights was the first part of Kennedy's legacy the new president wanted continued. "We have talked long enough in this country about equal rights. We have talked for one hundred years or more. It is time now to write the next chapter, and to write it in the books of law."

Those who knew Lyndon Johnson—understood his drive, his intellect, his intimate knowledge of congressional power, and his enormous persuasive abilities—knew that something powerful and historic was about to happen in Washington. Kennedy's advocacy of civil rights had been tentative and late in coming, reflecting the fallen president's lack of confidence in his relations with Congress. Johnson was a man of enormous insecurities, but he suffered from no deficit of confidence when dealing with Congress. In calling for passage of a strong civil rights bill—and in his private conversations with members of Congress and civil rights leaders in the days leading up to his speech—he was forceful and direct. He would see to it that Congress passed civil rights and he would use every instrument at his disposal to do it, including Kennedy's memory. "No memorial oration or eulogy could more eloquently honor President Kennedy's memory than the earliest possible passage of the civil rights bill for which he fought so long," Johnson told Congress.[1]

This is the story of the most significant and inspiring legislative battle of the twentieth century—the two decades of struggle in the halls of Congress that finally resulted in civil rights for the descendants of American slavery. It is the story of how political leaders in Washington transformed the ardent *passion* for freedom—the protests, marches, and creative nonviolence of the civil rights movement—into *concrete progress* for justice. It is a story of heroism and cowardice, statesmanship and political calculation, vision and blindness.

This story is not only about the triumph of freedom; it is also about the success of compromise and conciliation. The passage of civil rights laws is one of the finest examples of what good is possible when political leaders transcend partisan political differences and focus on more than the immediate judgment of the voters—when they consider also the ultimate judgment of history.

This story, however, does more than relate the victory—to quote Lincoln—of "the better angels of our nature." It is also the sad tale of a determined, powerful band of southern politicians who clung pitifully and shamefully to their region's brutal and oppressive past and, therefore, helped delay the march of equality for more than a decade. It is also the story of the beginning of the national Democratic Party's decline in the South as retribution for Lyndon Johnson's apostasy.

The question will naturally be asked: Could the Congress of the early twenty-first century address such an important and emotional issue in the same way? In other words, would the congressional leaders of 2006 conduct themselves with the sobriety, dignity, and statesmanship of Johnson, Hubert Humphrey, Everett Dirksen, and Robert Kennedy? Without a doubt, I believe the answer is that this story would be impossible in today's Congress. Washington is thoroughly infected with partisanship, and its political leaders are focused on short-term political aims and controlled or heavily influenced by lobbyists and political consultants. It is difficult to imagine the civil rights acts of 1964 and 1965 passing the modern House and Senate—institutions suffering from a severe deficit of statesmanship and an abhorrence of bipartisan cooperation.

When examining the passage of these bills, I was struck by the virtual absence of pollsters and political consultants from the equation. When political leaders like Johnson, Humphrey, Dirksen, and Kennedy sat down to negotiate the details of the civil rights laws, they did so without political consultants at their side and without the benefit of daily tracking polls guiding them on every nuance of the bill. Of course, these men and other leaders almost always had the political consequences of their actions in mind. They were acutely aware of public opinion, and they usually tailored their rhetoric in ways they thought most effective and appealing to the greatest number of voters. But they were not slaves to the polls, the consultants, or the lobbyists. Lyndon Johnson signed the 1964 civil rights bill in the full knowledge that it would destroy his party in the South. (Would a modern-day president do the same?) These leaders enjoyed what many politicians today have never experienced—a degree of latitude from their constituents to conduct business in ways they believed best for the nation without fear of immediate retribution. Their compromises were usually in private and reached only after considerable negotiation with ideological competitors who were also friends and neighbors, not enemies to be destroyed or investigated.

There was no C-SPAN, Fox News, or CNN featuring pundits and counterfeit journalists shouting insults and analyzing only the political ramifications of the bills, rather than their substantive details. Civil rights supporters marched in the streets and loudly picketed Washington, to be sure, but it was often the violent reaction to those protests—in Selma and Birmingham and other southern towns—that solidified public support for the bills. To the extent that the proponents and opponents of civil rights were organized to express their views to Congress—and they were organized on both sides—the expressions were generally heartfelt demonstrations of opinion, not the poll-driven and consultant-manipulated expressions the political operatives now call "grassroots lobbying."

Could the civil rights bills have passed the modern Congress? Probably so, because as Everett Dirksen said at the time, nothing can stop an idea whose time had come. Yet it is difficult to imagine these bills, in the current political environment, passing with any significant degree of dignity or high-mindedness. This is not to say that the debate was always dignified and responsible. But the worst behavior by southern racists was aberrant and often denounced or ignored.

Perhaps most significant—and, sadly, quaint—was the bipartisan nature of the civil rights bills. Leaders of both parties believed that these laws were best for the country and for the political health of their political parties; they willingly cooperated to ensure their passage, rarely attacking each other in public or in private during an arduous and politically perilous process. Nothing would have threatened passage of these bills more than an ugly partisan battle between Democrats and Republicans; nothing assured their success more than the willingness of political leaders to set aside their political weapons in pursuit of the most significant social reform since slavery's abolishment. To suggest that something similar could happen today is fantasy, and it is what makes this story all the more remarkable and instructive.

This book, then, is not just the tale of legislative battles of old; it is the story of a lost era when statesmanship was possible and when progress was achieved in ways that united the country and appealed to our highest principles, not our basest instincts. The era was far from perfect. Its leaders were deeply flawed in many ways. Yet, compared with the deplorable state of affairs in Washington today, the 1950s and 1960s were an age of enlightenment. Considering how partisanship and corruption have poisoned our political system, we would do well to study this period. To save our democracy, however, we must emulate it.

1

WE HAVE JUST STARTED OUR WORK

Two knees jutting from the shallow water along the riverbank attracted Robert Hodges's attention. The seventeen-year-old boy fishing in the Tallahatchie River just north of rural Money, Mississippi, wasn't sure what he had found. But it looked like a human body.

Shortly thereafter, on August 31, 1955, Tallahatchie County sheriff's deputies fished from the water a grotesque, decomposing body of a fourteen-year-old black boy. The body proved to be that of Emmett "Bobo" Till, a Chicago youth who had been abducted from his uncle's sharecropper's house by two white men in the early morning hours of August 28.

Several days before, Till had allegedly walked into Roy Bryant's Grocery and Meat Market in the small town of Money to buy some candy. Before leaving, according to Bryant's wife, Carolyn, Till asked her for a date and placed his hands on her waist. As he was leaving—this is one part of the incident corroborated by Till's companions—he said, "Bye, baby," and whistled at her. If Carolyn Bryant's testimony was truthful, Till's actions amounted to suicide by redneck—a dangerous and deadly breach of the South's Jim Crow code that violently protected the honor of white women against the sexual advances of black men.

If Till only whistled at Bryant, it was still a reckless and foolish act. Before he left Chicago for his summer vacation, Till's mother had instructed the teenager on the ways of her native Mississippi. "If you're walking down the street and a white woman is walking toward you, step off the sidewalk, lower your head," Mamie Till told her son. "Wait until she passes by, then get back on the sidewalk, keep going, don't look back."[1]

The exact circumstances of Till's encounter with Bryant are unknown. What is certain is that by the time twenty-four-year-old Roy Bryant returned to Money, much of the population of the rural county—black and white—knew about the incident. If he didn't defend his wife's "honor,"

Bryant knew he would be labeled a coward. Therefore, with the help of his half-brother, J. W. Milam, Bryant abducted Till, intending to "whip him . . . and scare some sense into him." In the face of Till's unrepentant and defiant attitude, the evening took an ugly and deadly turn. After beating Till to a bloody pulp, the two men used barbed wire to tie a seventy-five-pound cotton gin fan around his neck. After shooting him in the head, the men dumped his lifeless body into the Tallahatchie River, where Robert Hodges found him several days later.[2]

Bryant and Milam were soon arrested for kidnapping and later charged with Till's murder. Till's mother, meanwhile, notified reporters about her son's abduction and subsequent murder. She demanded her son's return to Chicago. When the body arrived, she overruled a written agreement with Mississippi authorities who insisted on a closed-casket service and forbade the funeral home from making her son's mutilated body more presentable. "Let the world see what I've seen," she told the funeral director. Later, she wrote, "The whole nation had to bear witness to this."[3]

The nation did bear witness. Mamie Till's determination to share her grief with the country—more than one hundred thousand mourners filed past Till's open casket in four days—turned her son into a worldwide martyr for human rights. Several weeks later, the summary acquittals of the two defendants by an all-white jury sparked a wave of outrage throughout the nation and the world, particularly among the U.S. news media, which had paid scant attention to the plight of southern blacks.[4] More important, the Till case aroused and emboldened blacks across the nation, who finally began to believe that perhaps—just perhaps—they might someday enjoy the rights of full citizenship denied for so long.

Only two months after the acquittals in the Till case, another dramatic incident further heightened the nation's consciousness about southern race relations. By refusing to carry her exhausted body to the back of an Alabama bus on December 1, 1955, seamstress Rosa Parks sparked a grassroots movement among blacks to secure their civil rights. Although the resulting citywide boycott of the Montgomery City Lines—led by twenty-six-year-old Baptist minister Martin Luther King Jr.—was among several stirrings of the modern civil rights movement, the constitutional and legislative questions about blacks and their rights as citizens had arguably been "settled," legally and constitutionally, for decades.

The Thirteenth Amendment to the Constitution, adopted in 1865, said:

Neither slavery nor involuntary servitude, except as a punishment for crime whereof the party shall have been duly convicted, shall exist within the United States or any place subject to their jurisdiction.

The Reconstruction Act of 1867 gave freedmen the right to vote. The Fourteenth Amendment to the Constitution, ratified in July 1868, said:

No State shall make or enforce any law which shall abridge the privileges or immunities of citizens of the United States; nor shall any State deprive any person of life, liberty or property without due process of law; nor deny to any person within its jurisdiction the equal protection of the laws.

In March 1870 the states ratified the Fifteenth Amendment, which strengthened the right to vote:

The right of citizens of the United States to vote shall not be denied or abridged by the United States or by any State on account of race, color, or previous condition of servitude.

Five years later, Congress passed a civil rights bill that declared:

All persons within the jurisdiction of the United States shall be entitled to the full and equal enjoyment of the accommodations, advantages, facilities, and privileges of inns, public conveyances on land or water, theaters, and other places of public amusement; subject only to the conditions and limitations established by law and applicable alike to citizens of every race and color, regardless of any previous condition of servitude.

In support of these measures, federal troops streamed into the South in the years following the Civil War. The rights of blacks were upheld, for a time, at the point of a gun. Gleeful with their newfound freedoms, most former slaves could not have imagined how the forces of Jim Crow would ultimately undermine their ostensible victories. In their euphoria, some black leaders even declared that the struggle for civil rights had ended. One leader triumphantly asserted: "All distinctions founded upon race or color have been forever abolished in the United States."[5]

As blacks soon learned, the postwar civil rights laws were, in the words of one historian, only "fragile legal props."[6] The truth was that racism was only in hibernation. When it awoke, white supremacy lurched into motion and roared with a brutal and violent fury.

Ignited by white southern leaders and fueled by the U.S. Supreme Court, white supremacy blazed across the South. It gutted the laws and constitutional protections that had briefly recognized blacks as citizens of the United States. In 1873, the Supreme Court ruled that the Fourteenth Amendment applied merely to *states*—not to individuals. Ten years later the court held that, because of its reliance on the Fourteenth Amendment, the Civil Rights Act of 1875 was unconstitutional. In language strikingly similar to arguments later used against modern civil rights legislation, the court declared that blacks could no longer be considered "the special favorite of the laws." These rulings—and others like them—nurtured an explosion of Jim Crow laws throughout the nation.

Southern states erected a variety of clever roadblocks to black voter registration, including literacy tests, cumulative poll taxes, and lengthened residency requirements. By 1900, black voters—once registered in greater numbers than southern whites—were almost nonexistent.[7]

In 1896 the Supreme Court again proved a reliable advocate for the white man when it sanctioned, in *Plessy v. Ferguson*, "separate but equal" facilities for whites and blacks. Two years later, the court upheld segregation again. Meanwhile Congress, which had passed the civil rights laws and sent the constitutional amendments to the states for ratification, retreated into a climate of hostility and indifference toward black suffrage and other rights. Some southern senators even demanded the deportation of blacks.[8]

Lynching was common in the South and also in Ohio, Illinois, and Indiana. From 1889 to 1918, more than 2,500 blacks and 702 others were reportedly lynched, many for minor offenses and "general principles."[9]

The Supreme Court's 1944 ruling in *Smith v. Allright*—declaring that the all-white Democratic primary in Texas was unconstitutional—provided the kind of sweeping change that helped blacks win back an important aspect of their citizenship. With the death of the white primary, the numbers of black voters exploded throughout the South. In 1940, before the ruling, an estimated 5 percent of eligible black voters in the South were registered. By 1947 that figure had more than doubled to 12 percent. Five years later, it was 20 percent. Despite these enormous gains, however, black registration lagged far behind that of whites: white registration in southern states ranged from 60 to 70 percent in 1952.[10]

Those who believed that increased black registration would result in greater attention and consideration from the white establishment were disappointed. Of an earlier era, historian Lerone Bennett Jr. had written: "They were a formless and shapeless mass, outgunned and out-manned, nine to one, by mean and determined adversaries who held all the high ground." Decades later, the conditions Bennett described seemed tragically immune to the march of time.[11]

Frustrated at every turn by implacable white supremacist forces in the states and in Congress—particularly the Senate—civil rights advocates took aid and comfort where they could find it. After three successive Republican administrations had ignored cries to end segregation in Washington's federal offices, President Franklin Roosevelt finally abolished the practice. Roosevelt also began integrating the armed forces and demanded that wartime industry follow equal opportunity employment practices. During his first two terms, he appointed 103 blacks to federal positions—though these were mostly clerical and lower-level executive posts. The first lady, Eleanor Roosevelt, was more outspoken about the need for civil rights and worked diligently to find federal jobs for blacks. She achieved impressive results. By 1946 the number of black federal workers had quadrupled since 1933. "The Negro had never before had this penetration into the government that he had under Roosevelt," said NAACP leader Roy Wilkins, "and he'd never had access to this many or this variety of government jobs that he had under Roosevelt."[12]

Federal employment opportunities were a step forward, but they did nothing to help the millions of black citizens straining under the weight of the South's oppressive segregation laws and customs. With the blessing of the Supreme Court, states erected all sorts of onerous restrictions on the rights and prerogatives of black citizens.

Black children were among the most pitiful victims of these statutes. In 1951 the laws of twenty-one states—most of them southern—and the District of Columbia required or permitted segregated schools. A 1944 study of the segregated South concluded that Mississippi and Georgia spent *five times* more on educating whites than blacks. Other southern states, on average, were better; the money they spent on educating white students was only three times what they spent on black schools. Salaries for white teachers were 30 percent higher than those of black teachers.[13]

With the president able to effect only incremental change and Congress unwilling to address the deplorable state of black America, civil rights advocates had only one branch of government to which they might turn. The once-hostile Supreme Court, they hoped, might now possess the will to restore the constitutional rights that southern leaders had dismantled or ignored throughout the previous seventy-five years.

As director of the NAACP's Legal Defense and Education Fund, Thurgood Marshall saw the federal judiciary as a legal crowbar. Used properly, the courts could pry open the doors of the South's whites-only schools, railroad dining cars, restaurants, and hotels.

Marshall and his legal team had been challenging specific violations of the Fourteenth Amendment throughout the country since 1936—with great success. He had argued and won the case that outlawed the all-white Texas primary in 1944. He had helped stop the use of racially restrictive housing covenants. In 1950, Marshall and his team had finally persuaded a more liberal Supreme Court to deal body blows to three aspects of segregation built upon the foundation of "separate but equal." In three cases handed down on the same day in June, the court held that physical facilities were not the only factors in judging the equality of a black law school; that universities could not deny their black students the free use of school facilities; and that segregation in railroad dining cars was unconstitutional.

The next year was a turning point. Marshall and his team finally found the cases they believed would revive the moribund Fourteenth Amendment. Consolidating five school desegregation cases from Kansas, Virginia, South Carolina, Delaware, and the District of Columbia, Marshall's team filed suit for a group of plaintiffs who maintained that segregated schools were unconstitutional. The cases became known as *Brown v. Board of Education of Topeka*. "The question," Marshall argued before the court, "is whether a nation founded on the proposition that 'all men are created equal' is honoring its commitments to grant 'due process of law' and 'the equal protection of the laws' to all within its borders when it, or one of its constituent states, confers or denies benefits on the basis of color or race."[14]

On May 17, 1954, the Supreme Court, led by its new chief justice, Earl Warren, handed down a unanimous ruling:

> We conclude that in the field of public education the doctrine of "separate but equal" has no place. Separate educational facilities are inherently unequal. Therefore, we hold that the plaintiffs and others similarly situated for whom the actions have been brought are,

by reason of the segregation complained of, deprived of the equal protection of the laws guaranteed by the Fourteenth Amendment.

The Supreme Court's imprimatur of racial segregation had suddenly vanished. Although it applied only to the segregation of public schools, *Brown* was an earth-shattering milestone in the nation's evolving civil rights movement. This monumental decision transformed race relations for the rest of the century. Blacks who marched for their rights became legitimate newsmakers, treated more respectfully by the national media. The decision was a powerful moral impetus for the desegregation of the nation's public schools. And it foretold of greater victories, holding forth hope to the embryonic civil rights movement that all forms of racial segregation and discrimination might eventually be hounded to extinction.[15]

Perhaps no group of Americans understood the potential consequences of the *Brown* decision better than southern politicians. Among this group, in the halls of Congress and in southern state capitols, reaction was swift and furious. With few exceptions, southern leaders proved that their devotion to segregation and white supremacy was far greater than the patriotic allegiance they routinely professed to constitutional government. Mississippi senator James Eastland, a fierce defender of segregation, warned that the South would not "abide by nor obey this legislative decision by a political court." Eastland defiantly warned that southern leaders would "take whatever steps are necessary to retain segregation in education." South Carolina governor James Byrnes, a retired Supreme Court justice, declared angrily that the court "didn't interpret the Constitution; it amended it" and implied the justices were tools of communism.[16]

Beyond Washington, a nationwide battle over civil rights followed with dizzying speed. White citizens' councils—some later called them "Ku Klux Klans without the sheets" or "white-collar Klansmen"—sprung up throughout the South and dedicated themselves to resisting the court's alarming attack on segregation. "We say to the Supreme Court and to the northern world," declared Mississippi judge Tom Brady, "you shall not make us drink from this cup." Brady's biblical allusion to Christ's entreaty before his death was not accidental. Many southerners believed they were about to be crucified by northern liberals, whose latest pawns were the justices of the U.S. Supreme Court.[17]

A year after the initial *Brown* decision, justices remanded the suits to lower courts with orders to oversee desegregation of public schools "with

all deliberate speed." Many southern school districts interpreted "deliberate" to mean methodical defiance, and they invented various schemes
to evade the court's decree. Virginia moved to replace its public schools
with a system of private schools; the state would pay tuition for white students. Other southern states completely ignored the court's order. Some
retrenched by adopting aggressive measures aimed at widening the scope
of segregation. In the years immediately following the *Brown* decision,
southern states enacted more than 450 laws and resolutions in reaction
to the "repulsive" notion that black children might be worthy to sit beside
white children in a public school classroom.

In some border states and in cities such as Washington, Baltimore, Lou-
isville, and St. Louis, schools quickly integrated with little controversy. The
Deep South was a vastly different case. Throughout the region, but particularly in Mississippi, reaction to *Brown* was ugly, hateful, and violent.
Three blacks were lynched in the state in 1955. Two NAACP leaders, Reverend George W. Lee and Lamar Smith, were killed for refusing to remove
their names from Mississippi's voter registration rolls.[18]

Despite such horrific repercussions, the *Brown* decision emboldened
blacks to believe that the times were changing. Nowhere was this more
evident than in Montgomery, Alabama, where a court, in December 1955,
convicted Rosa Parks of violating the state's bus segregation law by refusing to surrender her seat to a white passenger. Like Parks, growing numbers of blacks in Montgomery grew weary of the indignities forced upon
them each time they rode the city's buses. Expected to pay the same fare as
white passengers, they were treated rudely by drivers, forced to sit in the
rear of buses, and often had to relinquish their seats to white passengers.

Montgomery's civil rights leaders immediately saw Parks's case as their
best opportunity to win a legal challenge to the city's bus-seating law. For
many blacks, however, a drawn-out lawsuit seemed to fall considerably
short of the kind of visceral protest they had in mind. "There had been so
many things that happened," one woman later explained, "that the black
women had been embarrassed over, and they were ready to explode." Thus
was born the plan for a boycott of Montgomery's bus system. An estimated
30,000 to 40,000 black passengers boarded the city's buses each day—
about three-fourths of the total fares. If blacks refused to ride the buses,
the system could be crippled.[19]

The emerging boycott drew its strength from the black community's natural center—its churches. As long as the city's black ministers

supported the effort from their pulpits, tens of thousands of bus riders could be persuaded to avoid the buses. To lead the effort, activists chose the twenty-six-year-old pastor of the Dexter Avenue Baptist Church, the Reverend Martin Luther King Jr. A popular and eloquent minister, King had held his preaching position for only a few months and, according to one boycott leader, looked "more like a boy than a man." [20]

King was the son and grandson of preachers. His academic credentials were impressive, with degrees from Morehouse College and Crozer Theological Seminary and a doctorate in theology from Boston University. A devoted student of the teachings of Reinhold Niebuhr, the renowned American theologian, and Mohandas Gandhi, the Indian nationalist leader who had ended British rule through nonviolence, King firmly believed that blacks could best achieve civil rights with a peaceful approach. "We are not here advocating violence," he declared at the first of many mass gatherings to build support for the boycott. "We have overcome that . . . The only weapon that we have . . . is the weapon of protest." [21]

As the boycott enjoyed greater success—participants set up an impressive system of carpools to replace the buses—some of Montgomery's white radicals reacted violently. "Listen, nigger," growled an angry caller to King one evening, "we've taken all we want from you. Before next week you'll be sorry you ever came to Montgomery." King was deeply troubled. He had not asked to lead the movement. He had not wanted to become a lightning rod for the wrath of Alabama's white racists. The role had been thrust upon him. Three nights later, King's home was bombed during a boycott rally. [22]

Far from intimidating King and his followers, the incident renewed their commitment to the cause. For almost an entire year, Montgomery's resolute black citizens steadfastly refused to ride the city's buses. And they brought the Montgomery City Lines to its knees. A year later, on December 21, 1956, the U.S. Supreme Court upheld a lower court decision declaring Montgomery's bus-segregation law unconstitutional. The boycott was over. Thousands of triumphant blacks returned to the buses—and sat where they pleased.

Two peaceful days of integration were shattered violently in the early morning hours of Sunday, December 23, when the angry blast of a shotgun tore through the front door of King's parsonage. Later that morning, King calmly warned his terrified congregation that "some of us may have to die" in the fight for racial equality. "We have just started our work," he declared. "We must have integrated schools . . . That is when our race will gain full equality. We cannot rest in Montgomery until every public school is integrated." On that morning, with those words, King had transformed a simple, narrowly focused bus boycott into the first real battle of the modern struggle for civil rights. The historic boycott now represented not merely an end to bus segregation but the beginning of a popular national movement. From the innocent fatigue of a modest black seamstress, the nation's greatest civil rights leader had found his voice. The epic struggle for social justice was joined.[23]

2

TO HELL WITH THE SUPREME COURT

President Dwight Eisenhower's 1956 State of the Union message gave little comfort to southern members of Congress opposed to the advance of civil rights. "It is disturbing," Eisenhower told the House and Senate, "that in some localities allegations persist that Negro citizens are being deprived of their right to vote and are likewise being subjected to unwarranted economic pressures." Recommending an investigation of racial discrimination by a bipartisan commission, Eisenhower declared, "We must strive to have every person judged and measured by what he is, rather than by his color, race or religion."[1]

Despite that seemingly enlightened statement, Eisenhower was a cautious moderate who believed in pursuing civil rights advances gradually. No racist, Eisenhower was nonetheless the product of racist environments. Born in Texas and promoted through the ranks of a segregated army, he viewed the nation's racial problems through southern-tinted glasses. His 1952 election, in which he carried four of eleven southern states, marked the first time a Republican presidential candidate had earned substantial support in the South. Believing that black leaders often made unreasonable demands for civil rights, Eisenhower doubted that the federal government could eradicate prejudice by "compulsion." To an old friend he wrote that on all issues, including civil rights, he hoped to remain on "the path that marks the way of logic between conflicting arguments advanced by extremists on both sides."[2]

The *Brown* decision and its potential to incite turmoil in the South had troubled Eisenhower and helped to destroy his previously "cordial relations" with Chief Justice Earl Warren. Many southerners blamed Eisenhower for the decision because he had appointed Warren. Worried that the *Brown* case would cause southern states to abolish their public school systems, as some had threatened, Eisenhower refused to endorse the decision or to urge southern states to comply with it. This shameful lack of presidential leadership on civil rights only comforted and encouraged the growing massive resistance movement in the South. On the most important social issue of the century, Eisenhower was speechless.[3]

Any real progress on civil rights within the administration would come because of Eisenhower's attorney general, Herbert Brownell. A politically astute New Yorker, Brownell had been Eisenhower's campaign manager and chairman of the Republican party. He well understood the inherent political perils and benefits of advancing civil rights. In 1953 Brownell had been responsible for reviving two "lost" District of Columbia statutes making it a crime for a restaurant to refuse service to a black customer. He had also filed a friend-of-the-court brief with the Supreme Court in which he urged the justices to side with the plaintiffs in the 1954 *Brown v. Board of Education* cases.

On one hand, Brownell knew that a sympathetic stance on the issue might help stop the exodus of black votes from the Republican party that began during Roosevelt's New Deal. Going too far, however, might prevent Republicans from building on their southern successes of 1952.* In April 1956, with Eisenhower's reelection campaign on the horizon, Brownell prepared to take the risky step of presenting to Congress the draft of a Justice Department civil rights program.

Brownell's idea was not new. In fact, his program would eventually fall far short of the kind of activist legislation President Harry Truman had proposed as early as 1948. Nevertheless, if approved, the bill would become the first civil rights legislation enacted by Congress since 1875—and Eisenhower's party could claim much of the credit. As Brownell well understood, the Republican party already held tremendous advantages in large urban states in congressional and presidential elections. Attracting additional black support might help Republicans capture and hold dozens of marginal congressional districts.

Brownell undoubtedly realized that even if his bill failed, Republicans stood to inherit a windfall of black ballots. George Reedy, for one, theorized that Brownell's real strategy "was to send Congress a bill which could not be passed no matter which political party was in control." Reedy suspected that Brownell—"the most partisan politician I have ever met in either political party"—planned to "go before the country and talk about a

---

*In the 1952 elections, in addition to Eisenhower's election as president, the Republicans gained control of the House and the Senate.

forceful civil rights bill which was proposed by a Republican president and rejected by a Democratic Congress."[4]

After much discussion, Eisenhower finally gave Brownell his hesitant approval to "test" his bill before Congress. In April 1956 Brownell unveiled a six-point legislative draft. He asked Congress to create a bipartisan civil rights commission to investigate civil rights grievances; establish a civil rights division in the U.S. Justice Department; expand federal laws to prohibit the intimidation of voters in federal elections; authorize the attorney general to file civil injunctions for civil rights plaintiffs; permit individuals to take their civil rights complaints directly to federal courts; and allow the Justice Department to sue in cases of attempted jury or witness intimidation. Although the House eventually passed a version of Brownell's bill, Democratic senator and majority leader Lyndon Johnson of Texas—fearing the Republicans were about to steal the issue from them and that a civil rights debate would hopelessly divide Senate Democrats prior to their national convention—conspired with Russell and other southerners to keep the bill off the Senate floor.[5]

Like Johnson, Eisenhower avoided civil rights. Southern leaders, meanwhile, were encouraged not only by the president's ambivalence but by the Supreme Court's unwillingness to demand immediate compliance with its *Brown* decision. Resistance to desegregation of public schools stiffened. In Virginia, Senator Harry Byrd outlined his "doctrine of massive resistance" to integration. Scores of segregationist groups sprouted throughout the South. By 1956, the Ku Klux Klan alone boasted membership of more than 200,000.[6]

Besides passing new segregation laws, southern politicians revived constitutional challenges to *Brown* based on the philosophy of "interposition." A tenet of states' rights dogma, interposition was rooted in an interpretation of the Tenth Amendment's designation to the states and the people of all "powers not delegated to the United States by the Constitution." Employed more than a hundred years earlier by South Carolina and Virginia in an attempt to restrain federal powers, interposition enjoyed a sudden revival in southern capitols. It was the "constitutional" device of choice that the legislatures of Alabama, Georgia, Louisiana, Mississippi, and South Carolina used to challenge federal attempts to segregate their schools. Wrapping themselves in the banner of states' rights, southern governments sought to interpose the Tenth Amendment between the federal courts and their segregated schools. "The decision won't affect us at all," the superintendent of a Mississippi county had boasted after the *Brown* ruling. "That's because we're not going to observe it in our county. It will be 'to hell with the Supreme Court' down here."[7]

A controversial document conceived by South Carolina senator Strom Thurmond in early 1956 gave segregationists in Congress their first opportunity to formally declare war on the Supreme Court and its supporters. Never temperate in his approach to segregation, Thurmond proposed that southern congressmen issue a formal statement articulating their objections to the Supreme Court's *Brown* decision. Thurmond maintained the Court had misinterpreted the Fourteenth Amendment and had relied more on "the opinions of modern-day sociologists and psychologists." Furthermore, he argued, the Constitution did not mention education. Therefore, because the Tenth Amendment reserved to states all rights not accorded the federal government, education was none of the Court's business.

This, said Thurmond, meant that "public education is a matter for the States and the people to control." Thurmond wrapped all these sentiments into his draft. In a flourish, he concluded with eight declarations attacking the Court. He extolled the states that resisted the *Brown* decision, protested judicial activism, and urged "equal protection" for "all citizens where separate but equal public facilities are maintained."[8]

The leader of the southern senators, Georgia's Richard Russell, not only backed Thurmond's idea—he seized the initiative in hopes of softening Thurmond's extremist language. Assisted by Walter George of Georgia, John Stennis of Mississippi, Olin Johnston of South Carolina, and Sam Ervin of North Carolina, Russell drafted a more moderate statement that he hoped every southern senator would endorse. Even with the toned-down version, however, Russell failed to secure unanimous support of the southern bloc.[9]

George Reedy, an aide to Lyndon Johnson, regarded Thurmond's initiative as a hostile reaction to the gradual realization that "a civil rights act was inevitable." Senator Albert Gore of Tennessee agreed and recalled that Thurmond presented the text of the declaration to him on the Senate floor, "in full view" of reporters perched above in the press gallery. "I took one quick look at it and gave a flat 'No,' handing it back to him with some disagreeable emphasis because he already knew I would not sign it." Gore regarded the document "as the most unvarnished piece of demagoguery I had ever encountered."[10]

On March 12, 1956, Senator George rose on the Senate floor to read the statement, which became known as the "Southern Manifesto." (Its more formal title was the "Declaration of Constitutional Principles.") After announcing that nineteen senators and seventy-seven House members, representing eleven southern states, had signed it, George began reading the manifesto in his baritone voice:

> We regard the decision of the Supreme Court in the school cases as a clear abuse of judicial power. It climaxes a trend in the Federal Judiciary undertaking to legislate, in derogation of the authority of Congress, and to encroach upon the reserved rights of the States and the people.
>
> The original Constitution does not mention education. Neither does the Fourteenth amendment nor any other amendment . . .
>
> We commend the motives of those States which have declared the intention to resist forced integration by any lawful means . . .
>
> We pledge ourselves to use all lawful means to bring about a reversal of this decision which is contrary to the Constitution and to prevent the use of force in its implementation.[11]

Liberals quickly assailed the declaration. Senator Hubert Humphrey of Minnesota rose to discuss how the issue was undermining America's promotion of worldwide democracy. "If we persist in the course of denying people in America equal rights," Humphrey said, "we shall bring down upon our Nation the wrath of the world . . . If America ever hopes to give world leadership, we must set the pattern here in America. We have to set it unmistakably in a firm belief in human equality and equal justice under the law."[12]

The most significant aspect of the Southern Manifesto was not who signed but who *did not:* Albert Gore and Estes Kefauver of Tennessee, and Lyndon Johnson of Texas. The absence of the majority leader's signature attracted the most attention. Shortly after Walter George read the manifesto to the Senate, Senator Richard Neuberger of Oregon noted Johnson's decision. "If that is true, Mr. President, it is one of the most courageous political acts of valor I have seen take place in my life." An unabashed fan of the dynamic Senate leader, Neuberger perhaps exaggerated the extent of his colleague's valor. Johnson's decision was no surprise. Three days earlier, in a press statement, he claimed he had "neither seen this document, nor have I been asked to sign it." Because he was majority leader, Johnson explained, the manifesto's authors "did not want their statement to be constructed as an attempt to formulate senatorial or Democratic Party policy." He did not, however, denounce the manifesto or "the distinguished Senators" who signed it. "In my opinion, the solution of the problem cannot be found on the Federal level," Johnson said, "for it involves basic values reflected in the sovereignty of our states. It's my hope that wise leaders on the local level will work to resolve these differences."[13]

Privately, however, Johnson had struggled with the manifesto and the way in which it threatened to disrupt Democratic senatorial unity. "I'm damned if I do and damned if I don't," he reportedly told adviser Bobby Baker. "The Dixiecrats, and a lot of my people at home, will be on me like stink on shit if I don't stand up and bray against the Supreme Court's decision. If I *do* bray like a jackass, the red hots and senators with big minority blocs in the East and the North will gut shoot me."[14]

There was another important reason Johnson did not sign: he wanted to be president, a fact well known by his patron and mentor, Richard Russell, leader of the Senate's southern forces. In the weeks prior to the manifesto's release, Russell never pressured Johnson. "Russell was very determined to elect Johnson president of the United States," said George Reedy. "Obviously [he] knew that this would end it." In a memorandum to Johnson in June 1955, Reedy asserted "there is some evidence" that a southerner could be elected president, but not "if he were known as 'the Southern candidate.'" As Johnson surely understood, nothing would brand him an old-style southerner more than his signature on the radical Southern Manifesto. In essence, Johnson's southern colleagues let him off the hook. Senator John Stennis of Mississippi said that southerners wanted Johnson's support, but they recognized "that he wasn't just a senator from Texas, he was a leader and he had a different responsibility in that degree."[15]

Furthermore, Johnson seemed to believe that his position as majority leader—a post he assumed in 1955—required him to have a broader vision than when he had represented only his state of Texas. As early as November 1955, while still recovering from his heart attack of the previous summer, Johnson had delivered a widely publicized speech in which he unveiled his "Program with a Heart." The speech outlined a thirteen-point New Deal–style legislative agenda, including a constitutional amendment to outlaw the poll tax. Arkansas congressman Brooks Hays, who later regretted signing the manifesto, believed Johnson would not have signed it, even if pressured by Russell, not only because of his "new sense of responsibility from the national standpoint," but because he opposed the manifesto's aims. Humphrey agreed. "I knew he didn't want to classify himself in those days as a southerner."[16]

Perhaps most significant for Johnson was his growing fear that passions over civil rights would rip his party apart—a disastrous result in a presidential election year. With Eisenhower's attorney general preparing to submit a civil rights program, Republicans were making their first tentative overtures for the black vote. In a hotly contested election, Johnson knew that the issue might not only influence who occupied the White House but determine which party controlled the Senate.

The Southern Manifesto was a dangerous and foolhardy attempt to defy the Constitution as interpreted by a unanimous Supreme Court. It further separated the South from the rest of the nation and permanently stained the records of those who endorsed its racist appeals. Yet it is possible to conclude that the manifesto actually aided the progress of civil rights. Its presentation in March 1956 marked the first time that Lyndon Johnson publicly parted ways with his fellow southern senators in a substantive sense. Johnson's refusal to sign the manifesto was no endorsement of civil rights. It did, however, mark the beginning of Johnson's—and, ultimately, the nation's—long but steady voyage across the great philosophical divide that separated states' rights from civil rights.

3

THREE SENATORS

At the center of the congressional debate over civil rights stood three U.S. senators: Lyndon Johnson, Hubert Humphrey, and Richard Russell. Each a Democrat, they viewed the divisive issue through the prism of individual perspectives and unique personal experiences. Each had grown up immersed in politics; each the son of a father who served in elected office.

At fifty-eight, Russell of Georgia was the oldest, having been elected to the Senate in 1932, after serving as governor and speaker of the state House of Representatives. A dignified and reserved man, Russell commanded enormous respect among his Senate colleagues—liberals and conservatives, Democrats and Republicans. A committed bachelor, Russell had made his work his life. He understood the Senate's complex parliamentary rules and precedents better than any other senator—without exception. Armed with an encyclopedic knowledge of the rules and an unparalleled ability to employ them in debate, Russell had become one of the Senate's most respected and powerful members, as well as its most effective opponent of civil rights.

By the common definition of the word, Russell was a racist; that is, he believed in white superiority. Unlike many southerners, he did not base his opposition on any visceral hatred of blacks. Rather, he simply believed blacks were inferior to whites. "He wasn't a lyncher," said his friend and Johnson aide, Harry McPherson, "but he was certainly country bigoted in his views of blacks." Russell had supported many federal programs that provided economic and educational assistance to citizens of all races. But the success that Russell tolerated for black citizens was acceptable only in a strictly segregated environment.[1]

But unlike more-strident southern Democrats, Russell frowned on attempts to split the Democratic party over this one question. On most issues, he strongly agreed with the majority of his Democratic colleagues. As an ally and friend of President Franklin Roosevelt, he had supported most New Deal programs. Russell's leadership was largely responsible for the passage of the national school lunch program in 1946—an accomplishment he would always consider among his most important in public life. On programs like agriculture, public power, labor relations, and education, Russell was usually a Democratic stalwart. He disliked being labeled a conservative simply because he was a southerner and opposed civil rights. "It's a mistake to lump all of us southerners together," he once said, "just as it is wrong to expect people from any one section of the country to think alike." The only issue uniting southerners, Russell maintained, "is on the question of racial equality."[2]

What he saw as liberal attempts to impose a new, alien way of life on southern states deeply offended Russell. Over the years, Russell had gradually assumed greater leadership among his southern colleagues on civil rights. In 1952, hoping to prove that a southern could compete in national politics, Russell had declared his candidacy for the Democratic party's presidential nomination. He won the Florida primary, but by making civil rights such a significant part of his Florida campaign, Russell laid the groundwork for his eventual failure, highlighting the very issue that would cost him votes in every other region. Of his candidacy based primarily on opposition to civil rights, *Time* observed: "Florida showed that Russell is the candidate for the South; outside the South, he has almost no support and plenty of bitter opposition. There is no lesson of American politics clearer than that such a sectional candidacy has little chance of winning the presidency."[3] By the time of the July convention in Chicago, which awarded its nomination to Illinois governor Adlai Stevenson, Russell was an obvious sectional candidate with virtually no northern or western delegate strength.

Russell's failed candidacy demonstrated how completely the South had become isolated in presidential politics. Few men of his time were better qualified for the presidency than Richard Russell. Yet because of his position on one issue—civil rights—Democratic leaders in every region but the South summarily dismissed him as a viable candidate. While he had hoped to gain greater influence for the South in the nominating and platform process, Russell instead learned that many Democrats viewed him as an anachronistic Old South relic. The truth was now abundantly clear to Russell and other attentive southerners: No one who represented a former Confederate state could be elected president as long as he opposed civil rights.

Five years later, as the Senate debated the Civil Rights Act of 1957, the painful lessons of his 1952 campaign would guide Russell. His subtle acquiescence to Lyndon Johnson's efforts to pass that bill was born out of the bitter memories of his own failed presidential bid. Russell's failure and Dwight Eisenhower's election in 1952 eventually led Russell to conclude that Johnson might be the *only* southerner with any realistic hope of becoming president in his lifetime. In Johnson, his protégé, Russell would invest not only his presidential aspirations but also his abiding desire to restore his beloved South to the mainstream of American politics.[4]

Thirty-seven-year-old Hubert Horatio Humphrey was an ambitious, ebullient politician. He was well liked, always eager to make a new friend or win a new ally. A tireless worker, he often seemed to be juggling a hundred projects at once. "Hubert was like a whirlwind," said his friend, novelist Frederick Manfred. "He was everywhere at once, it seemed." But Humphrey cared deeply about *so many* issues. Consequently, he talked fast—and often too long. Humphrey could be eloquent at times. And when he was passionate about an issue, he rarely failed to inspire his listeners with the intense convictions that churned furiously inside him.[5]

The Minnesota senator's resolute convictions on civil rights were firmly grounded in his childhood. Born in 1911, above his father's drugstore in the small, windy prairie town of Wallace, South Dakota, Humphrey was the second of four children born to Hubert ("H.H.") and Christine Humphrey. Humphrey grew up emulating his father and his populist ideals. A devoted follower of the great populist William Jennings Bryan, H.H. regularly read Bryan's famous "Cross of Gold" speech to his children. "I heard William Jennings Bryan," H.H. once said, "and became a Democrat." Among the virtues the elder Humphrey taught his son were hard work, charity, an overflowing zest for life, and a strong sense of social justice.[6]

In 1939, after graduating from the University of Minnesota with a political science degree and a passion for the progressive New Deal politics of Franklin Roosevelt, Humphrey headed south to Louisiana. With his sights on a post-graduate degree and a teaching position, he went to Baton Rouge to pursue a master's degree in political science at Louisiana State University. He had never been to the South, but when offered a $450 fellowship to attend and teach at LSU, he accepted.

Life in segregated Louisiana quickly opened his eyes to the deplorable daily indignities suffered by southern blacks. "When I discovered the

WHITE and COLORED signs for drinking fountains and toilets, I found them both ridiculous and offensive," Humphrey recalled. "I remember my naive reaction: 'Why, it's uneconomic.' No one, I thought, could view black life in Louisiana without shock and outrage." Humphrey said the experience not only taught him about the evils of southern segregation; "it also opened my eyes to the prejudice of the North."[7]

Later, as mayor of Minneapolis in the mid-1940s, Humphrey reformed the city's official and unofficial discrimination practices against minorities. Under his leadership, the city established the nation's first enforceable municipal Fair Employment Practices Commission, and doors of opportunity began opening to blacks, Jews, and Native Americans. Humphrey also prodded his police department to show greater sensitivity to minorities. He helped establish a human relations course for police officers at the University of Minnesota. He backed up his rhetoric on tolerance with decisive action.[8]

As a candidate for the U.S. Senate in 1948, Humphrey and his allies helped transform President Harry Truman's troubled re-election campaign by persuading the Democratic National Convention to adopt a strong pro–civil rights platform plank. Truman and the party bosses opposed the plank, but Humphrey's eloquent speech to the convention was decisive. "My friends, to those who say that we are rushing this issue of civil rights, I say we are 172 years late!" Humphrey told the delegates in Philadelphia. "To those who say that this civil rights program is an infringement on states' rights, I say this, that the time has arrived in America for the Democratic Party to get out of the shadows of states' rights and walk forthrightly into the bright sunshine of human rights." To Illinois delegate Paul Douglas, who would soon enter the U.S. Senate with Humphrey, the speech was "the greatest political oration in the history of the country, with the possible exception of William Jennings Bryan's 'Cross of Gold' speech." Years later, many historians would consider it one of the most significant political speeches of the century.[9]

Elected to the Senate in 1948, Humphrey became friends with his Senate freshman colleague from Texas, Lyndon Johnson. During his Senate years, especially as majority leader, Johnson would never enjoy warm relations with the Senate's liberals; but he could not afford to dismiss them as irrelevant nuisances because he often needed their votes. In Humphrey, Johnson found a pragmatic ally, a friend, and, most important, a bridge to the liberals. Johnson admired—some thought he envied—Humphrey's speaking abilities, his intellect, and the cheerful enthusiasm he brought to any endeavor. "When I picture Hubert in my mind," Johnson said many years later, "I picture him with tears in his eye; he was always able to cry at the sight of something sad, whether it be a widow with her child or an old crippled-up man." Johnson also was often frustrated with Humphrey's impracticality and verbosity. "Your speeches are accomplishing nothing," Johnson once told Humphrey in the early stages of their friendship. "Support me and deliver your liberal friends. Otherwise . . . you'll be ignored and get nothing accomplished you want."[10]

Despite their differing styles and ideologies, Humphrey and Johnson shared common backgrounds. They were children of rural America. Their fathers were elected officials who had instilled in them an abiding respect for government service and a passion for politics. Each was elected to public office at an early age. They both distrusted the eastern political "establishment." Early in their careers, Johnson and Humphrey had been teachers and had gained important experience, prior to elective office, as administrators of New Deal programs.

Humphrey's constant appeals for cooperation with Johnson did not please the Senate's liberals, who, Maine's Edmund Muskie believed, would sometimes "rather get shot down in flames than just to get a small step forward." Never averse to taking a principled stand on an important issue, Humphrey was nonetheless "not one of those to get shot down in flames on every liberal cause," said Muskie. But, he added, "other liberals felt otherwise."[11]

By the mid-1950s, after a rocky start in Washington, Humphrey had become a respected and admired member of the Senate. Writing in the *New Republic* in 1955, journalist Robert L. Riggs astutely observed that Humphrey "has not retreated one inch from the liberal side while establishing a beachhead among Southern conservatives." Far from becoming Johnson's captive as some liberals feared, said Riggs, "Humphrey has bored from within to give liberals a means of presenting their demands to the leadership."[12]

The third senator at the center of the civil rights debate was the most significant. A tall, slender, earthy man, Lyndon Johnson, forty-eight, was consumed by ambition for power. The term "son of a bitch" seemed to roll effortlessly from the lips of those who knew him well. "He may have been a son of a bitch," said his long-time press aide, George Reedy, "but he was a colossal son of a bitch." Said aide Gerald Siegel: "He was sometimes a mean sonofabitch. He was petulant. He was capable of childish temper tantrums." Moments later, however, he could smother the object of his wrath with warmth and affection. To most, Johnson was almost entirely one-dimensional, caring only about politics and power. "The one thing that made Lyndon Johnson different from other people, I suppose," said his friend Virginia Durr, "was that when he started doing something, he poured every ounce of his energy into it and it became the great overriding thing of his life." Said boyhood playmate Sherman Birdwell: "His regular work was politics and his hobby was politics; his life was politics."[13]

A public school teacher in his early years, Johnson had once taught poor Mexican-American students in the small town of Cotulla, Texas, where he excelled at motivating his students to perform. "My students were poor and they often came to class without breakfast, hungry," he recalled years later. "They knew even in their youth the pain of prejudice." The experience had a lasting impact on Johnson. "Somehow," he said, "you never forget what poverty and hatred can do when you see its scars on the hopeful face of a young child."[14]

Elected to the U.S. House in 1937, the brash Johnson quickly befriended two of Washington's most powerful men—President Franklin Roosevelt and House Speaker Sam Rayburn. With Roosevelt's backing, he ran for the U.S. Senate in 1941, but lost by only 1,300 votes. Seven years later, he ran again, this time narrowly winning his Senate seat in an election that, most historians agree, was stolen.[15]

Johnson entered the Senate having never supported one civil rights bill. While his actions as a teacher, congressional aide, and New Deal administrator had demonstrated compassion for minorities, his voting record in Congress was "unblemished" by even one vote in favor of civil rights. He had voted against the antilynching bill in 1937 and again in 1940. In 1942, 1943, and 1945, he had opposed legislation to abolish the poll tax. In 1946 he had opposed an amendment to deny funds under the school lunch act to any state or school that discriminated on the basis of race. The same year, he voted to adjourn the House rather than consider legislation concerning a Fair Employment Practices Commission.[16]

In his congressional campaigns, however, he had never played on racial fears to win votes. He had paid perfunctory lip service to segregation, but had not made the issue a central theme. And unlike some southern members of Congress, he made no speeches to the House about the dangers that civil rights and racial integration posed to the Republic—a practice then widely known as "talking Nigra." In fact, Johnson never once discussed the issue of civil rights on the House floor during his twelve years as a congressman. "Except for his nay votes," journalist Leonard Baker said, "the issue might not have existed for him."[17]

To one-time staff member and longtime friend John Connally, Johnson was "far more liberal than he voted. But he recognized that to be an effective politician you have to survive." He was more than effective. He was, in those years, the perfect politician for his district. He worked hard to bring home all the dams and public works projects he could, while assiduously avoiding any discussion of civil rights. Politically, the strategy was sound. But for Johnson's more liberal associates and friends—chiefly his longtime friend from Alabama, Virginia Durr—his silence was not enough. She wanted action and would sometimes "bitterly" reproach him about his opposition to civil rights. Johnson always quieted her anger with a reassuring hug and the admonition, "You're dead right! I'm all for you, but we ain't got the votes. Let's wait until we get the votes."[18]

In the Senate, Johnson shamelessly courted Richard Russell, the powerful leader of southern senators. Russell saw Johnson as a new breed of southern politician with liberal *and* conservative credentials who might help transform regional stereotypes of the South. Russell's biographer, Gilbert Fite, believed that Russell saw Johnson as "someone who could bridge the gap between North and South" because of his ability to look moderate—sometimes almost liberal—while talking like a southern conservative. "I think Senator Russell recognized him as having everything that it took to be president," said Russell's aide William Darden.[19]

In other words, Russell probably saw in Johnson a steadfast opponent of civil rights who could relate to and move among the Senate's liberal coalition in ways no other southerner could. Most important, perhaps, was that Johnson—always playing the role of dutiful son—gave Russell every reason to believe that he would remain exceedingly deferential to the elder Georgian.

Exploiting his relationship with Russell, Johnson accumulated power with breathtaking speed. In January 1951, after only two years in the Senate, he was elected whip, the Senate Democrats' number-two leadership role. By 1953, with the defeat of Minority Leader Ernest McFarland of Arizona, Johnson became the Senate Democratic leader. When the Democrats took back control of the Senate in the 1954 elections, Johnson—after only six years in the Senate—became majority leader.[20]

While his energetic work habits became legendary, Johnson's amazing skill at winning votes and building majorities ultimately distinguished him as the most dynamic and successful Democratic leader ever. "He was about, face to face, as persuasive a man as you ever met," James Rowe recalled. "More persuasive than anybody I ever met. And he was a dangerous man in that sense. He could convince you black is white if you gave him enough time." Senator Russell Long of Louisiana was amazed that Johnson "could think of more reasons why you ought to vote that way sometimes than you could yourself." As he prowled for votes on and off the Senate floor, Johnson was relentless, crafty, and overpowering. Wyoming senator Gale McGee grew accustomed to Johnson's imposing frame "as he would tower over you and get his head down close to your nose, you know, and really work you over in terms of trying to convince you to take a position that he favored." The technique became known in Washington as "the Johnson treatment," because every encounter with Johnson over legislation was a physical as well as an intellectual experience. Said *Washington Post* editor Benjamin Bradlee: "When Johnson wanted to persuade you of something, when you got the 'Johnson treatment,' you really felt as if a St. Bernard had licked your face for an hour, had pawed you all over." Humphrey said Johnson won votes "by whispering in ears and pulling on lapels, and nose to nose. You have almost got to see the man. He'd get right up on you. He'd just lean right in on you, you know . . . He was so big and tall, he'd be looking down on you, you see, and then he'd be pulling on your lapels and he'd be grabbing you."[21]

Besides his imposing physical presence, Johnson seemed always to know *exactly* what argument to make or pressure point to apply with each colleague. "Johnson had almost everybody's number," marveled Howard Shuman, aide to Senator Paul Douglas. "He knew their weaknesses, whether it was women or drink, or whether they wanted a certain bill, a committee assignment, or whether they wanted more office space. He knew what almost everybody wanted." Johnson's "intelligence organization," said Washington senator Henry Jackson, "covered the Senate like the morning dew. I must say that he was a master of the doctrine that you better have your facts first before you make a move."[22]

From civil rights to farm policy, Johnson seemed to lack any overriding ideology to guide his actions or pursuits. Passing legislation and accumulating power seemed his only passions. "He didn't care whether his votes came from Joe McCarthy or Wayne Morse or Hubert Humphrey," said George Reedy. "Johnson would forget any political differences at any moment if he could get something done."[23]

At times—on issues such as housing, education, and social security—Johnson seemed to be a powerful force for progressive Democratic policies. But on oil and gas, civil rights, and labor legislation, he proved a reliable friend of the southern conservatives. When the Senate divided badly on an issue, Johnson's political philosophy—if he had one—rarely entered the picture. Rather, said Senator Herman Talmadge of Georgia, "he would work toward an area of compromise. Then he would normally get some senator who was not broadly identified with either side of the issue [to] offer some conciliatory amendment, which would normally bring the opposing factions together and succeeded in getting the consensus of the Senate in passing legislation."[24]

Another enormous factor in Johnson's success, said George Smathers, was his acute sense of timing. "He never wanted to get a bill defeated if he thought by playing it [at] the right time he could get it through," Smathers said. "He would wait 'till he heard that two guys were going to be out of town. Right away, that would go into Johnson's calculated mind and he would think: 'I'm going to bring up this vote at that time because those guys have already committed to make a speech.'"[25]

In the end, timing—combined with cold political calculation—was a strong factor in Johnson's decision to finally move on civil rights. The time for a civil rights bill had arrived.

4

GALLOPING WITH THE CROWD

The election of 1956 was Lyndon Johnson's wake-up call. The inability of the Democratic-controlled Congress to address civil rights helped send record numbers of urban and middle-class black voters flocking to Republican Dwight Eisenhower in that year's presidential election. Estimates varied, but most agreed that Eisenhower had increased his black support by almost 20 percent since 1952. The Gallup polling organization concluded that "of all the groups of the nation's population, the one that shifted most to the Eisenhower-Nixon ticket . . . was the Negro voter." More startling to Democrats was that Eisenhower carried *five* southern states while winning record numbers of black votes in a second landslide over Adlai Stevenson.[1]

Democrats were most alarmed that Eisenhower had won those southern states with the help of black voters. In 1952 Stevenson's black support had been strongest in the South. Four years later, however, the shift of blacks to the Republican ticket was most abrupt in the South. Attorney General Brownell's gambit in 1956—proposing a Republican civil rights bill—had paid great dividends. His dogged advocacy of civil rights had helped the Republicans in the North *and* the South. But Richard Nixon also deserved credit. In Harlem, the vice president had effectively appealed for black votes by arguing that the Republican party in Congress was "solidly behind" the administration's civil rights program. Nixon said if blacks supported Eisenhower "and elect a Republican Senate and House of Representatives, you will get action, not filibusters." At the Alfred E. Smith Memorial Dinner in New York, shortly before the election, Nixon declared that "most of us here will live to see the day when American boys and girls shall sit, side by side, at any school—public or private—with no regard paid to the color of their skin. Segregation, discrimination, and prejudice have no place in America." While Nixon, Brownell, and other Republican leaders recognized the potential that black votes held for continued electoral success—perhaps enough votes to make theirs the majority party—the victory did not seem to whet Eisenhower's appetite in the same way. He appeared doubly resolved to pursue an incremental, self-styled policy of "steady progress without rashness."[2]

Leaders of both political parties pored over the election returns with great interest. For Republicans, a stronger push for civil rights legislation in 1957 now seemed the clear path to greater victories in the future, perhaps even the key to winning control of the Senate in the midterm elections of 1958. For Democrats the results were more vexing. Despite the Republican presidential landslide, Senate Democrats had widened their slim majority by one vote—allowing Johnson to claim vindication for his often nonconfrontational legislative strategy. Yet a growing chorus of liberals ignored this minor triumph. They maintained that Johnson's refusal to challenge Eisenhower had, in fact, contributed to Stevenson's embarrassing defeat. Johnson and House Speaker Rayburn, they complained, had drawn no distinctions between the two parties and therefore had presented voters with no reason to reject Eisenhower.

Democratic National Committee chairman Paul Butler, an aggressive, sometimes strident liberal from Indiana, was a leading proponent of this criticism. Frustrated that Johnson and Rayburn usually disregarded the party platform and marched to their own legislative beat, Butler became an assertive spokesman for the party's liberal wing. In late 1956, hoping to unify congressional Democrats with their national committee, non-congressional Democrats such as Adlai Stevenson, Dean Acheson, Eleanor Roosevelt, Arthur Schlesinger, and John Kenneth Galbraith joined Butler to form a group known as the Democratic Advisory Council. These Democrats did not create the organization simply to challenge Johnson's leadership. Among other things, Butler and others merely wanted to prod Johnson and Rayburn into more aggressive action on the party's agenda. In that spirit, Butler invited Johnson, Rayburn, and a host of House and Senate members to join the new group. Only two—Humphrey and Kefauver—accepted. Johnson and Rayburn "thought that the place for the Democratic Party to set policy was in the Congress," said Stevenson's campaign aide Newton Minow, "and that the best politics was to go along with Eisenhower whenever possible, and fight with him only when they thought it was very, very important." Butler and other more combative liberals abhorred that strategy. Even Humphrey, Johnson's faithful liaison to the liberals, concluded that congressional Democrats must shed their legislative lethargy and begin advancing an aggressive liberal agenda.[3]

Although Humphrey had assured Johnson in a September letter that he expected to be "working *with* you" when the Senate convened in 1957, he was already preparing to side with Butler. Shortly afterward, a furious Johnson learned that Humphrey had not only joined Butler's advisory committee but had banded with other liberals to issue a sixteen-point "manifesto" containing the "new liberal program" they demanded of the Democratic leadership in the new Congress. Johnson angrily spread word among Senate Democrats that he no longer considered Humphrey a trusted member of his inner circle. In January, when Humphrey phoned to discuss routine Senate business, Johnson was distant. "You broke faith with me," he finally said. Humphrey protested. "Now, Lyndon, you know I wouldn't do that. You can get more votes out of this body than anybody can get. You are a great, great leader, Lyndon. I was simply trying to make you an even better leader."[4]

An anonymous memorandum to Johnson from an aide, probably George Reedy, reflected the seriousness of the threat to banish Humphrey. The memo's author cautioned Johnson to give "very serious thought" before "cutting off Senator Humphrey completely from any but the most formal contacts with the leadership." While condemning Humphrey's willingness to break with Johnson, the aide reminded Johnson that, of all the liberals, "he is about the only one who can be worked with to any real degree." Humphrey, the aide concluded, "is too important a prize to be lost." In the end, it appeared that Johnson had merely succumbed to one of his occasional temper tantrums. Humphrey indeed played too vital a role to be cast aside so casually. Within weeks the two men had returned to their usual friendly relations.[5]

Although he publicly denied it, the presidential election returns and the threat of a liberal revolt in his ranks *had* persuaded Johnson of the inevitability of some kind of civil rights bill. "One thing had become absolutely certain," Johnson later said. "The Senate simply had to act, the Democratic Party simply had to act, and I simply had to act; the issue could wait no longer." This realization did not mean Johnson had resolved the question of *how* he would finesse the issue without destroying his party or losing his majority leadership in an angry southern revolt.[6]

The previous fall, during a small party at the house of his aide Gerald Siegel, Johnson revealed the level of his anxiety and uncertainty when Siegel insisted that Johnson himself should move for consideration of the bill. Johnson scoffed at that notion. "You're crazy," he said. "What do you want me to do? Just move it, [and] resign from the Senate the next day?" Supporting a civil rights bill would be a dramatic reversal of Johnson's consistent opposition since 1937. While he often protested—truthfully—that he cared more about blacks than his voting record suggested, Johnson was by no objective measure a civil rights liberal. "I think it is fair to say," Paul Douglas observed, "that when Johnson was in the Senate, he opposed all methods and all attempts to liberalize the position of Negroes and other minorities." Thurgood Marshall, whom Johnson later appointed to the Supreme Court, never regarded Johnson as a liberal senator. For most of his congressional life, he was—in the words of Aaron Henry, a black civil rights advocate in Mississippi—"pretty much galloping with the [segregationist] crowd."[7]

That harsh view of Johnson, largely unchallenged, is primarily based on his congressional record and his public utterances. The reality was, however, as those who understood not only Johnson but the Senate itself knew, that no amount of dogged, inventive liberal leadership would likely vanquish Russell's southerners if they resolved to filibuster.

The name of the parliamentary device used to prevent a vote on a bill by prolonged debate derived from the Dutch word *freebooter,* meaning "plunderer" or "pirate." Nothing made Russell's southern troops more imposing on the Senate floor than their ability to pirate a debate, preventing any civil rights measure from coming to a vote. Although they used the tactic with skill, Russell's forces had not invented the filibuster; they merely adopted it from the Senate's liberals, who had made more frequent use of the weapon in pre–civil rights days.

For all of its negative connotations, the filibuster was actually a grand device steeped in Senate history and lore. The filibuster permitted the Senate to boast of its distinction as "world's most deliberative body." Legislation might be railroaded through the House, with its more restrictive rules of debate, but in the Senate cooler heads would ensure that most measures would not pass until properly and soberly considered. Until 1917, any senator with a strong will and a healthy bladder could wage a lonely battle against a bill he found offensive, unconstitutional, or dangerous to the nation. A crusading member, or group of members, could seize the floor and talk until exhausted. No Senate rule existed that could force them to relinquish the floor. Those senators from small states, with meager representation in the House, especially loved the filibuster. After all, the apprehensions of the smaller, rural colonies had led to the creation of the

Senate—the Great Compromise—an institution in which all states had equal representation regardless of size or population.

For most of its 160 years, the Senate had functioned with no rule for cloture, the process of ending or limiting debate. In 1917, however, the Senate came under attack from President Woodrow Wilson after a filibuster killed a bill to arm America's merchant ships against the Germans. Enraged that a "little group of willful men" had "rendered the great government of the United States helpless and contemptible," Wilson shamed senators into enacting a cloture rule.

From 1917 to 1949, Senate Rule XXII had required a two-thirds vote of senators *present and voting* to impose cloture. The Senate changed that in 1949, raising the bar for cloture by requiring a two-thirds vote of the entire Senate. Senators also liberalized the cloture rule slightly by subjecting "any measure, motion, or other matter" to cloture. This meant that the cloture rule required sixty-four votes—provided that all ninety-six senators voted—to stop a filibuster. By contrast, the filibusterers needed only thirty-three votes to stop any measure from coming to a vote. And so Rule XXII, the impenetrable parliamentary fortress, protected Russell and his southern troops from the growing ranks of civil rights proponents.[8]

No longer content to wait for Johnson's cautious, deliberate leadership on civil rights, the Senate's liberals declared their intent to wage an all-out fight to liberalize cloture at the beginning of 1957. On January 3, just after the Senate convened, New Mexico's Clinton Anderson moved to consider adoption of the rules. Liberals argued that a majority of senators could adopt new rules at the beginning of each Congress.*

Vice President Nixon, now courting black voters for his anticipated 1960 presidential campaign, rendered an "advisory opinion" supporting Anderson's motion. Hoping to avoid a partisan showdown with Nixon, Johnson cleverly moved to table the Anderson motion rather than challenge Nixon's opinion directly. Supported by Republican leader William Knowland,

---

*For as long as anyone could remember, tradition held that as a "continuing body," the Senate had no obligation to ratify its rules at the beginning of each Congress. The "continuing body" principle held that because only one-third of the Senate was elected every two years, the remaining two-thirds of its membership "continued" into the succeeding Congress. The point was important. Under a 1949 rules change, the Senate could not invoke cloture on a debate over changing any Senate rule. Therefore, the only way to force a vote on the issue was to assert the Senate's right to approve new rules at the beginning of each Congress.

Johnson's maneuver—having the Senate vote on a tabling motion rather than vote directly on Nixon's opinion—"let a lot of the Republicans off the hook," as Howard Shuman said. By a 55–38 vote, the Senate tabled Anderson's motion.[9]

Though the liberals had lost another round on cloture, the vote portended their ultimate success. The last time the Senate had decided the same question, in 1953, senators had voted 70–21 against Anderson's motion. That year, only five Democrats and one independent had joined fifteen Republicans in support of Anderson. This time, however, twenty-one Democrats voted with seventeen Republicans to support a change in cloture. In four years, the liberal movement had gained seventeen important votes. The additional support, Joseph Rauh believed, "began to be a tipoff to the southerners that if they gave us nothing, and they really filibustered the [civil rights] bill to death, we might beat the filibuster rule in '59." As George Reedy told Johnson in a memorandum, "the South must cold-bloodedly assess the situation . . . if it is to avoid punitive, vengeful and possibly even disastrous legislation." In another memorandum, Reedy was more direct: "If a reasonable bill is *blocked* in this session, the way will be paved to majority cloture and a really tough bill in the near future."[10]

Though Johnson clearly accepted Reedy's arguments for southern compromise, both men may have doubted that Russell would filibuster civil rights this time. In the fall of 1956, while Russell and Reedy attended a NATO conference in Paris, Russell had confided that "we can never make [Johnson] president unless the Senate first disposes of civil rights." Russell stopped short of saying that he regarded Johnson's presidential hopes as a greater priority than defeating civil rights, but he left Reedy with "the clear impression that such a thought was somewhere in his mind." More important, Johnson and Reedy now had good reason to believe that if Johnson could amend the bill to Russell's satisfaction, southern forces might wage only a perfunctory battle.[11]

Johnson knew that Russell wanted to help elect him president, but what about other southerners who cared less about Johnson's presidential ambitions? If these men refused to wage a vigorous fight, and a civil rights bill passed, how would they explain their refusal to filibuster when they returned home? If the southerners remained unified and determined, they could forestall any motion to consider a House-passed bill. But in the face of growing public support for civil rights, were they willing to face the consequences of bringing down another civil rights bill? How long could eighteen southern senators prevent the Senate from acting on one of the most pressing national issues? The answer largely depended on Russell.

Gambling that Russell's desire to see him elected president would be greater than his antipathy toward a weak voting rights bill, Johnson began to lay the groundwork for the first civil rights act in eighty-five years. On June 18 the House passed Eisenhower's civil rights bill—almost identical to the 1956 legislation—by the overwhelming margin of 286–126. As the Senate awaited the bill's arrival, battle lines were drawn.[12]

Russell, stalwart as usual, stood ready to lead his southern opposition in battle. As majority leader, Johnson quietly plotted his own legislative strategy. For now at least, he would adopt a furtive leadership role. Republican leader William Knowland would instead occupy the Senate's most visible position of leadership on civil rights.

Knowland headed an unprecedented coalition of moderate Republicans and liberal Democrats. Although Eisenhower's advocacy had sparked these Republicans' sudden willingness to support a civil rights bill, other forces were now at work. Historically allied with the southern opposition to Roosevelt and Truman's progressive agendas, some Republicans had wearied of the alliance. Said Reedy: "They did not, as a whole, throb to flood control, rural electrification, public power and parity farm programs that were absolutely essential to states that based their economies on cotton, rice and tobacco."[13] For Republicans from midwestern and northeastern states—whose small black populations posed inconsequential threats to the white majority—something vastly more significant overshadowed their old alliance with southerners against civil rights. They now worried more about the political fortunes of the national Republican party and its leader, Dwight Eisenhower. With dizzying speed, they abandoned their erstwhile southern allies on civil rights. In almost no time at all, Russell and the southerners had precious few allies outside the South.[14]

Two days after the House passed the civil rights bill, Knowland and his Democratic ally, Paul Douglas, launched their attack. They objected to the bill's referral to Judiciary. With the Senate version of the bill bogged down in committee, Knowland and Douglas had every reason to fear that a referral of the House bill would only ensure the slow death of *two* civil rights measures. At last, Douglas said, the liberals planned "to use the rules" to force action on the issue "instead of having the rules of the Senate continuously used to prevent the Senate from considering important issues." On June 20, when Russell objected to the Knowland-Douglas interpretation, the Senate overruled him, 45–39. Under the rules, the bill could now become the Senate's pending business by a simple majority vote.[15]

The roster of Russell's supporters on this vote was a curious mix of Republicans and Democrats, including several liberals and moderates: Clinton Anderson, J. William Fulbright, Albert Gore, Estes Kefauver, John F. Kennedy, Warren Magnuson, Mike Mansfield, Wayne Morse, James Murray, and Joseph O'Mahoney. Eisenhower snidely observed that those votes "struck me as rather odd" because the list included those who "normally proclaimed themselves champions of 'liberalism' and the 'little people.'"[16]

One other moderate Democrat joined in voting to sustain Russell's point of order—Lyndon Johnson. Certain that Douglas and Knowland would win, he bought time with his conservative Texas constituents by siding with Russell. To a constituent in Fort Worth, Johnson insisted he was "working to prevent the passage of legislation that would allow the Attorney General to haul our people into a federal court and prosecute them without a jury trial." While the day might soon come when Johnson would vote for a civil rights bill, a constituent uprising would only distract him from the important task of finding a reasonable compromise.[17]

As for the liberals and moderates who voted with Russell, some of their votes seemed to suggest a basic distrust of Republican leader Knowland. A former opponent of cloture, Knowland had few real civil rights credentials. His support for the bill seemed based entirely on the promise of a political windfall for his party. Among those most suspicious of Knowland was Clinton Anderson, who believed Knowland hoped the southerners would filibuster the bill to death. This, Anderson explained, "would permit him to blame the Democrats for its defeat and permit the Republicans, in future elections, to pose as defenders of the American Negro." Anderson and several other liberals wanted the bill to pass but were "wary" of what they believed were "Knowland's traps."[18]

Another, more intriguing motivation led several western Democrats—Morse, Mansfield, Murray, O'Mahoney, and Magnuson—to vote with Russell to refer the bill. All five apparently traded their votes in a deal brokered by Johnson, whereby a group of southern senators agreed to support a controversial dam and hydroelectric project on the Idaho-Oregon border.

For years, proponents had wanted the federal government to construct the dam at a site on the Snake River known as Hells Canyon. Western Republicans, the Eisenhower administration, the private power industry, and many business organizations had always opposed the plan, arguing instead for construction of three smaller, privately owned dams. In June 1956, with Johnson doing little to promote the project, the Senate had voted 41–51 to reject Wayne Morse's legislation to fund the Hells Canyon dam. At the heart of the debate was the perennial question of public versus private power. For many western politicians it was the crucial and most emotional issue of the day—far more important than civil rights.

Johnson understood the issue's importance better than most. But he also knew that the day might soon come when he and Russell's southern troops would need the goodwill and support of western moderates. So, on June 21—the day after the six Democrats supported Russell's attempt to send the civil rights bill to Judiciary—Johnson called for a vote on the Hells Canyon dam. This time, five southern Democrats who had voted against the dam in 1956 staged a sudden, "unexplained" about-face. To the utter amazement of their colleagues and the press, Russell, George Smathers, James Eastland, Sam Ervin, and Russell Long reversed their previous opposition to the project.[19]

What Johnson had accomplished was nothing short of brilliant. He had banked a tremendous amount of goodwill with western Democrats. "He made himself some friends on both sides of the issue," admitted Long, one of the southerners who had reversed his Hells Canyon vote. Years afterward, Johnson explained that he "began with the assumption that most of the Senators from the mountain states had never seen a Negro and simply couldn't care all that much about the whole civil rights issue." They did care, however, about Hells Canyon. "So I went to a few key southerners and persuaded them to back the western liberals on Hells Canyon." In return, Johnson now had grateful votes in reserve. He would spend them judiciously to secure the eventual compromise that he hoped would ultimately save the civil rights bill from defeat.[20]

All he needed now was a compromise.

5

THIS IS ARMAGEDDON

In March 1956, members of white citizens' councils throughout Louisiana embarked on an ambitious program to purge blacks from the state's voter rolls. The project was urgent, as the councils warned registrars, sheriffs, and other officials in a pamphlet: "The communists and the NAACP plan to register and vote every colored person of age in the South." Nowhere was the effort more relentlessly and successfully carried out than in Ouachita Parish, in northeastern Louisiana. Aided by the parish registrar, council members compiled a list of more than 3,400 black voters and filed affidavits challenging the voting qualifications of each. Although the affiants claimed to have examined the files of those whose registrations they challenged, the parish registrar knew better. Council members had failed to conduct a thorough examination of the rolls, and their affidavits were not sworn before the registrar or his deputy, as required by law.

The results of the council's examination were even more suspect. Each of the 2,389 black voters in Ward Ten was challenged, yet none of the 4,054 white voters was targeted. In Ward Three, the council filed affidavits against 1,008 of the ward's 1,523 black voters but only 23 whites.

Upon receiving the affidavits, the registrar dutifully mailed citations to challenged voters, instructing them to appear within ten days to certify their qualifications. The response was overwhelming. Black voters turned out in large numbers during April and May, forming lengthy lines at the parish courthouse. Sometimes they began queuing up as early as 5:00 A.M. This massive response evoked little sympathy from the registrar's office, which allowed only fifty people to plead their cases each day. As a result, most challenged voters never got the chance to prove their qualifications. The registrar summarily struck their names from the voter rolls. Those fortunate enough to have a hearing were presumed unqualified unless they proved otherwise. Furthermore, they could not call as witnesses people who lived in another precinct, those whose own voting qualifications had been challenged, or those who had been witnesses for other challenged voters.

The result was a holocaust of disenfranchisement for the hapless black voters of Ouachita Parish. In March, 5,782 blacks had been listed as voters. On October 4, after the registrar issued his ruling, only 889 remained on the rolls.[1]

Louisiana was not alone in its hostility toward blacks who wanted to vote. In one North Carolina county, the registrar gave literacy tests only to black applicants; the test required them to write the preamble to the U.S. Constitution using perfect spelling, punctuation, and capitalization. In another county the registrar required black applicants to answer a list of twenty questions. Among other things, they were required to name all candidates running for public office in the county, explain the meaning of primary and general elections, reveal their membership in the NAACP, and declare whether they would support the organization if it attacked the U.S. government. Some Alabama counties ordered blacks to calculate their age in years, months, and days. If they missed by one day, the registrars rejected their applications.

"The right to vote is the cornerstone of our representative form of government," Attorney General Brownell said as he presented the Eisenhower administration's civil rights bill to a Senate Judiciary subcommittee in February 1957. "It is the one right, perhaps more than any other, upon which all other constitutional rights depend for their effective protection." Despite his serious concerns over the white citizens' councils' assaults on black voters, Brownell and his Justice Department attorneys had no legal remedies they could employ to stop the practice. Their hands were tied. By law, they could intervene *only* when a registered voter complained that his voting rights had been denied on election day.[2]

There was much about the administration bill that southerners found objectionable. Even so, the fundamental right of adult citizens to vote—guaranteed by the Fifteenth Amendment—was not something Russell and his troops were eager to oppose on the Senate floor. "I had a sense that the southerners felt guilty about depriving the Negroes of voting," said George Reedy. "They didn't at all feel guilty about depriving them of jobs, they didn't feel sensitive about housing, but they were defensive about the vote. That they couldn't justify." Southerners treaded lightly around the bill. They would find aspects other than voting on which to base their objections.[3]

Almost a carbon copy of the administration's 1956 legislation, the new bill was divided into four parts. Although called a civil rights proposal, the bill created no new rights; it merely provided for more effective federal enforcement of laws and constitutional guarantees already on the books. Part I created a bipartisan civil rights commission, with a two-year life span, having the power to subpoena witnesses in its investigations of civil rights violations. Part II would give the Justice Department a new assistant attorney general who, Brownell pledged, would head a civil rights division. Part III would give the attorney general new injunctive powers to fight and prevent violations of voting rights and other civil rights. Part IV outlawed attempts to prevent individuals from voting in federal elections and empowered the attorney general to initiate civil actions for preventive relief.[4]

While they opposed the entire bill, many southerners particularly abhorred Part IV, which denied jury trials for defendants charged in criminal contempt actions arising from the legislation. Russell was concerned about the jury trial issue. But he was more alarmed by Part III, which gave the attorney general enormous new powers to initiate legal action against those who sought to deprive a citizen of voting rights or any other civil right. To southerners, this meant aggressive federal action to enforce the desegregation of public schools—possibly at gunpoint. Despite Russell's suspicions, it had not been school desegregation that Brownell had in mind when he wrote Part III into the bill. Emmett Till's brutal murder in Mississippi had demonstrated to Brownell "the lack of power of the attorney general . . . to act in matters of this kind." After searching the federal statutes, Brownell had been frustrated that his Justice Department was unable to identify any legal basis the federal government could use to "enforce the constitutional promise that had been made to our citizens" by the Fourteenth Amendment.[5]

Liberals, on the other hand, found Part III weak. Under its provisions, the federal government could not intervene until aggrieved individuals filed their own private lawsuits. "This meant," said Paul Douglas, "that the relatively poor and disadvantaged would have the heavy burden of initial costs and the grave danger of losing their jobs and their incomes at the hands of white rulers of their communities." Class actions were not allowed. That meant the Justice Department could not employ sweeping legal measures to address wholesale civil rights violations. Despite all its weaknesses, however, Part III was a far more potent weapon for civil rights than anything in current statutes.[6]

As it emerged from the House, the bill had remained virtually intact. While southerners had tried vainly to amend it to require jury trials for criminal contempt, few House members had complained about Part III and the vast new authority it gave to the attorney general. Ostensibly the provision merely gave the federal government injunctive power to stop illegal discrimination. "This seemed innocent enough," said Douglas, who admitted wondering why Justice Department lawyers had put it in the bill. However, Douglas added, "Dick Russell knew what it meant."[7]

On July 2, Russell rose on the floor of the Senate to speak on the civil rights bill that Knowland would call up for consideration in only a few days. His powerful speech would drastically alter the dynamics of the debate. Standing erect at his mahogany desk—directly behind Johnson's—Russell declared that approval of the House-passed bill "will cause unspeakable confusion, bitterness and bloodshed" throughout the South. In his usual low voice, he said, "If you propose to move in this fashion, you may as well prepare your concentration camps now, for there are not enough jails to hold the people of the South who will today oppose the use of raw federal power to forcibly commingle white and Negro children in the same schools and in places of public entertainment."

While proponents had characterized it as a right-to-vote bill, Russell asserted, "It is as much of an actual force bill as the measures proposed by Sumner and Stevens in Reconstruction days in their avowed drive 'to put black heels on white necks.' The powers are there, even though more cunningly contrived than the forthright legislation aimed at the South in the tragic era of Reconstruction." Furthermore and most significant, Russell explained, the Justice Department had grafted Part III to a provision of the civil rights laws that were enforceable by an 1866 statute empowering the president to use armed forces to "aid in the execution of judicial process . . . and enforce the due execution of the provisions" covered by the statute. "I unhesitatingly assert," he told the Senate, "that this section of the bill was deliberately drawn to enable the use of our military forces to destroy the system of separation of the races in the southern states at the point of a bayonet, if it be necessary to take this step." If the Senate persisted in retaining Part III, Russell hinted that he would lead a filibuster against the bill.[8]

In the wake of Russell's assault, southerners pounced on the bill, invoking horrific images of a second Reconstruction. "It would make of the southern states conquered provinces," Judiciary chairman James Eastland declared. "In its essence, it would deny to the southern states the fundamental base of the American system of government—and that is the right of self-government." Always eager to tie civil rights to the communist threat, Eastland said the bill "borrows the very worst form of Stalin tyranny" and would result in "forced integration by the use of the bayonet." The southern onslaught had its desired effect. Said *Time:* "After a while, many a conscientious Senator could no longer see the facts for the smoke." Russell's attack on Part III carried enormous weight in the Senate. "We were sunk," Douglas said. Douglas's aide Howard Shuman placed equal blame on Brownell and his lawyers, who had so "shrouded" the bill "in general language" that few understood its potential impact.[9]

Despite his apparent tactical victory, Russell knew that his southern troops were still very much on the defensive. In a story the day after the tirade against Part III, the *New York Times* observed that it was a time of "melancholy and the inner knowledge of ultimate defeat" for Russell. The irony of Russell's life, the *Times* said, "lies in the fact that he can be a primary leader only in [a] cause that he knows already to be lost in the unfolding movement of history. His mission thus cannot be to win any fight but only to lose fights as slowly as possible, one by one, and so to hold back a little longer the oncoming certainty of [a] compulsory federal civil rights program in his native South."[10]

On July 3, fifteen members of the southern bloc gathered to discuss legislative strategy in Russell's office. Russell was realistic. He stated the obvious: Despite the improving prospects that the Senate would remove the most potent provisions of Part III, the southern bloc was still under siege. Their numbers had dwindled to a core of about eighteen dependable members. Their once-loyal allies, the Republicans, had defected to the other side. With that in mind, Russell favored a nonconfrontational strategy by which southerners would not wage a futile battle to defeat the bill. Instead, he believed, they should work to so weaken it with amendments that its impact in the South would be minimal.[11]

Although South Carolina's Strom Thurmond and Olin Johnston dissented, Russell deftly guided the discussion toward a compromise rather than a divisive filibuster. While they would continue to use the specter of "extended debate" as a bargaining tool, Russell and the wiser members of the southern bloc understood the consequences of preventing the Senate from passing legislation that a majority outside the South regarded as desirable and inevitable. "I told them," Russell later said, "I would not [filibuster] because the threat of a filibuster was really more powerful than a real filibuster would have been." As the meeting ended, Harry Byrd of Virginia captured the prevailing sentiment of the group when he turned to Russell and said, "Dick, it's up to you." On Russell's recommendation, the group agreed to allow a vote on Knowland's motion to bring the bill up for consideration. "The extraordinary decision reached by the Southern group was made for a hard and simple reason," *Newsweek* observed. "They were licked from the start. Their only hope, they realized, was not to defeat the bill with parliamentary devices but to attempt to gain the best possible revision of the bill."[12]

That decision was unwelcome news for Douglas and the Senate's more dogmatic liberals. If liberal and moderate Democrats and Republicans remained a cohesive group, they could force their southern colleagues to choose between capitulation and filibuster. Either alternative was acceptable to the liberals. If they forced the southerners' hand, the best result would be a strong, effective bill. Yet if Russell's bloc filibustered the bill to death, liberals knew that civil rights would be a powerful issue in the 1958 congressional elections, perhaps resulting in an electoral mandate for a stronger bill. A compromise bill would blur the battle lines. The bill would be weaker, but it would allow the southerners to escape the wrath of most voters, even those who wanted stronger legislation.

After the July 3 meeting, Thurmond was the one member of the southern group most dissatisfied with Russell's strategy of compromise. A fervent believer in segregation, Thurmond seemed to neither grasp nor care about the dire political consequences of sinking a popular bill. Interviewed about the episode in 1989, Thurmond still seemed unable to comprehend the importance of passing a civil rights bill in 1957. He still believed that the southern group should have filibustered but had sacrificed its principles in order to elect Johnson president. "Johnson," Thurmond said, "had told them that to have a chance [at the presidency], he'd have to have a civil rights program and a civil rights bill."[13]

As the Senate approached the day it would vote to begin debate on the bill, Part III—the heart and soul of the Eisenhower-Brownell legislation—was in distress. Early on, House Judiciary Committee chairman Emanuel Celler realized that the heart of Part III was dead unless Eisenhower made an impassioned, articulate plea for its passage. That was something the president would not—or could not—do. "There seems to be no fight in the administration," Celler told reporters.[14]

In the Senate, meanwhile, Johnson exhorted his colleagues to meet the nation's lofty expectations. He avoided much of the preliminary debate, leaving the floor to Knowland and Russell, who led their respective coalitions in the early skirmishes over the bill. On July 12, Johnson began the Senate's day by paying tribute to the "high caliber" of debate on both sides. He also began to lay rhetorical groundwork for the ultimate compromise on Part III. "There will be some," he said, "who insist that it is little short of treason to dot a single 'i' or cross a single 't' in passing the civil rights bill. There will be others who will insist that it is the height of infamy to approve a single 'i' or cross a single 't.' But I think the American people have more sense than that."[15]

For some time, Johnson had known what it would take to stop the southerners from filibustering. Russell had presented his terms with unmistakable clarity: the gutting of Part III and approval of an amendment to Part IV providing for jury trials in criminal contempt cases. This was the price for southern acquiescence—to render the bill a toothless voting rights measure.[16]

Yet Johnson knew that he and Russell alone did not have the votes to pay this price. Most of the votes to kill Part III and amend Part IV would, of necessity, come from outside the southern bloc. Finding these votes would not be easy. Johnson would have to deal, call in favors, and issue threats. He would also have to keep the Senate debate dignified and, more important, civilized. Johnson feared that George Reedy's early assessment might be correct: "The thinking of both pro- and anti–civil righters is so polarized that *one side cannot vote for anything* and *the other side cannot vote for anything but everything.* The only solution in such an impasse is for reasonable men to emerge with a measure which may not satisfy the pro and the antis but *which is so demonstrably reasonable that it will satisfy the country.*"[17]

Achieving the compromise that Johnson and Russell needed—one that could muster a majority on the Senate floor—would require all of Johnson's immense powers of persuasion. In the Senate, every member had his or her own unique definition of *reasonable*. James Rowe, who volunteered his views in a July 3 memorandum, sized up the situation well when he observed, "This is Armageddon for Lyndon Johnson."[18]

On July 16, Johnson broke new ground. He rose to announce that he would support Knowland's motion to call up the civil rights bill. Yet he quickly added that he would also vote for three other motions: to refer the bill to the Judiciary Committee for seven days, to water down Part III, and to add a jury trial provision to Part IV. Although his position on the bill was not yet entirely clear—he insisted that his vote for Knowland's motion "should not be construed as a vote in support of the bill"—those who knew him understood exactly what he meant by the following admonition: "I think the members of this body should debate it, discuss it, amend it, improve it and then vote on it."[19]

On July 16, 1957, the decades-old coalition of southern Democrats and conservative Republicans died. The Senate finally voted, 71–18, for Knowland's motion to begin formal debate on the House-passed bill. When the presiding officer announced the tally, Johnson and Knowland leaned across the narrow aisle that divided the Republican and Democratic halves of the chamber and shook hands. Meanwhile, eighteen lonely southerners— abandoned by their former Republican allies and now exposed as the last defenders of the Old South—had weathered the prevailing national winds by voting to deny the Senate the opportunity to debate the bill. Despite the overwhelming vote, Johnson knew that much of the bill's support rested on shifting legislative sand. Russell's rhetoric after the vote was evidence of the precarious situation. The southern leader kept up his steady drumbeat of opposition. He ominously warned that his troops were "prepared to extend the greatest effort ever made in history to prevent passage of this bill in its present form." Russell dismissed the lopsided vote. His forces, he declared beforehand, would "muster nothing like our total strength."[20]

Johnson knew that Russell was at least partially correct. Although the southerners were massively outnumbered on civil rights, they held at least one significant advantage over the liberals: they were *united,* almost to a man, in their goal of weakening the bill. The liberals and Republicans, on the other hand, were anything but a cohesive group. Some Republicans— Irving Ives and Jacob Javits of New York, Clifford Case of New Jersey, and Charles Potter of Michigan—were prepared to resist any compromise at all. Others, such as Karl Mundt of South Dakota and Milton Young of North Dakota, seemed agreeable to almost any type of compromise proposal. In the middle were the vast majority of Republicans, open to compromise but unwilling to give the southerners *everything.* The nonsouthern Democrats were split, too. The dogmatic liberals led by Douglas equated compromise with treason, while western Democrats—such as Clinton Anderson, Bob Kerr, Frank Church, and Joseph O'Mahoney—were eager for a reasonable bargain.

With so many groups playing so many different political games, the southerners remained the Senate's most cohesive faction. If he could not find a way to resolve southern concerns over Parts III and IV, Johnson knew that the fragile majority supporting the bill would run headlong into a powerful, well-oiled southern filibuster machine.[21]

6

THE BEST WE COULD GET

"I think there is a way that you can finally put the other provisions through, and then the other southerners would have no real reason to go on with their filibuster." Those words from New Mexico's Clinton Anderson were music to Johnson's ears. He knew that the Senate must drastically weaken Part III to prevent a southern filibuster. Now, here was a trusted member of the liberal bloc volunteering to lead the fight.[1]

Anderson's civil rights credentials were impeccable, but he understood that the "best" legislation would have no effect at all unless it could win the votes for passage. For several days before the Senate voted to take up the bill, he had "glued" himself to his desk on the Senate floor, where he listened intently to the debate over Part III. Anderson concluded that "if you could just remove the southern fears that we would march an army into the South, it would be worthwhile." After a couple of days, Johnson sidled over to ask Anderson why he was so interested in this debate. When Anderson volunteered that he was considering an amendment to strike the most potent provisions of Part III, Johnson urged him to do it—and offered a suggestion. "He thought I should get a really good Republican to join with me." After surveying the Senate, Anderson selected two respected Republican moderates: George Aiken of Vermont and Francis Case of South Dakota.[2]

Johnson instinctively understood the benefit of a liberal westerner and two moderate Republicans proposing to gut Part III. Had Russell or another conservative southerner presented the same amendment, liberals would have held it up as a willful attempt to destroy the bill by eliminating its strongest provision. It would have been anathema to everyone but the small southern minority. For many liberals, an Anderson-Aiken-Case amendment was a different matter altogether. The liberal Democrats and moderate Republicans who supported Part III could not intimate that these men were allies of Richard Russell. Their amendment immediately disarmed liberal critics, making it exceedingly easier for Johnson to find the votes to pay the first installment of his agreement with Russell.[3]

The unexpected assistance from Anderson, Aiken, and Case also complicated matters for Russell's southern bloc. His sudden inheritance of liberal and moderate support foreclosed Russell's ability to filibuster. "If you were going to filibuster," George Reedy observed, "it's one thing to filibuster when nobody is agreeing with you, when you're standing there with your back to the wall. But when you start getting some reason and some cooperation from the other side, that puts you on a bad spot. You can't really filibuster then." From that point on, Reedy said, the southerners "laid down and they played dead."[4]

Nothing, however, furthered the effort to emasculate Part III more than Eisenhower's weak, faltering defense of his own bill. The day after the Senate voted to consider the bill, the president appeared before the White House press corps. At earlier meetings with the media, the president had undercut Knowland's leadership by admitting his ignorance of the House-passed bill. A question from reporter Rowland Evans sealed the fate of Part III. Evans asked if it would be "a wise extension of federal power" to permit the attorney general "to bring suits on his own motion, to enforce school integration in the South."

"Well, no," Eisenhower responded. "I have—as a matter of fact, as you state it that way, on his own motion, without any request from local authorities, I suppose is what you are talking about?"

"Yes, sir," Evans replied. "I think that that is what the bill would do, Part III."[5]

Through the fog of apparent ignorance of his bill, Eisenhower's signal was clear: He did not support Part III. Blindsided again by Eisenhower's inept defense of the legislation, Knowland did what he could to absolve his president of the blame. He argued, weakly, that "the details of the bill belong to this body and to the other body of Congress." With Knowland's leadership undercut by the White House, Johnson quickly moved to fill the void. He launched his strategy to weaken Part III and began rounding up the necessary votes to do it.[6]

Now Johnson supplemented daily exhortations for lofty, dignified debate with aggressive appeals for deleting the heart of Part III. "The vote on Part III is of crucial importance," he told the Senate on July 24. "It can well make the difference between achievement and futility." Minutes later, Johnson's brand of pragmatism prevailed. The Senate approved the

Anderson-Aiken-Case amendment, 52–38. Part III was dead. "I believe the bill was strengthened," Johnson told senators the next day. To the contrary, the bill was weakened. Only its chances for passage had improved. Liberals correctly asserted that striking the core of Part III would weaken it considerably. Yet the strong bill that Douglas and Knowland wanted would only have ensured a southern filibuster and a bitterly divided Democratic party.[7]

Throughout the debate, Johnson showed many faces to many people. He soothed Russell with sympathetic language: "These Negroes, they're getting pretty uppity these days and that's a problem for us since they've got something now they never had before, the political pull to back up their uppityness." With other conservatives he tried a different approach: "If you don't pass this moderate bill, you're going to have a bill crammed down your throat because Richard Nixon is very smart politically and he is courting black people right now and you're going to get something that you can't live with."[8]

Speaking to his friend Humphrey, Johnson ridiculed the ease with which northern liberals supported civil rights. "Hubert, it don't take any genius to be for civil rights from Minnesota," Johnson said. "How many black people you got in Minnesota?" "Well, we've got about 12,000," Humphrey replied. "Well," Johnson muttered, "you make me sick." With other liberals Johnson played an enlightened moderate who was forced to shoulder the embarrassing burden of his Neanderthal southern colleagues. Years after the 1957 Civil Rights Act became law, Harry McPherson still had vivid memories of the day Johnson burst into the Democratic cloakroom and said to Paul Douglas, "Paul, be ready. The civil rights bill, we're going to have it up at two o'clock. We got it worked out. You and your boys be there." Johnson left the cloakroom. Several minutes later he was back. This time he spotted Sam Ervin. "Sam," he said, "get everybody here at two o'clock. We're going to get the nigger bill up." McPherson thought Johnson's behavior was "appalling," but he understood Johnson's need to romance both sides. "This is a leader trying to keep everything in the air, keep it going, every day making a speech about how reasonable and moderate and modest" the bill was.[9]

The bill that Attorney General Brownell had conceived, President Eisenhower had endorsed, and Knowland and Douglas had promoted in the Senate now belonged to Lyndon Johnson. With the destruction of Part III, no one was more important to the bill's success. No one had more to lose or gain by its failure or passage. Despite the ease with which the Senate weakened Part III, Johnson dared not celebrate his victory for long. He had satisfied only half of Russell's terms. Southerners still demanded a jury trial amendment to Part IV.

The question was vividly simple: Should those who were tried for criminal contempt actions arising from violations of the legislation be guaranteed a jury trial? The answer, however, was far from simple. Southerners claimed that the bill violated the constitutional guarantee of trial by jury. Liberals, however, feared that trials with all-white juries would never result in convictions. The successful attack on Part III was bad enough; a jury trial amendment, they believed, was worse. It would completely gut the bill. Liberals, Reedy said, were not "going to permit the law to be nullified by what would have been routine acquittals of white offenders by Southern white juries."[10]

When the "full scope of the dilemma" became apparent to Reedy, he believed that "the world was finally going to get an answer to the old conundrum of what happens when an irresistible force meets an immovable object. There was no apparent 'give' on either side." Southern senators, already concerned about how their white constituents would view their decision not to filibuster, could not support legislation that would allow judges to jail people without a jury trial. Liberals and the White House, who had already swallowed one dose of bitter medicine in the Part III debate, could not face losing the debate over another important provision.[11]

In the House, at least, opponents of a jury trial amendment appeared to have the numbers and the facts on their side. After a spirited struggle, liberals had rebuffed southern proponents of such an amendment, 251–158. But as always, the Senate was another story.

When viewed through the prism of the southern electorate, a jury trial amendment seemed certain to inhibit a judge's ability to enforce his decrees. Simply put, if blacks were not registered to vote, they could not be selected to serve on southern juries, even in federal courts. All-white juries in 1957 were unlikely to convict any white person for violating the voting rights of a black citizen.

Southern supporters of the amendment had a remarkably straightforward argument, concisely summarized by Alabama's John Sparkman on a June television broadcast: "Running all through our Constitution and all through our legal texture is the rule that facts ought to be determined by juries and not by judges, unless a defendant is willing to have a judge determine the facts."[12]

While southerners trumpeted their case for the amendment in various public forums, Johnson worked furiously in the background for its passage. "I remember, in those days," said Idaho's Frank Church, "that he would sit at his desk in the Senate and plot ways and means to attract the necessary votes to cut this Gordian knot." Johnson so dedicated himself to passing the amendment that he rarely left the Capitol during a two-week period, often relying on Lady Bird to bring him a fresh change of clothes. When he learned that Eleanor Roosevelt was in town, he dispatched his aide Grace Tully, a former FDR employee, to bring the former first lady to the Capitol. "I'm here every single night, all night, day and night," Johnson complained to Mrs. Roosevelt, an outspoken liberal advocate of civil rights. "But where are all the liberals?" Frustrated that he was being forced to shoulder the burden—and eventually the blame—for weakening the bill so that it could pass, Johnson was sending a clear message to Roosevelt: The liberals wanted a civil rights bill, but they would not engage in the unseemly compromises necessary to assemble a majority. Someone else—namely Johnson—had to do their dirty work so that they could maintain their principled, vehement opposition to anything that might weaken the bill. Although Johnson understood his role and accepted it willingly, he was nonetheless irked that many liberals viewed him, according to Church, "as a kind of Machiavellian leader in the Senate who was doing his utmost to dilute and weaken civil rights legislation." That characterization, Church said, "was a great injustice to him, the kind of injustice that can only be done by those who take a self-righteous view of such issues."[13]

Johnson's determination to pass the jury trial amendment—and therefore ensure passage of the bill—"may well have justified his entire career," Reedy asserted, adding:

> he was absolutely determined that there would be a bill. He regarded the measure as a true starting point for reconciliation of North and South and he refused to move it from the floor—despite advice to do so from many of his colleagues. He pleaded and threatened and cajoled. He prowled the corridors of the Senate grabbing senators and staff members indiscriminately, probing them for some sign of amenability to compromise. He spent hours on the phone

in nonstop conversations with the most ingenious legal minds he knew . . . pleading with them for something to break the log jam. Virtually single-handed, he kept a large body of very strong-minded and willful men concentrating on a purpose which most of them thought could not be achieved.[14]

Finally, the means to cut the jury trial knot appeared in a liberal magazine, the *New Leader.* Essayist Carl Auerbach, a Wisconsin law professor and Humphrey's friend and adviser, defined the important differences between civil and criminal contempt in the federal judiciary. In his article, which Johnson ordered distributed to every senator, Auerbach argued that judges normally conducted criminal contempt proceedings when an individual ignored a court's order to comply with a federal law. In such cases, Auerbach maintained, the law had traditionally required jury trials.

Civil contempt proceedings were another matter. They did not deal with guilt or innocence; rather, they were held by judges seeking to enforce future compliance with a court order, not punish a past violation. Judges conducted these proceedings without juries because they could immediately dismiss a contempt citation whenever the defendant agreed to comply with the court's ruling. "So it is said in these cases," Auerbach wrote, "that the defendant 'carries the key of his prison in his own pocket.' He can open the prison door and walk out any time he pleases by obeying the court's order." Auerbach's conclusion was that "effective enforcement" of voting rights "can be secured through the civil-contempt proceeding" and its powers of coercion. When Johnson's New Deal friend Ben Cohen presented the article to him over lunch, the majority leader realized that the distinction between civil and criminal contempt might—in Church's words—be "the key to the passage of the bill itself." "Lord, he understood!" recalled Reedy. "He could have argued that before the Supreme Court."[15]

Johnson's challenge now was to persuade a majority of the Senate that the bill's *civil* contempt provisions would be a potent weapon to prevent voting rights violations in the South. Invigorated by the rhetorical ammunition supplied in Auerbach's persuasive essay, he instructed staff members Cohen, Gerald Siegel, and Solis Horwitz—assisted by lawyer Abe Fortas and former secretary of state Dean Acheson—to begin writing legislative language that simply amended Part IV to guarantee jury trials in all cases of criminal contempt, including labor disputes.[16]

Eisenhower, Knowland, and most of the liberal bloc opposed all amendments to Part IV. That meant the critical work of rounding up votes to pass the amendment—and thus forestall a southern filibuster—fell, as usual, to Johnson. One by one, he focused on key senators. Often he picked them off so quietly that Knowland and Douglas were oblivious to the steady erosion of their ranks.[17]

Johnson was winning, but time was running out. On Sunday, July 29, Humphrey went on a national news show to proclaim confidently that the amendment's supporters "haven't got the votes." Knowland, equally confident of victory, was now aggressively pushing for a vote. On July 29, he taunted the southerners to begin their filibuster. "Let's have it now and fight it out," he said.[18]

What Knowland did not know was that Johnson had gained a powerful new ally only the day before. At the Glen Echo amusement park outside Washington, one of Johnson's aides encountered Cy Anderson, the chief lobbyist for the twelve railroad brotherhoods. Because the amendment would require jury trials in all criminal contempt cases, including those arising from labor disputes, Anderson was a strong supporter. "Any labor skate who is against trial by jury ought to have his head examined," Anderson said as the two men discussed the jury trial issue. The offhand remark revealed another potentially important source of votes for the amendment, previously unknown to Johnson.

It was no coincidence three days later that Johnson announced on the Senate floor that the presidents of twelve railroad brotherhoods, all but two of them members of the influential AFL-CIO, had endorsed the amendment. The announcement destroyed the image of labor's solid opposition. While the AFL-CIO's executive committee officially opposed it, the amendment had garnered sudden, unexpected support from railroad unions, fifteen postal workers' unions, and the influential United Mine Workers president, John L. Lewis.[19]

Johnson gained additional votes with the help of Frank Church. As Church studied the politics of the amendment, he saw that the major obstacle for liberals was the expectation that southern authorities would not seat blacks on most southern juries. Church proposed an amendment to permit blacks to serve on federal juries even if they were not registered to vote. Johnson had been searching for some kind of sweetener that might entice the handful of Republican and Democratic moderates who were still undecided. Church's idea was just the nuance he needed. With Russell's tacit approval, Johnson persuaded O'Mahoney and Kefauver to accept Church's language.[20]

On the evening of August 2, Johnson—finally confident of victory— was ready to vote on the jury trial amendment. Yet Knowland, who had previously pressed for a quick vote, began stalling, the clearest indication to Johnson that his own side would prevail. Having once been confident of thirty-nine Republican votes against the amendment, Knowland now pleaded for two additional hours. He could only hope that two absent senators, Maine's Frederick Payne and Missouri's Tom Hennings, would arrive at the Capitol in time to cast their crucial votes.[21]

When voting ended, Johnson had prevailed, 51 to 42. Instead of thirty-nine Republican votes, Knowland had only thirty-three. He lost twelve crucial Republicans, while Johnson forfeited only nine of his forty-eight Democrats. The next morning, Johnson triumphantly declared that "we have strengthened the bill and we have strengthened the confidence of the American people in its provisions. That alone would justify the action we took." In the *New York Times,* William S. White characterized the amendment's passage as a "heavy defeat" for Eisenhower but "a great victory for a bipartisan coalition composed of Western liberal Democrats, Southern Democrats and a handful of traditional Republicans" headed by Johnson. *Time* called it "a shrewd political blow" to Eisenhower and Knowland's "prestige."[22]

Johnson deserved credit for winning the votes to pass the amendment, but he was greatly aided by Eisenhower and Brownell's ineffective advocacy. Remote and largely uninvolved in the details of the bill, Eisenhower left to play golf as the crucial negotiations over the amendment's final wording reached their climax. "Senators," columnist Doris Fleeson observed in the *Washington Evening Star,* "will not put more passion into his desires than he does." Making matters worse, Brownell departed for a bar association meeting in London during the most intense bargaining.[23]

While Eisenhower declared that the bill was now "largely ineffective," he refused to say whether he would sign it if the final product resembled the Senate version. To Vice President Nixon, the amendment's passage was "one of the saddest days in the history of the Senate because this was a vote against the right to vote." Knowland said the amendment had "greatly weakened" the bill. Oregon's Wayne Morse called the amended bill "a corpse." Although sorely disappointed, Knowland's Republicans knew their only option was to support the bill and wait for a House-Senate compromise to restore the provisions they had lost to Johnson's coalition. To vote any other way was to invite near-unanimous condemnation from liberals, black leaders, and the news media.[24]

Eisenhower's veiled veto threats startled the Senate's liberals. Suddenly the "weak" bill they once derided took on positive qualities that were previously unrecognized. If Eisenhower wanted to wield his veto pen, Humphrey and Douglas knew they must not make the decision easy for him by echoing his administration's criticisms. "This was the tipoff that the Democratic Party leaders felt they had the Republicans in a hole," David Lawrence wrote. "For it could now be demonstrated that the Democrats from both the North and the South wanted the legislation to pass and only those 'narrowly partisan' Republicans . . . were standing in the way."[25]

New York Republican Jacob Javits, a fierce opponent of the jury trial amendment, summed up the philosophical resignation of pragmatic liberals: "I'm disappointed in the bill as it is, but I want a bill and not a campaign issue." Indeed, the bill's utility, observed Ernest K. Lindley in *Newsweek,* was its spirit of honest compromise. "It is less than most of the northern Senators with large numbers of Negro constituents wanted or felt that they must strive for," Lindley wrote. "It is more than most of the southerners want—which is no bill at all. It is a compromise wrought chiefly by Senators who on this issue have some measure of political latitude."[26]

On August 7, after twenty-five long days of debate, the Senate made history. It passed the civil rights bill, 72–18. Five southern Democrats— Kefauver and Gore of Tennessee, George Smathers of Florida, and Ralph Yarborough and Lyndon Johnson of Texas—voted for it. Important to passage was a last-minute endorsement issued by the leaders of sixteen liberal organizations, including the National Association for the Advancement of Colored People and the Americans for Democratic Action. A day-long debate among the various leaders ended when Roy Wilkins, the respected chairman of the NAACP, finally concluded, "I can't see anything to do except say that this is better than nothing. Let's take it." Joseph Rauh— who admitted, "I was so mad at Johnson I was speechless, for gutting the bill so much"—finally adopted a pragmatic attitude toward the Senate product. "The best we could get was what they gave us."[27]

Two weeks of negotiations with the House produced a final compromise. House and Senate leaders, having wisely rejected a formal conference committee, presented Eisenhower with a slight modification of the jury trial amendment. On other aspects of the bill, primarily Part III, Eisenhower and the Republican leadership knew they had no choice but to capitulate to the Senate or face a certain filibuster by southerners. Although he insisted that they "unalterably opposed" the compromise, Russell said his troops would not filibuster the bill. On August 27, the House overwhelmingly passed the civil rights bill, 279–97.[28]

The following day, as the Senate debated the bill, South Carolina's Strom Thurmond—opposed to the jury trial compromise and still frustrated by Russell's refusal to orchestrate a southern filibuster—unexpectedly took matters into his own hands. Well rested and armed only with a handful of malted milk balls and throat lozenges, Thurmond asked for recognition at 8:45 P.M. "Mr. President," he said, "I rise to speak against the so-called voting rights bill, H.R. 6127." He then launched into a remarkable speech that lasted until 9:12 the next evening. Over twenty-four hours in length, Thurmond's talking marathon became the longest continuous oration ever delivered in the Senate.[29]

Having argued that a filibuster would result in stronger civil rights legislation and possibly provoke the Senate into liberalizing cloture, southerners had withheld their heavy filibuster artillery. Thurmond's grandstanding speech sent Russell and other southerners into a "cold fury," Reedy said. "They felt," wrote Jay Walz in the *New York Times*, "that Mr. Thurmond was leaving in the South a public image of a single Southern senator standing at barricades that had been deserted by the others." As Louisiana's Russell Long observed, the southerners believed Thurmond "was making a cheap campaign for his own reelection at the expense of the other guys." That, Long said, "caused [constituents] to say, 'What's the matter with you? That man's out there fighting for us and you're sitting on your ass [and] won't even help him.'"[30]

Less than two hours after Thurmond left the Senate chamber, the Senate passed the Civil Rights Act of 1957 by a wide margin: 60–15. On September 9 Eisenhower reluctantly signed the bill while on vacation in Newport, Rhode Island.[31]

In the wake of the historic vote, Johnson received rave reviews for his amazing skill in herding the bill through the Senate without a southern filibuster. Paul Douglas called it "a triumph" for Johnson's "policy of moderation over the [southern] extremists." At the time, William S. White believed the bill's passage set the stage for Johnson to dominate the 1960 Democratic National Convention and perhaps even win the presidential nomination. It was, White later said, "the most skillful single legislative job of leadership I ever saw." Noting that negotiations over the bill had been conducted under "volatile" conditions, Reedy maintained that without Johnson's leadership "there would have been no bill at all." In an effusive letter of praise Clark Clifford told Johnson, "There's no one else alive who would have stood the ghost of a chance to keep our party from splitting irretrievably."[32]

For Johnson, the bill was far more than a legislative triumph. It propelled him into a position of true national prominence. No longer did he wear the label of sectional leader. His informal alliance with Russell's southerners had seemingly ended when he voted for the bill's passage.

The bill had political implications for at least one other Democratic senator—John F. Kennedy. "It was curious," said Tom Wicker of the *New York Times*, "that both Kennedy and Johnson used that bill for their presidential purposes. And my recollection is that they did exactly the same thing for precisely the opposite purposes." Wicker was largely correct. Johnson had voted to delete Part III and to add a jury trial amendment; Kennedy, too, had supported the jury trial amendment, but had voted to *retain* Part III. Inherent in Johnson's efforts was his desire to become more acceptable to northern liberals. Kennedy, meanwhile, probably cast his vote for the jury trial amendment with an aspiring eye to the South. Kennedy "walked a teetering tightrope," observed James MacGregor Burns, who found himself fascinated by Kennedy's handling of the bill and its politics. "At the same time he was telling liberals of the effectiveness of a bill that included the [jury trial] provision, he was assuring worried Southerners that it was a moderate bill that would be enforced by *Southern* courts and *Southern* juries." While others, including Joseph Rauh, believed that Kennedy "hadn't quite made a final decision on where he was going" on civil rights, the 1957 bill was the beginning of a philosophical evolution that would eventually lead to his civil rights program as president in 1963. For Johnson, as well, the bill meant that he was well on his way to outright advocacy of the same civil rights proposal.[33]

While Johnson received many plaudits for his skill in guiding the legislation to passage, initial judgments of the bill itself were less than generous. Paul Douglas said that "it reminded him of Lincoln's old saying that it was like a soup made from the shadow of a crow which had starved to death." Most common was the view that the bill was only "half a loaf." To the NAACP's Thurgood Marshall, the bill was "just barely progress." Like many other liberals and black leaders, Marshall came to believe that "the smallest slice was good . . . because it was a strictly political move of getting something done." The 1957 act was important, insisted NAACP leader Clarence Mitchell, "because not only did it have substantive value, but it also represented a breakthrough. Up until that time, it had been assumed Congress could not and would not pass any civil rights legislation. We succeeded in passing it and that helped to let people know it could be done."[34]

In retrospect, the Civil Rights Act of 1957 clearly failed to conquer the racism of southern leaders determined to deny blacks the right to vote. Ultimately it would take passage of the Voting Rights Act of 1965 to fully enfranchise southern blacks. Nevertheless, the bill was *the* important first step in the evolution of modern civil rights legislation—and the starting point for the civil rights policies of presidents John F. Kennedy and Lyndon Johnson. "In real as well as in symbolic terms," Senator Clinton Anderson later observed, "I think it represented a genuine defeat for racism and the society of the Old South."[35]

At the very least, it was a good beginning.

7

A MEANINGLESS GESTURE

The ink on the Civil Rights Act of 1957 was barely dry when racially motivated violence threatened to erupt in Little Rock, Arkansas, in late September. Only weeks earlier, Russell had worried aloud that President Eisenhower might dispatch federal troops southward to desegregate public schools. Now the atmosphere of racial unrest in Arkansas barreled down a slippery incline toward Russell's once-implausible scenario. By year's end, the unrest in Arkansas would further polarize southern and northern members of Congress over civil rights, and much of the progress achieved by the century's first civil rights act would be lost in a dark cloud of bitterness and suspicion.

In early September, following a court-ordered plan to desegregate the city's public schools, the Little Rock school board prepared for the uneventful enrollment of nine black students at the city's Central High School. Sensing an opportunity to make political hay, Governor Orval Faubus—running for reelection the following year—elbowed his way into the controversy just as the school year began. Under the pretense of preventing violence, Faubus pandered to the most racist of Arkansas's white citizens when he ordered the state's National Guard to surround the school to bar the black students' entrance. Overnight, Little Rock became the next potential flash point in the nation's civil rights struggle.

Eisenhower initially refused to intervene. He calmly continued his vacation in Newport while aides kept him informed of all developments. But the president's indecision only allowed the crisis to worsen. By the time he became involved, nothing short of the U.S. Army could restore order in Little Rock.

Ten days into the tense standoff, Eisenhower reluctantly agreed to negotiate with Faubus. Their meeting in Newport, however, produced nothing but ambiguous and insincere promises by the governor that he would diffuse the situation. He removed his troops only when ordered by a federal judge and did nothing else to bring calm to the city. And he recklessly fanned flames of racism in Little Rock with extreme and demagogic language. On September 23, the passions he had exacerbated finally boiled over. An angry, screaming mob of several thousand white racists converged on Central High School to protest the scheduled enrollment of the black students. In the melee, two black reporters were attacked. As the mob spewed racial slurs and epithets, authorities quietly ushered nine terrified black children into a side door of the school to begin classes. When the crowd realized that the students were safely inside, they became even more enraged and rushed the building. Reporters heard cries of "lynch the niggers" from the mob. Finally, fearing for the black students' safety, Little Rock mayor Woodrow Wilson Mann ordered city police to remove them from the school.[1]

The next morning, a troubled Mann wired Eisenhower: "The immediate need for federal troops is urgent . . . People are converging on the scene from all directions. Mob is armed and engaging in fisticuffs and other acts of violence. Situation is out of control and police cannot disperse the mob." Several hours later, Eisenhower resigned himself to the inevitable: he would order federal troops into Little Rock to restore order. It was the first time a president had sent the U.S. military into the South for such purposes since Reconstruction. By day's end, forty-six giant transport planes roared into Little Rock Air Force Base, carrying more than a thousand paratroopers of the Army's 101st Airborne Division—the "Screaming Eagles." The next morning the troops, assisted by a federalized Arkansas National Guard, began dispersing the mob.[2]

Southern senators reacted with fury. South Carolina's Olin Johnston declared: "If I were governor and he [Eisenhower] came in, I'd give him a fight such as he's never been in before. I'd proclaim a state of insurrection and I'd call out the National Guard and then we'd find out who's going to run things in my state." Russell's junior Georgia colleague, Herman Talmadge, seemed equally disrespectful of the commander-in-chief, whom he compared to the Soviet communists who invaded Hungary in 1956: "We still mourn the destruction of the sovereignty of Hungary by Russian tanks and troops in the streets of Budapest. We are now threatened with the spectacle of the president of the United States using tanks and troops in the streets of Little Rock to destroy the sovereignty of the state of Arkansas."[3]

Southerners were not the only ones critical of the president. New York governor Averill Harriman, echoing the criticism of many northern liberals, observed that Eisenhower, "by his inaction, has contributed to the making of the present situation, and any trouble we have from now on can be laid at the door of the president's complacency and policy of appeasement of Governor Faubus while the crisis was developing."[4]

The violence in Little Rock destroyed much of the progress and harmony achieved by the passage of the civil rights bill. Southerners, once willing to grudgingly permit the passage of weak civil rights legislation, would now be expected to aggressively challenge—even filibuster—the next civil rights proposal. Although Eisenhower's use of troops was unrelated to the 1957 civil rights act, Russell's southerners risked looking like fools or traitors to their region if they dared to strike another moderate posture on the issue. Observed *Newsweek:* "Even the moderates, who had been persuaded by Johnson to go along with the civil rights bill, would now, for the sake of their political skins, have to turn their backs on moderation."[5]

The synergy of the civil rights act and the Little Rock crisis produced even more pronounced intransigence in Russell and other southerners. With the inevitability of increased black voting and the integration of public schools staring him in the face, Russell resolved to yield not another inch. Over time, his strident opposition to the Supreme Court's civil rights decisions had turned into irrational, unbridled hostility. In a February 1958 speech to the Georgia legislature, Russell warned that the Court was one of two great "threats" facing the nation. (The other was communism.) In a bitter diatribe, Russell attacked those justices who "profane the name of what was once our most respected institution of government" by "playing on unwarranted prejudice against the South and her white people."[6]

A year after the violence in Arkansas, the Supreme Court upheld the lower court's desegregation ruling in Little Rock, asserting that "the constitutional rights [of the children] are not to be sacrificed or yielded to the violence and disorder which have followed the actions of the Governor and the Legislature . . . Law and order are not to be preserved by depriving the Negro children of their constitutional rights." In response, Russell bitterly attacked the NAACP, Attorney General Brownell, and Chief Justice Earl Warren, who he said suffered from a "Messianic complex." Russell indirectly sanctioned continued defiance of the Court's rulings when he warned that the South's white people would not "surrender to the dictates of the NAACP merely because this organization is able to use the present Supreme Court as its mouthpiece and the powers of the Attorney General of the United States as its tool."[7]

In 1958 Russell's growing despair over the steady advance of civil rights led him to abandon his longstanding support for federal aid to education. His reasoning was simple: "I am completely confident that within a year or two at best we will be confronted with provisions on appropriations bills that will deny funds to states that do not integrate their schools." Perhaps the most telling evidence of Russell's alienation from his party's mainstream was his announcement in December 1958 that he would soon reintroduce his legislation "aimed at bringing about a more equitable distribution of the white and colored races throughout the United States." The legislation was the manifestation of Russell's strange belief that racial discord arose not from white racism but from the presence of large black populations in the South. Russell's objective—the massive relocation of southern blacks by a Voluntary Racial Relocation Commission—was an exceedingly unusual proposal by someone so thoroughly opposed to other social engineering programs. Despite his desire to guide the South back into the mainstream of American life, Russell was in fact prodding his region in the opposite direction. He and his southern colleagues were now as isolated as ever.[8]

The true philosophical divergence of Johnson and Russell on civil rights became apparent after the Civil Rights Act of 1957. Johnson—who had engineered the bill's passage and later offered only muted criticism of Eisenhower's actions in Little Rock—seemed prepared finally to embrace black voting rights and to accept the Supreme Court's dictums on school desegregation. Russell knew that nothing was likely to halt the advance of civil rights, yet he remained defiant, hoping at least to slow its progress. While genuinely alarmed at the new momentum the issue had gained—thanks in great measure to his Texas protégé—Russell still had faith in Johnson, for whom he still harbored presidential hopes. Russell may have believed that Johnson required *some* civil rights credentials to capture the 1960 Democratic nomination. As the debate over a quasi–civil rights proposal in 1958 showed, Russell—when he could afford to—remained ready to surrender some of his antipathy toward civil rights for Johnson's political well-being. Even so, circumstances would soon conspire to test his fealty to Johnson.

The congressional elections of 1958 proved a watershed year for liberals, with voters sending significant numbers of northern freshman Democrats into both houses of Congress. In just one election cycle, Senate Democrats increased their margin over Republicans by twenty-eight seats—from a narrow 49–47 edge to an astounding 64–34 advantage. In the House the results were equally spectacular. Democrats stretched their 234–201 lead over Republicans to 283–153.[9]

Historically, the party controlling the White House forfeited congressional seats in midterm contests. But this election was an unusually crushing one for Eisenhower's party. Several factors contributed to the dramatic swing: Senate Republicans had defended eight more seats—twenty-one to the Democrats' thirteen—and suffered from weakened party organizations in several states. Eisenhower had shown almost no interest in his party's electoral fortunes and offered little help to his beleaguered Republican congressional allies. The president—and by extension his party—bore ample blame for a severe economic recession, especially in agricultural states. Furthermore, Eisenhower's already sagging popularity slumped lower when his chief-of-staff, Sherman Adams, resigned under a cloud of scandal. "The responsibility for this disaster, when you come right down to it," said the *Wall Street Journal*, "must rest on President Eisenhower. It was he who had the sense of direction and lost it; it was he who should have nurtured a party to support his ideas and did not."[10]

Southerners were especially despondent over the results. "Time is short," the *Dallas News* said in an editorial. "The forces of conservatism in Washington are dwindling [to] men like Harry Byrd, [Barry] Goldwater. When they are gone, we are all gone." Speaking to the Georgia General Assembly in February 1959, Russell warned his state's lawmakers that southerners "simply do not have the strength" to pass legislation to restore the Supreme Court "to its proper place in our scheme of government." The southern bloc, he said, had "not only lost the support of many of those from other sections on whom we once relied, but the representatives from the states of the old Confederacy no longer present a common front." Russell's anxiety may have been overwrought, but southern influence in the Senate *was* shrinking. Throughout the 1950s, the southern ranks had been about equal to that of northern Democrats. After the 1958 election, nonsouthern Democrats outnumbered southerners by a huge margin—42 to 22.[11]

The election transformed the ideological complexion of the entire Senate Democratic caucus. Before 1958, nonsoutherners were a tidy balance of liberals such as Humphrey, Douglas, and Herbert Lehman with moderates such as Carl Hayden, Dennis Chavez, and Allen Frear. The historic 1958 elections swept ten new liberal-to-moderate Democrats into the Senate: Clair Engle of California, a seven-term congressman who filled the seat of Republican leader William Knowland (who had left to run—unsuccessfully—for governor); Howard Cannon of Nevada, who unseated two-term Republican George Malone; Thomas Dodd of Connecticut, a former congressman who defeated Republican William Purtell; Vance Hartke of Indiana, the mayor of Evansville, who filled the seat of retiring Republican archconservative William Jenner; Edmund Muskie of Maine, the first Democrat ever elected to the Senate from his state by popular vote; Philip Hart of Michigan, who beat incumbent Republican Charles Potter; Eugene McCarthy of Minnesota, a veteran congressman who defeated Humphrey's Republican colleague, Edward Thye; Harrison Williams of New Jersey, a former congressman; Stephen Young of Ohio, who defeated two-term incumbent Republican John Bricker; and Frank Moss of Utah, the Salt Lake County attorney who beat incumbent Republican Arthur Watkins.[12]

The liberals were ecstatic. "The election results," said Pennsylvania's Joseph Clark, "exceeded our fondest hopes." Before 1958, Johnson had often regarded the liberals as a yapping collection of impractical, impetuous bomb throwers. No more. The midterm elections, argued Humphrey's top aide, William Connell, transformed the Senate into "a liberal institution" in which Humphrey would conceivably control as many votes as Johnson. "If not equal partners," said Connell, "Humphrey became more important to Johnson after the 1958 election."[13]

Johnson now had a potentially unruly, restive majority to lead. "He was confronted with much more of the issue-oriented Senate than he had had before—much more of a Paul Butler–national party kind of Senate," Harry McPherson said. It would now be more difficult, he knew, to build majorities around incremental initiatives by uniting southern and western Democrats and moderate Republicans. Instead of staving off liberals and conservatives with his middle-ground, compromise-as-you-go approach, Johnson knew that Democratic unity in the new, liberal Senate would be more difficult than ever. "I'd just as soon not have that many Democrats," Sam Rayburn told Johnson. "Believe me, they'll be hard to handle. It won't be easy."[14]

On the other side of the aisle, Johnson now faced a dynamic new Republican leader—Everett Dirksen of Illinois. A pragmatic, skillful politician, Dirksen was the virtual antipode to his predecessor, William Knowland. "I am a man of principle," Dirksen once said. "And one of my basic principles is flexibility." Dirksen, said his biographer Neil MacNeil, "wanted power, influence and the prestige that comes with them, and he wanted to shape and temper the course of American political affairs." (That description could have comfortably applied to Johnson.) First and foremost, Dirksen was a master politician. He was the kind of man, recalled Utah's Wallace Bennett, "who was willing to sacrifice himself for the good of the party." A powerful and eloquent speaker, Dirksen occasionally resorted to excessively majestic verbiage, sometimes to his own embarrassment. Once, when defending the nomination of Clare Booth Luce as ambassador to Italy, his own oratory carried him away: "Why thrash old straws or beat an old bag of bones?" When his colleagues began to chuckle at the unfortunate choice of words, Humphrey, his friendly rival, rose to seize upon Dirksen's inadvertent slur. "I must rise to the defense of the lady." A very flustered Dirksen backtracked. "I am referring to the old bag of political bones," he said sheepishly, "those old canards." With Dirksen as his counterpart, Johnson would never again find it so easy to dominate his colleagues on the Republican side.[15]

In January 1959, Johnson moved forcefully to solidify his leadership and bolster his credentials with the burgeoning liberal bloc. The day before Eisenhower's annual State of the Union address, Johnson delivered his own speech to the Democratic caucus in which he outlined a bold, liberal New Deal–style agenda for the coming Eighty-sixth Congress. Johnson's laundry list included economic relief for depressed regions, water development projects for the West, and a housing and urban renewal program. He did not mention civil rights. Despite that one glaring omission, his progressive talk heartened the liberals. Johnson also moved to further separate himself from his former informal association with Russell and the southern bloc; he began attending meetings of the caucus of western Democrats.[16]

Johnson's leftward, westward shift may have heartened the Senate's liberals, but not for long. As the new Congress opened for business on January 7, liberals such as Douglas, Anderson, Humphrey, and New York Republican Jacob Javits were eager to test the strength of their swelling ranks. As in previous years, they planned to propose the adoption of new rules. The liberals' argument was familiar: The Senate was not a continuing body, and therefore it had the right to adopt its rules by majority vote at the beginning of each new Congress. But before Anderson and his allies could rise to make their motion, Johnson sideswiped them. Exercising his right as majority leader, Johnson captured the floor only minutes after Vice President Nixon convened the Senate. "From that moment on," reported *Time*, "it was all over but the shouting—and there was plenty of that." Hoping to head off the liberal efforts to relax the cloture rule, John-son offered a moderate proposal of his own. Cosponsored by the Demo-cratic and Republican leadership, Johnson's measure enabled two-thirds of senators *voting* to invoke cloture on any measure, including rule changes. Ostensibly, Russell and his southerners opposed any rule change—although Russell had proposed the same language as a compromise made the previous year. Privately, however, Russell knew that Johnson's pro-posal was a good deal, perhaps the southerners' only hope of heading off more stringent constraints on filibusters by the newly empowered liberal majority. While the southerners would not vote to liberalize cloture, they were realistic. Russell's bloc would not filibuster Johnson's motion.[17]

The Johnson resolution was just the kind of gradual modification liberals had always abhorred. It was "a meaningless gesture," Paul Doug-las complained. Nevertheless, Johnson knew he had the votes for his proposal, a fact that became evident when he "generously" expressed his willingness to permit a vote on Anderson's proposition. On January 9, the Senate tabled the Anderson motion, 60–36.[18]

Despite this defeat, the liberals did not retreat. On January 12 Douglas offered a substitute cloture rule that allowed a majority of senators to shut off debate fifteen days after the filing of a cloture petition. But Johnson still had his votes. The Douglas measure lost, 28–67. Later that day, the Sen-ate finally adopted—with the grudging support of most liberals—John-son's cloture modification, 72–22. "The South won a great victory," Douglas said on CBS's *Face the Nation* several days later. What bothered Douglas, he later said, was that "by acquiescence or otherwise, we may, somewhere along the route, be construed as having accepted the existing rules of the Senate." Moreover, he saw Johnson's cloture victory as an impediment to aggressive action on civil rights in 1959. "I think a majority of the country wants it," Douglas said, "but the power of the South to filibuster and the protection thrown around the filibuster by the small states and by the con-servative Republicans, I am afraid, is going to be such as to prevent it from being passed."[19]

Most observers interpreted the cloture-rule votes as ringing endorse-ments of Johnson's continued domination of the Senate, but closer analy-sis revealed widening fissures in his leadership. Although eight of fifteen Democratic freshmen—including liberals Thomas Dodd, Vance Hartke, and Howard Cannon—had supported Johnson on the tabling of Anderson's motion, seven of the new Democrats broke with the Democratic leader on their first important Senate vote. Risking reprisals, Clair Engle, Edmund Muskie, Philip Hart, Eugene McCarthy, Harrison Williams, Stephen Young, and Frank Moss had joined other liberal veterans to support Anderson over Johnson. Those votes portended even more liberal defections—and growing difficulties for Johnson.[20]

As always, freshman senators had been under intense pressure to support the leadership—if they knew what was good for them. Even the most uninitiated newcomer knew that Johnson, as majority leader, and Russell, as the most influential member of the Democratic Steering Committee, held absolute sway over committee assignments. Said Douglas's aide Howard Shuman: "I've never heard anybody say that [Russell] directly said to a new member, 'Vote with us or you don't get your [committee] choice.' But it was very clear what a new senator had to do." Muskie, whom Johnson later described as "chicken shit" for his leadership-defying vote, was relegated to two insignificant committees, while Johnson supporters such as Hartke got choice assignments. "The sugar plums," Paul Douglas observed, "went to the boys who went along."[21]

Despite the liberals' harsh judgment of his heavy-handed methods, Johnson was not quite the southern sympathizer they suspected. According to aide Solis Horwitz, Johnson had attempted to enlist Clinton Anderson's support for the compromise rules change. In exchange, Horwitz said, Johnson had promised to support an Anderson amendment to lower the cloture threshold from two-thirds to three-fifths of those voting. "Johnson was perfectly willing to take 60 percent and get rid of the issue," said Horwitz. But Anderson and the liberals rejected Johnson's offer. In the end, after rejecting Anderson's motion, the Senate turned down a subsequent amendment to reduce the votes needed for cloture to three-fifths. None of this would have happened, Horwitz insisted, if Anderson and his liberal colleagues had followed Johnson's lead. "That was another case of the liberals beating themselves," said Horwitz. To their detriment, the liberals simply could not overcome their immense distrust of Johnson to accept, in good faith, his efforts to reform the cloture rule.[22]

Another fissure in Johnson's leadership opened in February when Wisconsin Democrat William Proxmire—elected to the Senate in a special election in 1957—openly attacked his leader. In a Senate floor speech, Proxmire lamented that Johnson had grown so powerful "that the typical

Democratic Senator has literally nothing to do with determining the legislative program and policies of this party." Although only Oregon's Wayne Morse publicly endorsed this harsh criticism, Proxmire did receive hints of support from Douglas, Joseph Clark, and Albert Gore.[23]

Johnson would ignore the speech at his peril. Proxmire had expressed a growing sentiment among Democrats, many of whom were privately frustrated by Johnson's aggressive tactics. "Other senators were very, very reluctant to become involved personally," Proxmire later said. "In fact, when they called me about my speech, they would call me at home. They wouldn't call me . . . in the office. They were afraid the lines might be tapped. There was a real fear of Senator Johnson as the leader." McPherson believed there was "some justification" for Proxmire's criticism, even if Proxmire and other Johnson critics were often beneficiaries of his power. "Johnson's control of the machinery was complete," said McPherson. "When it was used to pass one's bills or to secure a choice committee assignment, it was welcome, but it was oppressive to those in opposition." Johnson's "constant pressure" for unanimous consent agreements, McPherson acknowledged, "often came close to harassment."[24]

Proxmire's attack outraged and offended Johnson. Privately, he called his unruly colleague "Senator Pissmire." Although he would never voluntarily relinquish his control over the levers of power, Johnson did agree to one minor reform: Worried that Proxmire's complaints might gain currency if not addressed, he agreed to hold a Democratic caucus meeting upon the request of any member. "Johnson assumed, correctly as it turned out," wrote political scientist Michael Foley, "that it would be the liberal group which would require additional caucuses and that ultimately the liberals would be the only members present at such caucuses."[25]

Publicly, Johnson responded that "this one-man rule stuff is a myth" and asserted that he had never tried to force his will on any senator. But he correctly suspected that Proxmire's attack was the early warning of more pronounced unrest among those in the liberal ranks who sought institutional reforms and more action on their legislative agenda—especially civil rights. Douglas, for one, had already confirmed this for Johnson in January, when he complained openly—albeit diplomatically—about the leader's ambivalence toward meaningful civil rights legislation. "This is the real world," he said on *Face the Nation*, "but I do think it is unfortunate that the image which the Democratic party gives to the country is the image created by the political necessities of Texas and the South."[26]

Johnson hoped the Senate could avoid the divisive and tiring issue of civil rights for several more years. Eventually, his aide Horace Busby and former secretary of state Dean Acheson persuaded him otherwise. Acheson argued persuasively that Johnson was "the one man in the Democratic Party whose rare gifts of leadership . . . make possible the solution of this seemingly insoluble problem." Gradually, Johnson came to realize that the relative impotence of the Justice Department under the 1957 act would inevitably spawn broader civil rights legislation by Senate liberals and the Eisenhower administration. Another civil rights bill, he realized, was a certainty. But the political questions facing Johnson were more vexing: Who would write the bill, how strong would it be, and who would receive the credit for its passage or failure? These were variables Johnson *could* control, but only if he took the initiative. If Johnson refused to take charge, he knew that a newly empowered coalition of liberal Democrats and moderate Republicans would almost certainly commandeer the civil rights issue—with uncertain and possibly dangerous results for the Democratic party.[27]

On January 20 Johnson submitted his own civil rights legislation, hoping he could hurriedly pass a mild bill before the issue became embroiled in the politics of the 1960 congressional and presidential elections. Too strong for Russell's southerners yet much too weak for the liberals, the bill's main features were an antibombing provision that barred interstate transportation of explosives; an extension of the Civil Rights Commission created by the 1957 act; subpoena powers for the Justice Department in voting rights investigations; and establishment of a Federal Community Relations Service to mediate local disputes over segregation and integration.[28]

The bill's centerpiece was the Community Relations Service, a compromise provision that fell far short of the aggressive federal action sought by liberals. Solis Horwitz acknowledged the provision's inherent weakness in a February 16 memorandum: "While the plan recognizes that the implementation of the Supreme Court decisions through the judicial process in the District Courts has not worked satisfactorily, it makes no change in existing law." The provision, Horwitz explained, "provides an additional method which is non-coercive and wholly voluntary in character."[29]

Not surprisingly, the NAACP's Roy Wilkins reacted coolly to the bill, charging, with some accuracy, that it was "an effort to block consideration of effective legislation in this field. We regard it as offering liniment to cure a tumor, for it omits entirely the paramount domestic issue of desegregation of the public schools." Calling for enactment of the 1957 act's erstwhile Part III provision, Wilkins said its omission from the Johnson bill "prompts the suspicion that it is a sugar-coated pacifier."[30]

Not to be outdone, the White House offered its own bill. Similar to Johnson's legislation, the Eisenhower program—actually seven separate bills—contained an antibombing provision and an extension of the Civil Rights Commission. But Eisenhower went further. His legislation, sponsored by Dirksen and Arizona's Barry Goldwater, would have made it a federal crime to interfere with a federal school desegregation court order. The White House program would have also empowered the Justice Department to inspect local voter records and prohibited their destruction; authorized technical and financial assistance to areas with school desegregation problems; and provided emergency schooling for children of armed forces personnel if an integration dispute closed their public school.[31]

The most extensive bill was, of course, offered by Douglas and a bipartisan group of seventeen senators. The chief provision of their legislation was the scuttled Part III provision of the 1957 bill, which empowered the attorney general to initiate civil suits for school desegregation on behalf of black students. The Douglas bill also authorized the federal government to develop and enforce school desegregation plans through the courts.[32]

Russell, predictably, opposed all of the bills. But his words—"I shall oppose all of this political legislation to the limit of my ability"—had begun to sound tired, even hollow. By summer the fate of all three civil rights programs rested with the southern-dominated Senate and House Judiciary committees. In the Senate, a Judiciary subcommittee, after a squabble over the controversial Part III provision, approved only mild legislation to extend the life of the Civil Rights Commission and require state and local election officials to preserve voting records for federal inspection for at least three years. By the time Congress adjourned for the year, in mid-September, the bill was moribund and hopelessly mired in committee. The only civil rights legislation to pass Congress was a last-minute measure to fund and extend the Civil Rights Commission until November 1961.[33]

Johnson seemed unaware of the liberals' determination to pass another civil rights bill. The 1957 act had satisfied only those conservatives and moderates who viewed the issue as a nuisance, not a moral crusade. Moreover, the law was proving extremely difficult to enforce. Federal judges had dismissed Justice Department voting rights suits in Alabama and Georgia. In the Georgia case, Judge T. Hoyt Davis ruled that one provision of the bill, which empowered the attorney general to seek preventive relief in voting rights violations, was unconstitutional. Yet some civil rights advocates charged that the difficulties with enforcement did not rest entirely with the legislation's inadequacies or with unsympathetic southern judges. The Justice Department's ambivalence, they said, was to blame. Indeed, by the end of 1959 the Justice Department had filed only four lawsuits under provisions of the act: three to address voter discrimination and one against an all-white primary in Fayette County, Tennessee.

Even a simple extension of the Civil Rights Commission had been an uphill struggle. Johnson resurrected the legislation only when liberals hinted they would delay the Senate's adjournment by offering civil rights provisions as amendments to the Mutual Security Appropriations Bill. Moving to head off an embarrassing year-end deadlock over civil rights, Johnson and Dirksen reluctantly mollified the liberals by extending the commission.[34]

The sputtering drive for a civil rights bill gained some impetus in early September. A Civil Rights Commission report on voter registration in the South revealed that in 1956 only a quarter of the nearly five million eligible southern blacks was registered, compared with 60 percent of voting-age whites. "Some method must be found," the commission declared, "by which a federal officer is empowered to register voters for federal elections who are qualified under state registration laws but are otherwise unable to vote." In a five-to-one vote, the commission recommended a process by which the president could appoint temporary federal voting registrars.[35]

Days later, in an important concession, the two Senate leaders promised to bring a civil rights bill to the floor early in 1960. On September 14, the day before adjournment, Johnson made the announcement: "I serve notice on all members that on or about twelve o'clock on February 15, I anticipate that some Senator will rise in his place and make a motion with regard to the general civil rights question." Privately, Johnson signaled liberals and conservatives that he would tolerate nothing stronger than a voting rights bill—in other words, he explained, "an effective bill that will satisfy the consciences of sixty-seven senators [the cloture threshold]."[36]

Russell regarded Johnson's move toward civil rights with disgust. Publicly, at least, he blamed the liberals. The various bills introduced in 1959, Russell told a Lions Club meeting in Dawson, Georgia, in December, "vary only in the degree of their vindictiveness. All of them are hostile to our concept of government and contrary to the spirit and intent of the Constitution." The "ultimate price" of such federal intervention, he warned, "would be totalitarianism." The most extraordinary aspect of an otherwise conventional speech was Russell's absurd assessment of race relations in the South, which he said "remain generally good. This has been brought about under our traditional social order which permits members of both races to live and work together in peace, harmony and mutual understanding."[37]

Six weeks later the more authentic nature of southern race relations manifested itself in Greensboro, North Carolina. On February 1, 1960, four black freshmen from North Carolina A&T College peacefully entered a downtown Woolworth's store. As they settled onto stools at the whites-only lunch counter, the black waitress refused them service. "Fellows like you," she angrily told them, "make our race look bad." Two days later, the impromptu protest blossomed. More than eighty A&T students, now coordinated by student leaders, were reserving times for their shifts in an organized sit-in at Woolworth's and the local Kress store. Similar protests quickly spread throughout the South. Within the span of three months, thousands of black and white students staged sit-ins at lunch counters in fifteen cities in five southern states. At almost every site, students sat at whites-only counters, demanded service, and left only when the store closed or when local police officers arrested them. While most of the demonstrations were peaceful, some resulted in violence.[38]

The civil rights movement, previously a well-mannered cause led mostly by clergy and directed primarily at school desegregation and voting rights, was now awakened by the infusion of thousands of energetic, indignant black college students who demanded their full rights as citizens. Astute politicians, including Russell, soon understood that this brewing unrest throughout the South would mean even greater pressure for tougher civil rights legislation in 1960.

Such a bill now seemed inevitable—as was the first personal strife between Russell and his protégé, Lyndon Johnson.[39]

8

A VICTORY FOR THE OLD SOUTH

Johnson's promise to take up a civil rights bill by February 15, 1960, was no idle threat. As the day approached, he reminded Russell of his plans. "Yes," Russell said coolly, "I understand that you let them jockey you into that position. I understand." Later Johnson mentioned his promise again. "Yes, I know that," Russell replied. "Go ahead, do whatever your judgment tells you. That's your business, your responsibility. I'm not the leader."[1]

With his 1960 reelection campaign on the horizon, Russell engaged in a complicated game of verbal gymnastics, declaring his unwavering opposition to legislation that he implied was inevitable. In an unusually vitriolic and defeatist speech to the Georgia Assembly on February 8, Russell charged that a "stable" of presidential hopefuls was "dancing to the tune of the pressure groups." He said that the Democratic party "has virtually abandoned us."[2]

Back in Washington, on the same day, Republican leader Dirksen introduced Eisenhower's civil rights bill. Virtually identical to the administration's 1959 proposal, it had one additional provision—a plan for court-appointed voting referees to force the registration of blacks who were unlawfully disqualified or purged. The bill did not, however, contain several stronger provisions that liberals still regarded as crucial, particularly the Part III language from 1957.[3]

The following day, on February 9, Russell again sounded the alarms in a speech to the States' Rights Council in Atlanta. Russell said that the "sponsors of these mis-called proposals have not the slightest regard for the Constitution or for the rights of the states. They are interested only in currying favor with the pressure groups who purport to speak for a sizable bloc of minority voters in key areas of the nation." Russell said that Humphrey and other liberals "must be running a race to see who can introduce the greatest number of bills and the most ingenious means for punishing the southern people."[4]

Russell was at least partially correct about the amount of civil rights legislation awaiting action. In addition to bills by Johnson, Eisenhower, and the coalition of Democratic and Republican liberals—all of which were carried forward from 1959—Humphrey and several other Democrats had introduced an alternative to Eisenhower's voting referee proposal. Humphrey's legislation and its companion bill in the House empowered the president, in certain cases, to appoint officials to register blacks for federal elections.[5]

On February 15, shortly after 11:00 A.M., Johnson surreptitiously moved to fulfill his promise to bring civil rights legislation to the Senate. Matter of factly, he asked for and received the Senate's unanimous consent to proceed to the consideration of a minor, noncontroversial House-passed bill, H.R. 8315. The legislation authorized the army to provide unused officers' quarters at a Missouri military base for students whose school had burned in 1959. Nothing about the legislation should have raised anyone's suspicions. Later that afternoon, however, Johnson's announcement almost jolted Russell out of his chair.[6]

"Mr. President," Johnson said, addressing the presiding officer, "the unfinished business now before the Senate, H.R. 8315, relates to the leasing of a portion of Camp Crowder to a school district in Missouri. Because there is, as yet, no civil rights legislation on the Senate Calendar, this bill has been selected as the one on which, in fulfillment of the Senate's pledge of last year, to begin discussion of civil rights proposals in this chamber." Johnson then invited senators to propose civil right amendments. "I hope all interested senators will offer in a spirit of constructive, responsible, and nonpartisan dedication to human rights, the proposals they believe will best serve the ends of protecting the constitutional rights of American citizens."[7]

Johnson's move was brilliant. Because he had opened a House-passed bill to civil rights amendments, Johnson had bypassed the Senate Judiciary Committee. In addition, as he knew, Senate amendments to a House-passed bill would return directly to the House floor, bypassing the Rules Committee. Johnson had given Russell plenty of warning that he would attempt to bring a civil rights bill before the Senate, but Russell never guessed that Johnson would go beyond a routine attempt to prevent referral of the bill to the Judiciary Committee. Russell expected that Johnson would merely offer a motion to take up the civil rights bill directly—which, of course, the southerners would filibuster. Weeks of debate on Johnson's procedural motion would occur, Russell assumed, before the southerners launched another series of filibusters over individual amendments.[8]

Johnson's clever tactic carried the double indignity that legislation reported out of Russell's own Armed Services Committee would now be transformed into a civil rights bill. "I rise to protest action of this sort," Russell said angrily. Later, his voice dripping with sarcasm, he asked whether Johnson and Dirksen "proposed to boil us in oil, or to burn us at the stake, or to fricassee us on some new kind of rack or wheel or simply to stick a bayonet into our bodies." His strongest words came moments later, when he decried Johnson's move as "a lynching of orderly procedure in the Senate of the United States. In other words, the end justifies the means— 'Let us at 'em, come the fifteenth day of February.'"[9]

In an acrimonious exchange with Russell, Dirksen staunchly defended his Democratic counterpart's maneuver. "I had wished, of course, that a civil rights bill might be on the floor or that we might have had one out of committee," Dirksen said. Sometimes, Dirksen added, "we have to pursue extraordinary procedure. In order to get the job done, I am willing to accept any castigation or blame for invoking an extraordinary procedure."[10]

Although furious that Johnson's sneak attack might open the door for consideration of all sorts of proposals, Russell may not have been as adamantly opposed to civil rights legislation as he seemed in front of Georgia audiences or on the Senate floor. In early February Russell had confessed to Johnson's aide Gerald Siegel that the administration bill, then slowly working its way toward House passage, might be acceptable. But for now, at least, the southerners would not allow Johnson, Dirksen, or anyone else in the Senate dictate the terms of a civil rights bill. They wanted instead to forestall Senate action until the House had a chance to pass the so-called "clean" administration proposal, without a Part III provision. Meanwhile the southerners had a problem. How could they kill time until the House acted?[11]

The smell of filibuster was in the air.

In 1957, before the Little Rock crisis, most southern senators had believed that their decision to forgo a filibuster in return for a weak voting rights bill was thoroughly defensible. This bill was different. "One of the main reasons why we filibustered against that 1960 bill," Herman Talmadge later explained, "is that we had been burned badly in 1957. We had been talked out of blocking that earlier bill by assurances that federal troops would not be used to enforce court orders." After Little Rock, Talmadge said, he realized that "we were pretty naive to have believed that." By 1960 these southerners, stung by criticism that they had not fought hard enough to defeat the 1957 bill, found themselves corralled into a filibuster by their own doomsday rhetoric. For example, Russell called the bill "the gravest threat to free national elections in this country since the stolen presidential contest of 1876." The legislation, Sam Ervin charged, would "single out certain groups of Americans on no basis but their race, and demand that they be given rights superior to those ever sought by or granted to any other Americans . . . in history."[12]

On February 16, Russell moved to postpone consideration of the civil rights issue for a week. He lost overwhelmingly, 28–61. Later that day, Wayne Morse, an Oregon liberal offended by Johnson's unorthodox parliamentary maneuver of the previous day, moved to discharge civil rights legislation that the Senate had already referred to the Judiciary Committee. But Johnson and the liberals remained in firm control, and Morse's motion failed, 4–68. Finally the Senate rejected, by voice vote, Morse's motion to discharge from the Rules Committee Humphrey's bill that authorized federal registrars. The actual question of civil rights was finally presented to the Senate on February 17, when Dirksen offered the Eisenhower administration's seven-part bill as an amendment to the House-passed Missouri school bill. Their resolve now growing stiffer by the day, southerners refused to yield an inch of ground. They permitted no votes, objecting even when Dirksen asked for unanimous consent to consider the bill's seven parts "en bloc."[13]

On Tuesday, February 23, after a week of running in place, Johnson knew it was time to spur the Senate to action. He announced that on the following Monday, February 29, the Senate would begin an around-the-clock, continuous session. If southerners wanted to prevent a vote, he would force them to wage a full-fledged filibuster—not the gentlemanly nine-to-five variety that had been the rule in recent years. If Johnson forced them to debate the bill for twenty-four hours a day, southerners could not claim that he had denied them ample time to air their views—a common argument against cloture.[14]

That day the filibuster began to take life. "We will resist to the limit of our ability, within the provisions of the rules," Russell said. Chief among the southern weapons, he announced, would be quorum calls "at awkward times" of the day and night. To more than one discerning ear, Russell was announcing the beginning of a filibuster. Johnson, meanwhile, hoped that the continuous session would force the southerners into an early capitulation. He did not, however, know that Russell and his troops were prepared to revolutionize the use of the modern filibuster.[15]

For decades, a filibuster usually meant that a handful of outnumbered senators talked until they reached the limits of physical and emotional endurance. Such tactics were most successfully employed near the end of a legislative session, when their members were eager to depart Washington and thus more agreeable to compromise.

This filibuster was different. Staged early in the session, it would not benefit from the same time constraints. Furthermore, the southern group, which included many of the Senate's oldest members, was not likely to prevail in any confrontation where physical stamina was as important as oratorical skill.* Nonetheless the southerners at least knew that history favored their cause: the Senate had *never* imposed cloture on a southern filibuster in a civil rights debate.

Ostensibly concerned about the physical strain that around-the-clock sessions would impose on the Senate's older members, Florida's sixty-seven-year-old Spessard Holland attempted to lay the potential blame on Johnson and Dirksen. "The responsibility," he said, "for the lives and health of certain members of the Senate who are of age and in feeble health is upon the hearts and consciences of the two leaders of the Senate." Johnson adamantly refused to accept such responsibility. "I am not the one who prevents the majority of the Senate from expressing themselves," he replied. Johnson noted that "if the majority want to adjourn at eight o'clock this evening, they can do so."

To prove his point—and to divest himself of responsibility for the possible collapse of an elderly senator—Johnson called the southerners' bluff. On February 26 he moved to adjourn the Senate the following Monday at 5:00 P.M. "I do not want to have on my conscience," Johnson said, "an individual decision that was not in accordance with the majority wishes of this body." Caught off guard by Johnson's sudden move, confused southerners began voting for adjournment. When Russell learned of Johnson's scheme, he moved quickly to deny the leadership a chance to display its

---

*Filibusters were often physically taxing because of the Senate rule that required members to stand while addressing the Senate. Any member who sat or left the chamber without yielding temporarily to another member lost his or her right to the floor.

true strength. Midway through the roll call, southerners stopped voting for adjournment and began voting to remain in session. Although Russell described the 67–10 vote against adjournment as merely "a straw man," a satisfied Johnson declared himself merely an agent of the Senate's will.

Assured of twenty-four-hour sessions for at least two weeks, southerners began to discuss how they might sustain a lengthy filibuster without exhausting themselves in the process. What they needed were not eighteen marathon runners but a well-conditioned relay team. Russell's Georgia colleague, Herman Talmadge, had just the idea. Relying on his experience "standing watch" in the navy, Talmadge devised a plan to "outfox" Johnson.[16]

"Look, Dick," Talmadge said, "this is as simple as ABC. We've got nineteen [actually eighteen] senators on our side. That's one general and eighteen troops. You divide those eighteen troops into three platoons of six men each. A platoon will go on duty for a twenty-four-hour period. You divide each of those platoons into squads of two men each. Those two men will be responsible for filibustering for eight hours. They can take turns talking and resting. Then, when the eight-hour watch is over, another squad will replace them. That means that each of us will be on duty for eight hours and then have two days off."[17]

In a meeting in Russell's office, at his large round table, the southern general gave the idea life and issued his marching orders. "Just remember," Russell told his colleagues, "that they didn't have any mercy on us and we won't have any on them." That, advised Russell, meant forcing Johnson and Dirksen to maintain a quorum to answer roll calls at every hour of every day. "Whenever you finish speaking," he said, "call for a quorum. Call for a quorum at the most inopportune time of the day for the great majority of senators."[18]

But quorum calls were more than just dilatory and bothersome. Under the Senate's rules, each senator could deliver only two speeches during a single *legislative day*. And legislative days, unlike twenty-four-hour calendar days, ended only when the Senate adjourned. Therefore, quorum calls were vital because, without a quorum (fewer than fifty senators), southerners could force adjournment and the advent of a new legislative day. As Talmadge explained, "The only way the opposition could hope to thwart us [short of cloture] was to keep the legislative day going until we all had given our two speeches. That meant preventing adjournment."

To make it difficult for Johnson and Dirksen to assemble a quorum, no southerners—except the filibustering senators on duty—would answer any quorum call. That would force the two leaders to draw at least forty-nine votes from their own ranks—a sometimes-impossible task at 3:00 A.M.[19]

In a matter of days, Russell succeeded in turning the tables on Johnson. Instead of wearing themselves down, Russell's forces turned the pro–civil rights senators into a fatigued and grumpy collection of middle-aged and elderly men who were forced to find precious moments of slumber on dozens of uncomfortable army cots placed just off the Senate floor. At all hours of the night, southerners demanded quorum calls. Bells rang loudly. Groggy, red-eyed senators would emerge from fitful sleep, stagger onto the Senate floor, answer the roll call, and stumble wearily back to their cots for an hour or two of sleep before the bells rang again. "They smothered us with quorum calls," recalled Jacob Javits. "Sleep became the unifying force in the drama," reporter Thomas Wolfe wrote in the *Washington Post*. During early-morning sessions, as the southern sentries conducted their lonely "debate," Wolfe observed that "sleep hung in the air like nerve gas."[20]

The southerners, meanwhile, were fresh and well rested. Because they purposely abstained from most quorum calls, all but a handful of them enjoyed a full night's rest throughout the filibuster. "We had a comparatively easy time," Sam Ervin recalled, "but the majority was run ragged." Said Talmadge: "We beat them to death." The southerners were more than a little amused at how easily they had put their pro–civil rights colleagues on the defensive. "You'd be surprised how much physical strain we could put on the opposition," Alabama's John Sparkman bragged years later. Said Paul Douglas's aide Howard Shuman: "A senator who was filibustering didn't have to show except every third day and didn't have to speak except every sixth day. The people who were trying to break the filibuster had to be around, fifty-one of them, at all times, to answer the quorum calls . . . The effect of it was to wear out the people who were trying to break the filibuster, rather than to wear out the people who were filibustering."[21]

Denying requests for unanimous consent was another dilatory tactic that Russell used skillfully to thwart the opposition. Under Johnson's regime, unanimous consent—a routine voice vote on noncontroversial matters—had become the bread and butter of the Senate's daily business. Russell now served notice that southerners would refuse almost all such requests for the duration of the filibuster. Like other weapons in the southerners' arsenal, this tactic was not simply an annoyance. Denying unanimous consent for routine motions—for example, to dispense with the reading of amendments or an entire bill—consumed time and gave the southerners a chance to rest their weary feet and voices. The southerners used other parliamentary weapons as well. They demanded roll calls on all sorts of procedural inquiries and posed convoluted questions to the presiding officer. To give a filibustering senator a brief respite or bathroom break, southerners sometimes posed questions lasting several minutes.

Throughout the filibuster, Johnson was on constant alert for surprise attacks from the southerners. If Russell or one of his men could catch the leadership dozing, they could do almost anything they wanted with a simple unanimous consent request. On one night in particular, Johnson suspected that Russell might attempt some parliamentary trick. Although he had placed a pro–civil rights senator in the chamber to guard against a southern surprise attack, Johnson worried that the senator might be caught off guard by Russell's suspected scheme. Sometime after midnight, Johnson dressed, put on his shoes, and walked over to the Senate chamber. "He looked around," Harry McPherson recalled, "and heard the southerners speaking and saw his watchman sitting there, his head nodding off. And at that very moment at the other end of the chamber he saw the door push open about two inches, and there was Dick Russell looking out, waiting for Johnson to pull a trick, cut this guy off and pass the bill." [22]

By March 5, southerners had filibustered for 125 hours and 31 minutes. Except for a single fifteen-minute recess, the Senate had remained in session for its longest continuous period ever. All Senate committees had suspended hearings. During that time, the Senate had held only one substantive vote: On March 2, the Senate tabled an amendment proposed by Russell Long of Louisiana to the bill's first section. [23]

The debate, though spirited, was surprisingly free of acrimony. And southern speeches were germane. But on March 5, an exhausted Johnson finally relented. "Every man has the right to a Saturday-night bath," he said as he sent his weary allies home for the evening. To Russell and the southerners, the recess meant only that they were winning. "I think we could have carried on . . . for the rest of the session if necessary," Ervin said, "because [Russell] had a very good system for conducting a filibuster." His troops, Russell told the press, were in splendid condition, and there was "no area of compromise." Such talk, however, was merely for show. A compromise, Russell Baker reported in the *New York Times,* "is palpably in the air and everybody knows it." But as Baker correctly noted, when and if the Senate reached a compromise, it was likely to be the northern liberals—not Russell—who relented.[24]

Three days later, a partial southern victory seemed assured. Johnson finally called off the continuous session when the bipartisan liberal group filed a cloture petition on March 8. Further evidence of the southerners' clout was the unsuccessful cloture vote on March 10. Johnson and Dirksen had both opposed cloture, arguing that they needed time "to find an area of agreement" that could "represent the views of sixty-seven members of the Senate [the two-thirds majority needed to impose cloture]." But Jacob Javits protested that Johnson should not force the Senate to wait until two-thirds of the body agreed. "The people of New York sent me here on the constitutional principle that it took a majority, not two-thirds, of the Senate to act." Douglas warned—accurately—that failure to impose cloture would send a signal that "strong measures" would never be part of the final legislation. "The result," he declared, "will be a truncated bill." The cloture vote that the liberals demanded only proved Douglas's point. A majority sided with Johnson and Dirksen. Senators rejected cloture, 53–42, opting to wait for a compromise.[25]

The vote, the first on cloture since 1954, was a blow to the liberals. Gone was their argument that an outmoded cloture rule was preventing the Senate from acting. They had not even garnered a simple majority. Another defeat came quickly on the heels of the cloture vote, when senators approved Johnson's motion to kill a Part III amendment in a 55–38 vote.[26]

As Johnson searched for a compromise, he faced the daunting challenge of appeasing at least two of the Senate's three competing factions: Russell's southerners, ostensibly opposed to all civil rights legislation but obviously willing to end their filibuster in favor of a mild compromise version of the administration's bill; the Democratic and Republican moderates, led by Johnson and Dirksen, who supported the administration proposal but were willing to compromise on some provisions, particularly exclusion of the Part III language; and the Democratic and Republican coalition of liberals—led by Douglas, Clark, and Javits—who were pushing legislation to strengthen the administration proposal by attaching amendments supported by the NAACP and the ADA. The liberal group was itself divided: Some Democrats hoped that the proposed amendments would help erase the Republican fingerprints left on the bill by the administration's proposals. Particularly dear to the liberals' hearts were proposals to permit the president to appoint federal registrars wherever the Civil Rights Commission certified that voting discrimination existed—a more aggressive approach to voting rights than the administration's referee provision.[27]

On March 4 the House finally began its long-awaited debate on the administration bill. On March 24, members voted 311–109 to send a watered-down version of the bill to the Senate. It included a provision, added during floor debate, for the appointment of voting referees—but only in areas where a federal judge determined that discrimination prevented black registration. The House had also eliminated the school desegregation and job discrimination provisions which southerners found most objectionable. In short, the House bill seemed just the kind of compromise that Johnson and Dirksen believed would short-circuit the southern filibuster.[28]

On March 24 Johnson moved to abandon the Senate legislation and refer the House bill to the Judiciary Committee with instructions to report it to the Senate by March 29. Although Judiciary Committee chairman James Eastland protested that his committee needed more time to consider the referee provision, the Senate overwhelmingly sided with Johnson. By an 86–5 vote, senators gave the committee only five days to do its work.[29]

In two days of hearings, Judiciary members recommended amendments to every section of the bill. On March 30 the Senate went into high gear. It voted 71–17 to begin consideration of the House-passed legislation. In rapid-fire succession, senators adopted eight amendments, most of them minor. Among the substantive changes, senators voted 68–20 to outlaw obstruction of *any* federal court orders, not just those relating to school desegregation. Suddenly the bill had gained unstoppable momentum.[30]

The Senate's final product seemed to satisfy only the moderates. Russell said that the bill "flies in the face of the Constitution; it absolutely destroys due process so far as the local election official is concerned." Yet liberals such as Joseph Clark believed that southerners had successfully weakened a strong bill. Clark, who would reluctantly support it, waxed melodramatic. "Dick, here is my sword," he joked shortly before the final vote. "I hope you will give it back to me so that I can beat it into a plowshare for the spring planting. Surely in this battle on the Senate floor the roles of Grant and

Lee at Appomattox have been reversed." Javits, another reluctant yes vote, called the bill "a victory for the Old South."[31]

On April 8, before a virtually deserted gallery, the Senate made history for the second time in three years. It passed the Civil Rights Act of 1960 in a 71–18 vote. In contrast to 1957, the vote was almost anticlimactic. After fifty-three days of debate, both sides had long since exhausted their arguments. House members, meanwhile, were in no mood for a contentious conference to resolve differences in the bill's two versions. "We're tired of this thing," said House Republican leader Charles Halleck. "We want to get rid of it and do something else for a change." Two weeks after Senate passage, the House agreed to the Senate's amendments, 288–95. Eisenhower signed the bill on May 6.[32]

Except for a few ideologues, the eighteen members of the southern group knew that Russell had negotiated a fair deal. In the Senate they had appeared reasonable, even progressive, for having "wisely" resisted the primal urge to continue their filibuster. At home, however, they were free to declare, as did Russell, that they had "defeated the most vicious schemes proposed by the South haters" and had "stricken out or modified other unfair and inequitable features." Johnson, too, could claim victory. Again he had broken the debilitating civil rights gridlock. Cries of despair from the extremists on both sides seemed proof enough that he had performed well.[33]

In the end the bill satisfied no one completely, least of all Russell. He recognized the legislation for what it was—another step in the slow but steady march toward a comprehensive civil rights act. "He can slow the onward course of the opposition," William V. Shannon wrote in the *New York Post* in March. "He can avoid surrender. But he cannot ultimately win a total victory."[34]

9

GO GET MY LONG RIFLE

As much as he wanted it, Johnson stood little chance of winning the Democratic presidential nomination in 1960. His southern roots and his reputation as a conservative made his candidacy almost impossible. It mattered not that he was responsible for passing two civil rights bills, the first such legislative feats in the twentieth century. Many influential liberals did not trust him. Their memories of his fealty to Russell's southern bloc were too powerful, and a couple of incremental voting rights bills could not capture their hearts.

By making his Senate leadership a central part of his campaign, Johnson only highlighted his reputation as a ruthless dealmaker whose passion was the art of compromise. When Johnson did venture out from Washington, his unpolished and earthy speaking manner often failed to inspire audiences, especially when compared with the refined, urbane demeanors of senators John F. Kennedy of Massachusetts and Stuart Symington of Missouri or the effusive eloquence of Humphrey. Explained Howard Shuman: "He knew Senate politics instinctively, but he didn't understand national politics, and he wasn't really attuned to national issues because of his focus on the Senate."[1]

A significant part of Johnson's problem with Democratic liberals—a key constituency—then-Minnesota governor Orville Freeman later concluded, was that he "had simply no time for the people who wanted to talk a good game but never get anything done. He really held them in great repugnance . . . And so, sometimes he would . . . fail to communicate with them even when he had really a very excellent liberal record." Freeman, who later was agriculture secretary under presidents Kennedy and Johnson, admitted that he was among those who had believed that Johnson was too conservative. While traveling to the Democratic convention in Los Angeles, however, he began reviewing Johnson's voting record, and he was "astounded" to learn that Johnson was far more liberal than he had imagined.[2]

By contrast, John F. Kennedy, forty-two, was a charismatic second-term senator who had almost been chosen as Adlai Stevenson's running mate in 1956. Although some branded him a liberal, he was actually a moderate. Mindful of potential southern delegates, he had displeased dogmatic liberals by his refusal to condemn Senator Joseph McCarthy's reckless pursuit of communists in the federal government in the early 1950s. On civil rights, despite his otherwise impressive voting record, some liberals still bitterly remembered his vote to send the 1957 bill to the Judiciary Committee and his support for the jury trial amendment. Liberals also may have been aware that Kennedy counted among his southern supporters men such as John Stennis and Herman Talmadge.

Many liberals not only opposed Johnson for president but despaired at the thought that Kennedy might choose him as his running mate. One ADA leader, Robert Nathan, recalled that members of his organization opposed Johnson because he "was not 'all out,' that he was attempting to compromise and take what he could get, so to speak." Johnson would probably have agreed with Nathan's characterization, and that was the problem. The liberals did not want a compromiser; they wanted a *real* liberal. What they could not admit publicly was that Kennedy's overall record was barely more liberal than Johnson's.[3]

Not long after he arrived in Los Angeles for the Democratic convention, Johnson knew the race was over. At Kennedy's hands, he learned a hard lesson: His strength in the halls of Congress—his ability to forge compromises and build consensus—was no advantage in the presidential arena. Had his congressional colleagues possessed the power to choose the nominee, Johnson would have won hands down. But they did not have such authority; the more liberal Democratic activists did. In their eyes, Johnson was merely a southern wheeler-dealer and protégé of Richard Russell. Too many influential liberals, black and white, simply doubted his loyalty to their causes, particularly civil rights.

Kennedy, meanwhile, enjoyed generous support among blacks and civil rights activists. One advantage was his near-perfect voting record on civil rights during his thirteen years in Congress. From his 1947 House vote for an anti–poll tax bill to supporting stronger amendments to the 1960 Civil Rights Act, Kennedy had been with the liberals on all but two major votes.[4]

To bolster his standing among black leaders, Kennedy had enlisted Harris Wofford, a Notre Dame Law School instructor, former staff member of the U.S. Civil Rights Commission, and the first white man ever to graduate from Howard University Law School. Although originally hired to advise Kennedy on Asian affairs, Wofford now became the campaign's adviser on civil rights. "We're really in trouble with Negroes," Robert Kennedy confessed to Wofford in May 1960. "We really don't know much about this whole thing. We've been dealing outside the field of the main Negro leadership and have to start from scratch." Despite John Kennedy's awkward relations with black leaders, his civil rights record was clearly superior to Johnson's—at least in the eyes of liberals and civil rights activists. As for Johnson, most black delegates regarded him as a halfhearted newcomer to the civil rights debate.[5]

There were some notable exceptions to this view. NAACP secretary Roy Wilkins confessed to Wofford that he regarded Johnson as a better friend of civil rights. "If you ask me who, of all the men in political life, I would trust to do the most about civil rights as president," he said, "it would be Lyndon Johnson." According to Wofford, Wilkins saw in Johnson a quality that eluded most liberals, "a deep, inner determination" about the need for civil rights "that stemmed from his intimate knowledge of the damage racial discrimination was doing not only to the South but to the whole country." Wilkins was correct. Despite all his dispassionate votes in favor of civil rights, Kennedy would never have Johnson's innate feel for the issue.[6]

Kennedy's fortunes with black delegates were further strengthened by his inadvertent but fortuitous support of a strong civil rights platform plank. The platform language was stunning in its commitment to bold action on civil rights. "The time has come," it declared, "to assure equal access for all Americans to all areas of community life, including voting booths, schoolrooms, jobs, housing, and public facilities." The platform pledged that a Democratic administration would use "the full powers" of the 1957 and 1960 civil rights acts to ensure the right to vote; "eliminate literacy tests and payment of poll taxes" as voting requirements; seek desegregation plans in "every school district" covered by the Supreme Court's school desegregation decision; empower the Justice Department to initiate civil suits "to prevent the denial of any civil rights"; make the U.S. Commission on Civil Rights a permanent entity; establish a Fair Employment Practices Commission; "use its full executive powers" to end racial segregation in the federal government; and end discrimination in federal housing programs, "including federally assisted housing."[7]

"It was like a child in a candy store," Joseph Rauh later said. "They just gave me what I wanted, all the way on the plank. It was unbelievable. Then, Kennedy campaigned that way. If anybody looks at the Kennedy campaign in 1960, you will see he just said any damned civil rights thing you suggested. I mean, it was perfect."[8]

In 1948, and perhaps in 1952, such a liberal platform would have sparked an angry walkout of southern delegates. Not in 1960. Many southerners who supported Johnson knew they would likely hand the election to the Republicans if they abandoned the convention. Instead of walking out, the southern platform committee members—including Spessard Holland, James Eastland, John Stennis, Sam Ervin, and Russell's close friend Charles J. Bloch—filed a minority report. "There is no 'constitutional requirement that racial discrimination be ended in public education,'" the delegates asserted, clinging hopelessly to their threadbare massive resistance philosophy. "All that the courts have said on this subject is that if a state chooses to establish and maintain a public school system, the children in the schools of that system may not be segregated by the standard of race or color." When the platform reached the convention floor, southern opponents were in no mood for a spirited challenge. Although they offered their minority report as a substitute to the civil rights plank, southerners wisely declined a roll-call vote. Delegates quickly rejected the southern substitute by voice vote.[9]

Such were the declining fortunes—and the increasing isolation—of the civil rights opponents. Several weeks later, the Republican National Convention that nominated Vice President Richard Nixon approved an equally forceful civil rights plank. "Although the Democratic-controlled Congress watered them down," the Republican platform stated in a partisan jab at Democrats, "the [Eisenhower] administration's recommendations resulted in significant and effective civil rights legislation in both 1957 and 1960."[10]

With Kennedy assured of the nomination, talk turned to the selection of a running mate. Despite Johnson's assurances to supporters that he was not interested in the position, and would decline it if offered, it was no secret that Kennedy *ought* to want Johnson as his running mate. He was, after all, the runner-up for the nomination. As the Senate majority leader, he was one of the party's most prominent and skilled leaders. In several southern states where Kennedy's Catholicism was a liability—in Texas, for example—Johnson could make the difference. As an astute politician, Kennedy understood that the electoral votes of Johnson's home state might give him the edge in a tight race with Richard Nixon. For those reasons, Kennedy offered Johnson the vice-presidential nomination.

Most of Johnson's advisers, as well as Kennedy's, were stridently opposed to the idea of a Kennedy-Johnson ticket. Kennedy aide Kenneth O'Donnell told the nominee that Johnson's selection was "the worst mistake you ever made." He argued that despite Kennedy's promises to "get rid of the old hack machine politicians," his first decision after his nomination was to "go against all the people who supported you" by choosing Johnson. Kennedy reacted angrily to O'Donnell's lecture. "I'm forty-three years old, and I'm . . . not going to die in office," Kennedy said. "So the vice-presidency doesn't mean anything. I'm thinking of something else, the leadership of the Senate. If we win, it will be by a small margin and I won't be able to live with Lyndon Johnson as the leader of a small majority in the Senate. Did it occur to you that if Lyndon becomes the Vice President, I'll have Mike Mansfield [Johnson's whip] as the leader in the Senate, somebody I can trust and depend on?" O'Donnell recalled that after Kennedy's outburst, "I began to soften and see things differently."[11]

With Congress set to return for a post-convention session in August— to consider housing, Medicare, and civil rights legislation—Kennedy needed peaceful relations with Johnson and Sam Rayburn. "If Johnson and Rayburn leave here mad at me," Kennedy told O'Donnell, "they'll ruin *me* in Congress next month. Then I'll be the laughingstock of the country. Nixon will say I haven't any power in my own party, and I'll lose the election before Labor Day. So I've got to make my peace now with Lyndon and Rayburn, and offering Lyndon the vice-presidency, whether he accepts it or not, is one way of keeping him friendly until Congress adjourns."[12]

Johnson was torn, but ultimately decided he had no choice but to accept. He voiced his dilemma to Congressman Homer Thornberry: If he turned down Kennedy, and Kennedy lost, "they'll blame me for it, and then my position as majority leader might be in jeopardy." Yet if Kennedy won, "they'll say, 'He won without your help,' and then I'll have some problems." Ultimately, Johnson told Thornberry that "I may owe a responsibility to try to carry this country for the Democratic party."[13]

Johnson may also have realized that his days as the Senate's dominant force were ending, given the number of restive liberals who now chafed under his leadership. Harry McPherson speculated that this realization weighed heavily on Johnson's mind. "Well, hell, I'm tired," McPherson imagined Johnson thinking. "I've been working hard as leader. I've had a heart attack. I think, instead of going through the frustrations and agonies of being on the short end of the stick down at the Hill and being kind of an errand boy for Jack Kennedy, I'll run with him. I'll be vice president and bide my time."[14]

In Los Angeles, as Johnson mulled his options in a hotel suite full of aides and friends, Oklahoma senator Bob Kerr burst into the room. He was livid. His eyes immediately fixed on Johnson. According to Arkansas congressman Oren Harris, Kerr shouted, "Lyndon, they tell me that Jack Kennedy wants you to be his running mate. If you accept, I'll shoot you right between the eyes!" Tennessee governor Buford Ellington remembered Kerr's first words differently: "I know what's up, and I'll go get my long rifle. It ain't going to happen!" Before Kerr could say more, Sam Rayburn herded him into the bathroom. Now a supporter of Johnson as running mate, Rayburn reasoned with Kerr for several minutes. When the two men emerged, Kerr walked calmly to Johnson and said, "Lyndon, if Jack Kennedy asked you to be his running mate, and if you don't take it, I'll shoot you right between the eyes."[15]

Later that day Johnson phoned Kennedy to inform him of his decision. Minutes later he stepped into the crowded corridor outside his hotel room and stood on a chair. "Jack Kennedy has asked me to serve," he announced. "I accept."[16]

Johnson and Kennedy moved quickly to calm liberals and black leaders who were outraged by Johnson's nomination. "Just give me a chance," Johnson pleaded at a caucus of black delegates near the close of the Los Angeles convention. "I won't let you down. I'll do more for you in four years in the field of civil rights than you've experienced in the last hundred years." Civil rights activists were dubious. James Farmer, head of the Congress of Racial Equality, considered Johnson's nomination "a disaster, because of his southern background and his voting record on civil rights."[17]

"Well, I'm here to tell you that all hell broke loose," Humphrey later said. Liberals such as Joseph Rauh and Michigan governor G. Mennen "Soapy" Williams "were just up in arms," said Humphrey, who was pleased with Johnson's selection. "I sat down and visited with [Johnson] a good long time," Humphrey said, "and then went to work amongst as many of the liberals as I could on his behalf." At the time, Humphrey said, few liberals were willing to voice their public support for Johnson. "All I know," grumbled Rauh about Kennedy's earlier pledge not to pick Johnson, "is that if a political promise is worth a damn, I had a broken promise." When he first heard the news of Johnson's selection on the convention floor, Rauh had grabbed an open microphone. To delegates and a national television audience, he bellowed, "Wherever you are, John F. Kennedy, I beseech you to reconsider."[18]

More practical liberals recognized the brilliance of Kennedy's selection. "The Democrats never carried Texas," observed Connecticut governor Abraham Ribicoff. "If Texas did not go for the Democrats, they could not win the presidency. Johnson was the only one who could bring him something." Orville Freeman, a last-minute convert to Johnson's camp, argued "very strongly" with his liberal friends "that Lyndon Johnson had an excellent liberal record, and that basically he was a populist in his political and economic and social orientation." In what turned out to be a remarkably prescient assessment, the *New Republic* insisted that "by changing Lyndon Johnson from a Texas to a national politician, Kennedy frees him to take more liberal positions if, as Johnson's old friends in Washington have always vowed, those are the true beliefs of the inner man."[19]

Johnson clearly understood that his political future hinged on whether he could carry the South for Kennedy. One southern conservative in particular was on his mind in the days following the convention. Would Richard Russell, who had not attended the convention and had openly worried about the leftward drift of his party, lend his considerable influence to a liberal ticket on which Johnson occupied the number-two spot?

Through his nephew Bobby, a Georgia delegate, Russell had advised Johnson to reject Kennedy's offer. He thought it unwise for Johnson to relinquish his majority leader's post for the ceremonial and powerless job of vice president. Russell also worried that Johnson's position on the ticket would amount to an endorsement of the liberal platform that he regarded as "a mess of unconstitutional vote bait."[20]

For his part, Johnson believed that Russell's endorsement was crucial to the ticket's chances in the South. At a "unity meeting" of southern governors called at his behest by Tennessee's Buford Ellington, Johnson spotted Robert Troutman, a Georgia-born lawyer who was a friend to both Kennedy and Russell. Later that evening, Johnson pulled Troutman aside. He was "very depressed," said Troutman, that southern leaders had not yet endorsed the Democratic ticket. Please go to Russell and Herman Talmadge, Johnson implored, and remind them that Kennedy had chosen him "with the expectation" that he could deliver the South for

Kennedy. Johnson, said Troutman, "felt that [Russell and Talmadge] were almost obligated" to publicly support him. In a rambling and emotional monologue, Johnson described the long and tangled history of his friendship with Russell.

Troutman did as Johnson asked. Shortly after the governors' meeting, he drove to Russell's Winder, Georgia, home. To Russell's "amusement," he recounted the entire conversation with Johnson. Yet Russell remained "very bitterly" opposed to Johnson's acceptance of Kennedy's offer and told Troutman that he had already "done a great deal to show his friendship in times past." Troutman left with the distinct feeling that Russell "was gonna sit it out."[21]

Russell indeed planned to watch the 1960 presidential race from the sidelines. He planned to lend Johnson two of his aides but nothing more. Although he personally liked Kennedy, Russell vehemently opposed the Democratic platform that promised to "implement these vicious [civil rights] provisions." On September 24 Russell issued a perfunctory and unenthusiastic statement: "On November 8, I shall vote the straight Democratic ticket as I have always done." Several weeks later, he left for a three-week inspection of U.S. military bases in Europe.[22]

Johnson, meanwhile, embarked on an old-fashioned whistle-stop tour of the South aimed at persuading the region's predominantly Protestant voters to give a Catholic candidate a chance. At stop after stop through eight states over five days, Johnson recounted Kennedy's heroic exploits as commander of PT-109 during World War II: "When he was savin' those American boys that was in his crew, they didn't ask what church he belonged to."[23]

Throughout the train trip, Johnson conveniently dispensed with his former identification as a southwesterner. On the LBJ Victory Special, Johnson was all southern. His drawl was deeper, and he laced his speeches with folksy adages. He was, he often noted, "the grandson of a Confederate soldier." He largely met the issue of civil rights honestly and directly. He rarely waited until questioned about the issue, broaching the subject himself in every major speech. "I say to you," he declared in numerous speeches, "we will protect the constitutional rights of every living American, regardless of race, religion, or region." Johnson's only acknowledgment of southern fears about civil rights was a promise that he and Kennedy would single out no "region"—meaning the South—for civil rights enforcement. The message was clear: Jack Kennedy and the Democratic party would *protect* or *guarantee* the civil rights of every American. Yet Johnson made no mention of his and Kennedy's explicit endorsement of a platform that pledged aggressive action to ensure desegregation of schools and federal housing and employment.[24]

Johnson's southern tour was a great success. As he attracted hundreds and then thousands of supporters at nearly every stop, state and local Democratic leaders began shedding their reluctance to support the ticket. In Florida, the Democratic nominee for governor declared Johnson "immensely qualified." Governors Ernest Hollings of South Carolina and John Patterson of Alabama warmly embraced Johnson's candidacy, as did senators Talmadge of Georgia and Eastland of Mississippi. By the time Johnson's train reached its final stop in New Orleans, an impressive array of Democratic officials was waiting, ready to present Johnson their enthusiastic endorsements.[25]

Besides helping blunt the issue of Kennedy's religion in the heavily Protestant Bible Belt, Johnson had also reassured many nervous southern Democrats that a Kennedy administration would not take a radical approach to civil rights. Yet it was just that question—how aggressively would Kennedy push for action on civil rights?—that plagued liberals and conservatives alike. Shortly after the convention, Johnson had advised Kennedy to be careful. To coax nervous southern states back into the Democratic column, Kennedy must play the issue with finesse. Kennedy was not so sure. While he wanted to avoid needlessly provoking white southerners, he understood that the growing black vote in the North and the South would be crucial to his election. Kennedy, however, was unsure how to court black voters. The strong Democratic platform would help, but the Republican platform was just as forceful. A well-publicized meeting with prominent civil rights leader Martin Luther King Jr. might help Kennedy prove his commitment to civil rights. The two men, however, had been unable to agree on the time and place.

Actually, many voters found it almost impossible to discern differences in the two parties' civil rights policies. A Republican president had proposed the civil rights acts of 1957 and 1960, but Democrats—minus their southern bloc—were the ones who provided the congressional leadership and the crucial votes to ensure their passage.[26]

In the end, it was Martin Luther King's arrest in October—and

Kennedy's inadvertent reaction to it—that would help transform the racial dynamics of presidential politics for the rest of the century.

On October 19 King joined black students in a peaceful protest at the all-white lunch counter of an Atlanta department store. Denied service, King and the students refused to leave and were arrested. Although police eventually released the students, King had more serious legal problems. In May he had been issued tickets for two minor traffic violations. He had paid the $25 fine, but the infractions carried a one-year probationary period. During that time, if King violated any federal or state law, he was subject to more serious charges. A segregationist judge in Atlanta was unmoved by King's protests that he had not known about the probation. He sentenced King to four months in prison.[27]

In Washington, officials of Eisenhower's Justice Department briefly considered court action to rescue King. Instead, Deputy Attorney General Lawrence Walsh merely drafted a sympathetic statement that Eisenhower declined to use. Richard Nixon's advisers also considered urging their candidate to express concern for King and his wife but concluded that this might alienate white voters.[28]

In Washington, Harris Wofford, a friend of King, had monitored the Atlanta situation for Kennedy's campaign. He urged his Atlanta friends to get King out of jail. Already Wofford's interest in the case had drawn his candidate into the controversy—although Kennedy had not personally lifted a finger for King. When Atlanta's progressive mayor, William Hartsfield, engineered the release of the student protesters, he gave Kennedy the credit. Wire services carried Hartsfield's statement nationwide.[29]

When Wofford learned of Hartsfield's statement, he protested to Atlanta lawyer Morris Abram: "But Kennedy knows nothing about my call. I told you I was acting on my own." Hartsfield himself tried to comfort Wofford, admitting that he "ran with the ball farther than you expected." But the mayor insisted that he was "giving [Kennedy] the election on a silver platter, so don't pull the rug out from under me." Scrambling to contain the controversy, Kennedy's campaign issued a brief statement claiming that the candidate had merely ordered "an inquiry" to obtain "the facts on that situation and a report on what properly should be done."[30]

Now that King faced a four-month prison term, Wofford worried that Kennedy risked looking ambivalent and ineffective. He urged a stronger statement to increase pressure on Georgia authorities to release their prominent prisoner. Kennedy's Georgia leaders were much more cautious. Any further intervention by the Democratic candidate, they advised, might cost them Georgia and several other southern states. Finally Governor Ernest Vandiver, husband of one of Russell's nieces, promised to get "the son of a bitch" out of jail if Kennedy made no more public statements.

Three days after the students' release, as King languished in jail, a frantic Coretta King phoned Wofford. Frustrated that he could not reveal the governor's promise and that Kennedy "could not make any public comment on the case," Wofford only informed Mrs. King that he was "doing everything possible." After the call, Wofford confessed his frustration to Louis Martin, a black former newspaper publisher.

"Who cares about public statements?" Wofford complained. "What Kennedy ought to do is something direct and personal, like picking up the telephone and calling Coretta. Just giving his sympathy, but doing it himself."

"That's it, that's it!" Martin said. "That would be perfect." [31]

That night the situation in Georgia worsened. Deputies awakened King abruptly at about 3:30 A.M., slapped handcuffs and leg irons on him, shoved him into the back of a car, and embarked on a harrowing two-hundred-mile trip to the Georgia state prison in Reidsville. When Wofford found out the next morning, he tracked down his close friend Sargent Shriver, Kennedy's brother-in-law and Illinois campaign manager. As luck would have it, Kennedy was in Chicago that morning. Wofford made his proposal: Kennedy should phone Mrs. King and express concern for her husband's safety. Shriver agreed and left immediately for Kennedy's hotel room. When he arrived, several other aides were in the room. One by one, they left. Finally Shriver and Kennedy were alone. "It was miraculous," he recalled, "because I had not wanted to bring up the idea of calling Mrs. King with the others there, because I knew it would precipitate a debate about the call's pros and cons."

Shriver broached the subject. "Jack, I have an idea that might help you in the campaign: Mrs. Martin Luther King is sitting down there in Atlanta, and she is terribly worried about what is going to happen to her husband. I have her home telephone number; I suggest that you pick up the phone, say hello, and tell her you hope that everything works out well."

Kennedy pondered Shriver's suggestion for about fifteen seconds. "That's a good idea," he said. "Can you get her on the phone?" Shriver placed the call and handed the phone to Kennedy, who spoke with Mrs. King for no more than three minutes. "I want to express to you my concern about your husband," he said. "I know this must be very hard for you. I understand you are expecting a baby, and I just wanted you to know that I was thinking about you and Dr. King. If there is anything I can do to help, please feel free to call on me." Before Shriver could report to Wofford, Coretta King called. "She was very moved and grateful," Wofford recalled. By day's end, she had given the story to the *New York Times*. Shortly after Kennedy's call, the judge released King on $2,000 bond.[32]

King told reporters he was "deeply indebted to Senator Kennedy." Although he stopped short of endorsing the Democratic candidate, King later praised Kennedy for having "moral courage of a high order." At a joyful gathering that night at King's Ebenezer Baptist Church, King's father, Reverend Martin Luther King Sr., was effusive in his praise of Kennedy. "Jack Kennedy has the moral courage to stand up for what he knows is right." Elated by his son's release and the role Kennedy had played in it, "Daddy" King—a Republican—later announced he would vote for Kennedy, even though the candidate was Catholic.[33]

On November 8, Kennedy was elected president by the razor-thin margin of 118,574 votes out of 68.3 million cast. More decisive was the Electoral College, where Kennedy defeated Nixon 303 to 219. In Texas, where more than two million voters went to the polls, Kennedy won by a margin of just 46,233 votes. It was the first time Texas had gone Democratic since 1948. Johnson won two elections that day, also beating Republican nominee John Tower by 364,000 votes to win reelection to his Senate seat.

Johnson's presence on the ticket, and his vigorous campaigning across the South, were at least partly responsible for an impressive string of southern victories. Seven former Confederate states fell to the Democrats: Alabama, Arkansas, Georgia, Louisiana, North Carolina, and South Carolina, and Texas. The rest of the South went to Nixon—except for Mississippi, whose voters gave a plurality to a segregationist candidate. Without Johnson as his running mate, said Mississippi's James Eastland, "Kennedy would not have carried any Southern state." House Republican leader Charles Halleck put it bluntly: "I don't think Jack Kennedy could have been elected if he hadn't had Lyndon Johnson with him."[34]

Difficult to imagine was a Kennedy victory without a southerner on the ticket. More difficult to imagine was anyone whom southerners would have found more acceptable than Johnson—progressive enough to appease disgruntled liberals and blacks yet conservative enough to calm uneasy white Democrats. In retrospect, Kennedy's controversial decision seemed brilliant.

Now that Kennedy had won, southerners worried. What would Kennedy do on civil rights given the activist agenda outlined in the party's platform? "I guess it is for the best," Russell told a friend several days after the election, "for I am confident that [Johnson] will be a power in the next administration. If he has any sense of loyalty (and I am sure that he does), he and Kennedy both will appreciate the fact that they would have been signally defeated without the South."[35]

How would the new president and vice president govern? How hard would they push the issue of civil rights? For the moment, no one was certain.

The teacher and his Mexican-American students. Johnson (*center*) with his fifth-, sixth-, and seventh-grade classes at the Welhausen Elementary School in Cotulla, Texas, in 1928 or 1929. *LBJ Library Collection.*

Standing between Georgia's two senators, Richard Russell and Walter George, Johnson faces the press after a White House meeting with President Eisenhower in 1953. *White House photo courtesy Richard B. Russell Library.*

Lyndon Johnson and Hubert Humphrey's friendship dated back to 1949, when they both entered the U.S. Senate. Humphrey, a fierce advocate for civil rights, was Johnson's bridge to the Senate's liberals. *LBJ Library photo by Yoichi R. Okamoto.*

The Southern General. Richard Russell of Georgia was not only Lyndon Johnson's mentor in the U.S. Senate but also leader of the southern forces against civil rights legislation. One of the most respected and powerful members of the Senate, Russell chaired the Armed Services Committee. *LBJ Library photo by Frank Wolfe.*

President Dwight D. Eisenhower signs the Civil Rights Act of 1957 while on vacation in Rhode Island. *White House photo courtesy of Eisenhower Library.*

Lady Bird and Johnson at the 1960 Democratic National Convention in Los Angeles. Johnson challenged John F. Kennedy for the Democratic presidential nomination and lost. Kennedy's selection of Johnson as his running mate helped the ticket carry several southern states, including Johnson's home state of Texas.
LBJ Library photo by Frank Muto.

Running mates. Senate Majority Leader Johnson and Democratic presidential nominee Kennedy together in the U.S. Capitol in August 1960. Johnson would not enjoy his time as vice president under Kennedy. "Every time I came into John Kennedy's presence," Johnson later said, "I felt like a goddamn raven hovering over his shoulder . . . I detested every minute of it." *LBJ Library photo by Frank Muto.*

President Kennedy speaks to a joint session of Congress in May 1961. Despite having served in the House and Senate, as president Kennedy was never confident in his relations with Congress. On civil rights, Kennedy favored executive action over legislation and only proposed a civil rights bill a few months before his assassination. *Photo courtesy of NASA.*

Friends and rivals. Despite his distrust of his former attorney general, Johnson campaigned for Robert F. Kennedy (*left*) when he ran for the U.S. Senate from New York in 1964. *LBJ Library photo by Cecil Stoughton.*

Rev. Martin Luther King meets with President Johnson at the White House in March 1966. *LBJ Library photo by Yoichi R. Okamoto.*

Kennedy and Sorensen. Robert Kennedy championed the civil rights cause during the Kennedy and Johnson administrations as attorney general. At a 1968 White House, now as U.S. senator from New York, Kennedy is joined by his brother's former adviser, Ted Sorensen. *LBJ Library photo by Yoichi R. Okamoto.*

Senate leaders. Senate majority leader Mike Mansfield (*left*) and Senate Republican leader Everett Dirksen. *LBJ Library photo by Yoichi R. Okamoto.*

Despite a mixed record on the issue during his congressional years, as president Johnson was a determined proponent of civil rights legislation.
LBJ Library photo.

Attorney General Nicholas Katzenbach served in the Justice Department under Robert Kennedy and Lyndon Johnson and helped develop the strategy for the passage of the Civil Rights Act of 1964. Johnson later appointed Katzenbach as attorney general. *LBJ Library photo by Yoichi R. Okamoto.*

Senator Russell Long of Louisiana (*left*) and Dirksen at the White House in 1965. While Long voted against the Voting Rights Act of 1965, he was among several younger southern senators who signaled their desire to end the perennial battles over equality for black Americans. *LBJ Library photo by Yoichi R. Okamoto.*

The Johnson treatment. Johnson and Richard Russell at the White House in December 1962. *LBJ Library photo by Yoichi R. Okamoto.*

Mansfield (*left*) and Senate Foreign Affairs Committee chairman J. William Fulbright at a White House meeting in 1966. Fulbright was among the most enlightened southerners in the Senate and yet voted against the civil rights and voting rights acts. *LBJ Library photo by Yoichi R. Okamoto.*

Former president Dwight Eisenhower and President Johnson aboard Air Force One in 1968. Although the two men were from different political parties, they worked well together. It was Johnson's legislative skills that ensured passage of Eisenhower's civil rights bill in 1957. *LBJ Library photo by Yoichi R. Okamoto.*

New Supreme Court nominee. U.S. Solicitor General Thurgood Marshall and Johnson in the Oval Office on June 13, 1967, prior to the announcement that Marshall would become the first African American appointed to the U.S. Supreme Court. *LBJ Library photo by Yoichi R. Okamoto.*

Johnson speaks to the nation from the East Room of the White House on July 2, 1964, before signing the Civil Rights Act. "We believe all men are entitled to the blessings of liberty," Johnson said. *LBJ Library photo by O. J. Rapp.*

Johnson presents ink pens to Hubert Humphrey and Everett Dirksen after signing the Civil Rights Act of 1964. He is flanked by dozens of civil rights leaders, cabinet members, and congressional leaders. *White House photo courtesy Minnesota Historical Society.*

Sidekicks. As the Senate's deputy majority leader, Hubert Humphrey was the lead strategist for the Civil Rights Act of 1964. The bill's passage was the crowning achievement of Humphrey's congressional career and persuaded Johnson to choose him as vice president. Now the vice president–elect, Humphrey joins Johnson for a horseback ride at the LBJ Ranch in November 1964 after the general election. *LBJ Library photo by Cecil Stoughton.*

Alabama governor George Wallace at the White House in 1968. After his turbulent meeting with Johnson in 1965 during the Birmingham crisis, Wallace remarked, "If I'd stayed in there much longer, he'd have had me coming out for civil rights." *LBJ Library photo by Yoichi R. Okamoto.*

Voting rights. President Johnson hands a pen to Rev. Ralph Abernathy after signing the Voting Rights Act of 1965. To the right of Abernathy stand Rev. Martin Luther King Jr., Clarence Mitchell, and Patricia Roberts Harris. *LBJ Library photo by Yoichi R. Okamoto.*

Triumph for freedom. Johnson poses with congressional leaders at the U.S.
Capitol after signing the Voting Rights Act of 1965. *From left to right:* Mansfield,
Humphrey, Dirksen, Johnson, and House Speaker John McCormick.
LBJ Library photo by Yoichi R. Okamoto.

Republican presidential nominee Richard Nixon meets with Johnson, the retiring
president, at the White House in July 1968. *LBJ Library photo by Yoichi R. Okamoto.*

Humphrey and Johnson meet in the Cabinet Room in April 1968, just days after Johnson announced he would not seek reelection. Shortly thereafter, Humphrey announced his candidacy for the Democratic Party's presidential nomination. *LBJ Library photo by Yoichi R. Okamoto.*

10

HOW DID WE LET THIS HAPPEN?

From the moment he became vice president, Lyndon Johnson was a miserable man. "Lyndon looked as if he'd lost his last friend on earth," recalled journalist Margaret Mayer. "Every time I came into John Kennedy's presence," Johnson later said, "I felt like a goddamn raven hovering over his shoulder . . . I detested every minute of it."[1]

Partly to preserve some semblance of his former power and importance, Johnson was reluctant to relinquish his role as Senate potentate to Montana's Mike Mansfield, the Democratic whip who was about to replace him as majority leader. Even the trappings of his former office were impossible to surrender. Normally Mansfield would have occupied the majority leader's roomy and lavishly decorated suite of offices in the Capitol, derisively known around the Senate as the "Taj Mahal." But Johnson retained the space, leaving Mansfield with an office only half the size of Johnson's.[2]

When Johnson confessed to former aide Bobby Baker that he and Mansfield had agreed that Johnson would become chairman of the Senate Democratic Caucus—and therefore its presiding officer—Baker was "both astonished and horrified." Johnson had not fully understood how many of his colleagues yearned to be free from the constraints of his oppressive rule. "Under Johnson, it was like a Greek tragedy," said Howard Shuman, Paul Douglas's longtime aide. "Nothing went on in the Senate that hadn't happened off the floor beforehand." Even Johnson's former whip, Florida's George Smathers, acknowledged the obvious: "Johnson had just thwarted the democratic concept of the Senate, because he was so powerful and worked so hard at it." To Harry McPherson, Johnson had been the right man for the times. But times changed. "Johnson was the ideal opposition leader," McPherson explained. "Mansfield would be the perfect team player." Many Democrats, especially the liberals, were thrilled to be playing for a new coach.[3]

Mansfield was different from Johnson in almost every way. A quiet, passive man, he was content to allow legislation to take its course. To Mansfield the leadership was "a moral post," said George Reedy. His philosophy, according to Gerald Siegel, was: "It's my role as leader to make it possible for every senator to do what he wants." Unlike Johnson, Mansfield rarely pressured his colleagues for their votes. "He was perfectly willing to explain a bill," recalled J. William Fulbright of Arkansas, "but he very rarely asked you, 'Say, would you please vote for a certain bill?'" Said Herman Talmadge of Georgia: "Mansfield was a moderator and not a leader."[4]

On January 3, 1961, less than three weeks before Johnson would be sworn in as vice president, Senate Democrats met to choose their new leaders. Mansfield made his proposal, one that would effectively make the majority leader a deputy to the vice president of the United States. For a moment, utter silence reigned. Finally Albert Gore spoke up. He was angry. "We might as well ask Jack [Kennedy] to come back up and take *his* turn at presiding." Another Johnson critic, Joseph Clark, also objected. At first red with embarrassment, Johnson's face turned ashen. He was astonished. Old cronies like Willis Robertson of Virginia, Olin Johnston of South Carolina, and Clinton Anderson of New Mexico rose to speak against Mansfield's proposal. They argued that the arrangement would violate the Constitution's separation of powers.[5]

Although most senators said nothing, the smattering of vehement opposition threatened to embarrass Mansfield just minutes into his term as majority leader. Worried about a larger revolt, he threatened to resign unless the caucus upheld him. The Democrats grudgingly approved his motion, 46–17, but their message was clear: Despite his "victory," Johnson knew the arrangement could not work. As Bobby Baker said, "They were inviting [Johnson] out of their Senate inner circle." Although the Constitution made him the Senate's president, Johnson's legislative powers had vanished. "He was no longer the majority leader," explained William Proxmire, "and there was no way he could discipline anybody. And I think it took a little while for people to really appreciate and understand that, they were so used to giving Johnson what he wanted."[6]

As he angrily left the meeting, Johnson reportedly snarled, "I now know the difference between a caucus and a cactus. In a cactus all the pricks are on the outside."[7]

The White House staff greeted Johnson with even greater indifference. Given oversight of the U.S. space program and appointed by Kennedy to chair the President's Committee on Equal Employment Opportunity, Johnson found little else of substance to consume his time and his enormous energies. He was uncomfortable around the urbane, well-educated hotshots on Kennedy's staff, and their disrespectful practice of calling him "Lyndon" offended Johnson. Most of Kennedy's aides and advisers— especially Attorney General Robert Kennedy—scorned the vice president. Johnson returned their scorn in kind.[8]

Despite the humiliation and isolation of his new job, Johnson remained exceedingly deferential to Kennedy. Conscious of the "provocations" at the hands of Robert Kennedy and others, James Rowe, for one, marveled at Johnson's restraint. "I thought his conduct was exemplary all through that period."[9]

Although Kennedy publicly portrayed his relationship with Johnson as intimate, the two men had at best an uneasy, distant arrangement. "They abided each other," said George Smathers, a friend to both men, "but they didn't like each other, really." Nonetheless, Kennedy always treated Johnson with respect and even reprimanded staff members who failed to do the same. "He understood Lyndon like the back of his hand," said Kennedy's appointments secretary, Kenneth O'Donnell. "[Johnson] was an insecure fellow and as long as you treated him right, he was all right."[10]

Yet Kennedy rarely discussed major decisions with his vice president, and Johnson almost never volunteered his opinion or advice unless Kennedy asked. "The president wanted to consult him," maintained Assistant Attorney General Burke Marshall, head of the Justice Department's civil rights division. "He just had a hard time getting the vice president to [speak up]. The vice president was very reluctant to tell the president what to do." At meetings with the cabinet or congressional leaders, Johnson sat silent and desultory. When asked his opinion, he was often a mumbling, muted shell of his former self. Rowland Evans and Robert Novak speculated that Robert Kennedy and other younger administration officials "misinterpreted" Johnson's silence during White House meetings "as a sign of inability to cope with the great problems of the day." Johnson's towering accomplishments as majority leader, they noted, were either unknown, forgotten, or dismissed. Johnson therefore "began to be marked down in a grossly unfair and wildly uncorrect appraisal as a lightweight." Johnson knew that he had become the butt of jokes around Washington. "Whatever happened to Lyndon?" was a common question. Such derision is standard fare for vice presidents. For someone of Johnson's enormous ego and hypersensitivity, however, the humiliation was almost unbearable. Johnson fell into a deep and conspicuous funk.[11]

Perhaps what made Johnson most unhappy was Kennedy's inexplicable refusal to use him as an administration lobbyist on Capitol Hill. As *Wall Street Journal* reporter Alan L. Otten noted in a July 1961 story, "Rather than applying his well-known legislative skill to pilot President Kennedy's program through Congress, [Johnson] is operating mainly as part of the policy-making apparatus within the executive branch." Noting that "at least a half-dozen" cabinet and staff members were more influential than Johnson, Otten observed that Johnson had "largely abandoned" the role of a legislative strategist "that everyone expected [him] to continue in the vice presidency." Perhaps Kennedy understood better than Johnson how the vice president's intimate involvement in legislative affairs would have ruffled the feathers of some congressional leaders. As one senator confided to Otten, "The Senate is a club and there's a thick curtain between active members and retired members."[12]

While Johnson languished in his sudden obscurity, Humphrey flourished in newfound prominence. With Kennedy and Johnson's support, senators elected Humphrey whip. To his liberal friends, Humphrey explained: "I have made mud pies and built dream houses long enough. Now I want to do something."[13]

Now, suddenly, their roles were reversed. Humphrey was in; Johnson was out. A fiery, liberal outsider, once scorned and ostracized by the Senate Club, Humphrey now stood near the pinnacle of that body's power and influence. He was now the Senate's number-two Democrat and a leading member of his party's steering and policy committees. Furthermore, his leadership role and his twelve years of seniority afforded him a new degree of legislative preeminence on three of the Senate's most important committees: Foreign Relations, Agriculture, and Appropriations. As a top congressional leader, he would now be an adviser and lieutenant to the president. He would meet with Kennedy often and would be a participant in the Wednesday morning congressional leadership meetings.[14]

Humphrey won the whip job for several reasons. Of all the senior liberals, he was the most pragmatic, the person most able and willing to trim his sails to achieve legislative victories for the new president. With his powers of persuasion, he could occasionally win over even the more dogmatic liberals. In addition, despite his liberal credentials on civil rights, Humphrey enjoyed cordial relations with almost every member of the Senate. His natural "warmth and his human qualities," said Harry McPherson, even appealed to conservatives like Russell and Kerr. "It would be impossible for any of those people, being men of quality themselves, to remain cold to Hubert Humphrey." Humphrey actually *cared* about his colleagues.[15]

Nothing, however, made Humphrey an effective leader in the Senate more than Mansfield's virtual abdication of the traditional leadership role of majority leader. "He tried to be effective without being oppressive," Humphrey said, diplomatically, of Mansfield. Because Mansfield was so passive, so unwilling to twist arms or lead his colleagues in the manner of Johnson, or even Rayburn and Dirksen, the duty fell to Humphrey. He viewed his job not simply "as a creature of the Senate," but "as a sometime-extension of the administration." As one liberal Democratic senator said in April 1961, "Mike Mansfield is a fine, sweet, lovable guy, but when you want something done in the Senate nowadays, you go to Hubert."[16]

Humphrey attacked the job with typical enthusiasm and good humor. Only three months after becoming the whip, his tally of legislative accomplishments included a minimum wage increase, an aid to education bill, and a compromise on Kennedy's farm program. By year's end, Kennedy adopted and Congress enacted a pet project of Humphrey's—the Peace Corps. Just as impressive was the skillful way Humphrey persuaded liberals to drop their opposition to the appointment of John Connally, Johnson's old friend, as secretary of the navy. He also kept southern conservatives from thwarting the confirmation of a black man, Robert Weaver, as administrator of the Housing and Home Finance Administration. In time, in the words of one *New York Times* reporter, Kennedy had "no more trusted ally on Capitol Hill." Dismissing the bitterness of their 1960 primary contests, Kennedy and Humphrey developed a warm and easy friendship. "It was kind of a fun relationship," Humphrey's aide David Gartner recalled. "They deeply respected each other, but on the other hand they just got along well." Humphrey was one of the few advisers who regularly teased the president.

Humphrey's usefulness to the White House and his willingness to forge a compromise when necessary are evident in his handling of Kennedy's legislation to provide aid to economically depressed areas. Although President Elsenhower had vetoed the bill twice, the legislation took on new life under Kennedy. Paul Douglas introduced the bill early in the 1961 session. But conservatives soon threw up objections over the legislation's funding mechanism—directly through Treasury instead of the yearly appropriations process. When Kennedy caved in to the conservative objections, Douglas's resolve stiffened. He refused to support the compromise Humphrey had crafted. Finally, in frustration, Humphrey told Douglas, "I'll bargain for you. I'm not so pure." With Humphrey's aggressive lobbying, the bill passed the Senate and the House. Kennedy signed it on May 1. The result was creation of the Area Redevelopment Administration.[17]

Humphrey firmly believed that his new job required him "to cajole and to persuade" in order to build "a consensus or majority to support a program." Yet some of his old liberal allies, especially those in the ADA, worried that Humphrey had become far too willing to compromise. "You can get away with a few things," one ADA leader complained in April 1961, "but it's going to catch up with Hubert if he keeps it up." Howard Shuman recalled that "Humphrey almost never failed to vote with us and support us on the crucial issues, but he was not as strong in his negotiating situation as we would have liked." Humphrey offered no apologies. "I don't have to prove I'm a liberal," he said the day after his election as whip. "After twenty years of sincere and conscientious effort, there is nothing more I can do. I don't have to tell people I didn't sell out. I won't waste my time talking to them if they think that."[18]

Harris Wofford had been standing on a Washington street corner one August morning in 1960 when John Kennedy spotted him. Kennedy pulled up in his red convertible and said, "Jump in." As the two men rode toward the Capitol, Kennedy instructed his civil rights adviser, "Now in five minutes tick off the ten things a president ought to do to clean up this goddamn civil rights mess."

Wofford had several ideas. First, the next president should sign an executive order ending racial discrimination in federally assisted housing. Only the previous year, Wofford had helped his former boss, Civil Rights Commission member Father Theodore Hesburgh, in the drafting of such a proposal. The commission had unanimously urged President Eisenhower to take that action, but the order was dormant and unsigned as the president prepared to leave office. As Kennedy and Wofford drove across town, Wofford ticked off several more proposals, all of them recommendations by the commission or commitments in the Democratic party platform plank on civil rights. "But the main theme," Wofford recalled, "was the great unused potential for executive action." As an up-close witness to the Eisenhower administration's inaction on civil rights, Wofford longed for a president who was willing to use "the enormous power" of the White House to effect change. Wofford believed "if you could get a president who really would use that power, it could make a major change and could open the way to legislation."[19]

Despite his seeming ambivalence and uncertainty about civil rights, Kennedy was not without feeling for the plight of black Americans. In his first debate with Richard Nixon, he displayed a profound *intellectual* understanding of the impact of racial discrimination. "A black child," he said, "has about one-half as much chance of completing high school as a white baby born on the same place on the same day, one-third as much chance of completing college, one-third as much chance of becoming a professional man, twice as much chance of becoming unemployed, about one-seventh as much chance of earning $10,000 a year, a life expectancy which is seven years shorter, and the prospects of earning only half as much."

In the second debate, Kennedy used a line that Wofford had supplied during their car ride in August. If elected president, he would, "by one stroke of the pen," issue the housing order that Eisenhower had refused to sign.[20]

On Inauguration Day, January 20, 1961, Wofford and millions of other hopeful Americans were stirred by Kennedy's eloquent speech in which he declared "that the torch has been passed to a new generation of Americans." Kennedy's support for a strong United Nations and his promise to help "break the bonds of mass misery" around the world was exactly the vision Wofford had hoped Kennedy would present. But Wofford was not so pleased by Kennedy's brief, almost cryptic mention of civil rights. Only the day before, Wofford had protested that the draft of Kennedy's speech did not mention civil rights, the nation's most divisive and controversial social problem. "You can't do this," Wofford said, mindful of the peaceful lunch-counter sit-ins that had begun in Virginia that very day. Kennedy's speech would lament human rights struggles in foreign countries, but he would not discuss the civil rights movement in his own nation. "You have to say something about it," Wofford insisted. "You have to."

Kennedy relented. To his declaration that the United States would remain opposed to human rights violations "around the world," Kennedy added only three words. Now the sentence would assert that America was "unwilling to witness or permit the slow undoing of those human rights to which this nation has always been committed and to which we are committed today *at home and* around the world."[21]*

Although Kennedy had avoided inaugurating his presidency with a vibrant call for action on civil rights, discrimination appalled him when he encountered it personally. For example, just a few hours after his brief, reluctant reference to civil rights—after the final float in the inaugural parade had passed the president's reviewing stand—Kennedy sought out his new assistant special counsel, Richard Goodwin.

"Did you see the Coast Guard detachment?" Kennedy asked. Goodwin was puzzled. He had no idea what Kennedy meant.

"There wasn't a black face in the entire group," the president said. "That's not acceptable. Something ought to be done about it."

Goodwin took the "observation" as "an order." Minutes later, he called incoming Commerce Secretary C. Douglas Dillon to convey Kennedy's wishes. By summer the Coast Guard Academy had hired its first black professor. The next year the academy enrolled four black cadets.[22]

In the early days of Kennedy's presidency, episodes like these only served to raise puzzling questions in the minds of civil rights leaders, congressional liberals, southern segregationists, and Kennedy's own staff. Was Kennedy *completely* committed to civil rights? Would he support legislation or simply follow the less-confrontational path of executive action? In the end, they wondered, would he live up to his promise of courageous, visionary leadership?

So far, judging by his conflicting actions and statements, no one knew for sure.

John F. Kennedy entered the White House having made thirteen separate promises of action on civil rights. Among other things, he had pledged to:

- push for enactment of the "Part III" legislation giving the attorney general full power to enforce all civil rights;
- "continue and strengthen" the U.S. Civil Rights Commission;

---

*Kennedy's inauguration was a groundbreaking event. For the first time, blacks participated fully in the festivities. Kennedy danced with black women at all five of his inaugural balls, the first time a president had done so. In addition, five blacks chaired inaugural committees and 500 served as committee members (Bryant, *The Bystander*, 210–11).

• end discriminatory poll taxes and literacy tests;
• "pass effective antibombing and antilynching legislation";
• issue the "long-delayed" executive order on housing; and
• enforce school desegregation orders.

His rhetoric in support of these proposals had not been tentative. Candidate Kennedy had firmly declared that the next president "must give us the legal weapons needed to enforce the constitutional rights of every American. He cannot wait for others to act. He himself must draft the programs—transmit them to Congress—and fight for their enactment." At a September press conference, Kennedy had gone a step further, asking Pennsylvania senator Joseph Clark and House Judiciary Committee chairman Emanuel Celler to draft legislation "embodying our platform commitments for introduction at the beginning of the next session" of Congress. "We will seek the enactment of this bill early in that Congress," Kennedy declared unequivocally.[23]

Now that Kennedy was president, millions of black Americans eagerly awaited the "moral and persuasive leadership" that he had promised. Despite all the rhetoric about action and his early indignation over segregation in the Coast Guard, Kennedy was far from committed to an all-out drive to fulfill his promises on civil rights. He was hesitant to dive headlong into a divisive fight over the issue in his administration's early months. His narrow election had been no mandate. Although he had often promised action on civil rights—and black votes may have guaranteed his razor-thin margin of victory—the issue had not been central to his campaign. Believing he had little popularity to spare in a divisive civil rights fight, Kennedy focused on other important issues such as tariffs, taxes, unemployment, education, the minimum wage, and depressed areas. "Handed an historic opportunity at the beginning of the 1960s to map out a trajectory for the country that could have carried millions of black Americans closer to freedom," wrote journalist and historian Nick Bryant, "he decided instead to adopt a policy of inaction."[24]

In May, White House press secretary Pierre Salinger suddenly disavowed the bills introduced by Clark and Celler, which had been created at candidate Kennedy's request. The bills, he announced, "are not administration-backed bills. The president does not consider it necessary at this time to enact new civil rights legislation." That announcement "floored" NAACP executive secretary Roy Wilkins, "because it amounted to telling the opposition, for example, in football analogy, that you weren't going to use the forward pass." Wilkins believed the time had come to "charge the opposition."[25]

Besides the normal hostility of southern conservatives, any Kennedy-sponsored civil rights bill would face other formidable institutional barriers. The cloture rule still required a daunting two-thirds vote—sixty-seven, if all 100 senators voted—to end a filibuster. Despite a Democratic platform pledge to liberalize Rule XXII, Kennedy thought that he could not afford to antagonize conservatives by taking sides in the biennial cloture fight in January.

Furthermore, despite the recent influx of new liberals into the body, southerners continued to chair most of the Senate's committees. While civil rights advocates and some congressional liberals viewed the world through the lens of one issue, Kennedy believed he was obligated to govern in a broader, more pragmatic fashion. He feared that alienating important southern committee chairmen by offering a volatile civil rights bill might be disastrous for civil rights and everything else Kennedy wanted from Congress. As one Kennedy aide explained to Anthony Lewis of the *New York Times,* "Suppose the president were to send up a dramatic message on civil rights and alienate enough southerners to kill his economic program in Congress? Would the Negro be better off or worse off? I think he'd be worse off."[26]

A disappointed Roy Wilkins believed that Kennedy's strategy demonstrated a poor understanding of Congress: "In the first place, any history would show that the opponents of civil rights legislation didn't give a hoot whether you introduced it or didn't introduce it as far as their attitude toward the major legislative proposals are concerned. They weren't going to let the major legislative proposals go through because the president did not introduce civil rights legislation out of their great gratitude and compassion and so forth, nor were they going to attack the proposals just because he introduced civil rights legislation."[27]

Kennedy's reluctance on civil rights was more deeply rooted in his own political insecurity. Because he had defeated Richard Nixon by so narrow a margin, Kennedy was unsure of his ability to bend members of Congress to his will. "He didn't feel he had a mandate," explained Assistant Attorney General Nicholas Katzenbach. The advice congressional leaders gave Kennedy reinforced this assessment. House Judiciary chairman Celler believed "the climate wasn't ready yet" for civil rights. There remained, he said, "a great deal of brush work to cut down the stumps of opposition." Kennedy received similar advice from Lyndon Johnson, Majority Leader Mansfield, and Bobby Baker, secretary to the Senate majority.[28]

At the time, Kennedy's tentative approach to civil rights deeply troubled Civil Rights Commission member Theodore Hesburgh. With more than thirty years of perspective, however, Hesburgh appreciated Kennedy's political dilemma. "I think the bottom line on Jack is that he's the same as any other president we ever had," Hesburgh said. "The day they walk in that front door of the White House, their next thought is, 'How am I going to stay here for eight years?'" Hesburgh speculated that Kennedy understood "as a northerner, that if you really wanted to commit political suicide, as a Democrat who'd been elected by a small handful of votes, the easiest way to do it would be to come out strongly on civil rights."[29]

To civil rights leaders, Kennedy was honest to the point of being blunt. "Nobody needs to convince me any longer that we have to solve the problem, not let it drift on gradually," Kennedy told Martin Luther King. "But how do you go about it? If we go into a long fight in Congress, it will bottleneck everything else and still get no bill."

Moderation meant no legislation, only executive orders to initiate or expand enforcement of existing civil rights statutes. Kennedy, said Wofford, "loved the idea of executive action." The absence of a legislative program led some to question whether Kennedy's commitment to civil rights was sincere. "I don't read it that way at all," Wofford insisted. "I think John Kennedy was inhibited, intimidated by Congress. He wasn't a real insider. He didn't feel confident in dealing with Congress. He estimated the opposition in Congress as very dangerous on civil rights." More important, according to Burke Marshall, "Everyone down in Congress told him that he couldn't pass a civil rights bill. So, he had a choice of not pushing one or pushing one but ending up with the defeat and wasting a lot of time."[30]

In his exhaustive study of Kennedy's civil rights record, Nick Bryant observed that "Kennedy's fear of alienating the Southern Caucus was bred as much of personal insecurity as political arithmetic." As a junior senator Kennedy had been "overawed by southern grandees like Richard Russell and Sam Ervin" and now "continued to view them in much the same way." Kennedy as well as his political advisers, Bryant argued, misread the changing political winds and underestimated his political strength. Despite having won "only" 49.9 percent of the popular vote, Kennedy carried seven of the eleven states of the Old Confederacy with 50.47 percent.

Furthermore, he did not comprehend that the Senate was growing more liberal and southern conservatives were "becoming increasingly isolated."

"Kennedy's retreat was in fact a monumental tactical blunder," Bryant wrote. "By publicly announcing his decision to back away from civil rights legislation he surrendered a crucial bargaining tool with southern Democrats." The southern Democrats were emboldened and civil rights leaders were gradually radicalized, "angry that the pendulum had swung away from them" and now determined to "adopt more aggressive tactics to win the new president's attention." As Bryant concluded: "The American public appeared favorably disposed toward reform, and many diehard segregationists seemed resigned to ultimate defeat. The possibility of progress was real. Compromise was inevitable, given the composition of Congress, but Kennedy had retreated too far."[31]

Executive action—the exercise of presidential authority already approved by Congress—ruled the day. In contrast to the lethargy of the Eisenhower years, the Kennedy administration, led by Attorney General Robert Kennedy, launched aggressive action on several fronts.

In March the president issued an executive order merging two former executive committees—the president's committees on Government Contracts and Government Employment Policy—into the President's Committee on Equal Employment Opportunity. "I intend to insure that Americans of all colors and beliefs will have equal access to employment within the government," Kennedy announced, "and with those who do business with the government." With Lyndon Johnson as chairman, the committee was empowered to fight discriminatory hiring practices by the federal government and by private companies with government contracts. Although Johnson adamantly pushed his committee staff to identify and weed out job discrimination, some critics contended that Johnson leaned toward a more polite cajoling of businesses, while Robert Kennedy and other administration officials supported greater initiative and more aggressive action.[32]

Kennedy's own hiring policy led him to appoint several blacks to high positions, including Robert Weaver to head the Housing and Home Finance Administration. A fifty-three-year-old, Harvard-educated civil rights activist, Weaver had served as national chairman of the NAACP, New York State's rent administrator, and vice chairman of the New York City Housing and Redevelopment Board. Not surprisingly, southern conservatives opposed his nomination. Mississippi's James Eastland charged that Weaver had been associated with several subversive organizations, describing him as "a man who has a pro-Communist background" and "belonged to half a dozen Communist-front organizations." On January 22 Louisiana's Allen Ellender declared that he had seen "some of the proof," supplied by the House Un-American Activities Committee, of Weaver's alleged Communist affiliations. Those charges lost their steam, however, when committee chairman Francis Walter announced the next day that no committee evidence linked Weaver to Communist activities. The Senate finally confirmed Weaver by a voice vote in early February.[33]

Kennedy appointed other blacks to government positions: George Weaver as assistant secretary of labor; Carl T. Rowan as assistant secretary of state for public affairs; Andrew Hatcher as associate press secretary; Lisle Carter as deputy assistant in the Department of Health, Education, and Welfare; and Frank Reeves to the White House staff. He named blacks to ambassadorial posts, including Clifton Wharton as ambassador to Norway, the first black to represent the United States to a predominantly white country. For the first time, two blacks—in San Francisco and Cleveland—were appointed as U.S. attorneys. "It got to be a kind of *sub rosa* joke around Washington, even among Negroes," recalled Roy Wilkins, "that Kennedy was so hot on the Department heads [to hire blacks] . . . that everyone was scrambling around trying to find himself a Negro in order to keep the president off his neck."[34]

Kennedy also named blacks to the federal bench, including the now-legendary NAACP lawyer Thurgood Marshall, to the Second Circuit Court of Appeals. Judiciary chairman James Eastland held up Marshall's nomination for many months. Eastland relented only when Kennedy agreed to appoint his law school roommate, Harold Cox, to a federal district judgeship. "You tell your brother," Eastland reportedly told Robert Kennedy, "that when I get Cox, he gets the nigger."[35]

Although the Democratic platform had promised "whatever action necessary" to eliminate literacy tests and poll taxes, Kennedy proposed no legislation in 1961. Robert Kennedy announced he would instead aggressively enforce the 1957 and 1960 civil rights acts, which gave him the authority to seek injunctions against voting rights violations. "We will enforce the law, in every field of law and every region," the attorney general bravely declared to a University of Georgia audience in May. "If the orders of the court are circumvented, the Department of Justice will act." The speech was Kennedy's first formal address as attorney general.

Although not one prominent Georgia public official was present, the crowd of 1,600 alumni and students applauded Kennedy enthusiastically when he finished.[36]

In April the Justice Department filed its first voting rights suit, against voting officials in Dallas County, Alabama. By year's end Robert Kennedy would file fourteen voting rights suits; by mid-1963, forty-two. (Eisenhower's Justice Department, by comparison, had filed only nine suits since the passage of the Civil Rights Act of 1957.) Even Martin Luther King argued that "suffrage" was the "central front" of his Southern Christian Leadership Conference. "If we in the South can win the right to vote, it will place in our hands more than an abstract right. It will give us the concrete tool with which we ourselves can correct injustice."[37]

As for school desegregation, the Democratic platform had promised to give the Justice Department new legislative authority—the language gutted from Part III of the 1957 act—to file suits against deprivation of *any* civil right. In this area as well, Kennedy would pursue no legislation—for now. Instead the Justice Department quickly entered a desegregation dispute in New Orleans, suing Louisiana officials for refusing to release federal school funds to the New Orleans School Board. Kennedy also sued the Louisiana legislature to prevent lawmakers from interfering with New Orleans school officials' desegregation efforts. With little fanfare, Kennedy sent Burke Marshall and other Justice Department lawyers to almost every school district slated for desegregation. Marshall offered to assist local officials in complying with court orders, and he established important lines of communication with political and community leaders throughout the South.[38]

All of this was appallingly insufficient to many liberals. Civil rights advocates suggested that the law did not require the government to wait until private citizens sued. The administration, they said, already had the legal authority to initiate school desegregation suits on its own. At his first press conference, on April 7, Robert Kennedy rejected the notion of a more direct approach. "I don't believe we do have that power," he argued. As for legislation to secure such authority, Kennedy said that he had not yet made "a final determination as to exactly what we will do."[39]

"You did get more vigorous action under [the Kennedy] administration, many suits filed by the Justice Department, more in a few months than the predecessor administration filed in several years," Martin Luther King later acknowledged. Yet King and others were not satisfied: "I don't think that his leadership really, at this point, grappled with the magnitude of the problem." Joseph Rauh, then general counsel for the United Auto Workers and a staunch Kennedy supporter, found himself sorely disappointed at the pace of civil rights action. "I feel that he was going too slow," said Rauh. Unimpressed by executive action and appointments of blacks to government posts, Rauh concluded—correctly—that the daunting challenge of negotiating with Congress intimidated Kennedy. "That is the political way," he said. "Do a lot of administrative things, but stay away from Congress."[40]

Kennedy seemed to understand the importance of a strong Civil Rights Commission—although its reports and recommendations sometimes caused considerable consternation at the White House. "In part because of Kennedy appointments," New York Times reporter Anthony Lewis wrote in October, "the commission has made a startling change from a prolix debating society to a firm advocate of prompt justice for the Negro." In a flurry of reports in 1961, the revitalized commission urged Congress to give every segregated southern school district six months to develop a desegregation plan; proposed an end to literacy tests for voting registration by requiring a sixth-grade education as proof of literacy; and urged Kennedy to issue an executive order ending discrimination in all federally aided housing.[41]

In their early months in the White House, Kennedy's people hoped they could contain and manage the building pressure for action on civil rights. They simply would not permit civil rights to intrude on more pressing domestic and international concerns. Instead Kennedy would rely on a deliberate, well-managed program of executive orders, Justice Department suits on voting rights and school desegregation, appointments of blacks to federal positions, and conciliatory meetings with civil rights leaders. He promised to do more—but only when the political climate improved.

His incremental policy of slow but steady action would never completely satisfy congressional liberals and civil rights advocates. The politician in Kennedy understood that. Yet because he saw the issue primarily in intellectual and political terms, the president seemed to underestimate the brewing forces of discontent among the downtrodden black citizens of the South. Before long, Kennedy began to learn something about the determination of black activists and their willingness to risk their lives in challenging segregation in the South.

In May 1961, the civil rights movement shifted from the peaceful resistance of lunch-counter sit-ins to more aggressive action. That month, groups of black and white college students left Washington and Nashville on buses bound for southern cities. These "Freedom Riders," some of them well trained in nonviolence, would goad southerners to violence in order to illuminate the failure of the southern states to comply with a 1960 Supreme Court decision outlawing segregation of public facilities in interstate commerce. At each bus terminal, they would attempt to integrate all-white waiting rooms, restaurants, and restrooms—all in violation of unconstitutional local and state segregation statutes. "We can take anything the white man can dish out," one rider said bravely, "but we want our rights. We know what they are—and we want them right now."[42]

As they made their way through Virginia, North Carolina, South Carolina, and Georgia, the nervous riders encountered little violence or resistance. Once they crossed into Alabama, domain of archsegregationist governor John Patterson, the climate changed. Angry, violent mobs accosted them at almost every stop. Near Anniston, a crowd of whites attacked the Greyhound bus, slit its tires, smashed the windows with pipes, and set it afire. Terrified and overcome by smoke, the riders found their way to a nearby hospital, where white attendants refused them medical treatment. A Ku Klux Klan–led mob attacked riders on another bus that managed to reach Birmingham. Local police waited a full ten minutes before they intervened. By then some riders were badly beaten.

In Montgomery, angry whites pummeled six riders with bricks and a garbage can. Others barely escaped serious injury by fleeing in taxicabs and private cars. In a rage, some in the white mob snatched the students' suitcases and smashed them against a wall of the bus station until their contents spilled out—and then they set fire to the heap of clothing and books. While trying to save one rider from the mob, the attorney general's personal emissary, administrative assistant John Seigenthaler, was beaten over the head with a metal pipe and kicked unconscious. Only when the Montgomery police belatedly fired tear gas into the crowd did the violence wane.[43]

"Obviously," *Newsweek* reported, "this was a total breakdown of law enforcement in Alabama." But Patterson and other Alabama authorities, unaware they were playing into the Freedom Riders' hands, remained defiant. "We respond to calls here just like anyplace else," said Montgomery police commissioner L. B. Sullivan, explaining why his men waited so long to intervene. "But we have no intention of standing guard for a bunch of trouble makers."[44]

Throughout the crisis, Attorney General Kennedy played mediator, working around the clock to persuade both sides to back down and leave the matter to the courts. Patterson's violation of his promise to protect the Freedom Riders outraged both Kennedys. With his racist white electorate in mind, Patterson was in no mood to compromise. "I'm getting tired of being called up in the middle of the night," he complained, "and being *ordered* to do this and *ordered* to do that." For two days, Patterson—the first southern governor to endorse Kennedy's candidacy—refused even to take phone calls from the president.[45]

The brutal response by locals and the negligence of Alabama authorities was *exactly* the reaction the Freedom Rides' organizers had hoped to provoke. The bloody violence made national news. Newspapers around the country—and as far away as Africa, Europe, and Asia—carried shocking accounts and photographs of the beatings. Said France's *Le Monde:* "The current toward racial integration has now acquired an irresistible force . . . Advocates of white supremacy . . . may retard evolution but they can't halt it." A *Daily Express* reporter told readers in London that the Kennedy brothers had proved to the world "that they are as ready to defend the ideals of individual liberty within the borders of the United States as they are to act outside." In the United States, public sentiment for legislative action on civil rights grew with every angry blow and racial slur hurled at the students. Governor Patterson deserved much of the credit. "If he had kept his mouth shut and accepted his responsibility to maintain law and order," *Time* observed, "the Freedom Riders would probably have passed through Alabama with little incident—just as they had passed through Virginia, North Carolina, South Carolina and Georgia."[46]

The Freedom Riders hoped that the crisis they provoked would move Kennedy to support comprehensive civil rights legislation. "I think we knew we were testing this new administration when we decided on the Freedom Rides," said John Lewis, a rider who was beaten by white thugs at a South Carolina stop. "I think it was right to test this young president early. The people associated with Kennedy gave us a lot of hope; there was something about the man that was the embodiment of change."[47]

Whatever encouragement the riders got from Kennedy was mostly inadvertent. At first unaware of the riders' plans, both Kennedys worried that the whole exercise would cast the United States in a bad light. It was not the kind of distraction the president needed as he dealt with the crisis in Berlin and prepared for a momentous summit with Soviet leader Nikita

Khrushchev in Vienna. "These things," Nicholas Katzenbach said frankly, "were seen as a pain in the ass."[48]

"Tell them to call it off!" John Kennedy bellowed to Harris Wofford in a phone call. "Stop them!"

"I don't think anybody's going to stop them right now," Wofford responded.[49]

Unable to persuade local and state officials to protect the Freedom Riders, Robert Kennedy finally ordered hundreds of federal marshals into Montgomery.[50]

As the marshals prepared to move in, more violence threatened to erupt at the Reverend Ralph Abernathy's First Baptist Church in Montgomery, where Martin Luther King arrived on May 21 for a massive rally. King and his mainstream Southern Christian Leadership Conference had not been responsible for the Freedom Riders' foray into the South. But now that this dynamic new assault on segregation had been unleashed, there was no turning back. King and other black leaders embraced the riders' cause. Even Thurgood Marshall, soon to become a federal judge, acknowledged that the pace of the civil rights movement had not been fast enough. "These kids are serving notice on us that we're moving too slow," he said. "They're not content with all this talking."[51]

In his speech to more than a thousand people, King demanded aggressive federal intervention to end segregation. "Unless the federal government acts forthrightly in the South to assure every citizen his constitutional rights," King declared, "we will be plunged into a dark abyss of chaos." Robert Kennedy could not have been pleased to learn that King had called for "a full-scale nonviolent assault on the system of segregation in Alabama," including a voter registration drive and attempts to integrate public schools, lunch counters, public parks, and theaters. "In short, we will seek to mobilize thousands of people, committed to the method of nonviolence, who will physically identify themselves with the struggle to end segregation in Alabama."[52]

As King spoke, an unruly mob gathered outside and began pitching rocks and bottles at the church. Undeterred by tear gas released by the federal marshals, the mob seemed on the verge of storming the church. One person shouted, "We'll get those niggers!" Another cried: "We want to integrate, too!" Trapped inside, the terrified congregation waited until the crowd finally dispersed early the next morning.[53]

Now the Freedom Riders were even more determined to press on. They ignored desperate pleas from Robert Kennedy to call off their mission in exchange for Kennedy's abstract promise of assistance. "People were going to be killed," Kennedy feared. But there were no more beatings, only arrests. When another group of fearless riders arrived in Jackson, Mississippi, Governor Ross Barnett avoided violence not by restraining angry whites but by promptly arresting all twenty-seven riders on charges of disorderly conduct. "I feel wonderful," Barnett bragged once the riders were behind bars, twenty-two of them choosing to remain in jail rather than pay a $200 fine. "I'm so happy that everything went off smoothly. The nation had its eyes on Mississippi today, and I think we showed them that we could handle our own affairs in an orderly manner."[54]

In the Senate, reaction to violence against the Freedom Riders was swift and emotional. Majority Leader Mansfield said the incidents in Alabama "should cause us—as a Nation—to hang our heads in shame." Humphrey called it "a sad day for Americans when some of our citizens are set upon as if they were enemies or as if they were not even human beings." The violence, Humphrey added, has "made a mockery of our democracy and of our national purpose, for the outbreaks have evidenced disorder and violence unworthy of a great nation. This problem is not confined to any particular area; it is a national problem."[55]

Southern conservatives condemned the violence but made it clear that they blamed the Freedom Riders and their provocations. "The self-styled freedom riders set out deliberately to create trouble at all costs," Strom Thurmond told the Senate. "Their avowed purpose, publicly expressed, was not to work toward the creation of better race relations, but to incite incidents." Perhaps the most shameful and hysterical response to the violence against the Freedom Riders came from Judiciary Committee chairman James Eastland. In a lengthy speech full of "exhibits" and other purported evidence, the Mississippi Democrat attacked the Congress of Racial Equality (CORE), which had sponsored the riders, as a Communist-front organization. "Since its inception," Eastland said of CORE, "its creed has been lawlessness and its tactics have followed the pattern-set by Communist agitators the world over." Eastland said he had been "informed" that the Freedom Rides were "devised deliberately as a prelude to various high-level meetings in Europe, as a propaganda method to embarrass the government of the United States in the handling of international affairs." CORE, he declared, "is carrying on the fight for a Soviet America."[56]

By the summer, Robert Kennedy responded to the Freedom Rides—but not with a civil rights bill. Under intense pressure from the Justice Department, the Interstate Commerce Commission ordered the desegregation of all interstate bus terminals, and the Justice Department began enforcing the order. (In 1955 the ICC had banned segregation on buses and trains and in railroad stations but had done nothing about segregation in bus terminals.) By year's end, all forms of segregated interstate transportation were abolished.

The ICC's order was an unmistakable victory for Kennedy's administration, but it did little to improve the president's standing with civil rights activists and other liberals. Although the president had helped to finally end segregation in interstate travel, the Freedom Riders and King had seen Kennedy as a reluctant and mostly silent supporter of their cause. Despite constant prodding by Wofford and others, Kennedy had stubbornly refused to issue a strong declaration of support for the riders.[57]

Days after racists in Alabama pummeled the riders, Kennedy had appeared at a joint session of Congress on May 25 to deliver his second State of the Union address of 1961. Although he declared in the speech that "we stand for freedom," he had refused entreaties by Wofford and Marshall to speak about the freedoms denied black citizens in the South. Instead Kennedy asserted that the "great battleground for the defense and expansion of freedom today is the whole southern half of the globe—Asia, Latin America, Africa, and the Middle East—the lands of the rising peoples. Their revolution is the greatest in human history. They seek an end to injustice, tyranny, and exploitation. More than an end, they seek a beginning." During the lengthy speech, Kennedy did not mention the civil rights struggle in the American South. As Wofford explained, the president undoubtedly suspected that Robert Kennedy's "actions had spoken louder than words, and he feared a white backlash in the South."[58]

As 1961 ended, Congress had little to show for its efforts on civil rights. Kennedy's proposal to elevate the Housing and Home Finance Administration to cabinet status ran up against a wall of southern opposition. The agency's administrator, Robert Weaver, was black—and would thus become the nation's first black cabinet official. Moreover, he was an outspoken advocate of integrated housing, or "open occupancy."[59]

In the Senate the venerable filibuster remained as strong as ever. As the session came to a close in September, senators rejected a proposal to lower the threshold for imposing cloture from two-thirds of those voting to three-fifths. An attempt to force a vote on the motion by invoking cloture failed miserably, 37–43. By year's end Congress had enacted only one civil rights measure—legislation extending the life of the U.S. Civil Rights Commission for two years. The Senate soundly defeated efforts to make the commission permanent.[60]

As the commission issued its mammoth, five-volume report for the year—offering recommendations on voting, education, employment, housing, and the administration of justice—veteran commissioner Theodore Hesburgh added a separate dissenting statement. It was a stinging, albeit indirect, rebuke of Kennedy's emphasis on foreign affairs over important domestic issues such as civil rights:

> Americans might well wonder how we can legitimately combat communism when we practice so widely its central folly: utter disregard for the God-given spiritual rights, freedom and dignity of every human person . . . Personally, I don't care if the United States gets the first man on the moon, if while this is happening on a crash basis, we dawdle along here on our corner of the earth, nursing our prejudices, flouting our magnificent Constitution, ignoring the central moral problem of our times, and appearing hypocrites to all the world.[61]

11

YOU'LL NEVER GET A CIVIL RIGHTS BILL

The early 1960s were bleak times for Richard Russell. The civil rights cause was on the march—literally—and Russell had little stomach for the momentous social changes he knew were inevitable. "We have come to evil days," he told a friend. "He was," observed longtime aide Proctor Jones, "out of step with what was likely to happen." [1]

With its bold commitment to civil rights legislation, Russell's beloved Democratic party had veered sharply to the left in the 1960 election. "My party . . . deviated from the past and has gone off and left me," he had complained during the presidential contest. In the Senate, Lyndon Johnson was gone, and Russell was no longer a hidden hand behind the leadership. Two liberals, Mike Mansfield and Hubert Humphrey, ran a much more progressive Senate. Mansfield, while always friendly and courteous, was not Russell's protégé and owed him no special debt. Russell's once-fearsome domination of the steering and policy committees had been eroded by Johnson's departure and by the addition of liberals such as Mansfield, Humphrey, Philip Hart, Edmund Muskie, and Joseph Clark. The southern bloc that Russell led was shrinking—and aging. Of the bloc's eighteen members, more than half were sixty or older, and four were over seventy.

As chairman of the Armed Services Committee and a senior member of the Appropriations Committee, Russell still wielded enormous power, but only within certain realms—defense, agriculture, and, to a rapidly declining degree, civil rights. Furthermore, because of age and his deteriorating health, Russell had simply lost some of his enthusiasm for waging legislative battles. He had rarely if ever been an offensive combatant in the fight against civil rights, but now he seemed more defensive and fatalistic than ever. He was afraid, he wrote to himself in 1960, that "my leadership has lost inspiration." [2]

None of this meant that Russell would ever capitulate to demands for civil rights. In early 1961 he led a surprisingly spirited fight against liberalization of the cloture rule and threatened a filibuster against the proposal. With no real support from the Kennedy White House, the rule change died.[3]

Except for agricultural policy, Russell found himself at odds with every major legislative initiative proposed by President Kennedy. His relationship with Lyndon Johnson was not much better. As vice president, Johnson now wholeheartedly supported Kennedy's program of executive action on civil rights. One of his first acts as chairman of the President's Committee on Equal Employment Opportunity had been to force the desegregation of the Lockheed plant in Russell's home state. Russell had hoped that Johnson, the southern moderate, would exert a moderating influence on the liberals in Kennedy's White House. He was mistaken. To the extent he had any influence, Johnson seemed to have become an all-out civil rights liberal. Russell, quite naturally, felt betrayed.

One Saturday afternoon, probably in 1962, William "Buddy" Darden witnessed Russell's growing disillusionment with his former protégé. A Capitol elevator operator under Russell's patronage, Darden (later a congressman from Georgia) was walking toward Russell's office when Johnson's chauffeur-driven limousine pulled alongside him.

"Hey, boy," Johnson shouted, "is Dick in?"

"Well, yes, sir," Darden replied.

"Well, tell him I'm out here in the car and I want to see him."

Darden scurried inside to deliver the message, but Russell was in no mood for Johnson that afternoon.

"You just tell the son of a bitch I'm not here. I don't want to fool with him today."

Darden was petrified. "Here I was, just walking in off the street, carrying a message from the vice president of the United States to the chairman of the Armed Services Committee, and I was supposed to go back and tell him that he wasn't in—yet I had already told him he was in." Not knowing what to do, Darden shuffled his feet and remained in Russell's outer office, hoping, he said, "that something would happen."

Before long, an impatient Johnson burst through the door and barged into Russell's office, where Russell received his old friend warmly. Darden said when he realized the two men "weren't going to come to blows, I exited and wasn't around there anymore."[4]

As few but Darden understood, the Russell-Johnson relationship was evolving.

Demands for progress on civil rights only intensified in 1962. "The president of the United States," New York Republican Jacob Javits declared from the Senate floor in January, "has apparently adopted the calculated policy of avoiding the Congress at this session on civil rights, and it cannot be done." By March Javits's frustrations boiled over. He finally gave public voice to a growing sentiment among civil rights advocates. "In my view," he told the Senate, "the President is appeasing southern members of his party who are in powerful committee positions, by his attitude on civil rights legislation, and as a result many parts of the administration's own program are getting absolutely nowhere." Javits's harsh criticism was close to the mark. It would have been difficult to imagine much of Kennedy's program faring any worse in Congress—even if he had introduced a strong legislative proposal on civil rights. Administration bills to create a Department of Urban Affairs and a Medicare system were stalled in committee, as was legislation to provide federal aid to education.[5]

Humphrey bravely defended Kennedy's civil rights policies, despite his personal concerns over Kennedy's reluctance to embrace the bold, comprehensive program he had promised during his campaign. On May 29, 1962, Humphrey rose in the Senate to deliver a lengthy defense of every portion of Kennedy's domestic and foreign policies. He passionately challenged those who claimed that Kennedy "has not even requested civil rights legislation or issued an Executive order ending racial discrimination in federally assisted housing." As Humphrey noted, Congress had extended the Civil Rights Commission in 1961 and was near enactment of a constitutional amendment banning the poll tax in federal elections. Furthermore, Humphrey declared, "the Kennedy administration has accomplished far more than its predecessor through administrative action—through lawsuits to compel voter registration, through negotiations on the successful integration of schools, through increased employment by federal agencies and federal contractors, and through action to end segregation in bus, airline and train terminals."[6]

At least one Kennedy-backed legislative proposal was making progress. Since 1949, Florida senator Spessard Holland—a tough, sometimes pedantic, seventy-year-old conservative—had bravely and repeatedly introduced a constitutional amendment to ban the poll tax. Once widespread, the poll tax was now an endangered species. Only Alabama, Arkansas, Mississippi, Texas, and Virginia still imposed a yearly tax as a voting requirement. But Holland, who wanted it abolished throughout the South, made destruction of the tax a personal crusade. In years past, both houses of Congress had approved some version of a ban, but they had never agreed on whether statute or constitutional amendment should end it.

By 1962 the times were finally catching up with the Florida Democrat. Desperate for some legislative progress on civil rights to appease restless liberals, Kennedy and Majority Leader Mansfield happily lent their support. On March 14 Mansfield called up a minor bill to establish the former home of Alexander Hamilton as a national monument. This legislation, he told the Senate, would serve as the vehicle for Holland's amendment. Russell's southerners, of course, objected. While he said he held "no brief for the poll tax," Russell complained that a constitutional amendment had no business as a rider to such a bill. The Senate disagreed. By a 58–34 vote, senators rejected Russell's constitutional point of order.

Passage of Holland's amendment was virtually assured. After all, the Senate had approved a poll tax ban in 1960 by a wide margin. (The House failed to act on the measure, favoring legislation over a constitutional amendment.) This year the only questions were how long the southerners would stall a vote and how strident they would become in defense of a decaying device of southern white supremacy. Past debates usually found southerners opposing civil rights legislation as unconstitutional infringements on the sovereign rights of states. Change the Constitution, they cried, but don't pass unconstitutional laws. Now Holland's amendment had called their bluff—and forced them to defend not the Constitution but the poll tax itself. In the end, much of the debate served only to portray the southerners as antiquated and ridiculous relics of the Confederacy.[7]

Mississippi's John Stennis, one of the more respected southern members, was most pitiful when he explained that the poll tax was only "misunderstood." Voting, he declared, "is a privilege; it is not a right. It has never been a right. I hope that in our form of government it will never be a pure right."[8]

On March 27, after a ten-day quasifilibuster, the Senate finally approved Holland's constitutional amendment, 77–16. Four southerners—Louisiana's Russell Long, Tennessee's Estes Kefauver, Florida's George Smathers, and Texas's Ralph Yarborough—joined Holland in supporting the amendment. Several other previously loyal allies abandoned the southern coalition on the vote, including West Virginia's Robert Byrd (a former Ku Klux Klan member) and Oklahoma's Bob Kerr. Every Republican but Lyndon Johnson's successor, John Tower, supported the measure. On August 27, the House approved the amendment, 295–86. Many House members had preferred a legislative ban over a constitutional amendment. In the end, however, they supported it because it was the only measure that could pass the Senate. "I am a pragmatist," House Judiciary chairman Emanuel Celler declared. "I want results, not a debate. I want a law, not a filibuster. I crave an end to the poll tax, not unlimited, crippling amendments. I say to you gentlemen and ladies, stretch your feet according to your blanket." In January 1964, upon ratification by the thirty-eighth state, the proposal became the Twenty-fourth Amendment to the Constitution.

Kennedy applauded the congressional vote and was happy to count the poll tax amendment as a civil rights victory for his administration. The vote, however, had never really been in doubt. Once a burning issue, the poll tax ban was now among the civil rights movement's lowest priorities. When ratified, it would have only minimal impact on black voting rights.[9]

More important was another civil rights measure that Kennedy supported. With administration backing, Majority Leader Mansfield and Minority Leader Dirksen introduced legislation based on a 1961 Civil Rights Commission recommendation to establish a sixth-grade education as proof of literacy for voter registration in states that employed literacy tests. According to a commission report, about one hundred counties in eight southern states excluded blacks from voting in "substantial numbers" because of their race. A "common technique" of barring black voter registration, the commission reported, was the "discriminatory application of legal qualifications for voters." White officials typically required would-be black voters to read and write, offer a "satisfactory" interpretation of the U.S. Constitution, calculate their ages to the day, and prove that they were of "good character." In one case cited by the commission, a registrar rejected a black schoolteacher for mispronouncing "equity" while reading a long passage.[10] Commission member Theodore Hesburgh, in a 1960 speech, had painted a particularly pitiful portrait of the humiliation suffered by thousands of blacks who attempted to exercise their Fifteenth Amendment rights:

> They would go down to the courthouse and instead of going in where the white people registered, they would have to go to a room in the

back where they would stand in line from six in the morning until two in the afternoon, since only two were let in at a time. Then, people with Ph.D.s and the master's degrees and high intelligence would sit down and copy like a schoolchild the first article or the second article of the Constitution. Then they would be asked the usual questions, make out the usual questionnaires, hand in a self-addressed envelope and hear nothing for three months. And then they would go back and do it over again, some of them five or six or seven times, some of them standing in line two or three days until their turn came.[11]

Mansfield monitored the political climate in the Senate. He doubted that a majority of his colleagues would support a literacy proposal that contained mandates on state and local elections. So, unlike the Civil Rights Commission's proposal, the Mansfield-Dirksen bill would apply only to federal elections. Under the legislation, registration officials could still use arbitrary literacy standards to exclude citizens seeking to vote in nonfederal contests.

In January, despite liberal protests, Mansfield sent his bill to the Judiciary Committee for hearings. Sensitive to concerns that Chairman James Eastland would "pigeonhole" the bill, the majority leader promised to attach the bill to a House-passed measure if the committee did not report it within sixty to ninety days. Sam Ervin's constitutional rights subcommittee held hearings in March and early April. Then, true to form, Eastland and Ervin sat on the bill and refused to report it out. As promised, Mansfield moved to bring the legislation to the floor. On April 24 he told the Senate he would attach the literacy legislation to a minor House-passed bill.[12]

Mansfield's move sparked an immediate filibuster. The southern opposition featured the standard bombast about the evils of cloture and the dangers of unconstitutional federal usurpation of the right of states to establish voting qualifications. Typical was Virginia's Willis Robertson, who maintained the issue was "whether Congress can say, *ipse dixit,* 'No matter what kind of dumbbell you are, if you stay in school through the sixth grade, mister, you qualify to vote.'" For two weeks Mansfield allowed southerners to wage what one *Congressional Quarterly* writer described as "a rather leisurely filibuster" during which neither side strictly enforced the rules of debate.[13]

Respecting his colleagues' aversion to the marathon debates of the 1950s, Mansfield ran the Senate more like a bank. The Senate convened, usually at noon, debated the bill—and other matters—for no more than six hours, and usually adjourned before 6:00 P.M. Mansfield ordered no weekend sessions. "The leadership gave up," said Pennsylvania's Joseph Clark. The debate, said *Time*, "had all the conviction of a professional wrestling match: everybody played his role for the crowd, but nobody got hurt."[14]

It was Mansfield's legislative judgment, not his accommodating leadership style, which deserved the most criticism. Before a May 10 cloture vote, Mansfield told the Senate that if the cloture motion failed, he would move to table the bill. It was a tactical error Johnson would never have committed. In making the announcement, Mansfield revealed his hand. Wavering moderates in both parties were off the hook, knowing that they could placate both sides by opposing cloture and then voting against Mansfield's tabling motion. Absent the knowledge of an impending tabling motion, the cloture question would have been all-important—a vote for or against the literacy bill. Now it was just a procedural question for those moderate Republicans and Democrats who hoped to appease the powerful southerners still chairing the Senate's most important committees.

The cloture motion failed as expected, 43–53. Twenty-three Republicans joined twenty-three southern Democrats and seven northern Democrats in supporting the filibuster. True to form, moderates of both parties effortlessly switched sides when Mansfield moved to table the bill. With even Mansfield voting against it, the tabling motion failed, 33–64. In other words, an overwhelming majority of senators supported legislation on which they were unable or reluctant to allow a vote. "This is the damnedest thing I ever saw," a reporter scoffed. "That bill hasn't got a chance and everybody knows it. Yet everybody's getting fat off of it." Mansfield tried—and failed—again on May 14 to get cloture.[15]

When critics suggested that the Senate leadership had bungled the bill, Mansfield countered that liberals and the Kennedy administration were more to blame because they were unwilling to aggressively fight for its passage. While New Jersey Republican Clifford Case took Mansfield to task for his failure to force the issue on the Senate, he reserved equal criticism for Kennedy—who, he said, "gave the matter a very low priority." Mansfield said that when he secured Kennedy's unenthusiastic support for the bill, he found little fervor for it among liberal organizations. "The liberal groups came in after ten days of doing nothing to ask me what they could do and I said in effect, 'You're too late. You could have helped before, but it's gone too far now.' And we were defeated."[16]

The failure to muster the votes to pass even an incremental, seemingly innocuous civil rights measure was a sobering defeat that only reinforced the perception—at the White House and now in the Senate—that civil rights was an impossible hurdle. Consulting with Mansfield after the vote, Assistant Attorney General Burke Marshall asked, "What should we tell people about the prospects for civil rights in the Senate?" "Tell them the truth," Mansfield replied. "What is the truth?" Marshall asked. Said Mansfield: "That you'll never get a civil rights bill with a Democratic president." A Democratic president, Mansfield believed, could "never persuade that many Republican senators to vote for cloture," even if he decided to "become involved" in the fight.

Given the legislative record of the previous five years, few could argue with Mansfield's logic. Congress had enacted civil rights measures in 1957 and 1960 because a Republican president, with considerable help from a strong majority leader, had assembled a coalition of northern and western Democrats and moderate Republicans. By themselves—without public support and White House leadership—the northern Democrats were powerless to enlist ambivalent western Democrats to join a civil rights coalition. Likewise, Republicans were unlikely to support civil rights bills that enjoyed only mild popularity and that the president himself was unwilling to actively champion. The failure of the literacy bill persuaded Marshall that "nobody cared" about a bill "that shouldn't have been controversial at all." The plight of black Americans, Marshall concluded, was "still pretty invisible to the country as a whole."[17]

While the civil rights filibuster thrived in the Senate, Kennedy's Justice Department continued waging its quiet war against voting rights violations and school segregation throughout the South. In June 1962 Robert Kennedy announced that the department had initiated investigations and legal actions in almost one hundred southern counties under provisions of the 1957 and 1960 civil rights acts. (One was Sunflower County, Mississippi, the home of Senator James Eastland.) Kennedy's department also actively encouraged civil rights organizations to undertake voter registration efforts. Assured that the federal government would protect their workers, Southern Regional Council leaders established the Voter Education Project, an outgrowth of Kennedy's determined belief that the power of the ballot would be far more effective than marches, sit-ins, and Freedom Rides. "If enough Negroes registered," he maintained, "they could obtain redress of their grievances internally, without the federal government being involved at all."[18]

Meanwhile, officials at the Department of Health, Education, and Welfare began an effort aimed at the gradual desegregation of public schools in the South. Relying on two 1950 laws, the administration said it hoped to establish desegregated schools in areas "impacted" by federal military or civilian activities. HEW secretary Abraham Ribicoff announced in March that the administration might begin implementing provisions of the 1950 legislation that allowed the federal government to establish on-base schools when no "suitable" schools were otherwise available for children living on federal property. The definition of "suitable," said Ribicoff, would now include "desegregated." At the same time, the Justice Department signaled its willingness to expand the scope of federal intervention by compelling desegregation of local school districts receiving federal impact funds. That, reasoned Burke Marshall, might lead to even more aggressive federal action. "If we have the power to bring suits to compel the desegregation of impacted area schools, it follows that within the limits of staff and time we are going to desegregate all impacted schools."[19]

While southern members of Congress opposed Ribicoff's plans, many of them could never have imagined just how far Kennedy and his Justice Department would carry their efforts to desegregate educational facilities in the South. The first bloody confrontation would occur, not surprisingly, in Mississippi.

The crisis began when the NAACP's Legal Defense Fund took up the cause of James Meredith. A twenty-nine-year-old black Air Force veteran, Meredith had first been rejected by the University of Mississippi in Oxford in February 1961. With the NAACP's help, Meredith sued the school in federal district court. He lost, but in September the U.S. Supreme Court upheld an appeals court ruling and ordered the school to enroll Meredith. The decision set Meredith and the federal government on a collision course with Mississippi governor Ross Barnett, a firebrand segregationist who had campaigned for office on a pledge to keep the state's schools "segregated at all costs." With his political fortunes sagging midway through his four-year term, this was a promise Barnett meant to keep—and exploit.

In September Barnett placed himself squarely in the middle of the controversy when he persuaded the university's trustees to appoint him as "special registrar" so that he could personally reject Meredith's admission. On September 20, shortly after Meredith arrived on campus, Barnett defiantly sent him away. The school's trustees were not so resolute. When threatened with federal contempt charges, they capitulated and agreed to enroll Meredith. Barnett, who instinctively understood the political benefits of his opposition to Meredith's enrollment, stood firm.

On September 25 Barnett physically blocked Meredith and two Justice Department officials from entering the offices of the state's college board in Jackson. "I hereby finally deny you admission to the University of Mississippi," Barnett announced after refusing to receive a federal court order enjoining him from further interference in Meredith's registration. As Meredith left the building, a gaggle of state legislators cheered Barnett and jeered Meredith and his entourage. According to one state senator, Barnett's defiant stand had been "the most brilliant piece of statesmanship ever displayed in Mississippi."

On September 26, accompanied by twenty-five unarmed federal marshals, Meredith approached the town of Oxford to make his fourth attempt at the court-ordered enrollment. This time the opposition to Meredith's enrollment would be a contrived confrontation, choreographed by Kennedy and Barnett during intense phone negotiations. The plan was simple: By refusing to enroll Meredith, Barnett would defend Mississippi's "honor" and keep his campaign promise to resist the forced integration of the state's schools. As part of the plan, two dozen U.S. marshals, one of them with his gun drawn, would then force Barnett to back down.

The next day, as Meredith and his escorts drove toward the campus, word came that an unruly, possibly violent mob of 2,500 citizens and about 500 state police officers had gathered on campus. Failing to get "satisfactory assurances" from Barnett that he would enroll Meredith, President Kennedy had already federalized the Mississippi National Guard and placed federal troops on standby in nearby Memphis, Tennessee. On Sunday, September 30, Barnett finally agreed to allow Meredith on campus. Barnett and the university would ostensibly bow to the superior and overwhelming federal forces. That evening four hundred federal marshals led by Deputy Attorney General Nicholas Katzenbach escorted Meredith onto the Ole Miss campus for his registration the next morning.

Realizing that Meredith was now on campus, a night of bloody violence unfolded. As federal marshals and highway patrolmen stood guard, the mob began shouting, "Go to Cuba, nigger lovers, go to Cuba!" Some threw rocks at the marshals and slashed the tires of nearby army trucks. As the rioting intensified, Barnett deplored the violence but did little to stop it. He and other state authorities stood by idly as most of the local police and highway patrolmen slowly disappeared, some of them derisively dismissing the federal marshals as "Kennedy's Koon Klan."

By dawn the rioters had gone, but not until they had inflicted heavy casualties and wreaked warlike havoc on campus and in town. Two people—a French newspaper reporter and a local jukebox repairman—were dead. Another 166 federal marshals had been wounded, 28 of them by gunfire. Forty soldiers and National Guardsmen were injured. Later that morning Meredith, unharmed and escorted by federal marshals, registered and began attending classes. As he headed for class, Meredith endured the taunts of white students: "Hey, James, how you like seeing what you did to your campus, nigger?" and "That blood is on your hands, nigger bastard!"

As the campus emerged from its violent stupor, 23,000 federal troops poured into Oxford to maintain order, imposing what *Newsweek* called "an undeclared state of military rule." Although Barnett was clearly responsible for having allowed the highway patrolmen to withdraw at a crucial moment, the governor shamelessly pointed his finger at the Kennedy administration and "inexperienced and trigger-happy" marshals.[20]

Among southern members of Congress, there was little support for Meredith and even less for President Kennedy's decision to send in troops. Louisiana's Allen Ellender declared his "full sympathy" with Barnett, who, the senator explained, "is doing his utmost to fulfill the campaign pledges and the will of the people of his state." Meredith had received "better offers from other schools," Ellender reported to the Senate. "His idea is to enroll in a strictly white school and it strikes me that his motives should be closely scrutinized." While deploring the violence at Ole Miss, North Carolina's Sam Ervin blamed Meredith for much of the unrest. "It seems to me that those who are engaged in fomenting litigation which has such a tragic aftermath might well meditate upon the words of St. Paul when he said: 'All things are lawful unto me, but all things are not expedient.'" In Birmingham, just days before the violence, Russell had voiced his enthusiastic support for "the great and courageous governor of Mississippi." Were he governor, Russell told a meeting of Alabama Democrats, he would take the same stand as Barnett. For good measure, he attacked the nation's highest court. "It is regretful," he said, "that we have no one in the Supreme Court that recognizes the fundamentals of democracy."[21]

Internationally, the incident was another human rights embarrassment for the United States—and for the administration's attempts to foster freedom and democracy around the world. In France, *Le Monde* noted that "each time the resistance [to desegregation] appears more anachronistic and more odious." State radio in Moscow solemnly observed that Meredith's registration at Ole Miss would not erase the "national shame" over segregation. The foreign critics were correct. America could hardly champion human rights abroad when the enrollment of a black citizen in a public university sparked a violent uprising that bordered on open rebellion. It is impossible, *New York Times* columnist C. L. Sulzberger argued in an eloquent October 3 essay, to defend "the downtrodden overseas while permitting a second class of citizens at home in the land of liberty." Those who hinder social progress, said Sulzberger, "serve only to aid our enemies and to inspire resentment among those who would be our friends."[22]

The consequences of the Oxford riot were not all negative. Ole Miss, after all, had been integrated—finally. Thanks to courageous federal judges—particularly those on the Fifth Circuit Court of Appeals—and the Kennedy Justice Department, whites in Mississippi and other southern states were beginning to realize that the Constitution would henceforth be applied to every citizen. "No American need be ashamed of the 'Oxford incident,'" a Massachusetts man insisted in a letter to the editor of *Time*. The bloodshed and violence, he argued, had overshadowed the fact that "the basic rights of one American—one quiet, unassuming citizen—were being infringed upon, and as a result of this infringement, the entire power, might and prestige of the U.S. Government went to his assistance . . . Americans abroad and at home need not hang their heads in shame. This was a proud day for Americans."[23]

President Kennedy's pledge to sign an executive order barring discrimination in public housing—"by a stroke of the pen," he had once declared—haunted him into the fall of 1962. Two years after his election as president, Kennedy stood accused of the same reluctance to act that had afflicted his predecessor. For months supporters of the long-promised order had ridiculed Kennedy's unfulfilled rhetoric by mailing thousands of ink pens to the White House. Not particularly amused, Kennedy ordered the pens piled in Harris Wofford's office. For the first twenty-two months of Kennedy's term, federal housing remained a bastion of racial discrimination, tacitly sanctioned by the federal government and practiced in virtually every American city.[24]

Kennedy delayed issuing the order for several reasons. As with other civil rights proposals, Kennedy hoped to avoid antagonizing the southern Democrats whose support he needed on a host of other domestic initiatives, including his plan to create a Department of Housing and Urban Affairs. Kennedy's advisers believed that the ultimate success of that proposal hinged on the tenuous, dwindling goodwill of southerners. If Kennedy won approval for the new department, Robert Weaver—head of Kennedy's Housing and Home Finance Administration—would become the first black person nominated to head a cabinet department. According to Burke Marshall, Kennedy concluded that the daunting task of winning approval for the new department, with Weaver as secretary-apparent, "would be much more difficult" if he issued the housing order first. Yet Congress had now rejected the proposal twice. By late 1962 creation of the new cabinet-level department appeared hopeless, effectively removing at least one of Kennedy's rationales for continued delay.[25]

There were more excuses for inaction. Other civil rights issues—the Freedom Rides, the Ole Miss crisis, school desegregation, and voting rights—also demanded Kennedy's time and attention. "We were up to our necks in civil rights," Robert Kennedy later observed, adding that "the amount of good that was going to be accomplished by [the housing order] was marginal." By the summer of 1962, the approaching congressional elections only complicated matters. Kennedy's advisers believed that issuing the controversial directive before the November elections would likely infuse a highly emotional civil rights question into the campaigns of southern Democrats, who were already on the defensive over Kennedy's other domestic programs.[26]

Finally, there was the question of the order's exact wording. Although it would prohibit discrimination in federally owned or operated housing, as well as housing built with federal loans or federally secured loans, other issues were not so clear. Should the nondiscrimination order apply, as the Civil Rights Commission recommended, to conventional loans and mortgages made by financial institutions that the federal government merely regulated? And should the order be retroactive—that is, should housing already built with federal money be included, or should the order simply apply to all such housing built in the future? Kennedy's advisers even debated whether the president should take the more dramatic step of demanding that the Federal Deposit Insurance Corporation and the Federal Home Loan Bank Board force their member banks and savings and loans to comply with the order. Kennedy doubted his ability to persuade the institutions' conservative board members to follow his lead, and he worried about the economic impact of such a sweeping order. A broad, retroactive directive, he feared, might dampen housing starts at a time when his priority was ensuring greater economic growth. "And the president finally decided," said aide Theodore Sorensen, "that we should make the order as broad as we were certain our writ would run and no further."[27]

On November 20, two weeks after the congressional elections and twenty-two months into his term, President Kennedy signed the long-awaited order. Its announcement—dispensed along with the dramatic news that Soviet bombers were leaving Cuba and another pronouncement on an Indian border dispute with China—was not a major news story. Limited in scope and not retroactive, the order required federal agencies to take all legal steps to prevent racial discrimination in the selling and leasing of federally owned or operated housing. Also covered was housing built with federal loans—including senior and community facilities and college housing—and single-family and apartment dwellings insured by the Federal Housing Administration or the Veterans Administration. "It is neither proper nor equitable," Kennedy said, "that Americans should be denied the benefits of housing owned by the federal government or financed through federal assistance on the basis of race, color, creed or national origin."[28]

While the presidential directive was welcome news to liberals and civil rights leaders, it failed to satisfy those who expected more of Kennedy. As Martin Luther King acknowledged, presidential leadership on civil rights was now much greater than under Eisenhower and Truman. "But that didn't mean," King added, "that [Kennedy] was giving the kind of leadership at that time that the enormity of the problem demanded." The violence sparked by the Freedom Riders in Alabama and James Meredith in Mississippi had given Kennedy grand opportunities to display support for basic civil rights, but his refusal to press Congress for a comprehensive legislative remedy fed the lingering questions about the degree of his sincerity and the strength of his commitment. To critics and even allies,

Kennedy seemed to pay attention to civil rights only when an issue or a crisis imposed itself on his administration.[29]

Active and eloquent on so many other fronts, Kennedy drifted aimlessly in the sea of civil rights, tossed back and forth by the rolling waves of competing interests and ideologies. The seas, meanwhile, only grew more tumultuous.

12

"WAIT" HAS ALWAYS MEANT "NEVER"

After two years in office, President Kennedy still had no comprehensive civil rights program and no prospects for one. Even if he overcame his hesitancy to send Congress a legislative proposal, his dismal record on Capitol Hill made passage an unlikely prospect at best. The president, said one Senate aide, "couldn't buy a bill out of Congress." While Kennedy and his men temporized and worried about alienating southern congressmen, events in the South spun out of control. The Freedom Rides, the violence at Ole Miss, and other ugly incidents slowly awakened the slumbering national consciousness and dramatized the plight of southern blacks.[1]

In February 1963, a Kennedy-requested Civil Rights Commission report, "Freedom to the Free," supplied another call to action, graphically documenting the pitiful progress of civil rights in the hundred years since Abraham Lincoln had signed the Emancipation Proclamation. Citizenship for blacks was not "fully realized," the commission declared. Blaming southern leaders for their dogged "resistance to the established law of the land and to social change," the commissioners reported that "subtler forms" of discrimination still existed in vast areas of the North: the "gentlemen's agreement" barring blacks from housing outside ghettos, discriminatory employment practices that kept blacks in menial jobs, and overburdened neighborhood schools that resulted in inadequate educational opportunities. Kennedy tried to put the best face on the damning report, and weakly pointed to the modest civil rights progress of the previous fifteen years. Despite "setbacks," Kennedy admitted that "we still have some length to go." To many, that was a vast understatement.[2]

Attorney General Robert Kennedy, meanwhile, was far more energetic. He aggressively touted the administration's achievements in "every area of civil rights—whether voting, transportation, education, employment or housing." The attorney general insisted that 1962 had been "a year of great progress in civil rights." Yet sadly, despite the administration's otherwise truly remarkable record of executive action, the crisis at Ole Miss was symbolic of Kennedy's passive approach to civil rights: aggressive enforcement of impotent laws and failure to propose new, stronger statutes. The Ole Miss debacle had only highlighted Kennedy's sometimes painful inability to tackle the intransigence of southern officials with anything less than military might.[3]

On civil rights the young president resembled a fire chief who waited until a smoldering situation burst into flames before acting. "Events," said Ramsey Clark, then a young Justice Department official, "outran leadership." Although Kennedy refused to admit it, the vigorous enforcement of powerful, comprehensive civil rights legislation—not yet on the books—was the only means to begin curbing the nation's escalating social unrest. There were simply not enough assistant attorneys general to shuttle between cities and disarm brewing racial violence, not enough federal troops to keep or restore the peace in dozens of southern locales. Executive action and military coercion were weak substitutes for strong, enforceable civil rights statutes. Absent tough federal laws, the Kennedy Justice Department was only a minor combatant in the civil rights fight. The struggle was, instead, waged in the streets and in federal courtrooms throughout the South. The NAACP sued; the courts ruled; and southern authorities often defied those decrees. In the worst of cases, the president finally dispatched U.S. marshals or federal troops to ensure compliance or quash the resulting violent uprisings. Even the federal courts were not always reliable on civil rights. Despite Kennedy's efforts to nominate liberals to judgeships, southern senators often foisted their segregationist friends on the president. "We came out with some bad appointments in the South," then–deputy attorney general Nicholas Katzenbach later admitted.[4]

Kennedy's cautious deference to southern members of Congress yielded him little legislative success. Most southerners opposed his domestic policies and vigorously protested his response to the unrest in Alabama and Mississippi. Kennedy's cautious, incremental approach seemed to please no one in the South, nor did it serve to calm racial tensions. Several cities appeared ready to ignite at the slightest spark. The growing disquiet in the South, George Reedy advised Vice President Johnson in a memorandum, was "spreading and a number of northern cities are dry tinder—ready to burst into flames at the least spark." After two years of delay, almost everyone but Kennedy's White House advisers understood that the president's policy of caution and executive action had failed—rather miserably. It was time for aggressive action.[5] Yet no civil rights bill, however popular, stood a chance of becoming law until Kennedy and Senate liberals found a way to deprive the southerners of their most potent weapon—the filibuster.

The biennial clash over cloture began on January 14 with Clinton Anderson's proposal to lower the cloture threshold from two-thirds to three-fifths of senators present and voting. Humphrey also entered the debate, filing a statement on behalf of fifty-one senators—thirty-six Democrats and fifteen Republicans—who wanted cloture invoked by "a lesser number" of votes. The southerners, of course, filibustered the motion to consider Anderson's resolution. In a debate on the motion, which lasted for twenty-four days, Russell and other southern leaders worked feverishly to stave off cloture. (The cloture rule, as amended in January 1959, no longer excluded from cloture those filibusters designed to stop proposed rule changes.) Freshmen senators eager for certain committees and veterans who longed for better committees found that Russell and other conservative steering committee members refused to make assignments until the Senate resolved the cloture question. "This," complained Pennsylvania's Joseph Clark, "held the sword of Damocles over the heads of all Senators" hoping for better committees. Russell also "reasoned" with small-state senators, persuasively arguing that the filibuster was their only protection from the tyranny of the majority.[6]

Meanwhile, as the Senate's presiding officer, Johnson refused liberal entreaties for a ruling on the constitutionality of changing the Senate's rules by majority vote. Liberals wanted the vice president to rule that the Senate was not a "continuing body" and could therefore rewrite its rules by a simple majority vote at the beginning of each new Congress. Had Johnson ruled in their favor—as Vice President Nixon did in 1959 and 1961—a simple majority of senators might have voted to uphold the ruling, clearing the way for another vote on lowering the cloture threshold. Johnson refused to take sides. He testily explained, "That is a question for the Senate itself to decide." Senators, not the vice president, he said, must rule on the constitutionality of changing the rules by simple majority.[7]

Harry McPherson, who assured Johnson that he had no right to make such a ruling, said he feared that if the vice president intervened as the liberals wanted, "Russell, old as he was, might climb right over [Senate parliamentarian] Charlie Watkins's wispy head and seek to throttle him." On January 31, with Majority Leader Mansfield on the sidelines, the Senate declined, 53–42, to consider the constitutional question as propounded by Johnson. One week later, in a cloture vote, senators refused to end the southern filibuster. Liberals fell 10 votes short of cloture, 54–42.[8]

Russell had won. The filibuster seemed safe, and civil rights only a faint hope.

In that vote, however, Russell could see his ultimate defeat. After the southerners prevailed, Joseph Clark ambled over to Russell. "Dick," he said, "here's my sword again. I guess fate has cast me in the role of Robert E. Lee and you as Ulysses S. Grant." Smiling sadly, Russell replied, "Dammit, Joe, it's beginning to look like I'm Lee and you're Grant. You're slowly eroding us away." As Russell understood, the fifty-four votes marked the first time liberals had mustered a majority for cloture. Like General Lee, *Newsweek* observed, Russell was now "burdened with a lost cause and a tragic destiny: to throw his monumental talents against the relentless mainstream of history." Leaders of both political parties sensed the shifting political sands on civil rights. Growing numbers of voters, in the North and the South, wanted Congress to act—some because they believed in equal rights for black citizens, others for fear that the violent social unrest in Alabama and Mississippi might soon engulf their peaceful cities.[9]

On January 31 a large group of House Republicans led by New York's John Lindsay introduced a surprisingly strong civil rights bill. Accusing Kennedy of failing to honor the Democratic party platform, Lindsay declared his legislation was "designed to pass," unlike the Democrats' "public relations" attempts. Lindsay's potent bill made the Civil Rights Commission permanent and empowered its members to investigate election fraud. Furthermore, the bill created a federal commission for equal opportunity in employment to investigate job discrimination by government contractors, authorized the Justice Department to initiate lawsuits in school desegregation cases, and made a sixth-grade education the standard for proof of literacy in voting registration. In the Senate, meanwhile, a bipartisan group of liberals led by Clark introduced school desegregation legislation. Kentucky Republican John Sherman Cooper and Connecticut Democrat Thomas Dodd also introduced a measure requiring states to impose uniform voting requirements to prevent the arbitrary and discriminatory application of voting laws.

The very fact that Republicans had beaten the Democratic president to the punch on civil rights was more than a little embarrassing to Democratic liberals. Kennedy still had no bill, not even a weak one. Morale was low among members of the Civil Rights Leadership Conference. One day when

NAACP lobbyist Clarence Mitchell arrived for a meeting of conference members, someone asked, "Can you cheer us up?" Mitchell responded, "Certainly. The Republicans are going to introduce some bills."[10]

President Kennedy finally joined the legislative debate over civil rights on February 28, sending Congress a voting rights bill with minor education provisions and a four-year extension of the Civil Rights Commission. But the bill's primary aim was to correct "two major defects" of the 1957 and 1960 civil rights acts: "the usual long and difficult delays" in obtaining court judgments in voting rights cases and the laws' failure to address the "abuse of discretion" by local voter registrars "who do not treat all applicants uniformly." In addition to permitting federal judges to appoint referees before the conclusion of a voting rights case, the bill required courts to give "expedited treatment" to voting rights cases; prohibited "the application of different tests, standards, practices or procedures" for different prospective voters in federal elections; and established a sixth-grade education as proof of literacy in voter registration. Kennedy's bill also created a program of technical and financial assistance for school districts implementing desegregation plans.[11]

The president's acknowledgment that his bill would not "constitute a final answer to the problems of race discrimination in this country" was clearly an understatement. As a voting rights measure, it was a moderate proposal; as a civil rights program, it was a pitiful substitute for aggressive legislative action. Martin Luther King, Joseph Rauh, and other civil rights advocates were dejected by Kennedy's refusal to offer a stronger, more comprehensive program. NAACP leader Roy Wilkins saw little value in the Kennedy bill. The bill was useful, he said, only because "it finally signaled that the administration recognized the necessity and efficacy of legislation."[12]

Although civil rights leaders viewed the bill as only a weak voting rights measure, Russell declared that it encroached on "almost every phase of social and racial relations." In a relatively mild attack, the Georgia senator unveiled a new criticism of the administration's attempts to desegregate restaurants, hotels, bus stations, airports, and other public accommodations. The fault, he asserted, rested not with white racists but with the unacceptable nature of blacks. "Not on a single occasion," Russell said in a prepared statement, "has the president called upon any of the members of such groups to make any effort whatever to improve themselves so that they will be more acceptable to other citizens who may have certain standards for their associates." Russell offered no advice on how blacks might better themselves, but he clearly spoke for many southern racists when he asserted that whites should grant full citizenship only to those blacks whom they found "acceptable." John Stennis was more severe in his assessment of the bill. The Mississippi Democrat branded its provisions "so extreme and unconstitutional that Congress should not seriously consider them." Mississippi congressman John Bell Williams was even more explicit and outrageous: "The whole kit and caboodle is nothing more or less than an attempt to turn the government over to the NAACP."[13]

Perhaps the most damning criticism of the bill came not from liberal Democrats or southern conservatives but from Republicans who, for now, were sponsors of the only comprehensive civil rights proposal before the new Congress. Gleeful at yet another opportunity to exploit divisions over civil rights within the Democratic ranks, Lindsay and other Republicans derided Kennedy's bill as a "thin" proposal. New York governor Nelson Rockefeller—whom Kennedy regarded as a prime contender for the 1964 Republican presidential nomination—dismissed the legislation as too little, too late. He noted that it addressed only five of the twenty-eight proposals recently made by the Civil Rights Commission. The real problem, said Rockefeller, was Kennedy's reluctance to fight for stronger legislation, which he said could pass "if the necessary leadership were forthcoming."[14]

The obligatory partisan swipes at their civil rights proposal did not alarm Kennedy's men. Far more troublesome was the restlessness in the Democratic ranks, especially in the Senate. To dejected liberals such as Douglas, Humphrey, and Clark, the Republican initiative seemed more than a little enticing. At weekly leadership breakfasts, Humphrey had become a minor nuisance with his constant pleas for strong civil rights legislation. Kennedy rebuked Humphrey on at least two occasions, but Humphrey stood firm. "The leadership for civil rights," he told Kennedy, "either has to take place in the White House or it is going to take place in the streets." For now, at least, Humphrey and the other liberals would grudgingly yield to White House pressure to support Kennedy.[15]

In Birmingham, meanwhile, Martin Luther King's followers prepared to take to the streets in fulfillment of Humphrey's ominous warning to Kennedy. By nature a moderate, conciliatory man, King had become the nation's leading voice for civil rights as president of the Southern Christian Leadership Conference. In the nine years since the Montgomery bus boycott, King's SCLC had become the preeminent civil rights organization in the South. King himself had become something of a living martyr of the civil rights movement. Racist white authorities had arrested and jailed him several times. His home had been bombed. In New York in 1958, a deranged assailant had stabbed him in the chest.

In 1963, King's aide Wyatt Tee Walker finally persuaded the civil rights leader to consider a dramatic showdown on civil rights. Only the year before, the SCLC had reluctantly abandoned a frustrating yearlong desegregation project in Albany, Georgia. King failed because Albany's white leadership, although racist and intransigent, was not dumb. Led by the town's savvy police chief, Laurie Pritchett, Albany had responded to King's demands with a firm yet nonviolent no. A dedicated white supremacist, Pritchett had learned the unmistakable lessons of the Freedom Rides and Ole Miss: If he prevented violence, he could avoid federal intervention in his town. As Pritchett no doubt understood, refusing black civil rights demands became untenable only when violence resulted in the unkind glare of national news attention. King's Albany protest finally fizzled in September 1962, largely because of Pritchett's determination to arrest black protesters with minimum incident and no brutality. The events in Albany had never generated sensational front-page news in the *Washington Post* or the *New York Times*.

Old-fashioned nonconfrontational protest had proved ineffective. And King and his advisers knew that their movement could ill afford another failure like Albany. "To take a moderate approach hoping to get white help, doesn't work," Walker insisted to King. "You've got to have a crisis." King and his aides finally acknowledged the folly of fighting local disputes with narrowly focused goals. What they needed, in the words of one historian, was "an American Bastille," the kind of confrontation that could result in a symbolic victory with national repercussions. As King's friend Bayard Rustin observed, "protest becomes an effective tactic to the degree that it elicits brutality and oppression from the power structure." In Birmingham, King's men gave the effort the appropriate name of Project C—for confrontation. In early March, several weeks after the Kennedy administration presented its civil rights program to Congress, King arrived in Alabama to organize a series of mass demonstrations aimed at desegregating several downtown department stores, a group of federal buildings, and a suburban shopping center.[16]

King's choice of Birmingham was significant. Among dozens of racially oppressive southern cities, none was more segregated and officially hostile to its black citizens. In the previous six years, Birmingham had suffered eighteen racially motivated bombings and fifty cross burnings. City parks had been closed since January 1962, when local officials refused to heed a court order mandating integration of all public playgrounds. Birmingham officials had even abandoned their minor-league baseball franchise rather than compete against integrated teams. In almost every way, the city's white community clung desperately to the South's racist traditions. It was, in King's opinion, the best place in the South to make a dramatic statement about the evils of racial segregation. Yet despite the severe nature of its racial divisions, the city was no caldron of black anger and resentment. In the words of a *Time* reporter, Birmingham's blacks were "docile" and "they knew their place: they were 'niggers' in a Jim Crow town, and they bore their degradation in silence."[17]

Viewed from another perspective, Birmingham's blacks were not willingly pacific but fearfully cowed into submission by the city's public safety commissioner, Eugene "Bull" Connor. A brutish racist, Connor had long ignored, perhaps even encouraged, violence against black leaders. Although he had recently campaigned for mayor and lost to a more-moderate opponent, Connor remained in complete control of the city's fearsome, all-white police force. With an eye on statewide office, the commissioner could not allow King and his black followers to humiliate or intimidate his department before all of white Alabama. He would hold the line. The defense of his city's racist mores would be forceful and unrelenting.

On April 3, the day after Birmingham's mayoral election, King and local minister Fred Shuttlesworth set their plan in motion: a gradual, deliberate escalation of organized protest. That day police arrested twenty black demonstrators at whites-only lunch counters at four stores. The next day authorities apprehended several more demonstrators in similar lunch-counter protests. King then declared that the foundation of the effort would be a widespread black boycott of Birmingham's white-owned department stores. Until these stores desegregated their lunch counters and hired more blacks in responsible positions, black shoppers would make their not-insignificant purchases elsewhere. "The Negro has enough buying power in Birmingham," King observed, "to make the difference between profit and loss in a business."[18]

A simple economic boycott would never give King what he wanted most—a dramatic confrontation with Bull Connor. Although the boycott held firm, Project C unfolded in near oblivion for almost a week. Most local black leaders, resentful of King's "outsider" status, initially wanted no part of his movement or the uproar it might bring to their peaceful and comfortable lives. King was resolute. He upbraided more than a hundred black ministers for "riding around in big cars, living in fine homes," yet refusing "to take part in the fight." Those unwilling to "stand up with your people," he declared, "are not fit to be a preacher." Despite King's passionate appeal, only a handful of the local pastors offered their enthusiastic support.[19]

Just as Project C appeared doomed at the hands of black apathy, Bull Connor came to its rescue. At the end of the first week, the police commissioner committed the first of many tactical blunders. On April 7 his officers arrested Reverend Shuttlesworth and forty-two others who joined a small band of peaceful black marchers on their way to City Hall. The next day, King's brother, A.D.—a local Baptist minister—led another small march from the Sixteenth Street Baptist Church toward downtown. Connor's men were on the scene again, now reinforced by a pack of vicious police dogs. This time an indignant crowd of black citizens lined the street in support of the marchers as the officers began making their arrests. When an onlooker charged at a dog with a knife, the dog attacked. Within minutes, other officers—some with dogs, others with clubs—turned on the crowd. Most of the terrified onlookers scurried for safety.

Wyatt Tee Walker instantly understood the significance of the brief scuffle. From now on, King would stage all demonstrations to provoke a brutal response from Connor, which would in turn attract national attention and create an outpouring of sympathetic outrage. He encouraged those unwilling or unable to march to lend their moral support by lining the streets as the protesters passed.[20]

On April 12 King defied a local court order and led a small march—supported by more than a thousand black spectators—from the Sixteenth Street Baptist Church. King had hoped the day's march would end in his arrest, thus ensuring wider popular support and notoriety for his cause. His wish was fulfilled. Police rounded up King and fifty of his followers after they marched only four blocks. King's arrest—he was placed in solitary confinement—finally began to focus the glare of the national news media on Birmingham. From his cell, in a letter published after his release, he answered his critics in the city's white religious community, who had condemned him as a troublemaking "outsider." In his now-legendary "Letter from a Birmingham Jail," King wrote:

> For years now I have heard the word "Wait." It rings in the ear of every Negro with a piercing familiarity. This "Wait" has always meant "Never." It has been a tranquilizing thalidomide, relieving the emotional stress for a moment only to give birth to an ill-formed infant of frustration. We must come to see with the distinguished jurist of yesterday that "justice too long delayed is justice denied." We have waited for more than three hundred and forty years for our constitutional and God-given rights.

In his letter, King acknowledged that his protest movement in Birmingham "seeks to create such a crisis and establish such creative tension that a community that has consistently refused to negotiate is forced to confront the issue. It seeks to dramatize the issue so that it can no longer be ignored." [21]

King languished in jail for more than a week. By the time he posted bond and resumed leadership of Project C on April 20, his movement was in crisis, sputtering toward a complete standstill. Almost a thousand protesters languished in the city's jails or were out on bond. Among participants on the outside, morale was low. Precious few demonstrators were joining King's ranks. To make matters worse, neither Connor nor the city's white business leadership had shown even the slightest willingness to accede to the demonstrators' demands. President Kennedy helped increase national awareness of the situation briefly when he phoned King's wife, Coretta, to express his concern during King's imprisonment. But Kennedy's involvement appeared only to have resulted in permission for King to phone Coretta. Again, the national news media—after a brief spurt of attention—largely ignored the story. [22]

"We had run out of troops," Wyatt Walker later explained. "We had scraped the bottom of the barrel of adults who could go. We needed something new." Finally King and his aides settled on a highly controversial and potentially dangerous strategy. Sometime in late April, King reluctantly approved a plan to enlist thousands of teenagers for the front lines of the protest movement. Organizers littered the city's black high schools with leaflets urging the students to "fight for freedom first then go to school." The youngsters responded, enthusiastically, by the hundreds. On the day of the first march, Birmingham's black schools were left virtually empty. [23]

On Thursday, May 2, just before noon, a large crowd of black onlookers gathered outside the Sixteenth Street Baptist Church. Nearby, Bull Connor's menacing forces assembled and waited for the anticipated march, which would—unbeknownst to Connor—forever change the nature and course of the nation's civil rights movement. Inside the church were the newest soldiers in the civil rights struggle, young people whose lives King would risk for the cause of freedom. Suddenly the students burst through the front doors of the church. They sang, shouted, and danced as they made their way toward downtown. They did not march far. Connor's men promptly arrested most of them, five hundred in all, without incident. Again, as King had hoped, Birmingham began to make national news.

The next day, before a large crowd of black onlookers and scores of newspaper and television reporters, a new corps of brave teenage marchers left the church in several waves as they chanted "We Want Freedom" or sang the hymn "We Shall Overcome." This time, one of Connor's captains commanded the youngsters to stop. Still chanting, the students ignored the order and marched headlong into the phalanx of officials, which now included firefighters equipped with high-pressure water hoses. As tensions mounted, onlookers shouted insults at the assembled police officers. Then bricks and bottles rained down from the roof of a nearby building. Two firemen and a news photographer were hit. In response, Connor called up police dogs to force back the encroaching throng of onlookers. Frightened by the snarling animals, the crowd edged nervously backwards. Others ran away. One nightstick-wielding officer on a three-wheel bicycle pursued fleeing protesters who ran from the scene. Stragglers were struck. "Look at 'em run!" Connor yelled gleefully. When he noticed that his officers were holding back a curious crowd of whites, Connor ordered them brought forward for a better view. "Let those people come to the corner!" he shouted. "I want 'em to see the dogs work. Look at those niggers run." Finally Connor called in the water hoses. Firefighters pummeled the protesters with streams of water under enormous pressure. The water toppled protesters like dominoes. Several were injured. A few brave souls got up and charged again, only to have a crushing blast of water knock them off their feet. The relentless pressure violently ripped clothes off the backs of some. In less than thirty minutes, the confrontation was over. The protest was quashed. Police had arrested 250 students—including a six-year-old girl.[24]

That night at a church rally, King implored his followers to continue the fight. "Don't worry about your children who are in jail," he cried. "The eyes of the world are on Birmingham. We're going on in spite of dogs and fire hoses. We've gone too far to turn back." King's emotional plea struck a chord. Day after day, hundreds of enthusiastic children appeared at the church, eager to march and well aware that they faced arrest or injury. On Friday, May 10, fewer than five hundred students marched out of the church before authorities sealed the doors. By day's end police had arrested more than 250 people after dispersing the marchers with water and dogs.[25]

Some of the worst violence occurred on Tuesday, May 7, when 2,500 black protesters swarmed out of the church and caught Connor's men by surprise. As the lounging officers scrambled into formation, the protesters broke through their lines. They surged into nearby Kelly Ingram Park and headed toward downtown, where they ran into department stores, singing and chanting. As police rounded up the demonstrators, an ugly confrontation unfolded in the park near the church. As hundreds of blacks lobbed bricks and bottles at them, police officers responded with blasts of water. This time firemen trained their hoses on one of the protest's top leaders, the Reverend Fred Shuttlesworth. Shouting defiantly at the officers as he stood in front of the church, Shuttlesworth was pounded by a bone-crushing blast of water that slammed him into the side of the building. Later, when Connor learned that Shuttlesworth had been carried away in an ambulance, he responded: "I waited a week down here to see that, and then I missed it. I wish it had been a hearse."[26]

Later that night, after city officials threatened to impose martial law, top business leaders and protest organizers began negotiating in earnest. Assistant Attorney General Burke Marshall helped them. On Thursday they announced the terms of their agreement. Demonstrators would cease marching if business leaders would promise to begin desegregating downtown stores and end discriminatory hiring practices. King hailed the settlement. "This day," he said, "is clearly a moment of great victory."

The spirit of harmony lasted barely two days. Radical whites denounced the accord, and Connor called for a boycott of the white stores whose owners had agreed to the deal. Alabama governor George Wallace scoffed at the agreement, declaring that he would never "be a party" to any compromise on segregation. On Saturday, May 11, after a large Ku Klux Klan rally, the bombing of the Reverend A. D. King's parsonage shattered Birmingham's uneasy peace. Neither King nor his family was injured. Minutes later, several bomb explosions rocked the Gaston Motel, which served as Martin Luther King's Birmingham headquarters. Four blacks were hurt.

Presumably the target of the blasts, King was out of town. The bombings sparked a round of riots that raged throughout the city for hours. Rioters burned houses and other buildings. Fifty policemen and rioters were injured in the violence. By dawn, a nine-block section of town was smoldering, virtually destroyed in the previous night's mayhem.[27]

The violence in Birmingham, especially Bull Connor's clumsy and ruthless tactics, made for sensational news on television and in newspapers across the country. "DOGS AND FIRE HOSES ROUT 3000 NEGROES," said the *Boston Globe* on May 4. The paper, like most others in the country, prominently featured shocking photographs of firemen blasting children with water hoses and a policeman gripping a stunned black youth while a menacing dog lunged at his exposed torso. "DOGS AND HOSES REPULSE NEGROES AT BIRMINGHAM," announced the *New York Times*. In the *Los Angeles Times,* a front-page story was headlined "ALABAMA RIOT: POLICE DOGS, FIRE HOSES HALT MARCH." *Time* and *Newsweek* devoted extensive coverage to Birmingham for several weeks. Said *Newsweek* on May 17: "The blaze of bombs, the flash of blades, the eerie glow of fire, the keening cries of hatred, the wild dance of terror in the night—all this was Birmingham, Ala." Overseas the headlines were worse. London's *Daily Mirror:* "RACE CLASH—1,000 CHILDREN JAILED." Moscow's *Pravda:* "MONSTROUS CRIMES OF THE RACISTS IN THE UNITED STATES." *Liberation* in Paris: "SAVAGES IN ALABAMA." [28]

In the Senate, southern segregationists loudly decried perceived violations of the Constitution. "None of us should be content to sit idly by in the face of this direct threat to historic constitutional principles," Mississippi's John Stennis declared. Of course, the constitutional principles about which Stennis and other southerners cared so deeply were the rights of states—not the civil rights of individuals, which had obviously been violated. Stennis had no complaints about Alabama authorities, who he said had functioned "fully and effectively." Later in the day, Oregon's Wayne Morse took the floor with a passionate rebuttal. "I say to my good friend from Mississippi," Morse said, "he need only turn the pages of *Life* magazine of last week for pictorial proof, if he is not already aware of it, of the shocking, inhumane, atrocious, horrendous conduct of the so-called Alabama state law officials and municipal law officials, be-spoiling the precious liberties of supposedly free Americans but of colored skin . . . There is no place in America for inhumanity to man." [29]

The resulting media coverage elated King. As Wyatt Tee Walker later explained, the blustering, uncompromising Bull Connor had been "a perfect adversary." In Walker's opinion, "Birmingham would have been lost if Bull had let us go down to the City Hall and pray; if he had let us do that and stepped aside, what else would be new? There would be no movement, no publicity. But all he could see was stopping us before we got there. We had calculated for the stupidity of a Bull Connor." Said CORE's James Farmer, "People . . . all over the U.S. sat in their living rooms, just finishing dinner or eating dessert and drinking coffee, and watched those abysmal scenes. [And they thought:] Those scenes are horrible; those little children—they haven't hurt anybody—those women. Bull Connor's a beast, we have to get rid of him; we have to put an end to this thing. This is not American. Give us some laws; let's have some laws. Laws that can be enforced and get this problem behind us . . . After Birmingham, the majority was with us; their consensus had arrived." [30]

President Kennedy, who had threatened to send in the National Guard to quell the May violence, urged Birmingham's white leaders to give some ground. On Capitol Hill, Humphrey must have found the president's words satisfying—yet maddeningly overdue. "There is an important moral issue involved of equality for all of our citizens," Kennedy said at a press conference. Until whites treated blacks as full citizens, Kennedy said, "you're going to have these difficulties . . . the time to give it to them is before the disasters come." It was precisely the point Humphrey had made to the president weeks earlier. [31]

From the beginning, King had hoped that the events in Birmingham would force Kennedy's hand by creating "such a crisis in race relations that it was an issue which could no longer be ignored." Perhaps, King later mused, Kennedy "came to see in a way that he had probably never seen— and in a way that many other people finally came to see—that segregation was morally wrong and it did something to the souls of both the segregationist and the segregated." Birmingham, Roy Wilkins observed, showed the White House "that perhaps the attack agreed upon was not as adequate as the president had thought at the outset." Most important, the alarming news stories and graphic images from Birmingham had awakened the nation to the brutal treatment that southern blacks usually encountered when they demanded their constitutional rights. [32]

"Blacks," Arizona congressman Morris Udall said later, "simply weren't going to shuffle along the dark side of the sidewalk anymore." At the urging of King and other leaders, blacks in Birmingham and elsewhere had taken to the streets, chanting "Freedom! Freedom! Freedom Now!" By the end of May, civil rights demonstrations had broken out in dozens of cities in Maryland, Illinois, Pennsylvania, North Carolina, New Jersey, and New York. But exactly what did King and his new legions of emboldened followers mean when they demanded their immediate "freedom"? "If the Negroes wanted something specific, the federal government might be able to find specific remedies," George Reedy told Johnson in a May 24 memorandum. "But the Negro revolt is not directed against the federal government. It is directed against the white governments they know—right in their own communities." There was, however, one "common denominator" among blacks and white supremacists, Reedy accurately argued. It was "a belief that the United States—in the person of the president himself—has not made a real moral commitment to the cause of equal rights and equal opportunity." By now it was clear to everyone that Kennedy's February legislative offering was woefully inadequate. No one could deny that the volatile situation now called for a much stronger, comprehensive package of legislative proposals. By May, Burke Marshall said, Kennedy himself arrived at that conclusion "without having a meeting or discussion about it." The president realized, observed historian Taylor Branch, "a bill to outlaw segregation by federal statute promised to resolve a hundred potential Birminghams from El Paso to Baltimore, and the clarity of inescapable tensions drew President Kennedy toward the relief of that single, huge gamble."[33]

Yet most of the president's advisers were far from enthusiastic about the prospect of their leader embarking on a controversial crusade for civil rights only seventeen months before the 1964 presidential election. Kenneth O'Donnell opposed it, as did congressional liaison Larry O'Brien. Ted Sorensen was described as "dubious." Majority Leader Mansfield and Bobby Baker doubted they could ever break a southern filibuster. Even Burke Marshall, the Justice Department's top civil rights official, was hesitant. Kennedy would be making civil rights his issue. "And doing that in 1963," Marshall said, "with the southern control of a third of the Senate, was a very, very serious undertaking." The bill "would tie up the Congress for months, for a year, maybe more than a year, making it impossible for him to get other legislation through." Marshall also worried that a strong civil rights program "would focus national attention on it, so that the failure to pass a bill would have been a failure of the Kennedy presidency" just before the 1964 presidential election. To Marshall, introducing a new civil rights bill was noble, but it amounted to Kennedy "betting" his presidency on one polarizing issue.[34]

Attorney General Robert Kennedy believed that, despite the forbidding odds, the president had no choice but to submit a comprehensive bill. Those who knew the president's pragmatic, often impulsive brother were not surprised by the advice he offered. Once he decided that the nation's racial problems could no longer be managed by executive action, the attorney general eagerly advocated altering the administration's course. As the president's brother, Kennedy had wide latitude. No other attorney general would have begun drafting a controversial civil rights proposal without the president's express permission. But on May 17, Robert Kennedy and Marshall ordered a draft of the bold legislation that the attorney general knew his brother would eventually offer to Congress. Several days later, at a May 22 news conference, the president confirmed reports that he was considering a new civil rights plan "which would provide a legal outlet" for blacks. He was vague about the legislation. "I would hope that we would be able to develop some formulas so that those who feel themselves barred, as a matter of fact denied equal rights, would have a remedy." [35]

As Justice Department attorneys began drafting the bill—in consultation with Kennedy's White House advisers—several provisions quickly emerged. The bill would almost certainly allow the federal government to withhold federal money from any discriminatory program or activity. It would create a Community Relations Service to help resolve local racial disputes and would establish a sixth-grade education as proof of literacy in voting registration. The bill would also provide for preferential and expedited treatment of voting rights suits and court-appointed voting referees in some pending voting rights cases. These provisions, however, would not make up the heart and soul of Kennedy's bill. Two others would be more important—and far more controversial.

Justice Department lawyers drafted a provision to permit the attorney general to initiate and file desegregation suits aimed at public schools and colleges. This was, in essence, the controversial Part III of the 1957 act. If included in the bill, this provision threatened to revive the kind of bitter opposition that erupted in 1957. Robert Kennedy was determined to draft this provision so narrowly that it would calm all fears of a reckless, vindictive attorney general given free rein to harass local school boards. [36]

Perhaps the bill's most controversial section was one that historians and southern blacks would come to view as the core of the legislation—a provision to require "equal access" to all public accommodations, including hotels, restaurants, theaters, and stores. It was the part of the bill for which President Kennedy had the most passion and enthusiasm. "He thought it was just outrageous to refuse to serve people because of their race," Burke Marshall recalled, adding that Kennedy "couldn't understand why that was a big issue." Kennedy told Ted Sorensen that reaction to this provision would be mild compared to that for other parts of the bill. Of course, because Kennedy was not a southerner, he failed to understand that the public accommodations provision would be the most disputed provision in the bill.[37]

Kennedy was firmly persuaded that the public accommodations section was an essential part of the bill. More vexing, however, was the constitutional basis for such a provision. Would it be grounded in the language of the Fourteenth Amendment, which prohibited a state from denying any of its citizens "the equal protection of the laws"? Or could Congress assert its power, under Article I, Section 8, "to regulate commerce . . . among the several states"? The question was the most hotly debated aspect of the public accommodations section. The president favored the more straightforward language of the Fourteenth Amendment. Justice Department officials disagreed. In enacting the Civil Rights Act of 1875—identical to the proposed public accommodations language in many respects—Congress had used the Fourteenth Amendment as its source of legislative authority. Eight years later the Supreme Court declared the law unconstitutional because, it said, the power of Congress under the amendment was limited to enforcing prohibitions against discriminatory actions by states. In a document prepared for the Senate Commerce Committee in 1963, Justice Department lawyers noted that "the Civil Rights Cases [of 1883] were decided 80 years ago and have never been questioned in subsequent opinions of the court. An expansion of the concept of State actions has occurred, but the basic 14th amendment distinction between governmental and private action has been consistently observed down to the present day."[38]

Finally, at Marshall's urging, the president agreed that the administration should construct the bill's language on a more solid foundation: the Constitution's commerce clause. Thus, discrimination in public places or businesses would be outlawed if goods, services, or accommodations were provided "to a substantial degree" to interstate travelers; if a "substantial portion" of the goods sold to the public had moved in interstate commerce; or if a business's activities "substantially affect" interstate commerce. The practice of discrimination by such businesses, the administration maintained, "obstructs interstate travel and the sale of related goods and services [and] restricts business enterprises in their choice of locations for offices and plants, because of their inability to obtain the services of persons who do not wish to subject themselves to segregation and discrimination." Actually, the administration would also apply the Fourteenth Amendment's prohibition on state-sanctioned discrimination. Segregation or discrimination in public accommodations would be specifically outlawed if carried out "under color of any law, statute, ordinance, or regulation; or . . . under color of any custom or usage required or enforced" by state or local officials.[39]

On May 24, as Justice Department lawyers continued to work on the bill, Vice President Johnson gave further rise to expectations that the Kennedy administration was about to make a significant and momentous proposal on civil rights. Johnson had become an outspoken and enthusiastic proponent of a comprehensive civil rights bill. His rhetoric was combative. In Detroit, in January, he had told a university audience: "To strike the chains of a slave is noble. To leave him the captive of the color of his skin is hypocrisy." Several weeks later, speaking before the Cleveland Urban League, he declared that the next hundred years "demand of us that we resolve the problems left unresolved when the Emancipation Proclamation freed the slaves." In mid-May, in a speech to the Capital Press Club in Washington, he said, "It seems to me that in the field of human rights, we are well past the stage where half a loaf will do."[40]

On May 30, in an eloquent Memorial Day speech at Gettysburg, Pennsylvania, Johnson hit a rhetorical crescendo in a speech that Hubert Humphrey or Paul Douglas could have easily delivered. In a way, the speech was a watershed in Johnson's evolution as a civil rights proponent and was the strongest pro–civil rights statement he had ever made in a public forum: "In this hour, it is not our respective races which are at stake—it is our nation. Let those who care for their country come forward, North and South, white and Negro, to lead the way through this moment of challenge and decision."[41]

13

A BILL, NOT AN ISSUE

Johnson had strong feelings about civil rights and the legislative strategy Kennedy ought to pursue. Making certain that Kennedy heeded his advice—or even heard it—was another matter. White House staff members often ignored him, and they severely limited his access to the president. Despite a presidential order to include Johnson in every White House meeting on civil rights, Lee White, Kennedy's civil rights assistant, sometimes forgot. "Now look, you work with Lyndon Johnson and make sure that he knows about all of these things," Kennedy ordered. "I want him here. I think he can do a lot." Despite the unmistakable nature of Kennedy's feelings about Johnson's involvement, White admitted that of eight meetings held by the White House and Justice Department staff to discuss civil rights, "There must have been two or three when I just clean forgot about the vice president—just forgot!" Of course, Johnson, extremely sensitive to such slights, did not attend any meeting to which Kennedy's men did not invite him.[1]

At one meeting to which the vice president was invited—a June 1 Oval Office meeting with Kennedy and his advisers—Johnson was largely silent and almost petulant. Asked by Kennedy for his thoughts on the proposed legislation, Johnson replied, "I haven't seen it." Kennedy shot back, "I haven't seen it either," the point being that the discussion was about what elements to include in the bill. Later, when asked again for his opinion on the matter, Johnson demurred, explaining that he was "not competent to counsel you." But finally, Johnson engaged the issue and offered Kennedy his best advice: "If we do that [propose a bill], then we got to go through with it and *pass* it. Gotta bear down . . . or else yours will be just another gesture."[2]

Shortly after the Oval Office meeting, Johnson asked appointments secretary Kenny O'Donnell for fifteen minutes alone with the president to discuss the issue. Kennedy responded by sending over Burke Marshall to hear his thoughts. Johnson talked with Marshall not about legislative strategy but about the importance of addressing the economic hardships endured by black citizens. Johnson never "came down hard one way or another" on whether Kennedy should offer a tough, comprehensive civil rights bill, Marshall said. "He'd talk around it, about the economic problems and his own experience with the [NYA] in the thirties, and so forth."[3]

Following his meeting with Marshall, Johnson again pressed O'Donnell for a private audience with the president. This time, on June 3, Robert Kennedy dispatched Norbert Schlei—the assistant attorney general in charge of drafting the legislation—to see Johnson. An agitated vice president "absolutely poured out his soul" about the bill, Schlei recalled. Ignoring the substance of the legislation, the vice president instead offered his strategic and tactical advice on the bill's presentation to the nation and its passage through Congress. Later that day, Johnson received a phone call from another administration aide, Ted Sorensen, a top adviser to the president who doubled as a speechwriter.[4]

By now, although he still had not seen a draft bill, Johnson vaguely understood the legislation Kennedy was prepared to submit to Congress; his information came mostly from a newspaper account. In a lengthy conversation with Sorensen (recorded by Dictaphone), Johnson repeatedly advised caution: "I think that we got to do our homework before we send a message, one, and we can't do that unless we spend some time on the message. Two, I think we ought to exchange some viewpoints [with members of Congress] on what legislation we can get." The president, Johnson counseled, should unveil his proposal in the South. As for the message Kennedy would eventually deliver to the nation, Johnson suggested that he not only declare his support for potent legislation, but establish a strong position of moral leadership on the issue. He suggested Kennedy go to the South and say:

> Now, I don't want to come here without talking about our constitutional rights. We're all Americans. We got a Golden Rule, "Do unto others as you would have them do unto you." Now I'm leader of this country. When I order men into battle, I order them men without regard to color. They carry our flag into foxholes. The Negro can do that, the Mexican can do it, others can do it. We've got to do the same thing when we drive down the highway at places they eat.

I'm going to have to ask you all to do this thing. I'm going to have to ask the Congress to say that we'll all be treated without regard to our race.

Johnson told Sorensen that such a message would "run some of the demagogues right into the hole." Yet he remained doubtful of Kennedy's ability to sell it to Congress. "I know the risks are great and it might cost us the South, but those sort of states may be lost anyway," Johnson said. "The difference is if your president just enforces court decrees, the South will feel it's yielded to force. But if he goes down there and looks them in the eye and states the moral issue and the Christian issue, and he does it face to face, these Southerners at least respect his courage. They feel they're on the losing side of an issue of conscience."

Reflecting counsel he had received in a memorandum from George Reedy a week earlier, Johnson told Sorensen that southerners of both races shared "one point of view that's identical":

They're not certain that the government is on the side of the Negroes. The whites think we're just playing politics to carry New York. The Negroes feel and they're suspicious that we're just doing what we got to do. Until that's laid to rest, I don't think you're going to have much of a solution. I don't think the Negroes' goals are going to be achieved through legislation and a little thing here on impact area or voting or something. I think the Negro leaders are aware of that. What Negroes are really seeking is moral force and to be sure we're on their side and make them all act like Americans.

Despite his doubts about the efficacy of Kennedy's proposal, Johnson believed that "he's got to have his bill." Referring to Kennedy's modest civil rights proposal in February, Johnson told Sorensen: "He's sitting over here, we've got six months, we haven't passed anything! I think he ought to make them pass some of this stuff before he throws this thing out . . . If I were Kennedy, I wouldn't let [the Republicans] call my signals. I'd pass my program, make them stand up and vote for it. While I was doing that, I'd go into the South a time or two myself. While I was doing that, I'd put the Republicans on the spot by making them buy my program."

Yet Johnson also advised caution, especially regarding the administration's relations with Congress. "We better just see what we want to do and be sure that everybody wants to do it and then go ahead," he said. "I don't think we're at that stage now. I told the Attorney General that, and I tell you that. Now, if you are at that stage [ready to introduce the bill], I'm making it abundantly clear I'm on the team and you'll never hear a [contrary] word out of me."[5]

In his 1965 memoir of the Kennedy presidency, Sorensen painted a different portrait of the administration's attempts to curry congressional favor for the bill. Sorensen accurately recalled that Kennedy and his aides "consulted frequently" with leaders of both political parties, but he gave Johnson no credit for having forcefully advocated this part of the president's strategy, and he did not mention his own lengthy discussion with Johnson. In an oral history interview with the John F. Kennedy Library in 1964, Sorensen falsely claimed "the vice president had a major role in the formulation of the legislation." Robert Kennedy was more forthcoming about Johnson's late involvement in the process. Kennedy recalled Johnson's advice "that we should do some work in Congress before the legislation was sent up, and that was a very wise suggestion." Heeding Johnson's counsel, the attorney general met with Richard Russell twice to explain the president's legislation. The president himself even talked with Russell. Courteous as always, Russell firmly informed both men that he would not only oppose the bill but would work vigorously to defeat it. Of course no one had expected that Russell would endorse the legislation. As Johnson understood, if the White House properly briefed Russell, he could not rise on the Senate floor—as he had in 1957—to accuse the Justice Department of subterfuge and deceit.[6]

On June 11, hours after Alabama became the last state in the nation to desegregate its state university, President Kennedy appeared on national television and radio to announce his civil rights legislation. Although Kennedy had planned a televised address only if violence erupted in Alabama, he abruptly decided to announce his program while the nation's attention was focused on civil rights. Kennedy's decision sent Sorensen into a last-minute speech-writing frenzy. Sorensen did his best, even though the bill's exact language was not complete and would not be ready for submission to Congress for another week. Just minutes before the broadcast, Kennedy still did not have the final draft of Sorensen's text. Sitting before the camera in the Cabinet Room, accompanied only by his brother Robert and Burke Marshall, Kennedy scribbled his own speech notes.[7]

At eight o'clock, Kennedy began his historic speech to the American people. The nation, he said, was confronted primarily with a moral issue. It is as old as the Scriptures and is as clear as the American Constitution. The heart of the question is whether all Americans are to be afforded equal rights and equal opportunities; whether we are going to treat our fellow Americans as we want to be treated.

If an American, because his skin is dark, cannot eat lunch in a restaurant open to the public; if he cannot send his children to the best public school available; if he cannot vote for the public officials who represent him; if, in short, he cannot enjoy the full and free life which all of us want, then who among us would be content to have the color of his skin changed and stand in his place?

Who among us would then be content with the counsel of patience and delay?

One hundred years of delay have passed since President Lincoln freed the slaves, yet their heirs, their grandsons, are not fully free. They are not yet freed from the bonds of injustice; they are not yet freed from social and economic oppression.

And this nation, for all its hopes and all its boasts, will not be fully free until all its citizens are free . . .

The fires of frustration and discord are burning in every city, North and South. Where legal remedies are not at hand, redress is sought in the streets, in demonstrations, parades and protests which create tensions and threaten violence—and threaten lives.[8]

Those who hoped that Kennedy's speech might calm racial strife in the South were shocked later that night by the cold-blooded murder of the NAACP's Mississippi field secretary, Medgar Evers. A tall, impressive-looking World War II veteran, Evers had recently gained prominence as the inspirational leader of several sit-ins and demonstrations in Jackson. That evening, just before midnight, as he entered his home, the crack of a high-powered deer rifle shattered the late-night silence. Evers lay wounded and bleeding in his driveway. His wife and three children rushed out of the house. "Please, Daddy, please get up!" his children cried. Evers died an hour later.[9]

Russell reacted to Kennedy's speech with predictable outrage and sorrow. "The outstanding distinction between a government of free men and a socialistic or communistic state," he said in a statement the day after Kennedy's speech, "is the fact that free men can own and control property, whereas statism denies property rights to the individual." Russell declared that he would oppose Kennedy's bill "with every means and resource at my command."[10]

Russell knew that he was fighting a losing battle. His southern bloc was shrinking and aging. In the coming months their public image would be unmistakable: graying Confederates waging a fierce battle not to win the war but only to stave off defeat as long as possible. Russell could not even be certain that he still had the overwhelming support of southern whites: In August a poll by Louis Harris showed that 54 percent of white southerners favored legislation to open public accommodations to blacks.[11]

Russell's only real chance of winning was to compromise or offer a reasonable alternative to Kennedy's legislation. Russell seemed to consider neither. As *Wall Street Journal* reporter Jerry Landauer observed in a June 19 column: "Richard Russell can summon a parliamentary precedent at the snap of a finger, yet there are some among his warm admirers who believe his 30 years in the Senate blind him to what's going on outside. Certain friends fervently hope that he will now bend somewhat to what they think is the Nation's mood for action."[12]

In Congress, Kennedy's bill would encounter many skeptics and enemies. None would prove more formidable than Russell. It was, for several reasons, a prospect that Kennedy and other admirers of the senior Georgia senator did not relish. In January, during a lengthy Oval Office meeting with *Atlanta Constitution* editor Ralph McGill, Kennedy had openly pondered Russell and his stubborn opposition to civil rights. "Here's a man of great gifts and great capacity for friendships and loyalties," Kennedy said. "The whole world is changing, and the whole nation is changing. And yet this gifted man remains adamant and defiant in the matters of any measures which tend to enter the field of race—civil rights." In an interview with the *New York Times,* Humphrey predicted that Congress would eventually enact a civil rights bill over Russell's opposition. "I only wish," Humphrey lamented, "that Dick Russell could have put his God-given talents to work on the side of constitutional guarantees of civil rights."[13]

Few northerners who despaired over Russell's intransigence fully understood the political mentality of the average southern politician. To many northern liberals, civil rights was one of many issues about which they felt strongly. For southern politicians, particularly those of Russell's generation, support for civil rights was not only political suicide—it was flat wrong and immoral. "It was just a very deep underlying conviction of his, a sincere conviction," said Ivan Allen, the progressive mayor of Atlanta, who doubted that politics influenced Russell's opposition to civil rights. Jimmy Carter, then a moderate Georgia state senator, also admired Russell because "he accurately mirrored the feelings of the Georgia people, [and] the southern people." CBS correspondent Roger Mudd said of Russell: "He was protecting and defending a way of life that he had been reared in and the majority of his people had been reared in, the majority of his constituents had been reared in, and that's what a man is sent here for—to defend the way of life that most people who sent him here enjoy. So I never faulted him for that."[14]

Whatever his motives, Russell vowed that he would oppose Kennedy's civil rights bill to "the last ditch." In the end, White House congressional liaison Larry O'Brien said, "we will just have to place the prestige and power of the president into the scales to see if they can outweigh Dick Russell."[15]

The prospects for Kennedy's bill, in the Senate at least, were grim. On June 27 Majority Secretary Bobby Baker reported to Majority Leader Mansfield that his "poll" of senators showed "conclusively that it is virtually impossible to secure fifty-one senators who will vote for the president's bill." Even if Kennedy found "a formula" on public accommodations acceptable to three key Republicans—Minority Leader Dirksen, George Aiken of Vermont, and Bourke Hickenlooper of Iowa—the chances for cloture were "50–50," Baker concluded.

In the House, meanwhile, Robert Kennedy had not helped his brother's cause. On June 20, during his first day of testimony before a House Judiciary subcommittee, he brusquely dismissed a Republican civil rights bill by telling New York Republican John Lindsay he had not found time to read it. That admission was unfortunate. With southern Democrats in opposition, the White House would need substantial Republican support in the House and Senate to pass the bill. "If we become too partisan," Baker had warned Mansfield, "we have no chance of passing a bill in the foreseeable future."[16]

Republicans held the key to the bill's passage, and many of them sincerely wanted to play a meaningful role in the process. Yet some of them were reluctant to back the bill's strongest provisions, suspecting that Kennedy might trade them away to gain the support of moderates in the Senate. That was no idle suspicion. Administration strategists—including Kennedy and Johnson—initially believed that several unspecified House provisions could be cast aside as the bill moved through the Senate. The Republican most leery of this strategy was William McCulloch of Ohio, a senior Judiciary Committee member who had aided passage of the 1957 and 1960 civil rights bills. Widely respected among congressmen of both parties, McCulloch was his party's point man on civil rights in the House—and one of the administration's best hopes for a bipartisan agreement. Following secret negotiations between McCulloch and Burke Marshall, the president agreed to two important conditions in exchange for crucial Republican support: First, the administration would oppose any attempts by conservative senators to weaken a House-passed bill and would not agree to amendments until McCulloch approved them. Second, Kennedy would publicly praise Republicans for their role in passing the bill. While the bargain buoyed hopes for House passage, the deal suddenly forced Justice Department officials to view their bill in a new light. Deputy Attorney General Nicholas Katzenbach and others now realized that the White House was unlikely "to get anything in the House of Representatives unless we were prepared to fight for it in the Senate." That realization, Katzenbach said, prompted them "to think more seriously of cloture than we ever had before."[17]

At the White House, President Kennedy launched a full-court press to generate public support for his bill, meeting with representatives of many civic, political, and religious organizations. On June 13 he conferred with nearly 300 labor leaders. Most of them endorsed the bill. Five days later, he met with 250 religious leaders. The meeting was a first. Never before had a large group of American religious leaders gathered to plot strategy for a major legislative initiative. Kennedy also lobbied a group of eight governors, more than 200 prominent attorneys, and representatives of 100 women's organizations.[18]

On June 22, three days after formally submitting his bill to Congress, Kennedy convened a White House meeting of the major civil rights groups. Although the president had not solicited advice from black leaders in drafting the legislation, he now asked for their support. In explaining the congressional maze that the bill must negotiate toward passage, Kennedy emphasized the difficulty of stopping the anticipated southern filibuster. Cloture would be impossible, he said, without the votes of midwestern Republicans. A proposed march on Washington, he told them, would only complicate matters and make it more difficult to win the support of ambivalent senators. "Some of those people are looking for an excuse to be against us," Kennedy said. "I don't want to give any of them a chance to say, 'Yes, I'm for the bill but I'll be damned if I will vote for it at the point of a gun.'" Johnson, normally reticent at such gatherings, spoke up. He agreed with Kennedy. To win about twenty-five crucial swing votes in the Senate, he explained, "we have to be careful not to do anything which would give those who are privately opposed a public excuse to appear as martyrs." Martin Luther King, A. Philip Randolph, and James Farmer disagreed. A mass demonstration in the nation's capital, King argued, "could serve as a means through which people with legitimate discontents could channel their grievances under disciplined, nonviolent leadership."[19]

As if to dramatize the serious nature of his own commitment to the issue, Kennedy pulled a piece of paper from his pocket. On it, he declared, were fresh poll numbers showing that his national approval rating had sunk from 60 percent to 42 percent in the days since he unveiled his bill. "I may lose the next election because of this," he insisted. "I don't care." No one ever found the figures he had cited, said Joseph Rauh, but Kennedy's point was clear: "It was a moral issue. It was a great speech he made to us. I felt from that moment he was terribly committed."[20]

Kennedy made another effective point during the meeting. He chided those who had harshly condemned Bull Connor's brutal tactics in Birmingham. "I don't think you should all be totally harsh on Bull Connor," Kennedy whimsically advised, revealing that he had fully understood the goals of the Birmingham demonstrations. "After all, he has done more for civil rights than almost anybody else."[21]

The unusual debut of Kennedy's program in the Senate spoke worlds about the treacherous journey it faced. On June 19 Majority Leader Mansfield submitted Kennedy's entire civil rights program in one bill. Cosponsored by thirty-seven Democrats and nine Republicans, it was promptly referred to the legislative domain of Judiciary Committee chairman James Eastland, one of the bill's most vociferous opponents. Although the legislation that Mansfield introduced contained public accommodations language, the majority leader immediately moved to assuage Republican leader Everett Dirksen. A vocal opponent of the public accommodations provision, Dirksen had refused to cosponsor the entire Kennedy program. Therefore Mansfield joined Dirksen as a sponsor of another bill that was identical to Kennedy's proposal in every way except public accommodations.

Dirksen was not the only powerful senator whom Mansfield courted. He joined Commerce Committee chairman Warren Magnuson in the introduction of a separate bill containing only the public accommodations section. Because it would regulate interstate commerce, the bill went to Magnuson's Commerce Committee, a more liberal and accommodating panel than Eastland's very conservative Judiciary Committee. In the House, meanwhile, Judiciary chairman Emanuel Celler, who had already begun hearings on the bills, introduced Kennedy's entire program on June 20.[22]

As the legislation began its deliberate pilgrimage, Kennedy and his aides worried that persistent outside pressure might complicate the task of selling their program to Congress. Despite the president's attempts at dissuasion, a group of ten national civil rights, labor, and religious organizations continued planning a massive civil rights rally in Washington for August 28. To the White House, the "March on Washington for Jobs and Freedom" would not build public support for the bill. It would instead threaten congressional passage. Although CORE leader James Farmer never heard Kennedy's people demand the march's cancellation, it was clear to him that "they wanted it called off" because they feared "that there would be violence and it would turn into a riot and so forth." Kennedy also worried that the march, with its implicit pressure on Congress to pass the administration's civil rights bill, might alienate some House and Senate members. Kennedy not only rejected addressing the rally—fearing an "adverse reaction" from the crowd—but also wisely turned down a meeting with march leaders before their rally at the Lincoln Memorial. Suspecting they would present him a lengthy list of demands that the administration could not honor, which would turn the march into an anti-Kennedy protest, the president instead welcomed the leaders to the White House following their rally.[23]

On the day of the march, official Washington was a ghost town. Fearing violence, most government workers stayed home. By late afternoon more than two hundred thousand people, including an impressive percentage of whites, gathered peacefully at the foot of the Lincoln Memorial and spilled alongside the enormous reflecting pool that stretched east toward the Washington Monument. With the brooding figure of Lincoln the Emancipator over their shoulders, speaker after speaker demanded freedom and greater economic opportunities for black Americans. Later, Humphrey and his Minnesota colleague, Eugene McCarthy, joined marchers in their walk to the Memorial Grounds. By the time Martin Luther King delivered his historic "I Have a Dream" speech, Humphrey said it finally seemed possible to him that Congress might pass the president's bill. Originally organized to highlight the need for greater economic opportunities for blacks, the march instead gave voice to the growing public support for Kennedy's civil rights program. When more than seventy senators and House members appeared on the memorial steps, shouts of "Pass the bill! Pass the bill!" greeted them. The event became, said march leader Bayard Rustin, "a call for the passage of civil rights legislation."[24]

In the House, meanwhile, Judiciary Committee chairman Celler lost control of Kennedy's bill. Ignoring advice from the White House on what kind of legislation could muster cloture in the Senate, Celler stubbornly clung to his own strategy. Goaded by the NAACP and the Leadership Conference on Civil Rights, Celler reported a much stronger bill out of his subcommittee—one laded with provisions he believed he could use as "trading chips" with southern Democrats and conservative Republicans in full committee. Celler had ignored the advice of more pragmatic legislative strategists. "We'd lost him," Robert Kennedy later said. The White House had, for now at least, also forfeited the crucial support of McCulloch. "It's a pail of garbage," McCulloch muttered. He predicted that the full committee would never approve the stronger provisions written in subcommittee.[25]*

In an ironic twist, southerners cleverly seized Celler's subcommittee bill in hopes they could muscle it through the full committee and onto the House floor—where it would face almost certain defeat. Celler's clumsy miscalculation now placed the White House in the awkward position of publicly demanding milder legislation. "What I want is a bill," Robert Kennedy told the full Judiciary Committee in October, "not an issue." Although some civil rights groups accused Kennedy of a "sellout" to House conservatives, the president held firm to his original legislation. His goal was not just a bill that could pass the Judiciary Committee but one that could pass the gatekeeper for all legislation on its way to the House floor— the crucial Rules Committee, controlled by archconservative Howard

---

*Among other things, the subcommittee bill applied the administration's voting rights provisions to federal and state elections; widened the administration's public accommodations provision to outlaw discrimination in any accommodation that operated under state authority or license; gave the attorney general much broader authority to initiate lawsuits in civil rights cases (the long-desired Part III language); made the U.S. Civil Rights Commission permanent; and established an Equal Employment Opportunities Commission with powers to end discriminatory hiring practices in all but the smallest businesses.

Smith of Virginia. "Can Clarence Mitchell [the NAACP's Washington lob-byist] and the Leadership [Conference on Civil Rights] group deliver three Republicans on the Rules Committee and sixty Republicans on the House floor?" the president angrily asked his aides. "McCulloch can deliver sixty Republicans. Without him it can't be done."[26]

After lengthy negotiations, and with Johnson's assistance, Kennedy persuaded Celler to alter his strategy in favor of a bipartisan approach and then wooed McCulloch back into the fold. On October 29 the Judiciary Committee rejected Celler's subcommittee legislation and reported the bipartisan product to the full House by a 23–11 vote. Robert Kennedy hailed McCulloch and House Minority Leader Charles Halleck for having saved civil rights from defeat in committee, but the experience left some civil rights leaders feeling betrayed. "Today's events are no cause for rejoic-ing but a challenge to work to strengthen the bill," NAACP leader Roy Wilkins declared, seemingly oblivious to the fact that Celler's subcommit-tee bill would have certainly died in full committee. "It wouldn't have got-ten through the House," Burke Marshall flatly declared. "We would have lost the Republicans, and we had to have them to pass it."[27]

Russell knew that the coming debate would be the fight of his life. His troops, as always, would be well prepared for battle. In early August he had summoned eighteen of his southern colleagues to the Armed Services Committee Room to begin mapping strategy. For ninety minutes they reviewed the legislation they expected from the House and discussed how they would employ the filibuster, their only real weapon. As in the debate over the 1960 Civil Rights Act, the southerners would split themselves into three teams. While two-thirds of the southerners rested, one team would handle the day's debate. This highly effective tactic had broken the back of Lyndon Johnson and the northern liberals once before, and Russell expected it would work again. "We were not without hope," Russell said after the meeting, declaring the mood of his colleagues was one of "grim optimism."[28]

Like many southern politicians of his generation, Russell was still a philosophic captive both of his archaic racist beliefs and of the notion that his constituents would never accept the social changes that John F. Kennedy had in mind. Yet other southerners had reached different con-clusions. Two of the nation's most prominent Georgians had now publicly endorsed Kennedy's bill. Secretary of State Dean Rusk declared that the bill's failure would cause the rest of the world to doubt the "real convictions of the American people." Besides, Rusk said, "racial discrimination is wrong." More significant was the support of Atlanta mayor Allen, who endorsed the bill in late July. When asked by Kennedy to testify before the Judiciary Committee, Allen hesitated. Black leaders in Atlanta urged him to remain quiet out of fear an endorsement would result in his defeat. Allen was almost certain that his city's voters would not reelect him if he endorsed the bill. (He was mistaken.) Yet he summoned the courage to speak out—and did so forcefully. Segregation, he told the committee, was "slavery's stepchild." Failure to enact public accommodations legislation, he said, "would amount to an endorsement of private business setting up an entirely new status of discrimination throughout the country. Cities like Atlanta might slip backward." Businesses and rural communities ought to be given some time to desegregate voluntarily, but he stressed that "now is the time for legislative action." [29]

Of course, Rusk and Allen were not the most prominent southerners supporting the bill. That distinction went to Lyndon Johnson. In the White House and in the Senate, Johnson had awakened from what many people believed was a political hibernation. Civil rights appeared to be the issue that had triggered his resurrection. From his intense strategy discussions with Burke Marshall and Ted Sorensen to his active involvement in White House negotiations with the House Judiciary Committee, Johnson became a forceful, useful, and wise adviser and legislative strategist. "I don't know what's got into Lyndon," an anonymous southern senator told the *Washington Post* in late August, "but he's out-talking Bobby Kennedy on civil rights." [30]

He was also, it appears, a true believer in the need for a strong civil rights bill. Little of this, however, mattered to most black leaders. Lyndon Johnson—prominent southerner, former Senate majority leader, and now vice president—was one of the most powerless people in the government. Most civil rights groups ignored him or took his support for granted. Some suspected that his motives for supporting civil rights were more political than personal. In any event, there was simply not much he could do for their cause. [31]

After November 22, 1963, however, every civil rights leader and congressional liberal—indeed every black American yearning for freedom—suddenly saw Lyndon Baines Johnson in a brand new light.

14

I WANT THAT BILL PASSED

The news of President Kennedy's murder hit Washington during the lunch hour. When Russell heard the first reports, he went directly to the ornate Marble Room, just off the Senate chamber. Several minutes later, CBS correspondent Roger Mudd found him there, hunched over the Associated Press and United Press wire machines. Mudd was moved by what he saw: Russell, tears streaming from his eyes, reading the news aloud to a stunned group of senators and staff members. Later Russell joined Majority Leader Mike Mansfield in the radio-TV gallery—a rare appearance for the camera-shy Georgian. "It was very hard for Dick to get through it," Mudd recalled. "And he damn near didn't get through it." Mudd said it was a scene he would never forget. "Considering how stately and self-collected Dick Russell always was, he just really came apart that afternoon."[1]

Later that day, in his office and surrounded by his staff, Russell's thoughts turned to his friend and protégé—the new president. "Well, Lyndon Johnson has all of the talents, the abilities and the equipment to make a very good president of this country, a very good president." Then Russell added, "And of course old Lyndon is going to enjoy being president. He'll enjoy every minute of it, every hour of it."[2]

Across town, Humphrey and his wife Muriel had been attending a luncheon at the Chilean embassy. Standing alone in the embassy's library, Humphrey received the news in a phone call from White House aide Ralph Dungan. Humphrey tried but failed to fight back tears. Struggling to regain his composure, he numbly staggered into the dining room, where he delivered the dreadful news to the assembled guests before the tears engulfed him. Leaving the embassy, Humphrey and Muriel headed straight for the White House. Upon their arrival, Humphrey spotted Kenny O'Donnell, perhaps Kennedy's closest aide—and burst into tears again. Humphrey gained control of his emotions only after a lengthy, solitary walk in the Rose Garden.[3]

That evening, when Air Force One touched down at Andrews Air Force Base bearing Johnson and the casket with Kennedy's body, Humphrey was waiting for his old friend, the new president. As Lady Bird disembarked, she greeted Humphrey and Muriel warmly with a kiss. "We need you both so much," she said quietly. Later that evening Humphrey and other congressional leaders huddled with Johnson in the Old Executive Office Building, where Johnson simply and humbly asked for their help and guidance.[4]

It was understandably the most overwhelming day of Johnson's life—a day when he would need the advice, counsel, and comfort of his oldest friends and advisers. Stepping onto the tarmac at Andrews, he had searched the crowd for his mentor from Georgia. "Where's Dick?" he asked. Russell had avoided the chaotic airport scene. Johnson phoned him several hours later, and the two men talked for ten minutes. The next day Johnson summoned Russell to the White House for lunch.[5]

In the days following the assassination—in discussions with friends, associates, and former adversaries—Johnson was modest and deferential. In conversation after conversation, meeting after meeting, he reached out for help and guidance. He asked Kennedy's grieving staff, as well as his cabinet, to stay on board. He made amends with his old friend Jim Rowe, with whom he had quarreled during the 1960 campaign. He renewed friendships with former advisers and associates such as Clark Clifford, Dean Acheson, and Adlai Stevenson. Most of all, Johnson was humble. In phone conversations on the night of the assassination with Justice Arthur Goldberg and Allen Hoover, son of former president Herbert Hoover, Johnson insisted that he was "inadequate" for the job.[6]

Yet he was *more than adequate*. He was arguably the most qualified vice president ever to assume the office upon the death of a president. No person had ever inherited the presidency with more experience, more confidence, and a better understanding of the nature of power and how to use it. From the moment of John F. Kennedy's death, Lyndon Johnson was in complete control of the federal government. He did not waver. He did not hesitate to issue orders or make decisions. He was now the nation's chief executive, and he used the powers of his office to the fullest extent. Gardner Ackley, then a member of the President's Council of Economic Advisors, watched Johnson dominate a November 25 meeting called to discuss economic matters. "To me," Ackley wrote in his notes of the meeting, "the most impressive thing was the confident way in which he approached the whole problem—not necessarily implying that he knew the answers, but he knew the score, and that the problem could be solved." From the beginning, Johnson made it clear that he would finish what Kennedy had started. That meant, among other legislative priorities, a civil rights bill. "The first priority," he told Jack Valenti and Bill Moyers, "is passage of the civil rights act." On the night Johnson became president, he told Valenti he was eager "to get civil rights off its backside in the Congress and give it legs."[7]

As he prepared for his speech to a joint session of Congress on November 27, Johnson telephoned several civil rights leaders. He was, he assured them, sincerely devoted to their cause. To National Urban League director Whitney Young, Johnson confided that he would challenge Congress to pass the civil rights bill. Young was pleased, saying, "I think you've just got to make a date for [its passage] and point out that . . . hate that goes unchecked doesn't stop just for the week."

Johnson enthusiastically seized Young's point. "Dedicate a whole page on hate, hate international, hate domestic and just say that this hate that produces inequality, this hate that produces poverty. That's why we've just got to have civil rights. It's a cancer that just eats out our national existence." Perhaps most encouraging to Young was Johnson's rock-solid determination to push for the bill's passage. Although Johnson cautioned, "Let's not move with that ball until we know where we're going," he exuded a resolve and tenacity that must have delighted Young. "Let's go and go right on through the goal line . . . [We] might get run out of bounds a time or two—but [we'll] keep coming." The situation, Johnson said, reminded him of the person who asked, "What's the difference between a Texas Ranger and a Texas sheriff?" The answer was, Johnson said, "Well, when you hit a Ranger, he just keeps coming. So, that's kind of the fight we want to get in. We want to just keep coming when we start." The next day, when Martin Luther King told him that passage of Kennedy's "great progressive policies" would be "one of the greatest tributes that we can pay" to the late president, Johnson replied, "Well, I'm going to support them all and you can count on that and I'm going to do my best to get other men to do likewise and I'll have to have ya'll's help . . . I never needed it more than I do now."[8]

Under Kennedy, civil rights leaders had been supplicants who struggled to win the president's tentative support for their cause. Now, under Johnson, the same men became lieutenants and advisers in a newly energized crusade. In an Oval Office meeting with NAACP leader Wilkins, Johnson could not have been more emphatic. "I want that bill passed," he said. Wilkins believed him.[9]

Johnson's demeanor with King, Wilkins, and Young was no patronizing bluster. From the beginning he believed passage of a civil rights bill would require a fierce and protracted legislative battle. On November 25 he told his economic advisers, "The only way you could lick this was to stay in continuous session . . . It's too bad that the deliberative process has to come down to an endurance contest, but that's the way it is." Within days of assuming office, Johnson began devising his legislative strategy for the Senate, even though the civil rights bill was still mired in the House Rules Committee. When he first quizzed Marshall about the legislative strategy, Marshall confessed, "I didn't have the foggiest idea how we were going to get it through the Senate, though I was sure, and I told him I was sure, we could get it through the House." When the bill arrived in the Senate, Johnson wondered, would the liberals be on their mettle for a fight with the southerners? "Some of the liberals make a few good speeches on the floor," Johnson remarked on November 25, "and then run off to make speeches and collect their honoraria."[10]

For now, Johnson had a speech of his own to deliver. Appearing before a joint session of the House and Senate on November 27—with his black family cook, Zephyr Wright, seated prominently in the gallery—the new president reassured a nervous world and a grieving nation and challenged Congress to help him finish the domestic and foreign policy initiatives that Kennedy had started. Standing at the rostrum in the House of Representatives, he spoke softly and deliberately. "No memorial oration or eulogy could more eloquently honor President Kennedy's memory than the earliest possible passage of the civil rights bill for which he fought so long," Johnson said. "We have talked long enough in this country about equal rights. We have talked for one hundred years or more. It is time now to write the next chapter, and to write in the books of law." Johnson argued that Kennedy's death "commands what his life conveyed—that America must move forward. The time has come for Americans of all races and creeds and political beliefs to understand and respect one another. So let us put an end to the teaching and the preaching of hate and evil and violence. Let us turn away from the fanatics of the far left and the far right, from the apostles of bitterness and bigotry, from those defiant of law, and those who pour venom into our Nation's bloodstream." When Johnson finished his speech, the House chamber erupted in boisterous, sustained applause. Even the southerners joined the standing ovation. (Most of them, including Russell, had refused to applaud Johnson's call for a civil rights bill.)[11]

The speech was enormously reassuring to uneasy liberals and civil rights leaders. As black comedian Dick Gregory quipped afterwards, "As soon as Lyndon Johnson finished his speech before Congress, twenty million of us unpacked." Paul Douglas viewed the speech with bittersweet irony: "It remained for Lyndon Johnson, who as senator had been the most subtle and determined opponent of all civil rights legislation, to become, as president, the evangelist for the movement." Although Douglas vastly exaggerated the president's former opposition to civil rights, Johnson's passionate embrace of Kennedy's civil rights proposal was not enough to persuade some liberals of his sincerity. Johnson knew that the most dubious liberals would ultimately respect only accomplishments, not words. For now, many of them remained wary of their new president.[12]

Many southern conservatives were not as doubtful about Johnson's determination to enact a tough civil rights bill. "People were probably a little more fearful," said Mississippi lieutenant governor Paul Johnson. "They were fearful because they knew that Lyndon Johnson was probably a hundred times smarter than Jack Kennedy was—smarter from the standpoint of being able to handle the Congress." Yet strangely, Johnson's speech did not alarm or shock most of the southerners. After all, it was the first presidential call for civil rights ever uttered in a bona fide Dixie drawl. "The essential difference in Johnson's civil rights approach," observed journalist Tom Wicker, "was in the overtures he was able to make to the South *at the same time.* Kennedy could not have done that, nor Nelson Rockefeller, and perhaps not even Dwight Eisenhower; certainly not Barry Goldwater."[13]

In a White House meeting with Russell on December 7, Johnson conveyed his determination in unmistakable terms. "I'm not going to cavil and I'm not going to compromise," he warned Russell. "I'm going to pass it just as it is, Dick, and if you get in my way I'm going to run you down. I just want you to know that, because I care about you."

"Mr. President, you may be right," Russell responded. "But if you do run over me, it will not only cost you the South, it will cost you the election."[14]

Russell knew Johnson was deadly serious—and he knew that Johnson's skills in passing legislation were unmatched. "He knows more about the uses of power than any man," Russell told a reporter. Recalling Johnson's success as majority leader, Russell observed, "Johnson could get three votes when all he had to offer was one office room the [three] senators [all] wanted to use."[15]

In the days and weeks after Kennedy's death, Johnson also reached out to prominent liberals, many of whom had distrusted him well before he engineered the compromises of the 1957 Civil Rights Act. Johnson asked Walter Heller, the liberal chairman of the Council of Economic Advisors, to "tell your liberal friends . . . that I am an old-fashioned FDR liberal and that I want to work with them, and that they will have an ally here in the White House." In early December, Johnson began courting Joseph Rauh, one of his most dependable, longtime critics. When New York senator Herbert Lehman died, Johnson invited Rauh to accompany him to the funeral on Air Force One. Throughout the early months of his administration, Johnson consulted civil rights leaders—who were generally more eager than their white liberal counterparts to believe that the new president would back up his strong rhetoric with equally decisive action. "I had always said I always felt," Whitney Young recalled, "that if ever I turned on the radio and heard the president of the United States speaking with a deep southern accent that I would panic. But I did not feel that way at all. I felt by that time that Lyndon Johnson would do exactly what he did."[16]

Johnson's immediate concern was the House, which was still in session at the president's behest despite the approaching Christmas holidays. There, the civil rights bill, H.R. 7152, was stranded in the Rules Committee, the domain of "Judge" Howard Smith, an eighty-year-old veteran congressman from Virginia. A segregationist and fierce opponent of civil rights, Smith steadfastly refused to grant a rule for the bill's floor debate. Smith's intransigence sent Johnson into a rage. "There's all this stuff going on [protests] and we've been talking about this for one hundred years," Johnson complained in a phone conversation with former Treasury secretary Robert Anderson. "But Howard has just gone off to his farm and tells the Speaker, 'I won't even give you a hearing on it' . . . Says, 'Hell, no. Go eat cake, goddamn it. Don't mess with me until next year.'"

Johnson was equally frustrated with Republicans who refused to sign a discharge petition, a parliamentary device to bypass Rules and force the bill onto the House floor. He mused about issuing these Republicans a challenge: "Now, you're either for civil rights or you're not. You're either the party of Lincoln or you ain't. And this, by God, put up or shut up." Johnson, the legislative strategist, understood why the discharge petition could become so important to the bill's ultimate success in the Senate. As he explained to *Washington Post* publisher Katharine Graham on December 2, "If we could ever get that signed, that would practically break [the southerners'] backs in the Senate because they could see that here is a steamroller that could petition it out."

Although he quietly pushed for the bill's speedy consideration in the House, Johnson was quick to avoid optimistic expectations. Kennedy had tried for almost a year without success, he told Graham. "Now, I hope in twelve months I can be, but he tried since May on civil rights and he hasn't been successful, so they better not be too quick to judge it."[17]

Meanwhile Johnson wisely handed over tactical control of the bill to Attorney General Kennedy, Deputy Attorney General Katzenbach, and Assistant Attorney General Marshall. "I'll do on the bill just what you think is best to do on the bill," Johnson told Kennedy. "We'll follow what you say we should do on the bill." While Kennedy appreciated Johnson's willingness to rely on the judgment of Justice Department attorneys, he suspected an ulterior motive. Kennedy suggested that Johnson "didn't want [himself] to be the reason, to have the sole responsibility" if the bill failed. If Kennedy plotted the bill's strategy and Johnson only followed instructions, Kennedy reasoned, Johnson "could always say that he did what we suggested."[18]

In the end Johnson was spared a fight with Chairman Smith over his refusal to report the bill out of the Rules Committee. Public opinion, largely driven by the emotional reaction to Kennedy's death, finally forced Smith's hand. Polls showed that more than 60 percent of the nation supported the bill. Johnson himself enjoyed an impressive 79 percent approval rating. Smith had no choice. "You'll have to run over us," he defiantly told the bill's supporters when he finally called for hearings on the bill. Smith knew the ultimate outcome. "We know we'll be run over."[19]

On January 30 Smith's committee voted, 11–4, to send H.R. 7152 to the House floor under an "open rule." House members could offer amendments to every section. During floor debate, Judiciary chairman Celler and his Republican counterpart, McCulloch, held their ground. Bolstered by vocal support and active lobbying from the White House, the Justice Department, the major civil rights and religious organizations, and organized labor, the bill emerged intact. Southern opposition was surprisingly listless and unorganized. During nine days of debate, southern opponents failed to add even one major weakening amendment to the bill.[20]

The bill that passed the House on February 10—by a 290–130 vote— was much broader and more potent than President Kennedy could have ever imagined. The "Part III" and fair employment provisions added by the

Judiciary Committee remained, as did provisions on public facilities and the withholding of federal funds from discriminatory programs. It was, in the words of *Congressional Quarterly*, "the most sweeping civil rights measure to clear either house of Congress in the 20th Century." [21]

The House victory invigorated Johnson. Minutes after its passage, he phoned two of the bill's chief lobbyists, his old detractor Joseph Rauh and the NAACP's Clarence Mitchell. "All right, you fellows, get on over there to the Senate and get busy," Johnson said, "because we've got it through the House and now we've got the big job of getting it through the Senate." [22]

The Senate, as usual, proved a curious beast. Like the body that Johnson commanded during the 1957 civil rights debate, the Senate of 1964 divided into three distinct groups: pro–civil rights Republicans and Democrats, Russell's southern Democrats (joined by far-right Republicans John Tower of Texas and Barry Goldwater of Arizona), and moderate Republicans. By themselves, the pro–civil rights forces could produce the fifty-one votes needed to pass a civil rights bill. But unless they found sixteen additional votes to invoke cloture, their bill would never come to a vote.

It was the support of the third group—moderate, mostly midwestern senators who made up about two-thirds of the Senate's thirty-three Republicans—that the Senate's liberals desperately needed to pass civil rights. On their own, Mike Mansfield's Democrats were dead. With a two-to-one advantage—at 67 to 33, their largest majority since 1939—the Democrats could conceivably invoke cloture anytime, but *only* if they voted as a bloc. With Russell's southerners in their ranks, that would never happen. During the forty-seven years of the cloture rule's existence—in eleven separate votes—liberals had never forcibly ended a southern filibuster of a civil rights bill.

With precious little hope that the Senate could stop a southern filibuster, Johnson gambled on an audacious strategy. He approved the Justice Department's plan for a bold, frontal assault in the Senate. The administration would neither seek nor entertain any compromise with southerners and conservative Republicans. "It would be a fight to total victory or total defeat without appeasement or attrition," Johnson later said, explaining that the "slightest wavering" on the bill "would give hope to the opposition's strategy of amending the bill to death." As Johnson and his Justice Department advisers knew, any agreement that weakened the bill in the Senate would probably result in its defeat once it returned to the House. McCulloch would make certain of that. When asked about possible weakening amendments in the Senate during Rules Committee hearings, McCulloch replied, "I would never be a party to such a proposal. My head is still bloody from 1957. I feel very strongly about this."[23]

Johnson knew that he could not maintain his credibility as a strong and true advocate of civil rights if he began consorting with Dirksen or Russell to weaken the bill simply to avoid a filibuster. "I knew that if I didn't get out in front on this issue, [the liberals] would get me," he later said. "I couldn't let that happen. I had to produce a civil rights bill that was even stronger than the one they'd have gotten if Kennedy had lived. Without this, I'd be dead before I could even begin." The matter was simple: There was no room for compromise. The strategy was not only sound legislative politics; it had now become a matter of principle.[24]

For the first time, finding sixty-seven votes for cloture on a civil rights bill was not a hopeless objective. By Katzenbach's informal count, liberals might have as many as seventy-four votes. Johnson was not so sure. At best, he estimated, there were fifty-eight votes—nine short of cloture. Katzenbach bluntly told the president, "If you do anything publicly but indicate that we're going to get cloture on this bill, we can't *possibly* get cloture on this bill. And the only way we can get it is for you with your experience to express absolute confidence, publicly and privately, that we're going to get cloture on this bill." Katzenbach also reminded Johnson that several conservatives had abandoned their absolute opposition to cloture in 1962 when they cast their first-ever votes to shut off a filibuster (waged by liberals during debate over the communications satellite bill). They can't oppose cloture on principle anymore, Katzenbach explained, expecting to gain "some additional votes" from the conservative ranks.[25]

Johnson endorsed the Justice Department's cloture strategy, but he continued to urge Majority Leader Mansfield to turn up the heat on southerners by holding the Senate in around-the-clock sessions when the expected filibuster began. Mansfield knew that this strategy was unwise. In 1960, that approach had failed to exhaust the southerners, enhanced their leverage, and resulted in passage of a weakened civil rights bill. During that debate, Mansfield explained, "it was not the fresh and well-rested opponents" of civil rights "who were compelled to the compromise. It was, rather, the exhausted, sleep-starved, quorum-confounded proponents who were only too happy to take it." As White House aide Mike Manatos explained to Larry O'Brien, Johnson's chief congressional lobbyist, "Night sessions make it necessary for at least fifty proponents to be within a few minutes of the Senate chambers while only three to four southerners need be on hand."[26]

Mansfield was rarely a headstrong man. On this point, however, he would not be bullied by Johnson or the civil rights activists. He feared that twenty-four-hour sessions would kill some of the Senate's older members. As Johnson later declared, the eventual administration strategy was simple and straightforward: "We would win, by securing cloture, or we would lose."

Although Mansfield helped set the overall tone for the coming debate, he remained a reluctant leader. He had no interest in assuming the day-to-day duties of managing the bill during floor debate. He awarded that role to Humphrey. Honored and somewhat overwhelmed to be entrusted the fate of legislation he had championed for so long, Humphrey realized the coming debate "would test me in every way." As he already knew, his performance on civil rights would serve as an audition for the role of Johnson's running mate in the fall presidential elections. As the Senate leader for civil rights, Humphrey would be thrust into the national limelight as never before. In the coming months, his vice-presidential ambitions and the fate of civil rights would be inextricable.[27]

Johnson gave Humphrey little or no advice about how to campaign for the vice presidency, but he had plenty of ideas about how to pass civil rights. Early in the year Johnson summoned Humphrey to the White House for a pep talk. "You bomb-throwers make good speeches, you have big hearts, you believe in what you say you stand for, but you're never on the job when you need to be there. You spread yourselves too thin making speeches to the faithful." Humphrey later said that Johnson's diatribe would have offended him "if he hadn't been basically right and historically accurate." Humphrey said he knew that Johnson "had sized me up. He knew very well that I would say, 'Damn you, I'll show you.' One thing about Johnson was that even when he conned me I knew what was happening to me. It was kind of enjoyable. I mean I knew what was going on, and he knew I knew." Johnson gave Humphrey another piece of important advice. "Now you know that this bill can't pass unless you get Ev Dirksen. You and I are going to get him. You make up your mind now that you've got to spend time with Ev Dirksen. You've got to let him have a piece of the action. He's got to look good all the time."[28]

Humphrey took Johnson's advice to heart. In a March 8 appearance on NBC's *Meet the Press*, Humphrey heaped generous praise on the Republican leader. "He is a man who thinks of his country before he thinks of his party. He is one who understands the legislative process intimately and fully, and I sincerely believe that when Senator Dirksen has to face that moment of decision where his influence and where his leadership will be required in order to give us the votes that are necessary to pass this bill, he will not be found wanting." Watching Humphrey's interview was Johnson, who called him afterwards. "Boy, that was right. You're doing just right now. You just keep at that. Don't you let those bomb throwers, now, talk you out of seeing Dirksen. You get in there to see Dirksen! You drink with Dirksen! You talk to Dirksen! You listen to Dirksen!"[29]

As everyone in Johnson's White House well understood, Dirksen was the key to beating the southern filibuster. "We knew we could not pass it with Democratic votes," Katzenbach argued. "We could not pass it with Democratic votes, plus liberal Republican votes. We *had* to have the leadership of the Republican party with us in order to get that legislation passed." The path to the votes to enact civil rights, said Humphrey's aide Raymond Wolfinger, "went through Dirksen."[30]

Before 1964 virtually every civil rights filibuster was strictly a one-way affair. Russell's southern troops engaged in lengthy monologues and colloquies while proponents of civil rights watched from the sidelines. Occasionally they sparred with the southern conservatives. Usually they relinquished the Senate chamber, appearing only for quorum calls and roll-call votes. Every time, the southern troops were more organized and better versed in the details of the legislation.

This time Humphrey meant to alter that equation. Working closely with Minority Whip Thomas Kuchel—a California liberal whom Dirksen had appointed Republican floor manager for the bill—he devised a system by which the proponents of civil rights would aggressively challenge, refute, question, and debate the southerners on every major point. Toward that end, Humphrey appointed rotating four-member groups of senators— known as the Civil Rights Corporals' Guard—to remain always in the Senate chamber. "We determined early not to let the Southerners occupy the press," Humphrey recalled. "So, in the very opening days, starting with the March 9 motion to take up [the bill], we proceeded to debate the Southerners . . . In other words, we were active, at no time passive, and at all times challenging the opposition."[31]

For each of the bill's major titles, Humphrey appointed a floor captain to organize and lead the response to the southern opposition: Joseph Clark would defend the fair employment practices provision, Commerce Committee chairman Warren Magnuson the public accommodations section, and Michigan's Philip Hart the voting rights section. As Humphrey explained, "When each senator has had a chance to debate the bill, title by title, they also had an opportunity to get some press for themselves, to be known as part of the team fighting for civil rights. This was not only good for the issue itself, but also for the senators and their public relations and they seemed to like it." Humphrey even suggested radio and television programs on which senators might argue the merits of the bill.[32]

Each morning Humphrey, Kuchel, their floor captains, and a Justice Department official—usually Katzenbach—met in Humphrey's Capitol office to discuss and coordinate the day's tactics. At least two days each week, Clarence Mitchell and Joseph Rauh joined them. The results were impressive. In April, Murray Kempton reported in the *New Republic* that "one result of this concern for detail is that for the first time in memory a civil rights debate has turned out to be almost lively; and at the very least Humphrey and Kuchel have improved the theater available to the visiting schoolchildren. At the most they have made the filibuster an inconvenience for those who practice it."[33]

To build solidarity among the civil rights proponents, Humphrey published a bipartisan civil rights newsletter. Every morning each pro–civil rights senator received a summary of the previous day's debate, complete with responses to the most recent attacks leveled by the southerners. "For the first time, we are putting up a battle," Humphrey bragged to the Senate after John Stennis demanded to know, "Who writes these mysterious messages?"[34]

Making the Humphrey-Kuchel coalition even more impressive was its sophisticated system for answering quorum calls. For years the suggestion of the absence of a quorum had been the southerners' favorite way to harass the majority. Quorum calls gave the filibustering senators time to sit and rest their feet and voices. They also served an important parliamentary purpose. Under the Senate's rules, each senator could deliver only two speeches per subject in a legislative day. If Humphrey and Kuchel failed to muster fifty-one senators, the Senate could adjourn and a new legislative day would begin, allowing the southerners to make more speeches. Failure to produce a quorum might also suggest that Humphrey's side lacked the resolve needed to beat the filibuster. As Humphrey knew, many undecided senators would stop thinking about a compromise with Russell only when liberals proved that their determination to endure was greater than that of the southerners. That meant aggressively debating the southerners, voting down their weakening amendments, and, most important, appearing for every quorum call.[35]

Humphrey addressed the quorum problem by taking a page from the southern playbook. He divided his Democratic troops into two platoons, each with about twenty-five members. Each day Humphrey notified members of one platoon that their names were on the duty roster. They were expected to answer all quorum calls. Added to their total were Humphrey, his floor captains, the few southern Democrats who were always in the chamber, and Kuchel's reliable but less-structured Republican forces of about sixteen. Throughout the months of debate, Humphrey's platoon system failed only once to muster a quorum when called.[36]

In the early weeks of the debate, Humphrey also enlisted the active participation of the nation's religious leaders. Prominent Protestant ministers, Catholic bishops and priests, and Jewish leaders were influential with undecided senators, and their active support was instrumental in transforming the political issue of civil rights into a moral question. Protestant, Catholic, and Jewish clergy planned a prayer vigil at the Lincoln Memorial for April 19. It would continue twenty-four hours a day until the Senate passed the bill. Other religious leaders prepared for a national convocation at Georgetown University on April 28. "It was the first time," said James Hamilton of the National Council of Churches, "that I ever recalled seeing Catholic nuns away from the convents for more than a few days. There was an agreement among religious groups that this was a priority issue and other things had to be laid aside." Commenting on the unprecedented convocation, the ecumenical publication *Christian Century* rejoiced, "The unequivocal stand taken by the religious leaders encourages the hope that the church at large is at last beginning to wake from its long slumber and assume its duty in solving the nation's racial problem."[37]

Because of Humphrey's imagination and legislative skills, the civil rights forces were organized as never before. From the beginning it was evident that his appointment as floor leader had been a wise one—for several reasons. Well respected for his intelligence and his understanding of the legislative process, he was the most eloquent and passionate spokesman for the cause of civil rights in Congress. Furthermore, Humphrey was enormously popular with his colleagues. Even the most racist of southern conservatives found it impossible to dislike him. "Everybody liked Hubert," declared William Hildenbrand, secretary of the Senate from 1961 to 1981. "If you opposed him, you didn't do it with a great deal of fervor. You just voted no and that was the end of it. You didn't really get up there and try to embarrass him or anything like that." Mike Mansfield could not have placed the civil rights bill in more capable hands.[38]

Russell and his southern forces comforted themselves with the knowledge that liberals had never invoked cloture on a civil rights bill. History was on their side—but not much else. Russell's strategy for the coming debate was simple. Knowing he could never defeat the bill outright, he declared that he would still fight it "to the last ditch." He would not repeat his success in winning backroom concessions from Lyndon Johnson, as he had in 1957. This time, he knew, compromise would come only if he sustained a filibuster through the summer. On CBS's *Face the Nation* in early March, Russell dismissed any suggestion of negotiating with Humphrey's liberal forces. "It seems to me," he said, "that we are just about to come to a state where it will be necessary for us to fight this bill to the bitter end." Russell's Georgia colleague, Herman Talmadge, explained the strategy differently: "We knew that there was no way in hell we could muster the necessary votes to defeat that civil rights bill, but we thought we could filibuster long enough to get the other side to agree to amendments that would make it less offensive."

Russell could always hope that the filibuster—"extended debate," as he called it—would enlighten the American public to the "evils" in the bill. Several months of illuminating debate—combined with spreading racial violence and the increasing volume of protests around the country—might turn public opinion around and evaporate support for civil rights. That scenario was far-fetched. It was certainly nothing around which to construct a winning legislative strategy.

Russell's strategy of delay was about all he had. There were no attractive alternatives to his last-ditch resistance. Even if he could negotiate a compromise with Dirksen, such an agreement guaranteed him the support of only a handful of Republicans. Unless he lured more Republicans to his side, he would still fall short of the thirty-four votes needed to sustain the filibuster. Yet any compromise on civil rights might leave Russell vulnerable to mutiny from incendiary southerners such as Thurmond and Eastland. Russell had only one hope for at least a partial victory: He must filibuster indefinitely and hope that an impatient White House and exhausted Senate liberals would eventually plead for a truce.[39]

Apart from himself, Russell commanded nineteen soldiers: eighteen southern Democrats and Republican John Tower of Texas. He would divide them into three platoons of six, led by Allen Ellender, John Stennis, and Lister Hill. Each platoon would see action every third day of debate. Each member would be responsible for talking only four hours a day—which, as a *New York Times* reporter observed in February, "is a mere throat-clearer for an accomplished southern orator."[40]

Just below the surface, Russell was in serious trouble. He knew that he could sustain a filibuster only if he prevented Johnson and Humphrey from seducing Dirksen. Humphrey, meanwhile, was busy courting Dirksen with a shameless, religious fervor. "I was his Jiminy Cricket," Humphrey later said, "visiting with him on the floor, in the cloakroom, in the corridors and on the elevators. I constantly encouraged him to take a more prominent role, asked him what changes he wanted to propose, urged him to call meetings to discuss his changes." Russell had other woes. Some members of the southern bloc, it seemed, were less than passionate about the strategy of fighting civil rights "to the last ditch." Talmadge, Long, Fulbright, and Smathers were not in the same league with segregationists like Russell, Eastland, Stennis, and Thurmond. Younger, less regional in their view of the nation, these more moderate southerners would dutifully deliver their speeches and otherwise feign a passionate fealty to the spirit of an Old South that they knew was dying. They would do little else, however, to help Russell. Some of them were tired of being outcasts in the Democratic party and weary of swimming against the tide of history. Others realized that their opposition to civil rights was no longer a surefire way to win elections.[41]

As Russell Long—always refreshingly frank about his political motives—explained many years later:

That black vote was getting to be a very significant vote and I was getting it all. Now, you read those speeches, I don't think you'd find anything in there where a person could stir up blacks to get angry at me. I think I said that these people deserve a better break than they're getting and I want to see them have it, but I don't think this is the way to do it . . . I didn't want to say anything that was going to alienate the blacks . . . because they had always been for me.[42]

Analyzing the younger, moderate southerners, journalist Murray Kempton called it a case "of age resisting youth; and a cause is hardly healthy when the realistic young think of a separate peace and only the principled old think of resistance to the end."[43]

Giving Russell even more reason for distress were adverse political developments back home. In January, when he learned that the Georgia Senate had approved legislation to abolish the state's poll tax, Russell announced to his colleagues that the vote was "a source of humiliation to me." Those who supported the amendment in Georgia belonged to a "pernicious drive to enforce coercion and conformity" on other southern states. In a March 1 appearance on *Face the Nation*, Russell acknowledged "an increase in sentiment" favoring civil rights in Georgia. "My people are not immune from brainwashing," he explained. "A great many of them have been brainwashed and they have forgotten the first constitutional principles and have failed to see the dangers of passing legislation on the threat of demonstrations."[44]

In April, when Russell again proposed legislation to subsidize the relocation of southern blacks to other states, the *Atlanta Constitution* ridiculed him for "[exposing] for all the nation to see an image which Southerners are trying to overcome, the callous attitude that Negroes can be moved about like chess pawns." The proposal even emboldened one member of the legislature to openly criticize Russell. State senator Lamar Plunkett observed that "the people of Georgia are now going forward with a little different beat of the drum. Those who are not thoroughly conversant with it may lose the beat." As journalist Meg Greenfield wrote in the *Reporter*, Russell's behavior "go[es] a certain way to disprove a current theory that [he] is only leading the fight against the administration's civil rights bill in the Senate to make a show for the folks back home. If anything, political wisdom would seem to dictate a little more circumspection on Russell's part."[45]

But Russell believed his cause was just. "I realize there is a group in the South and in some places in Georgia that is yielding to overwhelming force even if they don't like the trend," Russell said in March. "They think it is not worth it to carry on the fight. They've quit fighting. I haven't." As for why he was leading a losing battle, in April Russell told *Business Week*: "I'm not an anthropologist, but I've studied history. And there is no case in history of a mongrel race preserving a civilization, much less creating one."[46]

Russell lost his first skirmish of 1964 early in the debate. On February 26 the Senate rejected his objection to placing H.R. 7152 directly on the Senate calendar. Using the same rule that liberals had employed to bypass the hostile Judiciary Committee in 1957, Majority Leader Mansfield easily won in a 54–37 vote.[47]

On March 9, after almost two weeks of mostly lackluster debate, Mansfield made his next move. He propounded a motion to begin formal consideration of the civil rights bill. "I implore the Senate," Mansfield said, "when this bill is taken up, to debate it, to debate it as long as is necessary for views to be presented and argued. But then, Mr. President, I implore the Senate to vote on it, to do whatever is necessary so that, in the end, it may be voted up or down." Although they insisted they were not yet filibustering the bill, southerners delayed the vote on Mansfield's motion for more than two weeks.[48]

From the first days of debate, southern rhetoric took on an air of excited desperation. On March 21 Eastland told Humphrey that the bill "takes us back to Stalin, Khrushchev, Nasser, Hitler and a dictatorship."

"What is closer to Stalin and Hitler and Khrushchev," Humphrey replied, "is discrimination on the basis of race."

"I know of no discrimination on the basis of race," Eastland angrily shot back. "I disagree with the Senator on the definition of discrimination, of course." Minutes later, Eastland charged that the legislation "amounts to a destruction of the American system of government."[49]

Eastland was not alone in making wild, irrational statements that could only erode southern credibility. On a *CBS News* program in March, Strom Thurmond told Humphrey that "such a law would do nothing more than enslave a minority. Such a law would necessitate a system of federal police officers such as we have never before seen. It will require the policing of every business institution, every transaction made between an employer and employee."[50]

Despite his reputation as a dispassionate and dignified debater, Russell was not immune to hysterical rhetoric, especially regarding the equal employment opportunity provision. "This is mere socialism," he declared to the Senate on April 20. "Anybody who is familiar with the operations of state machinery in lands where all industry has been taken over by the government knows that the state tells the individual whom he must hire, whom he must promote, who shall be laid off, who shall fill that position. Then it cannot be long until the government takes over the remainder of the operation of the business." While Russell said he would not allege that the "well-meaning" supporters of the bill "are all Socialists," he noted that "every Socialist and Communist in this country has been supporting the proposed legislation since it was first dreamed up and submitted to the Congress."[51]

There *were* substantive arguments made against the bill. Americans, the southerners argued, had a constitutional right to rent or sell their property, merchandise, or services to those of their choosing. "Americans now possess the liberty to consider the matter of race, and even to prefer persons of their own race over members of another race, in their business dealings with others," North Carolina's Sam Ervin told the Senate on January 29. This bill, Ervin and others maintained, was unconstitutional because it conferred upon blacks new "privileges superior to those ever granted to any other Americans in history." As Russell argued on March 9, there could not be "any such thing as compulsory equality. To attempt to bring it about is to curtail the talented without assisting the stupid. The attempt to mold every American into a common form, if it succeeds, can only curse us forever with the drabness of forced similarity."[52]

Furthermore, the southerners claimed, basing the bill's public accommodations section on the Constitution's commerce clause was unsound. Observed Alabama's John Sparkman: "This type of police regulation is one which, without a doubt, should be left to the state and local governments." As for the fair employment provisions, Russell argued that they gave the federal government too much authority over the hiring practices of private businesses. "I state unhesitatingly that no member of the Reconstruction Congress, no matter how radical, would have dared to present a proposal that would have given such vast governmental control over free enterprise in this country so as to commence the processes of socialism."[53]

On March 26, after what *Time* called "sixteen days of drone-and-drawl talk," the civil rights bill finally became the Senate's pending business. Russell realized that a continued filibuster of the motion to consider the bill might only provoke the Senate to impose cloture. Without a fight, he permitted a vote. Mansfield's motion to take up the legislation passed, 67–17.[54]

Oregon's Wayne Morse then moved to refer the bill to the Judiciary Committee until April 8. "This bill is going to remake the social pattern of this country," Dirksen said in support of Morse. "Nobody should be fooled on that score." Mansfield was more persuasive. He argued that when the

Judiciary Committee returned with the bill, it would no longer be the Senate's pending business. Instead it would go back on the Senate calendar, where a motion to call it up would be debatable—and therefore subject to another filibuster. "How many days would we have to repeat the ordeal of the last two-and-a-half weeks?" Mansfield asked. By a 50–34 vote, senators rejected Morse's motion. "We lost a skirmish," Russell said after the two votes. "Now we begin to fight the war." [55]

"This is no longer a battle of the heart for [the southerners]," Humphrey told a reporter after the debate began. "They simply have to die in the trenches; that's what they were sent here for. They're old and they haven't any recruits. They know it—one of them said to me, 'You simply have to overwhelm us.' And so we have to beat them to a pulp. No one can make peace. They have to be destroyed." [56]

Thus began the longest debate in the Senate's history.

15

AN IDEA WHOSE TIME HAS COME

Shortly after noon on Monday, March 30, 1964, Humphrey stood at his mahogany desk in the Senate chamber and began the long-awaited formal debate on the civil rights bill. Although reporters, staff members, and tourists packed the galleries, only a half-dozen senators were present as Humphrey launched a comprehensive discussion of the bill. His speech was long, even by Humphrey's loquacious standards. He talked for three and a half hours.

"We are participants," he said, "in one of the most crucial eras in the long and proud history of the United States and, yes, in mankind's struggle for justice and freedom which has gone forward since the dawn of history. If freedom becomes a full reality in America, we can dare to believe that it will become a reality everywhere. If freedom fails here in America, the land of the free—what hope can we have for it surviving elsewhere?"

Discussing Title II, the public accommodations section, Humphrey offered his colleagues a graphic yet tragic example of racial discrimination in the South. He quoted from two travel guides. One listed motels and hotels in the South that accepted pets; the other listed establishments that accepted black guests. "It is heartbreaking," he declared, "to compare these two guidebooks. In Augusta, Georgia, for example, there are five hotels and motels that will take dogs and only one where a Negro can go with confidence. In Columbus, Georgia, there are six places for dogs and none for Negroes. In Charleston, South Carolina, there are ten places where a dog can stay, and none for a Negro."

To Humphrey, the bill was "moderate" but "long overdue." Yet he insisted that "moderate as it is, it insures a great departure from the misery and bitterness that is the lot of so many Americans." It was a misery, Humphrey lamented, that "has found remarkably quiet methods of expression." Far from faulting blacks for their urgent demands for strong civil rights legislation, Humphrey said he "marve[led] at the patience and self-control of Negroes who have been excluded from the American dream for so long." The Civil Rights Act of 1964, Humphrey said, "has a simple purpose":

> That purpose is to give fellow citizens—Negroes—the same rights and opportunities that white people take for granted. This is no more than what was preached by the prophets, and by Christ Himself. It is no more than what our Constitution guarantees.
>
> One hundred and ninety years have passed since the Declaration of Independence, and one hundred years since the Emancipation Proclamation. Surely the goals of this bill are not too much to ask of the Senate of the United States.

Humphrey directed his passionate speech at every member of the Senate, but Everett Dirksen—sitting quietly at his desk—was his primary target. To move Richard Russell or any one of the southern bloc would have been nothing short of miraculous. It would not happen. But to win Dirksen's heart—now that was a real possibility![1]

Even as he plotted to lure Dirksen to his side, Humphrey realized that he must first persuade his own troops to stay in the battle. On Saturday, April 4, Humphrey suffered an embarrassing setback: His side failed to assemble a working majority when the southerners suggested the absence of a quorum only forty minutes after the day's opening gavel. When the clerk tallied the roll, only forty-one senators were present. The civil rights forces fell ten short of a quorum. Of the fifty-nine absentees, seventeen were Republicans, seventeen were southern Democrats—but *twenty-five* were northern Democrats who claimed to support the bill. The Senate was unable to function because the bill's own proponents refused to show.[2]

The situation elated the southerners. Although Russell could have moved to adjourn, he did not, leaving it to Mansfield to pick up the pieces. The normally tranquil majority leader was livid. He angrily denounced the truancy as "a travesty on the legislative process" and moved to recess the Senate until the following Monday morning "in order to prevent this situation from turning into a farce." Although Mansfield and Humphrey had strongly urged their colleagues to attend the Saturday session, many had gone home to campaign for reelection; others were out of town delivering speeches.

Humphrey moved quickly to embarrass the absentees. Over the weekend he made certain that the news media knew and published the names of those senators who had failed to attend the Saturday session. "I'll bet there are so many senators here on Monday," he told the *New York Times*, "that you will think each state sent four." Later, Humphrey observed, "That was the end of that . . . We had the problem licked."[3]

By April 11 Humphrey could count on the regular attendance of a solid, dependable majority. On that day he produced a quorum in less than ten minutes. By then the civil rights proponents were organized so well that Humphrey, Mansfield, Dirksen, Russell, and several other senators confidently left the Capitol on April 13 to attend the Washington Senators' first home baseball game. If the southerners suggested the absence of a quorum, Humphrey knew that his aide, David Gartner, would phone the stadium's manager. Humphrey had even composed the message for the public-address announcer. Barely three innings into the game, Gartner called. "Attention, please," the announcer said, "there has been a quorum call in the United States Senate. All U.S. senators are requested to return to the Senate chamber immediately." As Humphrey, Mansfield, Dirksen, and others scurried for the exits—where a police escort awaited them—one senator remained immersed in the game between the Senators and the Los Angeles Angels. Russell, said a colleague, "never moved."[4]

Humphrey's determination to keep at least fifty-one senators within twenty minutes of the Senate floor did more than prove the iron will of the civil rights proponents; it also magnified the antagonism these senators had for the southerners. "This made them all the more unhappy when the filibuster was under way," Humphrey said, "because it meant they had to be away from their duties back home and be present in Washington only to answer quorum calls and, frankly, to get very little else done." If the southerners used the filibuster to foment public outrage over the supposed evils of the bill, Humphrey would play the same game. He would attempt to "arouse the public" over the way the southerners had hijacked a popular civil rights bill, "to create a sense of wrath and indignation in the public, and also in the Senate."[5]

No senator was more valuable to Humphrey than Dirksen. Renowned for his legislative and political artistry, Dirksen was, in many ways, a Republican version of Lyndon Johnson. Few members of the Senate were more pragmatic and flexible in their approach to legislation. "I am not a moralist," Dirksen once explained. "I am a legislator." On most major issues, Dirksen was willing to negotiate. At some point, Humphrey suspected, he would be ready to bargain for the best possible deal. Humphrey knew something else about his colleague: The Illinois senator was an eloquent, theatrical orator who relished the starring roles made possible by his leadership post. "He was the greatest actor I had ever seen in or out of the theater," observed Georgia's Herman Talmadge. "He was one of the few senators who could draw a crowd of other senators just to hear him speak." Dirksen was happiest when at the center of a grand drama such as the civil rights debate would provide. To win his crucial support, Humphrey knew that he must address Dirksen's substantive concerns about the bill while guaranteeing Dirksen a share—perhaps more than his share—of the glory and acclamation for the bill's passage. As one aide to the Democratic leadership confided to a reporter, "We are carving out that statesman's niche and bathing it with blue lights and hoping that Dirksen will find it irresistible to step into it."[6]

Dirksen, meanwhile, worried that he might not persuade enough Republicans to vote for cloture. "Getting cloture is going to be as difficult as hell," he confessed. "I don't know that we can do it."[7] In truth, Dirksen and his Republican colleagues had plenty of compelling reasons to support the bill. According to at least two national opinion surveys, more than 60 percent of the nation supported the House-passed legislation. Even without polling data, Dirksen could discern the political wind direction as well as any other member of the Senate. In a presidential election year, he knew that his party could suffer significant losses if the public viewed Republicans as obstructionists or, worse, as racists. After all, Republicans were the party of Lincoln, inheritors of a grand legacy that Dirksen knew he could preserve or destroy. Moreover, Dirksen's hands were tied by the knowledge that any substantial weakening of the bill would almost certainly result in fierce opposition from William McCulloch and his liberal Republican colleagues in the House. Dirksen had very little latitude on civil rights. His options were scarce.[8]

At heart, Dirksen was a conservative. From the beginning he had candidly acknowledged his qualms about the bill, particularly its public accommodations and fair employment sections. Although President Kennedy had once endorsed a separate fair employment bill, he had not included those provisions in his 1963 proposal—largely out of deference to Dirksen. The Republican leader had reciprocated by joining Mansfield as cosponsor of a pared-down Senate bill without fair employment or public accommodations language. If he could, Dirksen wanted to make the bill more palatable to his conservative Republican colleagues. On April 7 he submitted forty fair employment amendments to members of the Republican policy committee. The next day he shared the amendments with the entire Republican caucus. The changes he sought to Title VII, the equal employment opportunity provisions, were severe. They would prohibit the proposed Equal Employment Opportunity Commission from seeking court injunctions to end discriminatory hiring practices and would allow state fair employment agencies to preempt the federal EEOC. Harsh as they were, Dirksen's proposals were music to the fiercely conservative ears of Bourke Hickenlooper of Iowa, chairman of the Republican policy committee. Like Russell and the southern conservatives, Hickenlooper believed that Title VII gave the EEOC too much power over private businesses. He also believed that it would create serious conflicts with the twenty-five states that had fair employment laws—including Dirksen's state of Illinois. "This is a vulnerable section," Dirksen told a press conference. "I'd like to strike it altogether." As for how he would amend Title II, the public accommodations section, Dirksen was mum.[9]

Dirksen's remarks about Title VII and his laundry list of amendments sparked a vigorous debate among the liberals, moderates, and conservatives who made up the thirty-three-member Republican caucus. "My gracious sakes alive," liberal Republican Clifford Case of New Jersey protested on *Face the Nation*, "the Republicans are letting themselves be put in a position which is really not an accurate position when it looks as though they are opposing a strong civil rights bill." Dirksen insisted that he was trying to save the bill, not kill it, by attracting Republican votes through weakening amendments to the fair employment provision. "I have a fixed polestar to which I am pointed," Dirksen declared, "and this is: first to get a bill, second to get an acceptable bill, third to get a workable bill, and finally to get an equitable bill."[10]

Dirksen cautiously waded into the debate on April 16 when he presented ten Title VII amendments to the Senate. Dirksen's effort must have disappointed Russell. The Republican leader's amendments fell far short of his earlier stated desire to eliminate Title VII altogether. The proposed changes did not seek to eliminate the EEOC's injunctive powers, nor would they give state fair employment agencies preemptive powers over federal law. Instead Dirksen proposed only minor modifications to the bill, one of which stipulated that only aggrieved parties or an EEOC member could file fair employment complaints.[11]

Humphrey responded to Dirksen with patience and deference. When he first learned of Dirksen's lengthy list of proposed amendments—during a meeting with Burke Marshall, Joseph Rauh, and Clarence Mitchell—he remained calm. Don't be antagonistic, Humphrey advised the group. "The Republicans must carry the fight," he explained. "Let the Republicans argue it out with their own leader. Dirksen told me that if he did not get support, he would retreat." Humphrey's initial appreciation of Dirksen's situation was wise and correct. The Republican leader, at Humphrey's quiet urging, had unceremoniously retreated from at least forty of his amendments—some of which would have gutted Title VII. What remained was a collection of minor proposals.[12]

Dirksen's amendments, however, alarmed civil rights leaders, particularly Clarence Mitchell, who feared Humphrey might not be able to control the Republican leader—or would compromise with him. "We don't plan on letting them pass," Humphrey promised. "Don't you break out in a sweat, Clarence."

Later, when Mitchell began pressing Humphrey for around-the-clock Senate sessions to wear out the southerners, Humphrey resisted. "Nobody won a war starving the enemy," Humphrey said. "We must shoot them on the battlefield."

"You are shooting your friends if you trade with Dirksen," Mitchell replied.

"We don't have 65 votes for cloture," Humphrey replied. "Unless we are ready to move our clothes and our shavers and turn the Senate into a dormitory—which Mansfield won't have—we've got to do something else."

As if to further impress upon Humphrey the high-stakes nature of the debate's outcome, Martin Luther King told a *Face the Nation* audience on May 10 that without the employment discrimination and public accommodations provisions, he "would rather have no bill at all."[13]

As the southern filibuster droned into its fourth week, a vital new force entered the civil rights debate. A continuous prayer vigil by Catholic, Protestant, and Jewish seminarians had begun at the Lincoln Memorial on April 19. Students from seventy-five seminaries from around the country made a pilgrimage to Washington to pray for the bill's passage. On April 28, 6,500 people from various faiths gathered in support of civil rights at a National Interreligious Convocation at Georgetown University. Then, over the next few days, the religious leaders fanned out over Capitol Hill to lobby members of Congress.[14]

Humphrey not only understood the potential of the religious organizations and their sprouting political involvement; he also helped to guide it. Religious leaders had organized the Georgetown convocation at his suggestion. "The secret of passing the bill is the prayer groups," Humphrey confided to Rauh and Mitchell. To a reporter, he boasted: "Just wait until [senators] start hearing from the church people."[15]

Actually, some religious groups had been laboring for the bill for many weeks. At the behest of the National Council of Churches—which would spend $400,000 in its grassroots lobbying effort—clergy from all over the nation had been writing letters to House and Senate members. Some scheduled appointments with senators who came home during the Easter recess. Spearheaded by the council's Commission on Religion and Race, the lobbying effort was based primarily in midwestern states whose congressmen and senators were uncommitted and represented only negligible numbers of black constituents. Although these states had no natural constituency for civil rights, the religious organizations created one. In Nebraska, Iowa, and Minnesota, commission staff members taught church leaders and members how to lobby their members of Congress for support.[16]

During the House debate, the gallery sometimes seemed to overflow with ministers, priests, and rabbis—most of them voluntary watchdogs, or "gallery watchers," who tracked the votes and other activities of House members. Rauh, who spent many hours with Mitchell observing the debate from their perch in the gallery, recalled, "You couldn't turn around where there wasn't a clerical collar next to you."[17]

The clerical network was effective. On Saturdays and Sundays the rabbis, ministers, and priests preached in favor of human rights. By week's end senators received hundreds, sometimes thousands of letters urging them to support the bill or vote for cloture. While the public outpouring might not have made immediate converts in the Senate, undecided senators could no longer ignore the issue. Celebrating the powerful new unanimity among religious leaders, the national Catholic weekly *America* noted "the great and cheering fact" that "the Christian churches and the synagogues are, with only a few lamentable exceptions, speaking with a single voice. Is it any wonder that so many members of Congress have been impressed?"[18]

By late April Humphrey thought that he had gained the upper hand. Senators and the American people were growing tired of the southern talkathon. "No one can justify the filibuster," Humphrey indignantly declared on *Face the Nation* on April 26. "What is going on now demeans the Senate, insults the American citizens. And the American citizen is going to ask his senator and the Senate of the United States to stand up and to be counted on this vital issue of our time."[19]

But just as Humphrey began to detect a growing national impatience with the filibuster, groups of black militants began undercutting the bill's support. In New York, the Brooklyn chapter of CORE announced that its members would disrupt the opening day of the World's Fair, where Johnson was scheduled to deliver a speech. The CORE members said they planned to jam the Long Island Expressway with hundreds of "stalled" automobiles. Elsewhere other militants engaged in senseless and destructive protests. Radical black protesters entered an Atlanta restaurant and urinated on the floor. That act prompted a speech by former mayor William Hartsfield entitled "Is Urination Nonviolent?" In a Berkeley, California, supermarket, demonstrators piled groceries into shopping carts and then abandoned them. A New Orleans CORE official publicly warned of dire consequences if the civil rights bill died: "It is frightening to think of what will happen. There might be armed rebellion—and I wouldn't say one word to discourage it."[20]

National civil rights groups—including the NAACP, CORE, and the Urban League—recognized the potential for a white backlash against the bill and strongly condemned the militants. CORE suspended its Brooklyn chapter and forced it to cancel the threatened "stall-in." At the White House, Johnson was quick to speak out. "We do not condone violence or taking the law into your own hands, or threatening the health or safety of our people." Humphrey and Kuchel, equally distressed over the radical nature of the protests, issued a joint statement: "Civil wrongs do not bring civil rights. Civil disobedience does not bring equal protection under the law. Disorder does not bring law and order." The "unruly demonstrations," they said, "are hurting our efforts in Congress to pass an effective civil rights bill." If such protests continued, Humphrey knew that the southerners would begin exploiting them to heighten white anxiety over the bill.[21]

On April 21, thirty-seven days after they began their filibuster, the southerners finally made a tactical move. Talmadge called up his amendment to require jury trials in criminal contempt cases arising from any provision of the bill. Suddenly the debate shifted from the larger civil rights question to the venerable jury trial issue—a reprise of the most contentious portion of the 1957 act. The Talmadge amendment did more than simply narrow the debate. It lured Dirksen into direct negotiations with the Democratic leadership.

Three days later, on April 24, Dirksen made his first substantive movement toward cooperation with the pro–civil rights forces. He and Mansfield offered a substitute to Talmadge's amendment. They proposed limiting the bill's penalties for criminal contempt to thirty days in jail or a three-hundred-dollar fine, unless a jury convicted the defendant. Russell was unimpressed with Dirksen's effort at compromise. The amendment, he told reporters, imposed an arbitrary limit on criminal contempt proceedings that would guarantee only partial constitutional rights to defendants. Dirksen's proposal was "just a mustard plaster on a cancer," he said.[22]

The importance of Dirksen's amendment lay not in its impact on jury trials but in the fact that Dirksen had begun cooperating with the civil rights proponents. He was finally mapping strategy with Mansfield and Humphrey. By April 29 he was voicing frustration with Russell's absolute refusal to permit votes on *any* amendments. Dirksen told the Senate that if the southerners did not loosen their grip on the bill, he would join Mansfield in seeking cloture on the jury trial amendment.

Mansfield, while still opposed to around-the-clock sessions, had nonetheless begun turning up the heat on the southerners. Gone were the usual banker's hours. Now Mansfield convened the Senate at ten in the morning and usually held it in session until midnight. The always-bubbly Humphrey was also becoming irritated by the filibuster. "When we get around to the latter part of April," he told reporters, "we'll start spelling 'filibuster' in capital letters."[23]

Humphrey's and Mansfield's increasing impatience with the filibuster did not surprise Russell. Dirksen's sudden restlessness, however, was more troubling. Although any chance that Dirksen would ultimately side with the southerners on cloture was fading fast, Russell knew not to give up all hope. He quickly announced that a cloture vote might not be necessary. Emerging from a meeting with Russell on April 29, Dirksen told reporters that Russell would probably allow the Senate to vote on the jury trial amendment by May 6.[24]

While taking his first tentative steps toward direct negotiations with the Democratic leadership, Dirksen still hoped for an even better deal— some kind of sweeping compromise with Johnson. Rumors of such a deal swirled around the Capitol. Perhaps Alabama governor George Wallace's unexpectedly strong showing in the Wisconsin Democratic presidential primary meant that support for the bill was waning and that Johnson would be eager to strike the best possible bargain for quick passage of the bill. After all, how could the Great Compromiser resist the primal urge to broker an agreement that would ensure passage of a bill of such enormous importance?

He could, and he would. "I had seen this moderating process at work for many years," Johnson later said, conveniently omitting any mention of his role as a facilitator of that very "process." "I had seen it happen in 1957. I had seen it happen in 1960. I did not want to see it happen again." That meant no compromise, no deals, and no high-profile involvement by the president. Johnson explained that while he "gave to this fight everything I had in prestige, power and commitment," he had "deliberately" toned down his personal involvement "so that my colleagues on the Hill could take tactical responsibility—and credit; so that a hero's niche could be carved out for Senator Dirksen, not me."[25]

Believing that his special relationship with Johnson might lure the president into direct negotiations, Dirksen scheduled an April 29 meeting at the White House in order to make his case. Continued pursuit of a bill with no substantive changes, he would say, would almost certainly result in the bill's defeat in the Senate. If Johnson would only agree to bargain, Dirksen believed he could deliver as many as twenty-five votes for cloture. "Now it's your play," he would tell the president. "What do you have to say?" Dirksen expected that Johnson, the pragmatist, would have no choice but to deal. Johnson had other plans. "I'm going to tell him that I support a strong civil rights bill," Johnson told Mansfield by phone before the meeting. Johnson, offended that Dirksen previewed his demands of the president to the press, complained: "I don't know what's happening to him here lately. He's acting like [a] shitass!"[26] When he met with the president, Dirksen found Johnson resolutely unwilling to negotiate. Dirksen left the Oval Office disappointed and empty-handed.[27]

Johnson's refusal to negotiate forced Dirksen to face grim reality. Unless he was willing to join Russell's filibusterers—a politically unattractive option—there appeared to be no chance for a grand compromise, no watered-down bill to resolve his dilemma. In a matter of weeks, Dirksen's thirty-two Republican colleagues would choose between the positions of the racist, intractable southern filibusterers and the supporters of a bill so popular that it was a memorial to a martyred president. In the end the decision would not be difficult for a man with Dirksen's acute sense of history and intuitive feel for politics.

All the while, Humphrey kept the pressure on Dirksen to come to the bargaining table. "Well, Dirk, when do you think we ought to meet and talk over some of your amendments?" Humphrey asked.

"Well, give me a couple more days," Dirksen answered. "It isn't time yet." [28]

By Tuesday, May 5, Dirksen was ready. That morning he finally began full-scale negotiations with Mansfield and Humphrey. They were joined by Robert Kennedy and Nicholas Katzenbach from Justice, Commerce Committee chairman Warren Magnuson, and Republican senators Kuchel, Hickenlooper, and Aiken. Dirksen entered the room well armed. His aides lugged in their notebooks full of research and copies of the bill that Dirksen had carefully annotated during a lengthy hospital stay in February. Although he initially shocked Humphrey and Mansfield with the number of his requests—about seventy amendments—the two men soon realized that most of what Dirksen wanted amounted to face-saving technical alterations to the public accommodations and fair employment sections.

Dirksen did propose some substantive changes. For example, he wanted to amend the public accommodations and fair employment sections to limit the attorney general's power to intervene in cases of discrimination. In fair employment cases, he proposed giving state agencies at least thirty days to act before federal intervention. In both sections, Dirksen wanted proof of a clear "pattern or practice" of discrimination before the Justice Department acted. After the first meeting, Dirksen explained to reporters his sudden willingness to negotiate: "I'm trying to unscrew the inscrutable." [29]

As Dirksen and the Democratic leadership inched toward a deal, Russell temporarily dropped his objection to votes on southern amendments. On May 6, in five roll calls, pro–civil rights forces turned away two alternatives to the Mansfield-Dirksen jury trial substitute. But just when the Senate's pace quickened, Russell applied the brakes. Later that day the debate halted. With several southerners leaving town to tour poverty-stricken areas of Appalachia with President Johnson, Russell made it clear that the day's votes were the extent of his accommodation. [30]

Russell's turnabout infuriated Humphrey. "The whole procedure is disgusting," he complained after the filibuster—by now almost seventy calendar days—had become the longest in the Senate's history. "All that is being accomplished here is a display of adult delinquency. Any intransigent minority can run the Senate if a majority stands around with jelly for a spine." As he made clear, Humphrey was not simply angry with the southern "obstructionist tactics" that he said "were to be expected." He was angrier at those who professed to support the bill but continued to withhold their votes for cloture. The usually mild-mannered Mansfield agreed. "We are witnessing a travesty on the legislative process," he growled. "The majority is being told what it can do and what it cannot do." The *New York Times* lent its voice, reprimanding both the "arrogant" southern refusal to allow votes and "the spinelessness of Democrats and Republicans from outside the South" who were permitting "the Dixiecrat minority to frustrate action indefinitely."[31]

The debate exhausted Mansfield's abundant patience. On May 11 he announced that he would turn up the heat on Russell's troops. The Senate would "stay in session if it takes all year" to pass a bill. He would also resume holding the Senate in session until midnight. Russell was defiant. "That doesn't scare us," he replied. "We're ready for it."[32]

Off the Senate floor, in Dirksen's office, the ad hoc civil rights group moved steadily toward a compromise. After four intense meetings, they neared an agreement, finding common ground on many substantive issues and purely technical points. "The trick was to be sure you got it agreed to before too much bourbon was drunk," Katzenbach recalled with a laugh, "or else you had to do it again the next night." The group's fifth meeting, on May 13, was the turning point. Only two major differences remained. Dirksen was still holding out for further weakening amendments to the fair employment section. He also wanted to eliminate the Civil Rights Commission's authority to investigate voting fraud. On this point Robert Kennedy said that he agreed with Dirksen—the provision should not have been added to the bill—but he had promised McCulloch that it would remain. Removing it now might jeopardize support for the bill in the House.[33]

On the fair employment changes, Humphrey knew he must hold the line, especially after Joseph Clark of Pennsylvania angrily protested Dirksen's proposals to gut the fair employment provision. Storming out of the room, Clark complained loudly, "It's a goddam sellout!" Humphrey turned to Dirksen. "See what pressure I'm up against? I can't concede any more on this point." Dirksen reluctantly dropped his demands. By day's end the group emerged from Dirksen's office to announce an agreement.[34]

Standing before the assembled reporters, Dirksen gleefully took the lead. "We have a good agreement," he declared. Robert Kennedy concurred.

"This bill is perfectly satisfactory to me." Humphrey added, "And it is to me, too." The changes to which they had agreed "would not weaken the bill," Humphrey insisted. "We have done nothing to injure the objective of this bill."[35]

The major changes to the House bill were:

- elimination of the attorney general's unfettered authority to initiate court action in public accommodations and fair employment cases; the Justice Department could only sue when the attorney general had "reasonable cause to believe" that a "pattern or practice" of violations existed;
- in the thirty-four states with public accommodations and fair employment laws, the bill would require that complaints first be filed with state or local authorities;
- in the school desegregation section, the bill would specify that it did not authorize federal courts or officials to order the busing of schoolchildren to eliminate de facto segregation;
- the cutoff of federal funds to discriminatory programs would be limited to the particular political subdivision "or part thereof" in which a violation took place.

Most of Dirksen's amendments were to the fair employment section: Employers with seasonal workers would be exempted; American Indians on or near reservations could discriminate in favor of hiring Indians (the leaders wrote this amendment to secure the tenuous support of South Dakota's Karl Mundt); no outside groups, such as the NAACP, could file complaints for a worker; and courts would be required to rule that defendants had "intentionally" discriminated before granting relief.[36]

Dirksen was satisfied with his product. The House bill, he believed, had given the attorney general too much discretion over the bill's enforcement and would invite the Justice Department to involve itself in local disputes and harass small businesses. Because of his changes, the Justice Department would be restrained. Even the attorney general agreed that the House bill gave him more enforcement powers than he wanted.

The Dirksen amendments, though far from meaningless, would neither cripple nor substantially alter the bill. Rauh, not entirely pleased with Humphrey's willingness to deal with Dirksen, later admitted that the modifications were "minor face-saving changes" designed to give the impression that Dirksen had exacted major concessions from the liberals.

The vast majority of Dirksen's amendments, Rauh noted, "were 'ands' and 'buts.'" Journalist Murray Kempton observed that "Dirksen had done no small thing. He had acted out the ritual of initial distrust, long deliberation and final acceptance for all the dubious Republican senators who have appointed him their agent." Kempton marveled at Dirksen's ability to persuade some Republicans that his amendments "were substantive changes even while he was converting them into refinements of punctuation."[37]

Dirksen's role in the compromise made him an instant hero—just the role Johnson and Humphrey had first envisioned for him in February. That evening, Johnson called to thank—and flatter—Dirksen. "I saw your [Illinois's] exhibit at the World Fair, and it said 'The Land of Lincoln,' so you're worthy of the 'Land of Lincoln.' And a man from Illinois is going to pass the bill, and I'll see that you get proper attention and credit."[38]

To *Time*, the bill was now "Ev's Law." Reporters who had previously ridiculed Dirksen for his lack of principles now viewed the Republican leader as a statesman. Downplaying the hero's role yet relishing the praise and attention it generated, Dirksen insisted that civil rights was only one in a long series of inevitable social reforms. At a May 19 meeting with reporters, he quoted Victor Hugo, who Dirksen claimed had written in his diary on the night he died: "No army is stronger than an idea whose time has come." Actually, no diary of Hugo's exists. The quotation, from Hugo's *Histoire d'un Crime*, was different from Dirksen's version: "A stand can be made against invasion by an army; no stand can be made against invasion by an idea." Nevertheless, Dirksen had chosen an appropriate axiom, which he eventually adopted as his own. "Let editors rave at will and let states fulminate at will," Dirksen later said, "but the time [for civil rights] has come, and it can't be stopped."[39]

Most of the Senate's thirty-three Republicans quickly fell in line behind their leader. "Dirksen was the darling of the conservatives within the Senate," recalled William Hildenbrand, then secretary of the Senate. "So when he took that kind of position, it made it extremely hard for the others to take a different position." Not all conservatives were persuaded. Policy Committee chairman Hickenlooper complained that the amendments "don't go far enough to meet the real evils of this bill." Wyoming's Milward Simpson compared Dirksen's effort to hash. "They've just warmed it over," he said, "to make it more palatable."[40]

That certainly wasn't Humphrey's view. "We've got a much better bill than anybody even dreamed possible," he told Johnson on May 13. "We haven't weakened the bill one damn bit; in fact in some places we've improved it. That's no lie; we really have."[41]

Liberals weren't particularly overjoyed by the product of Humphrey's negotiations with Dirksen, but as a White House aide bluntly told *Newsweek*, "Where the hell else can they go? We're about ready to come out with a good bill."[42]

On May 26—after three months of seemingly endless floor debate—Mansfield, Dirksen, Humphrey, and Kuchel introduced a seventy-four-page substitute bill containing the Republican leader's amendments. "I doubt very much whether in my whole legislative lifetime any measure has received so much meticulous attention," Dirksen observed. Humphrey announced that a cloture vote would finally occur, probably on June 10. Dirksen stated, "I believe we can get cloture. And I think we have to have cloture now." With imposition of the dreaded "gag rule" staring him in the face, Russell was suddenly willing to allow more votes on jury trial amendments. On June 2 Russell gave Mansfield all of twenty minutes' notice that he was ready to begin voting. Mansfield saw Russell's announcement for what it was: a ploy to relieve the growing pressure for shutting off debate. Confident of victory, Mansfield told Russell that he was "talking to the winds." Despite Russell's charge that the liberals were now engaged in a time-killing filibuster of their own, Mansfield held firm. "Why does he wish to go over until next week?" Russell asked the Senate. Acknowledging that the civil rights leadership was not prepared to vote, Humphrey replied, "Simply because we need more time to nail down those cloture votes."[43]

Part of the problem was a minor mutiny in Dirksen's Republican ranks, led by Policy Committee chairman Hickenlooper. Dirksen's refusal to seek modifications to several of the bill's provisions displeased Hickenlooper. Humphrey suspected less noble motivations. "He was resenting the publicity and the play that Dirksen was getting," Humphrey said. Hoping to undermine Dirksen's position, Hickenlooper had convened several furtive meetings of conservative Republicans, at least one while Dirksen was at home ill. Concerned about reports that Hickenlooper might be "picking up strength," Humphrey went to Dirksen. Don't worry, the Republican leader told Humphrey. He was certain that he still had at least twenty-six votes for cloture.[44]

On Friday, June 5, Hickenlooper—claiming the support of seventeen to twenty Republicans—emerged to list his demands. He wanted cloture moved back by one day, to June 10, to accommodate senators who would attend a governors' conference in Cleveland. Next he wanted votes on three key changes to the bill: an amendment by Thruston Morton of Kentucky to give all criminal contempt defendants (except in voting rights cases) the right to a jury trial; an amendment by Norris Cotton to limit the application of the fair employment section; and an amendment of his own to eliminate training for school personnel in desegregation cases. While Humphrey predictably opposed the weakening amendments, he was still short of the sixty-seven votes he needed for cloture. An agreement with Hickenlooper might help him pick up a few more votes. First, however, he demanded solemn assurances from Hickenlooper that three Republicans—Mundt, Cotton, and Roman Hruska—would vote for cloture. With those votes duly promised, Humphrey approved the deal. It was a good bargain. Morton's jury trial amendment narrowly passed, 51–48, and Humphrey agreed to substitute it for the Mansfield-Dirksen jury trial amendment.

In two other roll calls, the leadership easily mustered the votes to defeat the Cotton and Hickenlooper amendments. Humphrey maintained that his willingness to satisfy the last-minute requests by conservative Republicans "brought us the extra votes we needed for cloture."[45]

Humphrey's bargaining with Hickenlooper struck Russell as unfair. After all, the goal of the southern filibuster was to force liberals to deal with Russell. In earlier days, when the alliance between southern Democrats and conservative Republicans was still intact, Russell would have undoubtedly been part of Hickenlooper's negotiations. By 1964, however, the two groups no longer fought civil rights in concert. Humphrey said that Russell complained "quite bitterly" that the civil rights leadership had refused to cooperate with him only days earlier when he had wanted to vote on jury trial amendments. "Well, Dick," Humphrey replied candidly, "you haven't any votes to give us in cloture and these fellows do."[46]

Now Humphrey knew he would have the votes to shut off debate. On the evening of Tuesday, June 9—the night before the scheduled vote—Humphrey phoned Johnson to give him the news: He had sixty-eight votes for cloture. Johnson questioned Humphrey intently about his count. Despite abundant optimism, Humphrey continued lobbying past midnight. He rounded up three more votes.[47]

That evening at 7:38, West Virginia's Robert Byrd, a former Ku Klux Klan member and future majority leader, stood on the Senate floor to begin what would be a fourteen-hour, thirteen-minute speech. The bill, Byrd defiantly declared, "would impair the civil rights of all Americans. It cannot be justified on any basis—legal, economic, moral or religious." Byrd ended his speech at 9:51 A.M. on June 10. Nine minutes later, the Senate's leaders began their final remarks on the cloture vote.[48]

Mike Mansfield went first, reading a letter from a twenty-nine-year-old constituent in Montana. Near the end of her long, poignant letter, the woman wrote:

> At night, when I kiss my children good night, I offer a small prayer of thanks to God for making them so perfect, so healthy, so lovely, and I find myself tempted to thank him for letting them be born white. Then I am not so proud, neither of myself nor of our society, which forces such a temptation upon us . . .
>
> I am only one person, one woman. I wish there was something I could do in this issue. I want to help. The only way I know how to start is to educate my children that justice and freedom and ambition are not merely privileges, but their birthrights. I must try to impress upon them that these rights must be given, not held tightly unto themselves, for what cannot be given, we do not really have for ourselves.[49]

Russell was next. Despite his strong opposition to cloture, he seemed to have little passion left for the fight. It appeared, one observer said, "that we were witnessing the end of an era." Ridiculing Mansfield's emotional appeal for the bill, Russell insisted the legislation had "no more emotional appeal than that which could be made for a purely socialistic or communistic system that would divide and distribute among all our people every bit of the property and wealth of the people of the United States." He derided the immense influence that religious leaders had exerted throughout the debate. "I cannot make their activities jibe with my concept of the proper place of religious leaders in our national life . . . They have sought to make [the bill's] passage a great moral issue. But I am at a loss to understand why they are 200 years late in discovering that the right of dominion over private property is a great moral issue."[50]

As Russell slumped into his seat, Mansfield yielded two minutes to Humphrey. Buoyant as usual, sporting a red rose in his lapel, Humphrey was a changed man. He had worked so hard during the arduous debate that he lost twenty pounds. His skillful management of the bill since February 26—through more than three months of debate—had transformed him into a national figure; he was now the leading prospect for the Democratic party's vice-presidential nomination. Characteristically, he chose to view the day and the impending cloture vote in the most optimistic light. Cloture would signal not merely an end to southern domination over civil rights in the Senate, but the dawn of a new day for the United States. "I say to my colleagues of the Senate that perhaps in your lives you will be able to tell your children's children that you were here for America to make the year 1964 our freedom year. I urge my colleagues to make that dream of full freedom, full justice, and full citizenship for every American a reality by their votes on this day, and it will be remembered until the ending of the world." It was perhaps the shortest formal speech Humphrey had ever delivered on the Senate floor. But it may have been the most satisfying.[51]

Finally it was Dirksen's moment. Weakened by a peptic ulcer that had plagued him throughout the debate, Dirksen showed the strain of the long hours he had spent in negotiations with Humphrey and Mansfield. He rose slowly from his seat and removed his glasses. "His face," one observer noted, "looked like a collapsed ruin, drawn and gaunt." Paraphrasing Hugo again, Dirksen declared, "Stronger than all the armies is an idea whose time has come. The time has come for equality in sharing in government, in education and in employment. It will not be stayed or denied. It is here."

Before Dirksen could complete his speech, presiding officer Lee Metcalf of Montana rapped his gavel. The hour had arrived for the vote. It was 11:00 A.M. As Dirksen took his seat, Humphrey stepped across the aisle to shake his hand. Then Metcalf propounded the question: "The chair submits to the Senate, without debate, the question: Is it the sense of the Senate that the debate shall be brought to a close? The Secretary will call the roll."[52]

Before a packed gallery, Secretary of the Senate Felton Johnson began the historic roll call. "I never heard the chamber so silent," Mansfield said later. "Mr. Aiken. Mr. Allot. Mr. Anderson. Mr. Bartlett. Mr. Bayh . . . " Senators responded with either "aye" or "no." When Johnson arrived at the name of Clair Engle, all eyes fell upon the frail, wheelchair-bound Democrat from California whom aides had escorted into the chamber. Crippled by two brain operations, Engle had not appeared in the Senate since April. Everyone knew he was dying from a brain tumor. Engle tried to answer the roll, but he could not speak. Finally he struggled to lift his partially paralyzed left arm. He pointed to his eye. "Aye!" declared the clerk. The scene moved many senators to tears. As Engle slowly left the chamber, the roll call continued.[53]

As the clerk reached the name of John Williams, Republican of Delaware, the count stood at sixty-six votes for cloture, twenty against. When Williams softly answered "aye," another senator exclaimed, "That's it!" Mansfield relaxed. Russell frowned and began scribbling on a yellow legal pad. Humphrey stuck his tally sheet into his mouth, bit down, and beamed. To a *Life* reporter, he looked "like a schoolboy who had just scored 'A' on a tough exam."[54]

Suddenly Arizona's Carl Hayden emerged from the Democratic cloakroom. Hayden was eighty-six, the dean of the Senate and its president pro tempore. The beginning of his service in Congress predated the 1917 cloture rule. In his long Senate career, he had never voted for cloture. But now he was grudgingly prepared to give Lyndon Johnson and Mike Mansfield his vote. As Hayden hobbled down the aisle, Mansfield intercepted him. "It's all right, Carl. We're in." Relieved, Hayden voted no.[55]

By the time the roll call ended, the tally stood at 71–29. Forty-four Democrats and twenty-seven Republicans had supported cloture. Only twenty-three Democrats, most of them southerners, joined six Republicans in opposing the historic motion. It was the first time the Senate had invoked cloture on a civil rights bill.[56]

Russell was a sore loser. He bitterly informed senators that he would now insist on calling up hundreds of southern amendments that were still eligible for roll call votes under the Senate rules. Later, as the Senate began voting down the amendments—southerners had submitted about 560 before the cloture vote—Russell complained angrily, "We are confronted with the spirit of not only the mob but of a lynch mob in the United States. Senators are paying no attention to what they are doing . . . There is no need for us to expect any fairness." Contrary to Russell's regrettable and intemperate assertion, senators knew *exactly* what they were doing. They had spent more than three months debating a single bill. They were more than a little frustrated by Russell's dilatory tactics, and they were eager to vote on final passage.[57]

While Russell fumed, Humphrey staggered numbly through the last few days of debate. Two days before the historic vote, misfortune struck the Humphrey household. On the afternoon of June 17—just after the Senate had approved a motion to substitute the Mansfield-Dirksen amendment for the House-passed bill—Humphrey left the Senate floor to take an urgent phone call from Muriel. One of their sons, Robert, had recently entered a Minnesota hospital for tests after complaining of swelling in his neck. When Humphrey answered the phone, a tearful Muriel gave him the awful news. Robert had a malignant growth in his neck. He would undergo immediate surgery. "It was exactly as if I'd been hit in the head with an iron hammer," Humphrey said. As he sat crying in his whip office, Rauh and Mitchell burst into the room, joyous over the overwhelming 76–18 vote on the substitute amendment. "Their joy disappeared as they shared my gloom and fears," Humphrey recalled. "Three grown men trying to savor the fullness of our success after decades of failure were instead sharing bitter tears."[58]

Humphrey was torn. Should he rush to Robert's side or fulfill his duty to the Senate and the nation? Consumed by "a kind of selfish guilt," Humphrey knew that if he left the Senate "we might lose the legislation." More than two hundred amendments were pending. "I was the only man who knew the whole story of the bill, knew all the amendments—and one little slip and we'd be gone." Perhaps Humphrey recalled the question Lyndon Johnson had posed early in his Senate career: "Hubert, do you want to be a good family man or a good senator?" Robert's operation was a success, and he enjoyed a full recovery. But the ordeal dampened Humphrey's joy over what would become his greatest legislative triumph. "So much pleasure on top of so much pain," he later said. "It sharpens both—brings out the tartness of life."[59]

On June 19, after 106 roll call votes on southern amendments—Senate leaders accepted only a handful of minor changes—the Senate adopted the civil rights bill, 73–27. The vote came almost four months after the debate had begun—and exactly one year after President Kennedy's civil rights program had first been submitted to Congress.[60]

After a brief debate, House members accepted the bill, voting 289–126 on July 2 to approve the measure as amended by the Senate. Later that day Johnson staged a nationally televised signing ceremony in the East Room of the White House. "We believe all men have certain unalienable rights," Johnson said, "yet many Americans do not enjoy those rights. We believe all men are entitled to the blessings of liberty. Yet millions are being deprived of those blessings—not because of their own failures, but because of the color of their skin . . . Our Constitution, the foundation of our republic, forbids it. The principles of our freedom forbid it. Morality forbids it. And the law I will sign tonight forbids it."[61]

Humphrey called the bill's final passage "the culmination" of his fifteen-year struggle for civil rights and of "a lifetime in politics in which equal opportunity had been *the* objective above all others." To many observers—despite Dirksen's heroic leading role—Humphrey deserved most of the credit for the bill's passage. As Democratic whip and as one of the nation's most prominent liberals, he had been the perfect choice to manage the bill in the Senate. His legislative skills had proved superb. The liberals were never so well organized and disciplined. Furthermore, Humphrey's good humor and boundless optimism had been a priceless resource. "There were many times when less patience and good humor on Humphrey's part might have changed the situation," *Congressional Quarterly* observed. True to his nature, Humphrey never allowed the debate to dissolve into personal recriminations. He and Mansfield had wisely resisted the advice of Johnson and many liberal leaders to play hardball with the southerners by holding the Senate in around-the-clock session. Humphrey's conduct and demeanor impressed even Russell, who told NAACP lobbyist Mitchell that "if it had not been for Senator Humphrey's fairness in giving a full opportunity to the opposition to present its view," the bill would not have passed.[62]

While Humphrey may have been the big winner, no one's loss seemed greater than Russell's. His thirty-two-year fight against civil rights had ended in total, humiliating defeat. Russell had opted for a risky all-or-nothing strategy—and lost everything. *Newsweek* observed, "Had Russell not played for time—banking on his mistaken belief that the Senate would not vote cloture—the Southerners probably could have softened the bill." Russell's purely defensive strategy puzzled Humphrey. "Frankly," he said, "I was rather surprised at the Southerners' tactics. I never could quite understand why they didn't let us vote more often because they had so many amendments in. If they had done so, they could have insisted that the legislative process was working, that amendments were being voted on. Instead of that, they just kept talking and talking. It seemed to me that they lost their sense of direction and really had little or no plan other than what they used to have when filibusters succeeded." By the time the Senate imposed cloture, it was too late for compromise. Russell's bargaining power had vanished. He watched helplessly as the Senate defeated hundreds of southern amendments in lopsided roll calls. "Dick Russell just couldn't believe that so many of his friends would desert him," said an aide to one southern senator.[63]

Russell's strategy had been curious. He had privately acknowledged the bill's inevitability, so why did he choose an unimaginative filibuster over conciliation and quiet negotiation aimed at softening the bill's most "egregious" provisions? Perhaps he hoped that Humphrey's liberal coalition would fall apart as the debate dragged on. He may also have anticipated that Dirksen would do the dirty work of compromise for him and negotiate amendments to substantially weaken the bill's public accommodations and fair employment sections. Russell may have gambled that Dirksen would never compromise with Humphrey and Mansfield—or that, if he did, he would be unable to persuade more than a handful of his Republican colleagues to follow his lead. Perhaps Russell, fully aware of the bill's inevitability, fought mostly for show. He reportedly told Mitchell "that if the opponents had not put up the fight they had, the bill would never have been enforceable in the South." Exactly what Russell might have meant by that assertion is not clear. Humphrey, however, speculated that Russell "thought it was important to have satisfied the people of the South that everything that could have been done had been done in opposition." [64]

If Russell was putting on a show, it was too often a bad one. Throughout the debate, the usually dignified Georgian had presented the most unattractive sides of his personality. He was sarcastic, shrill, and arrogant—sometimes all at once. When the bill became law, however, he was his usual responsible and gracious self. "I have no apologies to anyone for the fight that I made," he said. "I only regret that we did not prevail. But these statutes are now on the books, and it becomes our duty as good citizens to live with them." When Johnson read Russell's conciliatory comments, he praised his old friend effusively: "As the acknowledged leader of the opposition to the Civil Rights Bill, your reputation and your standing could not be higher in those areas where the adjustment to the bill will be the most difficult. Your call for compliance with the law of the land is, of course, in keeping with your personal code and I am confident it will have a great impact. It was the right and courageous thing to do." [65]

Russell and the southerners were not the only losers in the debate. One of the bill's most prominent Republican opponents was Arizona senator Barry Goldwater. As the presumptive presidential nominee, Goldwater had been under tremendous pressure from Dirksen and others in his party to support the legislation. "Barry, this is a dreadful mistake," warned Jacob Javits after Goldwater's Senate speech attacking the bill. Most agreed that Goldwater's vote against the bill showed, in the words of *Time*, "just how far he is removed from the mainstream of U.S. and Republican Party thinking." While Goldwater's opposition to the Civil Rights Act of 1964 only exacerbated his image as a philosophical extremist, the vote helped him and his party considerably in the South. As John Kennedy and Lyndon Johnson had known, civil rights marked the beginning of the end of the Democratic party's dominance in southern presidential politics. Before 1964, Republican presidential candidates had carried southern states only 7 percent of the time; from 1964 to 1992, Republicans would win southern states 70 percent of the time. Johnson remarked to an aide shortly after he signed the bill into law, "I think we delivered the South to the Republican Party for your lifetime and mine."[66]

Although many credited Dirksen and Humphrey for the bill's passage, Russell thought it was Johnson who "had more to do" with the bill's success "than any other man." In a way, he was correct. More than anyone else, it was Johnson who had skillfully transformed the bill into a memorial to his slain predecessor. Without his effective, dogged leadership and his steadfast refusal to compromise with Dirksen, the debate would almost certainly have dissolved into partisan bickering. In highlighting his commitment to the passage of civil rights, Johnson had also put his legislative agenda on hold for more than three months while the Senate debated the bill. His patience and determination paid off. His wisest decision had been to leave the day-to-day negotiations and the lobbying for the bill to Robert Kennedy, Humphrey, Mansfield, and Dirksen. Becoming publicly involved, he knew, would only inject presidential politics into the debate and complicate Humphrey's efforts to reach a bipartisan agreement. Therefore Johnson played only a minor public role in the debate, periodically issuing strongly worded statements in support of the bill's overall objectives. Privately, however, Johnson had been an enthusiastic strategist. He talked with Humphrey by phone constantly. Every week, over breakfast with the congressional leaders, he eagerly discussed legislative strategy. His aides constantly fed him information about the debate.[67]

In the end, Johnson had made the most arduous of philosophical journeys. As Humphrey noted, it was Johnson who—as Senate majority leader—had wisely allowed the southerners "face-saving victories while he established the principle of federal intervention." Because of Johnson's leadership in the 1950s, Humphrey explained, "the most venomous" southerners had been isolated, and the southern bloc began falling apart "with its own help." Johnson's leadership in shepherding through the 1957 and 1960 civil rights bills, though not landmark achievements, had paved the way for passage of the 1964 legislation.[68]

As Johnson put his pen to the bill during the East Room ceremony, he thought of Gene Williams, his black employee who had been reluctant in 1951 to drive Johnson's pet beagle back to the Texas ranch. "It's hard for me to get a place to stay, much less the dog," Williams had explained to Johnson. As Johnson noted later, "That had been the day I first realized the sad truth: that to the extent Negroes were imprisoned, so was I. On this day, July 2, 1964, I knew the positive side of that same truth: that to the extent Negroes were free, really free, so was I. And so was my country."[69]

16

DO YOU WANT TO BE VICE PRESIDENT?

After only one day in office, Lyndon Johnson had begun contemplating whom to choose as his running mate for the 1964 election. In a phone conversation with Johnson on November 23, 1963, Florida senator George Smathers stressed the importance of nominating a liberal. Smathers mentioned only one name. "Most of the southerners," he advised, "would be for Hubert."[1]

Humphrey himself began entertaining thoughts of the vice presidency, a position he had wanted as early as 1948, soon after Johnson took office. Only hours after Kennedy's death, Humphrey's friends began calling to urge him to seek the vice presidency. His answer, he said, had been brief: "I had no plans; whatever Lyndon Johnson wanted, Johnson would get." Humphrey tried to remain a passive participant in the draft-Hubert movement, at least in the months immediately following Kennedy's death.[2]

Viewed objectively, a Johnson-Humphrey ticket made perfect sense: Johnson, a son of the South and former leader of the Senate establishment, and Humphrey, a fiery northern liberal admired and respected by liberals and conservatives alike. Johnson enjoyed good rapport with the nation's business chieftains; Humphrey had excellent support among labor leaders. Of course other men with similar voting records or liberal credentials were available—most notably Robert Kennedy, Humphrey's Minnesota Senate colleague Eugene McCarthy, Connecticut senator Thomas Dodd, and Peace Corps director Sargent Shriver (brother-in-law of the late president). None, however, approached Humphrey in his almost unique combination of celebrity, legislative accomplishment, and friendship with Johnson. Yet Humphrey could afford to take nothing for granted. "The capricious part of Johnson's nature," Max Kampelman observed, "made it impossible for Humphrey ever to relax about the relationship."[3]

From the earliest days of 1964, Humphrey understood that his management of the civil rights bill would be a test of his leadership and his worthiness for the vice presidency. Throughout the months of debate, Johnson closely watched and measured him. In the spring Johnson first broached the subject of the vice presidency, telling Humphrey that he would choose him "if nothing arose that put an obstacle in his way." Johnson quickly added, however, that nothing was certain. Humphrey tried not to get his hopes up. "If it comes, it'll come," he said, almost nonchalantly, after his discussion with Johnson.[4]

Another strong indication of Johnson's interest in Humphrey came from Jim Rowe, a friend of both men, who came to see Humphrey early in 1964. "Are there any skeletons in your closet?" Rowe asked Humphrey. Humphrey replied that nothing in his past would embarrass the president. As Ted Van Dyk put it, Johnson had issued Rowe "a hunting license" to find a candidate. Rowe told Humphrey that Johnson expected him to build support for his candidacy. "If he could prove himself an asset to the ticket, and so on, he'd be considered," Van Dyk said, adding that Johnson "was going to offer the same choice to others."[5]

Heeding Johnson's instructions, Humphrey quietly began seeking support for his candidacy among labor and political leaders, journalists, and influential businessmen. Kampelman's group routinely sent favorable articles and polls to party leaders, labor officials, and potential convention delegates. Dwayne Andreas, a wealthy businessman and Humphrey's close friend, helped him build stronger relationships with the business community. Humphrey's aides funneled information about all of his activities to the White House.[6]

Throughout the spring and early summer, Johnson floated several trial balloons concerning other possible nominees. Each only added to Humphrey's anxiety. At one White House dinner, Johnson leaned over and playfully whispered to Humphrey that he planned to "drop Mike Mansfield's name into the hopper," explaining that besides flattering Mansfield, "it will give a lot of people something to talk about." In a matter of days Washington was abuzz with rumors of Mansfield's candidacy. The speculation amused Mansfield, who quickly disclaimed any interest in the position. Johnson continued dropping names, including those of New York mayor Robert Wagner and California governor Edmund Brown.[7]

In his search for a running mate, Johnson cast a wide net. He discussed the selection with dozens of cabinet members, governors, political consultants, and party officials. He consulted public opinion polls. Finally, he reached two conclusions: First, every potential running mate only weakened the ticket; Johnson would have been strongest running alone, if he could. Second, although Humphrey ran behind other contenders in the polls, he was the most popular second choice. "I had the feeling most of that summer," Humphrey later recalled, "that I would most likely make it. But I also knew that Johnson was a very pragmatic man and that if it looked to him like I couldn't be of any help to him or might be a hindrance to him or a load to carry, I don't think he'd have hesitated a minute to have said, 'Good-bye Hubert.'"[8]

For a brief while, Johnson insisted that he wanted to balance the ticket with a Catholic, preferably Shriver or McCarthy. During a meeting in the spring of 1964, Johnson convened a group of aides and advisers to discuss the vice-presidential nomination. At Johnson's direction, an aide produced a poll. "It was just made up in their office about fifteen minutes before," insisted Kenneth O'Donnell, a former Kennedy aide who had remained on staff to help Johnson. According to the "poll," Johnson might lose to presumptive Republican nominee Barry Goldwater if a Catholic was not on the Democratic ticket.

As Johnson debated the respective qualities of McCarthy versus Shriver, he turned to O'Donnell. "What do you think about it?"

"Mr. President," O'Donnell replied, "I thought we licked that in West Virginia—religion. I never voted for anybody for their religion in my life, and do you know what? I don't know any Catholic in the country that gives a damn where the guy goes to church. Whoever gave you that poll, you ought to get your money back. Because personally, I'm for Hubert Humphrey. He deserves it. He has worked hard for the party all these years, and you cannot pick the junior senator [McCarthy] over the senior senator. If you pick him just on religion alone, which will be written in every paper in the United States of America, you will blow the election. I think I would be totally opposed to it."

Johnson turned to Jim Rowe. "My hands are not clean," Rowe confessed. "I'm for Hubert Humphrey. I've been for Hubert Humphrey for years and years, so I happen to agree with Kenny, but I'm not going to say anything."

Johnson consulted several more advisers. All expressed support for Humphrey. "Now Lyndon was furious, furious!" O'Donnell recalled, adding that except possibly one person, "everyone in the room was a Catholic."

Following the meeting, Johnson pulled O'Donnell aside: "All right, you've got him and you can go leak it if you want. I'm committed to Humphrey. So forget it."[9]

In August, when Humphrey arrived in Atlantic City for the Democratic National Convention, he was the acknowledged front-runner. Johnson had eliminated most other candidates, including Attorney General Robert Kennedy, with his declaration in late July that he would not consider cabinet members for the job. The only two men now ostensibly in contention were Minnesota's two senators, Humphrey and McCarthy. After Humphrey appeared on NBC's *Meet the Press* with McCarthy on the Sunday before the convention, Rowe told him, "I can't predict what Johnson is going to do for certain, but it looks like you're the man."[10]

Just as Humphrey began to savor the impending realization of his longtime dream, Johnson threw up another potential obstacle. He wanted Humphrey to play mediator in a credentials dispute over which group of delegates would represent Mississippi at the convention—the all-white delegation led by Lieutenant Governor Paul Johnson (who had once joked that the NAACP stood for "niggers, alligators, apes, coons and possums") or the mostly black Mississippi Freedom Democratic Party. The black delegation, claiming to represent 450,000 black Mississippi citizens who had been systematically denied the right to vote, demanded that the convention seat its members instead of the state's all-white "official" delegation. Johnson gave Humphrey his charge: Use your considerable influence with the civil rights community to head off a potentially embarrassing fracas. "I always had the feeling, and it was implicit," said Van Dyk, "that if Humphrey messed this up, Johnson was not going to make him the running mate. It was a kind of test for Humphrey . . . If he couldn't do it, so much for Humphrey."[11]

Johnson worried that a failure to resolve the dispute to the satisfaction of civil rights leaders would help Goldwater. "Try to see if the Negroes [the black Mississippi delegation] don't realize that they've got the President, they'll have the Vice President, they've got the law, they'll have the government for four years," Johnson told Humphrey by phone on August 14. "Why in the living hell do they want to hand—*shovel*—Goldwater fifteen states?"

Humphrey replied: "We're just not dealing . . . with emotionally stable people on this, Mr. President."[12]

Humphrey's role in settling the dispute was ironic, and more than a little uncomfortable. After all, his dogged advocacy of a strong civil rights platform at the 1948 convention had catapulted him into national prominence. Sixteen years later, as an established national leader, his political future hinged on his ability to diffuse a potentially embarrassing confrontation over the same issue.

To help with the negotiations, Johnson sent Humphrey White House aide Walter Jenkins and Washington attorney Thomas Finney. Humphrey also summoned two trusted friends of his own, Minnesota attorney general Walter Mondale and UAW president Walter Reuther. After several days of difficult negotiations among members of the Mississippi Freedom Party, the official state delegation, and the credentials committee, Humphrey announced a compromise that failed to delight anyone: The credentials committee would seat only those delegates willing to take an oath pledging support for the ticket in the fall election. Two Freedom Party delegates would be seated with the Mississippi delegation, each with one vote. The convention would seat the rest of the black delegates on the floor as "honored guests." The agreement also included a rule, applied to future conventions, that would bar the seating of any state delegation that excluded blacks. The agreement "wasn't a bad offer," acknowledged Joseph Rauh, who had represented the Freedom Party in its negotiations. In protest, the Mississippi and Alabama delegates walked out of the convention hall. Yet Humphrey's negotiating skills and his stature as a strong advocate of civil rights had averted a larger southern walkout and a potentially embarrassing floor fight over credentials.[13]

Rauh was most impressed with Humphrey's unwillingness to urge his liberal friend to capitulate. "Five times I saw him and five times he would have had a chance to say, 'Joe, moderate your views, give in for me.' Never once, when the president of the United States was pushing Hubert to push me, never once did Hubert ever, ever ask for any concession on this basis . . . All I can say, for a guy who wanted to be vice president never once to ask for anything in that regard, I consider about as fine a thing as could have been done." More difficult to understand was Rauh's apparent unwillingness to help his loyal friend achieve a lifelong dream. Although Humphrey never publicly complained about Rauh's stubborn reluctance to compromise, he did lament the way that liberals took him for granted. "Nobody has to woo me," he told the New Republic in July. "I'm old reliable, available Hubert."[14]

The morning after the compromise was sealed, McCarthy withdrew his name from consideration. Soon Rowe arrived with more good news. Johnson wanted Humphrey in Washington later that day so that he could formally offer him the vice presidency. Later, before Johnson and Humphrey left for Atlantic City, Johnson finally broke his silence in an impromptu news conference. "Boys," he said, "meet the next vice president." Humphrey beamed.[15]

Later, many delegates agreed that Humphrey's acceptance speech, with its robust attacks on Goldwater's conservative voting record, was far better than Johnson's lackluster effort. To the enthusiastic cheers of the partisan crowd, Humphrey declared: "During the last few weeks, shrill voices have tried to lay claim to the great spirit of the American past, but they long for a past that never was. In their recklessness, in their rationalism, they distort the American conservative tradition. Yes, those who have kidnapped the Republican Party have made it this year not a party of memory and sentiment but one of stridency, of unrestrained passion, of extreme and radical language."[16]

By his own admission, Humphrey enjoyed "every exhausting moment" of the campaign. For the first time in his political career, Humphrey traveled in style—crisscrossing the country in a four-engine Electra, which his campaign dubbed "The Happy Warrior." "He went out and sang the liberal line and attacked Goldwater as an extremist and loved it," said Van Dyk. Years later, Van Dyk said, people often asked him, "What was the high point of Humphrey's vice presidency?" His answer was always the same: "It was the night he was nominated. Everything from there went downhill."[17]

Hoping to limit Democratic losses in the South, Johnson sent Lady Bird on an eight-state, twelve-hundred-mile whistle-stop tour from Virginia to Louisiana. Accompanied by her daughters, Lynda and Luci, Commerce secretary Luther Hodges (a former South Carolina governor), and House majority whip Hale Boggs, the first lady bravely faced crowds of hostile southerners still angry over Johnson's support for the Civil Rights Act. Some crowds were worse than others. South Carolina and Georgia were the most antagonistic. At the last whistle stop in New Orleans on October 9, the president joined Lady Bird for a rally at the city's train station. Johnson told tens of thousands of supporters, including many blacks, "I am going to repeat here in Louisiana what I have said in every state that I have appeared in, and what I said the night that I walked to the White House to take over the awesome responsibilities that were mine: As long as I am your president, I am going to be president of all the people." At a fund-raising dinner that night, Johnson refused to paper over his support of civil rights. To prolonged, enthusiastic applause, he declared: "Whatever your views are, we have a Constitution and we have a Bill of Rights, and we have the law of the land, and two-thirds of the Democrats in the Senate voted for it and three-fourths of the Republicans. I signed it, and I am going to enforce it, and I am going to observe it, and I think any man that is worthy of the high office of President is going to do the same."

To the dismay of his staff and many of his southern supporters, Johnson departed from his prepared text and recalled the story of a young Sam Rayburn and his visit to a dying Texas state senator, Weldon Bailey. As Johnson told the story, Bailey, a Mississippi native, said, "Sammy, I wish I felt a little better. I would like to go back to [Mississippi] and make them one more Democratic speech. I just feel like I have one in me. The poor old state, they haven't heard a Democratic speech in thirty years. All they ever hear at election time is 'Nigger, Nigger, Nigger!'"[18]

At first many in the audience were stunned. "It was a physical thing," recalled Johnson's aide Jack Valenti. "Surprise, awe; ears heard what they plainly could not hear, a cataclysmic wave hit everyone there with stunning and irreversible force." The audience reacted with thundering applause.[19]

On Election Day the Johnson-Humphrey ticket piled up what was then the largest victory ever in American presidential politics. Johnson won 61 percent of the vote and carried 44 states and the District of Columbia. In the South, Johnson's results were mixed. He won Arkansas, Florida, North Carolina, Tennessee, Texas, and Virginia. In the Deep South, however, he fared badly. Of the six states Goldwater carried nationally, five were southern: Alabama (where officials kept Johnson's name off the ballot), Georgia, Louisiana, Mississippi, and South Carolina. In Mississippi, where most blacks could not vote, the Johnson-Humphrey ticket suffered its worst defeat: The president received 53,000 votes to Goldwater's 360,000. Outside the South, Goldwater's only victory came in his home state of Arizona.

In 1957 Richard Russell's covert compromises with Lyndon Johnson had resulted in passage of the first civil rights bill of the twentieth century. Russell had hoped that a civil rights bill would release Johnson from the shackles of his heritage and hasten the day when a southerner—preferably Johnson himself—could be elected president of the United States. Now, almost eight years later, when fate presented Russell with the historic opportunity to help his protégé achieve that goal, he had demurred. In spite of pressure applied by some Georgia Democratic leaders, Russell told constituents, "I do not intend to take any part in the national campaign."[20]

Notwithstanding his earlier exhortations to constituents to peacefully obey the civil rights law, Russell explained that he could not bring himself to actively support a presidential ticket that pledged support and enforcement of what he called "the Federal Force Bill of 1964." To Georgia state senator Jimmy Carter, who had written urging Russell to participate in the campaign, Russell replied that even his friendship with Johnson would not lure him onto the stump. "I do not believe that even he would ask me to stultify myself by getting out now and supporting a campaign platform endorsing and assuring enforcement of a system which changes the form of government that we have heretofore known in this country." Furthermore, Russell said, he could not support Humphrey because the nominee had consistently opposed the cloture rule. "He is one of the most attractive personalities I have ever encountered and I know of no man who is a more fluent and eloquent speaker—in fact, he can 'charm the birds right down out of the trees'—but the fact remains that his philosophy is different to mine and is contrary to that the president always expressed as a member of the Senate." Goldwater, on the other hand, was "a real states' righter who believes in integration but thinks that it is a matter that should be determined by each state."

Despite his historic landslide election elsewhere in the country, Johnson lost Georgia by 94,000 votes out of more than 1.1 million votes cast. Although Johnson apparently had never asked Russell to lend his considerable influence to the campaign, Lady Bird had. On three separate occasions Russell politely rejected the first lady's entreaties to join her campaign swing through Georgia. His objections to Humphrey's liberalism, he explained, were simply insurmountable. When the Johnson-Humphrey ticket won, Russell seemed almost dispirited by the outcome and by the overwhelming endorsement of Johnson's liberal platform implicit in the election returns. While he blamed the most "radical" portions of the party's platform on Humphrey, Russell surely understood that virtually no word of the document would have been included without Johnson's support.[21]

Most likely, it was neither the election nor the platform that really bothered Russell. He was still smarting from passage of the civil rights bill and resentful that Humphrey, the bill's chief proponent and floor manager, was now the vice president. "The political wounds inflicted by the overwhelming forces, not only in the Senate, but in the communications media and throughout the land, led by vice president–elect Humphrey, were still bleeding," he later admitted. The prospects for 1965 and later were even more appalling. To his friend Senator Willis Robertson of Virginia, Russell confessed, "They have overtaken and overwhelmed us." [22]

17

WE ARE DEMANDING THE BALLOT

For years, southern members of Congress fought to defeat civil rights measures by arguing that such pernicious legislation would inevitably lead to violence and dangerous social upheaval in the former Confederate states. The balance between whites and blacks, they argued, was simply too delicate to alter suddenly with sweeping federal legislation. The passage of the Civil Rights Act of 1964 proved what many liberals had suspected: Such arguments were not based on legitimate concerns about maintaining peace and harmony; they were merely insincere excuses for preserving the South's brutal status quo in race relations.

Those who had accepted the threadbare southern arguments against the bill must have been greatly surprised by southern reaction to the legislation's passage. While Democrats suffered significant electoral losses in the South, the five southern states that Goldwater carried hardly qualified as the electoral disaster predicted by Russell and others. Furthermore, response to the dreaded public accommodations provisions was surprisingly benign: An extensive fifty-three-city survey conducted by the Community Relations Service found "widespread compliance" with the bill's provisions. "What is most important," Johnson said in reaction to the report, was that "it shows the law is being obeyed in those areas where some had predicted there would be massive disobedience." In New Orleans two hundred business leaders—including the manager of the well-known Roosevelt Hotel—put their names on a newspaper advertisement urging compliance with the law. Elsewhere in New Orleans, blacks quietly and peacefully desegregated downtown movie theaters and dined at French Quarter restaurants for the first time. The Jackson, Mississippi, Chamber of Commerce called on its members to obey the law "pending tests of its constitutionality in court." In Birmingham, where Mayor Albert Boutwell refused to use the city's resources to enforce the act, blacks and whites ate together in several downtown restaurants; the city's hotel and motel associations said they would obey the law. Holiday Inns of America told its 488 motels to observe the law. The South's largest cafeteria chain, Morrison's, announced it would do the same.

There was resistance. The city of Greenwood, Mississippi, drained its white and black community swimming pools rather than allow blacks and whites to swim together. Despite the peaceful integration of three hotels in Jackson, the Robert E. Lee Hotel closed its doors on July 6, four days after the bill became law. The Mississippi legislature unanimously praised the hotel's owners for their "courageous" decision.

There was scattered violence. In Moss Point, Mississippi, a sniper's bullet wounded a nineteen-year-old black woman as she sang the civil rights anthem "We Shall Overcome" at a voter registration rally on July 7. That day, in Bessemer, Alabama, a band of white men wielding baseball bats assaulted a group of blacks that asked for service at a department-store lunch counter. The most prominent resistance to the bill came on July 3 in Atlanta by Lester Maddox, owner of the Pickwick Restaurant. Aided by angry white customers waving ax handles, Maddox produced a revolver and chased three blacks from his establishment. Three days later, when another black bravely demanded service, Maddox again refused. He called the police, who took away the would-be patron.

In late July a three-judge panel in Atlanta ordered Maddox to obey the law, a decision that was affirmed by the U.S. Supreme Court in December. In writing for the 9–0 majority, Justice Tom Clark said that Congress possessed clear constitutional authority to enact laws removing obstructions to interstate commerce. "How obstructions in commerce may be removed— what means are to be employed—is within the sound and exclusive discretion of the Congress," Clark wrote.

For Maddox, the unfavorable Supreme Court ruling was not a total defeat. He became a hero among Georgia's white racists. In 1966 the voters of Georgia—aided by the state legislature—rewarded his violent racism and his contempt for the law of the United States by electing him governor.[1]

As the Supreme Court ruling of December had shown, the civil rights act's public accommodations provision had sharp teeth. By contrast, the act's voting rights provision proved a toothless, ineffectual instrument to guarantee black voting rights. Despite three separate acts—the 1957, 1960, and 1964 civil rights bills—Congress had so far been unable to break down the barriers to significant and widespread registration of blacks in the South. Under Dwight Eisenhower, the Justice Department had often been hesitant to employ the meager legal weapons issued by the Congress in the 1957 act. As the Kennedy administration proved with its more determined enforcement of the 1957 and 1960 acts, assertive executive action was severely limited without potent legislation. Because the Justice Department could enforce these laws only through the federal courts, hostile or indifferent southern judges controlled the fates of many voting rights cases.

"The avenues for opposition through litigation were so manifold," observed Stephen Pollak, an attorney in the Justice Department's Civil Rights Division, "that the pouring of the Civil Rights Division's total resources into voting discrimination" had resulted "in only minuscule advances." The existing voting rights statutes, Nicholas Katzenbach said, "were all sort of hopeless, the way judges down there were reading them and administering them. It just never got anybody registered." Katzenbach, now attorney general, quickly learned "that you're never going to get anywhere going case by case."[2]

The voting rights provisions of the 1964 act were designed primarily to accelerate the consideration and appeals of voting rights cases. Voting rights suits would be heard expeditiously by a three-judge panel and could be appealed directly to the Supreme Court. The bill also prohibited the unequal application of voter registration laws, outlawed disqualification for insignificant errors or omissions, and stipulated that a sixth-grade education was adequate proof of literacy. But the law applied only to voting in federal elections.

Despite these stronger provisions, black registration in November 1964 was much lower than white registration in every southern state. Across the South, only 43 percent of eligible blacks were registered, compared with 73 percent of eligible whites. The greatest disparities existed in Mississippi, where 70 percent of eligible whites were registered but only 6.7 percent of eligible blacks; in Alabama, with 71 percent of whites registered to 23 percent of blacks; and Louisiana, with 80 percent of whites and 32 percent of blacks.[3]

This deplorable state of black voter registration had lured about nine hundred idealistic college students from northern campuses to Mississippi during the summer of 1964. Under the auspices of the Council of Federate Organizations (COFO), an association of major civil rights groups, the students came flocking southward to participate in a voter education and registration effort known as the Freedom Summer Project. Led by Robert Moses of the Student Nonviolent Coordinating Committee (SNCC), the students—mostly whites—went door to door in rural Mississippi, hoping to persuade nonvoting blacks to attend voter education seminars at local churches. After being educated in the art of passing a voter registration test, the would-be voters—at least those with enough courage—were ready to present themselves to the county registrar.

For most of the students, Freedom Summer was no vacation. Resistance among black citizens was high—and rightly so. As Civil Rights Commission member Theodore Hesburgh later remarked, "In some areas, just attempting to vote is tantamount to suicide." Freedom Summer exacted an awful toll: six murders, thirty homes and buildings bombed, thirty-five churches burned, thirty-five shooting incidents, eighty beatings, and thousands of arrests. The events of the hot Mississippi summer not only highlighted the near-impossibility of black voter registration but exposed the woeful inability of the federal courts and the FBI to register and protect blacks in the South.[4]

From the White House, Johnson watched the Mississippi summer with concern and dread—fearing that events might force him into another divisive civil rights battle in the new session of Congress. Eager to focus on other aspects of his Great Society agenda, Johnson was reluctant to engage in another civil rights battle so soon after the arduous struggle of 1964. In a December 18 White House meeting, Martin Luther King urged Johnson to quickly propose a strong voting rights measure. "I'm going to do it eventually, but I can't get voting rights through in this session of Congress." The social programs Johnson wanted, he argued, would help black Americans "as much as a voting rights bill." As long as he pushed civil rights, Johnson believed the southern bloc in the Senate would prevent progress on his other initiatives.[5]

If necessary, however, Johnson would be ready with a bill. At his behest, Attorney General Katzenbach had begun drafting voting rights legislation just days after the Civil Rights Act had passed. "I could have shot him," Katzenbach later said. "I was so tired of being down in the halls of the Congress on the '64 act." The charge from Johnson: "I want you to write me the goddamndest, toughest voting rights act that you can devise." After all, it was Johnson's sincere belief that ballots paved the path toward full civil rights for blacks. As he told Humphrey, when the blacks get the vote, "they'll have every politician, North and South, East and West, kissing their ass, begging for support."

Whatever and whenever Johnson proposed his legislation, he wanted it to be entirely his bill. "He wanted something," Katzenbach explained, "that was purely Lyndon Johnson." Soon, the tragic events in a small town in central Alabama would force Johnson's hand and make his voting rights bill a national priority.[6]

Selma. An obscure town on the Alabama River in Dallas County was destined to become the civil rights battleground for 1965. Although the countywide voting-age population of 29,515 was almost 58 percent black, its voter rolls were overwhelmingly white. Of 9,877 registered voters, only 355 were black. Of the 795 blacks who attempted to register between May 1962 and August 1964, officials had enrolled only 93. During that period, registrars had added 945 of 1,232 white applicants to the county voter rolls.[7]

Its sheriff personified the county's oppression of black citizens. James Clark, a large, short-tempered, forty-three-year-old bully, would soon prove that Bull Connor was not the only inept lawman in Alabama. Clark would become to voting rights what Connor was to the 1963 civil rights debate—a vivid symbol of official southern racism and hostility toward blacks.

Dallas County had first attracted the attention of the federal government in 1961, when the Justice Department sued to prevent the county's registrars from discriminating against prospective black voters. By 1963, despite a federal injunction against that blatant discrimination, little had changed. Shortly after the passage of the Civil Rights Act of 1964, Sheriff Clark's deputies, wielding electric cattle prods, arrested fifty black citizens who appeared at the county courthouse to register to vote.[8]

By late 1964 Selma beckoned Martin Luther King and the Southern Christian Leadership Conference. King suspected that in Selma, as in Birmingham, the authorities would be unable to respond peacefully when blacks marched and attempted to register in massive numbers. On January 2, 1965, King launched his Selma campaign, telling a crowd of seven hundred that Alabama's blacks would take their appeals for voting rights to Governor Wallace, the state legislature, and ultimately the federal government. "We must be willing to go to jail by the thousands," he warned his audience. "We are not asking, we are demanding the ballot."[9]

Although King depended on another overreaction by local authorities, the Selma campaign would be markedly different from his 1963 Birmingham project in one significant respect. This time he would successfully articulate one simple and distinct goal: the right to vote. While Birmingham had helped sway public opinion in the general direction of the Civil Rights Act of 1964, King's numerous objectives there had been obscure. Blacks in Birmingham had articulated a diffuse collection of demands, including better jobs and desegregation of businesses, restaurants, and public facilities. In the end, however, Birmingham produced little immediate action in Washington. Kennedy was moved to propose legislation, but Congress reacted sluggishly. Not until Kennedy died and Johnson entered the White House did civil rights gain real momentum. In the words of civil rights historian David J. Garrow, although Birmingham "deeply affected the [Kennedys], there was no widespread national outcry, no vocal reaction by the nation's clergy, and no immediate move by the administration to propose salutary legislation."[10]

In Selma the demand was focused, forcefully expressed, and easily understood. The black citizens of Dallas County simply demanded the right to participate in the most fundamental exercise of the American democratic process.

In the weeks that followed, Sheriff Clark arrested Selma's blacks by the hundreds as they marched to the Dallas County Courthouse to register as voters. On January 19 the sheriff ordered a large group of blacks to wait in an alley near the side entrance of the courthouse. When they resisted this indignity, Clark arrested more than sixty of them on charges of unlawful assembly. Clark had walked into King's trap. The arrests energized Selma's fledgling protest movement. The next day another group of blacks appeared at the courthouse. Clark blocked their way. Armed with a billy club and a cattle prod, he stood defiantly in the courthouse doorway and issued his order: Wait in the alley! Clark promptly ordered the arrests of 150 citizens who disobeyed his order. The following week King turned up the heat again. The protests escalated. On February 1, King led 265 blacks to the courthouse, violating the city's parade permit. This time Selma's police officers arrested them all, including SCLC leaders King and Ralph Abernathy.

When almost 160 black children poured out of Selma's schools to protest the arrests, Clark played into King's hands again. With county jails already overflowing with black citizens, Clark ordered his deputies to herd the children toward the Fraternal Order of Police Lodge, six miles outside Selma. Clark's men waved billy clubs and cattle prods. They forced the terrified youngsters to march out of town at a quick trot. "You like to march so much, so we'll let you!" Clark shouted. The forced march lasted for three miles, until the deputies allowed the weary and frightened children to "escape." By week's end Clark had imprisoned more than 2,600 of Selma's black citizens. In an open letter to the *New York Times,* King pointed to the tragic irony: "There are more Negroes in jail with me than there are on the voting rolls." Meanwhile, in nearby Marion, Alabama, state troopers arrested nearly seven hundred black students who had peacefully marched to the courthouse to protest the county's voting rights and public accommodations violations.[11]

Events in Selma unfolded before a horrified national audience. Most graphic and disturbing was an Associated Press photograph taken of Clark as he brought down his billy club on a black woman whom two deputies had wrestled to the ground. True, the woman had landed the first punch to Clark's left eye, but the photographer did not capture that blow on film. The next day the photograph ran on the front pages of newspapers across the country. As *Newsweek* observed, the picture was "worth more to Martin Luther King's registration drive than all the thousands of words" that accompanied the story. Television cameras captured another violent incident involving Clark. When a black preacher, C. T. Vivian, called the sheriff "an evil man" for forcing twenty-five blacks to stand outside the courthouse in a rainstorm, Clark punched Vivian in the face and knocked him to the ground. "One of the first things I ever learned," Clark later bragged, "was not to hit a nigger with your fist because his head is too hard." As Selma's more temperate police chief later observed, King and the SCLC were manipulating Clark "just like an expert playing a violin."[12]

On February 5, Dallas County authorities released King from jail. He was now more defiant and determined than ever. The voting rights protests would spread across the South, he pledged, but he had particular designs on Alabama. He would work to triple the number of black voters in Alabama for the 1966 congressional elections and would "purge Alabama of all Congressmen who have stood in the way of Negroes." The next day President Johnson's press secretary, George Reedy, announced that the administration had decided to act. Johnson would soon be sending Congress a "strong recommendation" for a voting rights bill.[13]

King left Selma for Atlanta, but the protests continued. In nearby Marion there was more trouble. When four hundred protesters left the Zion Methodist Church to march through town, a small group of Marion policemen, backed up by fifty Alabama state troopers and a motley collection of angry white thugs, was waiting for them. Also in the group was Sheriff Clark, dressed in civilian clothes but wielding a billy club. Ordered to disperse, the marchers refused. Police and troopers tore into the crowd, beating the marchers at random. "They didn't have to be marching," recalled one witness. "All you had to do was be black." In the melee, the police and troopers injured several newspaper reporters and television cameramen. One victim was Cager Lee, an eighty-two-year-old man. Shouting "Nigger, go home," one of the troopers dragged Lee into the street and kicked him. Several state troopers assaulted Lee's daughter. Her son, Jimmie Lee Jackson, was shot in the stomach trying to save his mother. He died eight days later. The *Alabama Journal* (Montgomery) declared, "Alabama is, once again and worse than ever before, disgraced by mindless 'police work' and blood."[14]

With Jackson's death, the reinvigorated Selma project had a martyr. King immediately announced a fifty-mile march to Montgomery, where blacks would stage a dramatic rally for voting rights at the State Capitol. "I can't promise you that it won't get you beaten," King told his followers. "I can't promise you that it won't get your house bombed. I can't promise you that you won't get scarred up a bit. But we must stand up for what is right!"[15]

On the afternoon of Sunday, March 7, over six hundred blacks and a few whites gathered at the Brown Chapel African Methodist Episcopal Church. Despite orders from Governor Wallace prohibiting the march, the group was eager to begin its trek toward Montgomery. Armed only with bedrolls and knapsacks, the marchers wound their way through town and headed for the Edmund Pettus Bridge, which traversed the Alabama River. Along the way the marchers sang the Baptist hymn that had, by now, become the anthem of the civil rights movement:

> We shall overcome, we shall overcome,
> We shall overcome someday.
> Oh, deep in my heart, I do believe,
> We shall overcome someday.

As the marchers walked along U.S. Highway 80, an imposing unit of sixty state troopers blocked their way about four hundred yards short of the bridge. Headed by Colonel Al Lingo, the troopers were a menacing sight as they stood shoulder to shoulder in several rows, armed with revolvers, billy clubs, helmets, and gas masks. Nearby, spoiling for trouble, were Sheriff Clark's well-armed men, some of them on horseback. A bloodthirsty crowd of white townspeople was not far away.

As the marchers approached the phalanx of troopers, state police major John Cloud bellowed into his bullhorn: "Turn around and go back to your church! You will not be allowed to march any further! You've got two minutes to disperse!" When the marchers refused to turn back, Cloud gave the order: "Troopers—forward!" In an instant, the heavily armed troopers donned their gas masks and launched themselves into the crowd.[16] A *Newsweek* reporter described the rest:

> The front ranks of the column fell like dominoes before the first rush of state troopers; John Lewis, national chairman of the Student Nonviolent Coordinating Committee, went down with a mild skull fracture. At a half-walk, half-run, troopers shoved and clubbed the marchers into retreat. Behind them, the sheriff's cavalry mounted a Cossack charge into the scattering column. A fresh wave of troopers laid down the first volley of tear-gas canisters. A thick, acrid, blue-gray cloud spread over the highway. Billies flailed, horses dashed in and out, Negroes sprawled and choked and wept and screamed: "Please, no! God, we're being killed!" And across the road, in front of the Chick-N-Treat cafe, a gallery of whites whooped and cheered.[17]

By now the march had disintegrated into a frantic and bloody retreat. The terrified marchers fled toward town. But Clark's deputies fiercely pursued them. They were spared only when Selma police chief Wilson Baker ordered Clark to keep his men back. "Everything will be all right," Clark angrily told Baker. "I've already waited a month too damn long!" By day's end the troopers and deputies had beaten the marchers so badly that seventy-eight black citizens required hospital treatment.[18]

Television and newspaper cameras captured the entire ghastly scene. On Monday morning almost every newspaper in the country played the bloody Selma incident on its front page. The national outcry was deafening. In Detroit ten thousand people—led by the city's mayor and Michigan's governor—took to the streets in a peaceful but angry protest. Marchers also turned out in Toronto, Illinois, New Jersey, California, Wisconsin, Connecticut, New York, and Washington, D.C. At the White House, Johnson said he "deplored the brutality" in Selma but urged both sides to moderate their actions.[19]

Congress reacted viscerally to the news from Selma, in what *Newsweek's* congressional reporter, Samuel Shaffer, called "a wave of indignation greater than any episode in the long civil rights struggle." Suddenly lawmakers appeared eager to enact tough, meaningful voting rights legislation. In the Senate, Ralph Yarborough of Texas cried, "Shame on you, George Wallace, for the wet ropes that bruised the muscles, for the bullwhips which cut the flesh, for the clubs that broke the bones, for the tear gas that blinded, burned and choked into insensibility." In the House, Ohio congressman Wayne Hays proposed cutting the number of the Alabama delegation in half. Another Ohio congressman, Charles Vanik, suggested closing all of Alabama's defense and space installations as long as the state "chooses to declare war on the U.S. Constitution." Vanik declared, "The shame of Selma is the shame of America."[20]

In Atlanta, King said that as a "matter of conscience and in an attempt to arouse the deepest concern of the nation," he would lead another march to Montgomery on Tuesday, March 9. He issued an urgent call for white clergymen from around the nation to join him. The response surprised even King. The next day more than four hundred ministers, priests, and rabbis streamed into Selma from all regions of the nation. Despite a federal court order postponing the march, King agreed to abide by a secret compromise brokered by the president's emissary, Community Relations Service chairman LeRoy Collins. Alabama authorities would permit King's followers to march, but only to the bridge where the previous trek had ended in violence. At that point they would be allowed to kneel, pray, and then turn around.

On Tuesday afternoon King led 1,500 people from Brown Chapel toward the now-infamous Edmund Pettus Bridge. As he confronted the mass of state troopers, King halted the march. Again Major Cloud stood between the marchers and the long road to Montgomery. "You can have your prayer and then return to church if you so desire," Cloud told King. The crowd knelt and prayed for fifteen minutes. "We come to present our bodies as a living sacrifice," Ralph Abernathy said. "We don't have much to offer, but we do have our bodies, and we lay them down on the altar today." As the marchers finished their prayers, Cloud issued an unexpected order: "Troopers, withdraw!" Suddenly Highway 80 was clear. Governor Wallace had hoped to bait King into violating the court order against the march. King was more disciplined than the Alabama authorities. "Let's return to church and complete our fight in the courts," he said, as the marchers slowly began to reverse course.[21]

That night King tried to put the best face on his partial victory. "At least we had to get to the point where the brutality took place," he told the gathering at Brown Chapel. "And we made it clear when we got there that we were going to have some form of protest and worship. I can assure you that something happened in Alabama that's never happened before. When Negroes and whites can stand on Highway 80 and have a mass meeting, things aren't that bad."

The day would not be free of violence and tragedy. That night a white Unitarian minister from Boston, James J. Reeb, was attacked as he and two other ministers left a black-owned café near downtown Selma. "Hey, niggers!" a group of whites shouted as they pursued the three ministers. All three were beaten, but Reeb sustained the worst injuries. He died two days later in a Birmingham hospital.[22]

To many observers, it appeared that President Johnson had been only a passive, even indifferent observer of the events in Selma. On March 9, Johnson complained about King to his aide Bill Moyers. "Looks like that man's in charge of the country and taking over."[23]

Outside the White House, six hundred demonstrators protested the administration's perceived inaction by chanting, "LBJ, just you wait. See what happens in '68" and "LBJ, open your eyes, see the sickness of the South, see the horrors of your homeland." At the Justice Department, demonstrators were evicted after staging two sit-ins to protest Johnson's response to events in Selma. Inside the White House, twelve demonstrators on a regular tour of the mansion began an embarrassing sit-in to protest Johnson's civil rights policies.[24]

Johnson's indecision over Selma was mistaken for indifference. At the president's direction, Justice Department officials had been working for weeks on a voting rights bill that Johnson hoped would attract bipartisan support in the Senate and the House. Several times Johnson had talked with prominent civil rights leaders to assure them of his commitment to congressional action on voting rights. In his State of the Union address in early January, the president had urged Congress to pass voting rights legislation, although he had yet to decide whether he would propose a voting rights bill or a constitutional amendment.[25]

The violence in Selma outraged Johnson, although he complained privately that King and his marchers would be more successful "if they were in Washington, working on their senators, getting a voting bill passed." Master strategist that he was, though, Johnson instinctively understood that Selma had thrown open a window of opportunity through which he could now push strong voting rights legislation. Many liberals and some civil rights leaders were not as strategic in their approach to Selma. They urged Johnson to send federal troops to restore order, a course that would only have complicated matters for the president.

Attorney General Katzenbach, despite his own initial eagerness to dispatch the military, strongly advised Johnson that he lacked authority to make such a decision unilaterally. Katzenbach's counsel was wise. Had Johnson sent troops to Alabama without a request from state or local officials, he might have provoked further violence and ruined all chances for passage of his voting rights bill. For now he would reluctantly defer to Katzenbach, even if that caused him to appear indifferent to Selma's violence. Even so, the unrelenting protests outside the White House, along with the harsh criticism by civil rights leaders and some liberals, hurt Johnson deeply. "Once again," he later said, "my southern heritage was thrown in my face."[26]

In Selma, King demanded permission to lead a march all the way to Montgomery. The compromise trek to the Pettus Bridge had been only a temporary solution. Although Johnson wanted to avoid further violence, he would not protect King's marchers with federal troops unless Alabama officials explicitly requested them. He waited for Wallace to make the next move. "Make it clear we're not going to give an inch," he told aides. "Now that Wallace, he's a lot more sophisticated than your average southern politician, and it's his ox that's in the ditch. Let's see how he gets it out." Meanwhile, he told Katzenbach, "let's have that voting rights bill ready to go to Congress just as soon as we give the word."[27]

On March 11 Wallace gave Johnson an opening. When the White House learned that the Alabama governor had indicated his desire to meet with the president, Johnson quickly sent word of his willingness to set up an appointment. On Saturday, March 12, Wallace entered the Oval Office for a three-hour meeting. The six-foot-three Johnson invited the diminutive governor to sit on the sofa. Johnson took a seat in a nearby rocking chair. As Wallace's small figure sank into the cushions, Johnson leaned his imposing frame forward. He almost touched Wallace's nose with his. "Well, Governor, you wanted to see me?"

For fifteen minutes Wallace anxiously explained to Johnson the need to preserve law and order, quell troublemaking by outside agitators, and keep federal troops out of his sovereign state. "I saw a nervous, aggressive man," Johnson recalled, "a rough, shrewd politician who had managed to touch the deepest chords of pride as well as prejudice among his people." When Wallace finished, it was Johnson's turn. He focused on Wallace's nervous eyes.

"Now, tell me, how come the Negroes in Alabama for the most part can't vote?"

"They can vote," Wallace replied.

"If they're registered," Johnson said.

"White men have to register, too."

"That's the problem, George; somehow your folks down in Alabama don't want to register them Negroes. Why, I had a fellow in here the other day, and he not only had a college degree, but one of them Ph.D.s, and your man said he couldn't register because he didn't know how to read and write well enough to vote in Alabama. Now, do all your white folks in Alabama have Ph.D.s?"

"Those decisions are made by the county registrars, not by me," Wallace replied.

"Well then, George, why don't you just tell them county registrars to register those Negroes?"

"I don't have that power, Mr. President, under Alabama law—"

"Don't be modest with me, George, you had the power to keep the president of the United States off the ballot [in the 1964 election]. Surely you have the power to tell a few poor county registrars what to do."

"I don't. Under Alabama law they're independent."

"Well then, George, why don't you just persuade them what to do?"

"I don't think that would be easy, Mr. President, they're pretty close with their authority."

"Don't shit me about your persuasive power, George. Why, just this morning I was watching you on television . . . And you was attacking me."

"Not you, Mr. President, I was speaking against federal intervention—"

"You was attacking me, George. And you know what? You were so damn persuasive that I had to turn off the set before you had me changing my mind. Now, ordinarily I'm a pretty strong-minded fellow, just like them registrars. Will you give it a try, George?"

Wallace, the former bantamweight boxer, emerged from the lengthy meeting looking slightly punch-drunk, as if he had gone too many rounds with a much larger heavyweight. "Hell," he said later, "if I'd stayed in there much longer, he'd have had me coming out for civil rights."[28]

At an impromptu press conference in the Rose Garden, Johnson strode confidently before the waiting microphones. "Never in his sixteen months in office," wrote a reporter for *Time*, "was he more in command of the situation." First Johnson announced that he would send Congress a voting rights bill early the following week. Next he forcefully condemned the violence in Selma: "It is wrong to do violence to peaceful citizens in the streets of their towns. It is wrong to deny Americans the right to vote. It is wrong to deny any person full equality because of the color of his skin." With Wallace standing somberly just behind his right shoulder, Johnson informed reporters that he had "advised the governor of my intention to press with all the vigor at my command to assure that every citizen of this country is given the right to participate in his government at every level through the complete voting process."[29]

He was, he said, committed to maintaining law and order. "If the state and local authorities are unable to function, the federal government will completely meet its responsibilities." He had also told Wallace "that the brutality in Selma last week must not be repeated. I urged that the governor publicly declare his support for universal suffrage in the state of Alabama and the United States of America."

Despite having applied his considerable persuasive talents to Wallace, Johnson had really wanted only one concession, which he got: Several days later Wallace officially notified the president that his state was unable to bear the financial burden of protecting King's marchers on their five-day journey from Selma to Montgomery. Johnson in turn federalized the Alabama National Guard. Federal troops would be used, but not because the president had unilaterally ordered them into action; they would be mobilized because the state could not afford them. As Johnson explained, "They were not intruders forcing their way in; they were citizens of Alabama." That, Johnson later said, "made all the difference in the world."[30]

18

WE SHALL OVERCOME

With the new voting rights bill ready for introduction, Johnson's major concern was how best to present it to Congress. On Sunday evening, March 14, he met in the White House Cabinet Room with Humphrey and the House and Senate leadership to discuss whether he should present his bill to a joint session of Congress. Dirksen and Mansfield opposed a joint session.

"Don't panic now," Dirksen advised. "This is a deliberative government. Don't let these people say, 'We scared him into it.'"

Others—Speaker John McCormack, House Majority Leader Carl Albert, and Humphrey—urged Johnson to take his bill directly to Congress. "Logic is what you are saying," the vice president argued. "But emotions are running high. A message of what this government is doing—simply—is what is needed." Johnson, who had already decided he should personally present the bill to Congress, readily agreed. In minutes, Humphrey drafted a statement from the congressional leaders: "The leadership of the Congress [has] invited the president to address a Joint Session of Congress on Monday evening to present the president's views and outline of a voting rights bill."[1]

Going before Congress in this way had its risks. Johnson would be placing much of his considerable popularity and power behind a single bill whose passage was likely, but by no means assured. Since Harry Truman had appeared before a joint session in 1946 to request special legislation to end a national railway strike, no president had appeared in the House chamber to present his request for a specific bill. But the drama that the historic speech would produce was exactly what Johnson wanted. As Johnson later explained, "I felt I had to reassure the people that we were moving as far and as fast as we could. I knew this reassurance would not be provided by the cold words of a written message."[2]

Ninety-six years after the states had ratified the Fifteenth Amendment, Johnson would bring Congress a bill to breathe life into Section I of the moribund constitutional amendment, which declared that "the right of citizens of the United States to vote shall not be denied or abridged by the United States or by any State on account of race, color, or previous condition of servitude." In contrast to previous voting rights bills, Johnson's legislation would not rely on federal district courts for enforcement. Instead the president would ask Congress to establish uniform voting standards in those states with the worst histories of voting rights violations. The bill would abolish literacy and other qualification exams in states and jurisdictions where less than half the voting-age citizens had voted in or registered for the November 1964 general election. In those states, federal registrars could assume responsibility for voter registration. States that blocked federally registered voters from the polls could have their ballots impounded by the courts.

Under the bill's provisions, the federal government would immediately send voting examiners into at least six southern states whose voter turnouts in the November election had been below 50 percent: Mississippi (33 percent), South Carolina (38 percent), Alabama (36 percent), Virginia (41 percent), Georgia (43 percent), and Louisiana (47 percent). Thirty-four counties in North Carolina and one county each in Arizona and Maine would qualify for voting examiners. Another important provision required states in which the bill nullified voter-qualification laws to submit all subsequent changes in voting statutes to a three-judge District of Columbia panel.

The existing voting rights laws—despite considerable litigation by the Justice Department under Kennedy and Johnson—had produced only minor progress in the seven years since the Civil Rights Act of 1957. Johnson now proposed what one Justice Department official called an "almost revolutionary" change: The Justice Department would no longer seek relief from deliberate or hostile federal district courts. Rather, the government could send federal voter registrars directly into states or jurisdictions when the attorney general certified to the U.S. Civil Service Commission that voting rights violations existed.[3]

On the evening of March 15, at nine o'clock, Johnson stood at the lectern in the House of Representatives. The speech he was about to deliver was hastily prepared. Speechwriter Richard Goodwin had feverishly labored since morning, under intense pressure, to produce a polished text. Even as Johnson stood before the assembled members of Congress, the speech was not yet on the TelePrompTer. Johnson would read the first twelve pages from his loose-leaf binder before aide Jack Valenti could crawl across the floor of the House well and nervously thread the speech tape onto the machine.[4]

Not every member of Congress was in the House chamber as Johnson began his speech. The Mississippi and Virginia delegations staged a boycott, as did several other southern members. None of this troubled Johnson; his audience was the entire nation, not southern members of Congress.[5] Beginning his speech forcefully, Johnson immediately placed the voting rights issue into its larger, more significant context:

> I speak tonight for the dignity of man and the destiny of democracy. I urge every member of both parties, Americans of all religions and of all colors, from every section of the country, to join me in that cause.
>
> At times, history and fate meet at a single time in a single place to shape a turning point in man's unending search for freedom. So it was at Lexington and Concord. So it was a century ago at Appomattox. So it was last week in Selma, Alabama.
>
> There, long-suffering men and women peacefully protested the denial of their rights as Americans. Many were brutally assaulted. One good man, a man of God, was killed.
>
> There is no cause for pride in what has happened in Selma. There is no cause for self-satisfaction in the long denial of equal rights of millions of Americans.
>
> But there is cause for hope and for faith in our democracy in what is happening here tonight.
>
> For the cries of pain and the hymns and protests of oppressed people have summoned into convocation all the majesty of this great government of the greatest nation on earth.

The issue, Johnson declared, is "the harsh fact that in many places in this country, men and women are kept from voting simply because they are Negroes." Current laws, he insisted, "cannot overcome systematic and ingenious discrimination. No law that we now have on the books—and I have helped to put three of them there—can ensure the right to vote when local officials are determined to deny it." The Constitution, Johnson said, is clear: No one can be denied his voting rights because of his race or color. "We have all sworn an oath before God to support and to defend that Constitution," he declared. "We must now act in obedience to that oath."

On Wednesday, he said, he would "send to Congress a law designed to eliminate illegal barriers to the right to vote." And he noted that the last civil rights bill passed "after eight long months of debate." This time, Johnson insisted, "there must be no delay, or no hesitation or no compromise with our purpose . . . We ought not, we must not wait another eight months before we get a bill. We have already waited a hundred years and more and the time for waiting is gone. So I ask you to join me in working long hours, nights and weekends, if necessary, to pass this bill. And I don't make that request lightly."

With his next words, Johnson elevated himself and his presidency to a higher plane—linking himself inextricably with the noble cause of civil rights:

> But even if we pass this bill, the battle will not be over. What happened in Selma is part of a far larger movement which reaches into every section and state of America. It is the effort of American Negroes to secure for themselves the full blessings of American life.
>
> Their cause must be our cause, too. Because it is not just Negroes, but really it is all of us, who must overcome the crippling legacy of bigotry and injustice.

Then—for one brief, dramatic moment—Johnson paused. Raising his arms like an evangelical preacher certain of the righteousness of his message, Johnson declared:

> And we shall overcome![6]

For a split second, the chamber was quiet. Perhaps his audience was ever so stunned that the president of the United States had, as Richard Goodwin said, "adopted as his own rallying cry the anthem of black protest, the hymn of a hundred embattled black marches." Suddenly the entire chamber exploded in spontaneous, rapturous applause. Congressmen, senators, cabinet members, and Supreme Court justices leapt to their feet in an emotional, thunderous ovation. House Judiciary Committee chairman Celler cheered wildly. Tears welled in the eyes of Majority Leader Mansfield. In the gallery, blacks and whites wept openly. Watching the speech in far-away Selma, Martin Luther King cried. Next to Harry McPherson sat a glum southern congressman, who, shocked by Johnson's words, simply sputtered, "Goddamn!"[7] The real hero of the civil rights struggle, Johnson continued,

is the American Negro. His actions and protests, his courage to risk safety and even to risk his life, have awakened the conscience of this nation. His demonstrations have been designed to call attention to injustice, designed to provoke change, designed to stir reform. He has called upon us to make good the promise of America. And who among us can say that we would have made the same progress were it not for his persistent bravery, and his faith in American democracy.

As he ended his forty-five-minute speech, Johnson recalled for his audience his first post-college job, as a teacher at a Mexican-American school in Cotulla, Texas:

Somehow you never forget what poverty and hatred can do when you see its scars on the hopeful face of a young child.

I never thought then in 1928 that I would be standing here in 1965. It never even occurred to me in my fondest dreams that I might have the chance to help the sons and daughters of those students and to help people like them all over this country.

But now I do have that chance and I'll let you in on a secret. I mean to use it. And I hope that you will use it with me.[8]

When Johnson finished, the assembled members of Congress rose for another standing ovation. As he walked out of the chamber, down the center aisle, Johnson came face to face with Celler.

"Manny, I want you to start hearings tonight."

Celler was stunned. "Mr. President, I can't push that committee or it might get out of hand. I'm scheduling hearings for three days next week, beginning Tuesday."

Johnson was persistent. "Start them this week, Manny. And hold night sessions, too."[9]

Then, Johnson walked away. In the words of *Time:* "He strode from the chamber a changed man, confident . . . that he had launched the U.S. itself inexorably toward a new purpose."[10]

When Johnson delivered his historic speech, Richard Russell was a thousand miles away. Following more than a month's confinement at Walter Reed Army Hospital, Russell had left town to recuperate in Puerto Rico, then in Florida, and finally in his hometown of Winder, Georgia. He suffered from a pulmonary edema, a condition in which his emphysema-damaged lungs became congested with fluid and restricted his breathing. Despite intensive medical treatment, his condition had worsened. Doctors were finally forced to perform a tracheotomy to assist his breathing.[11]

Although Russell would eventually recover and move aggressively to head off any challenge to his Senate seat, his impact on the voting rights debate would be negligible. His illness aside, it is difficult to imagine how even a healthy Russell could have altered the dynamics of the debate over an immensely popular bill. In truth, Russell no longer exercised a disproportionate influence on most legislative questions; his voting record on major issues now placed him outside the Senate's mainstream. In the previous two years, for example, he had voted against a host of successful Johnson administration proposals besides civil rights, including the nuclear test-ban treaty, the War on Poverty bill, the Manpower Training Act, tax reduction legislation, federal aid to higher education, and a wheat deal with Russia. In Russell's absence, southern leadership had fallen to Allen Ellender, the seventy-five-year-old senator from Louisiana who was the most senior southerner after Russell. Although colleagues respected Ellender for his intelligence and integrity, in the end he would provide the same unimaginative and purely defensive leadership that had characterized Russell's efforts in 1964.

Passage of the Civil Rights Act of 1964 had left the southerners reeling. Now, just as they had begun to recover, Johnson and the Senate's liberals came charging again with an extremely popular voting rights measure. "The Senate is like the South after Grant took Richmond," a liberal senator told the *Saturday Evening Post* in March. "The southern generals are still brilliant, but their troops are old and tired, and there simply aren't enough to go around."

The liberal Democratic ranks had grown by two seats in the 1964 elections; Democrats in the Senate now held a 68–32 advantage over Republicans, their largest margin since 1940. Unlike their aging southern conservative counterparts, the liberals had energized their ranks with the addition of young men in their thirties—Edward Kennedy of Massachusetts, thirty-three, and Joseph Tydings of Maryland and Birch Bayh of Indiana, both thirty-seven.

A particular cause of the southerners' gloom was the cloture triumph of 1964. The filibuster's absolute failure had crippled their ability to mount another offensive against civil rights in 1965. Russell believed, in the words of one friend, that once the southerners had "lost their virginity," cloture would be easily repeated in 1965. That sentiment was echoed by an aide to another southern senator, who candidly explained to the *Wall Street Journal*, "They're tired. Many of them have been sick. And the civil rights fight last year really took the heart out of most of them."[12]

Adding to the southerners' helpless distress was the way that Johnson's brilliant speech energized the supporters of a strong voting rights bill. Typical was the review of journalists Rowland Evans and Robert Novak, who called it "the best, most genuinely moving speech" that Johnson had made as president. Eloquently written and brilliantly delivered, the speech capitalized on the powerful emotions that Selma had generated. In only forty-five minutes, Johnson transformed the nation's raw outrage over violence in Alabama into an undeniable determination to secure—with powerful legislation—the voting rights of all Americans.[13]

The guardians of the Old South were further disturbed by a growing apostasy in their own ranks. Louisiana's Russell Long, elected to succeed Humphrey as Democratic whip, signaled that he might find the courage to support the bill. On March 17, the morning after attending a private party at which Long was present, White House aide Jim Jones informed the president that Long had "spoken in strong support of the Voting Rights bill (although he said he would work for some amendments)." Long suggested he could persuade eleven of twenty-two southern senators to support the bill, and, Jones reported, "he will carry these eleven votes into the Southern caucus in hopes of thwarting a big filibuster attempt." At least two other erstwhile civil rights opponents, George Smathers and J. William Fulbright, appeared to have little stomach for a spirited filibuster. Even Harry Byrd, Virginia's venerable segregationist, seemed to have lost his zest for the fight. Asked by *Newsweek*'s congressional reporter, Samuel Shaffer, if he would participate in the southern filibuster, Byrd replied, "Yes, I'll have to do my part, but you know you can't stop this bill. We can't deny the Negroes a basic constitutional right to vote."[14]

As Byrd's extraordinary statement demonstrated, the southerners' reflex to oppose all civil rights legislation usually overpowered their professed loyalty to the Constitution. Even though they opposed the bill—on Constitutional grounds, they argued—most southern senators were never fond of fighting voting rights legislation. "It simply was not a respectable argument to make [that blacks should not vote]," Attorney General Katzenbach said, "and none made it."[15]

On March 18 Mike Mansfield asked the Senate to refer the voting rights bill to the Judiciary Committee with instructions to report it by April 9. "That is a pitiful thing," complained John Stennis before the vote, "if we really mean to study a proposal of this magnitude." Judiciary chairman Eastland, whose committee had never willingly reported a civil rights bill, unwittingly provided the Senate ample reason to impose Mansfield's deadline. "Let me make myself clear," Eastland declared. "I am opposed to every word and every line in the bill." Later that day senators voted 67–13 to give Eastland's committee no more than fifteen days to return with a bill. Despite its chairman's vehement opposition, there was little doubt that the committee—which now included a solid, influential bloc of nine liberals—would favorably report the legislation.[16]

Meanwhile in the House, Attorney General Katzenbach began his testimony for the legislation, telling the Judiciary Committee that the administration bill represented a "new approach, an approach which goes beyond the tortuous, often ineffective pace of litigation . . . a systematic, automatic method to deal with discriminatory tests, with discriminatory testers, and discriminatory threats." Although some Republicans complained that the bill was too narrow to eradicate small pockets of voter discrimination, Chairman Celler was now in firm control of his committee. Applying the lessons of his near-debacle in committee the previous year, he now said he would not allow the bill to become "freighted down" with amendments that might jeopardize its passage. Despite Celler's concerns, House passage was inevitable. Following the 1964 elections, the Democrats now controlled 295 seats to the Republicans' 140—an advantage of 155 seats and the largest Democratic majority since 1938.[17]

Three days later, on March 21, Martin Luther King and 3,400 followers embarked on the first leg of a four-day, fifty-four-mile march from Selma to Montgomery. The marchers—protected by 1,000 U.S. military police, 1,900 federalized Alabama National Guardsmen, U.S. marshals, and FBI agents—arrived in Montgomery on Thursday, March 25. As they converged on the Capitol grounds for a massive rally, Governor Wallace cowered in his office. He reneged on a promise to meet with a small group of demonstrators. Instead Wallace meekly peeked through his tightly shut Venetian blinds and muttered to aides, "That's quite a crowd." King, in his speech, reminded the marchers that they had overcome powerful odds in their trek to Montgomery. "And there were those who said that we would get here only over their dead bodies, but all the world today knows that we are here and that we are standing before the forces of power in the state of Alabama, saying 'We ain't goin' let nobody turn us around.'"[18]

In Washington the Senate and House Judiciary committees quickly put their imprints on the voting rights bill. Remarkably, both panels approved bills that were much stronger than the original administration version. In the Senate the Judiciary Committee added a ban on poll taxes in state and local elections and an additional trigger mechanism that would authorize the appointment of federal voting registrars in states or voting districts where fewer than 25 percent of eligible minority citizens were registered. The Senate committee did, however, weaken the bill slightly in other areas. At Dirksen's behest, and with administration support, Judiciary members narrowly voted to permit states with literacy tests and low turnout to escape from the bill's automatic trigger mechanism if less than 20 percent of their voting-age population was nonwhite. Dirksen also persuaded the committee to exempt a state or locality from the bill if its voting participation in the most recent presidential election exceeded the national average or at least 60 percent of the voting-age residents were registered. This provision meant that the bill would not apply to any state or political district outside the South. Some liberals found this particularly bothersome. They argued—accurately, it turned out—that more crafty southern states might try to release themselves from the bill's grip simply by increasing their white registration. Another Dirksen amendment changed a provision that would have allowed states and counties to exempt themselves from the bill by persuading a three-judge court in Washington that they had not practiced discrimination during the preceding ten years. Dirksen insisted on reducing that time by half.[19]

Dirksen's negotiations over the bill's specifics differed from his 1964 effort in one significant respect: This time, after the events in Selma, the Republican leader's ultimate support for the voting rights bill had never been in doubt. At first he had discounted the need for a voting rights bill, believing that the provisions of the 1964 act were sufficient. But the brutality of the authorities in Alabama shocked and deeply offended him. After Selma he told his aides that he would support "revolutionary" legislation to guarantee the right to vote. Initially Dirksen recoiled from the idea of sending federal registrars into the South, preferring more aggressive enforcement through the federal courts. Yet he kept an open mind, conferring often with Johnson and Katzenbach while Justice Department attorneys drafted the bill in February. "My real concern," Dirksen said, "is not to put anyone in jail, but to get people to vote." Finally Dirksen acknowledged that many federal courts in the South could not be trusted to enforce the law. He reluctantly agreed to support the registrar provision, but only if the bill called them "examiners" and only if the trigger provision applied to just seven southern states.[20]

Dirksen's approach to voting rights was strikingly similar to his negotiating style throughout the civil rights debate of 1964. Joined by aides to Mansfield, Justice Department officials engaged in intense negotiations with several Dirksen aides, including his chief representative, Neal Kennedy. For days the group reviewed "every line of the bill" in response to the many questions that Kennedy raised for Dirksen. Ultimately the administration yielded little of substance. Rather, as one Justice Department participant observed, the tedious negotiating process primarily permitted Dirksen "to come forward with a changed bill so that he could justify to his party moving from a skeptic position, or an opposition position, to a supporting position." Attorney General Katzenbach later remembered Dirksen's role less charitably: "He was demonstrating his power. [He believed that] he was the important guy, you needed him. It was something of an ego trip." Dirksen of course saw his own role in the most favorable, altruistic light. He quoted Abraham Lincoln to justify his evolution from civil rights opponent to one of its most vocal champions: "The dogmas of the quiet past are inadequate to the stormy present. The occasion is piled high with difficulty and we must rise with the occasion. As our case is new so must we think anew and act anew."[21]

While he tinkered with the bill at its margins, Dirksen was genuinely concerned about two provisions. He wanted to restrain the bill's power to dispatch voting registrars to the South, and he worried about the constitutionality of its poll tax provision. On the poll tax question, Johnson, Mansfield, and Katzenbach shared Dirksen's concerns. They feared the negative consequences in the South if the Supreme Court eventually ruled that Congress could ban poll taxes only by constitutional amendment. Congress had previously taken that route in 1962, when it passed an amendment banning poll taxes in federal elections. There were also Supreme Court precedents to consider. In 1937 and in 1951 the Court had rejected the notion that poll taxes were de facto violations of the Fifteenth

Amendment. In fact, not every state that imposed a poll tax (Vermont, for example) used it to exclude black voters.[22]

On April 30 Mansfield and Dirksen offered a substitute for the Judiciary Committee bill. It became the Senate's pending business. Although very similar to the committee draft, the leadership proposal was different in two important respects. First, with Dirksen's reluctant approval, it eliminated the "escape clause" that would have released states from the bill's provisions when at least 60 percent of their adult residents were registered. Second, it dropped the poll tax ban. In its place, Mansfield and Dirksen inserted language authorizing the attorney general to initiate "forthwith" court proceedings against enforcement of any poll taxes used in a discriminatory fashion.[23]

The Senate's liberals generally favored the leadership bill. Michigan's Philip Hart, the only senator to have participated in the day-to-day negotiations between Justice officials and Dirksen's staff, argued that the bill "is stronger and better balanced than the original legislation sent to Congress. But it is our intention to improve it." That meant insisting on the poll tax ban, despite administration warnings that such an amendment might eventually render the bill unconstitutional. Even Humphrey could not reason with his former liberal colleagues; they remained determined to press for an amendment to restore the anti–poll tax provision.

Led by Massachusetts freshman Edward Kennedy and New York's Jacob Javits, the liberals believed that the Judiciary Committee's outright ban was indeed constitutional. "There is no purpose in leaving this issue to the Supreme Court rather than seeking an act of Congress," Kennedy said, "if, admittedly, the congressional finding is to the effect that we believe, in 1965, that poll taxes have the effect of discriminating against many citizens and depriving them of their constitutional rights."[24]

Dirksen was a notoriously flexible man. On the poll tax question, however, he refused to budge. He had already relinquished his "escape clause" provision during his negotiations over the leadership substitute. Now he declared flatly that if the bill contained a poll tax ban, "I would have difficulty going to any other senator and asking him to vote for cloture. Then it would be a fielder's choice. It would be every man for himself." Katzenbach shared Dirksen's views on the poll tax issue and knew he could not afford to lose the minority leader's crucial support. "If we had not opposed the flat ban," he later explained to Johnson, "I believe Senator Dirksen, Senators Aiken and Prouty of Vermont, and other Republicans would probably [have been] lost for cloture. With only 45 Democratic votes, we could not prevail without these Republicans." Injecting himself into the Senate debate for the first time, Johnson announced that, although he sympathized with Kennedy and Javits, he supported Mansfield and Dirksen. "I have always been opposed to the poll tax," the president said. "I am opposed to it now. [But] I have been advised by constitutional lawyers that we have a problem in repealing the poll tax by statute."[25]

Except on this one issue, the leadership commanded a solid majority of the Senate, as evidenced by the first vote on a southern amendment on May 6. North Carolina's Sam Ervin took direct aim at the heart of the bill— the automatic appointment of voting examiners—with an amendment to give federal district courts the power to authorize their appointment. The trigger provision, some southerners argued, invested too much power in the hands of the attorney general. "People shout about the powers of the Attorney General," Dirksen finally said in frustration. "I wish someone would tell me who in our form of government is to enforce the Constitution and the law if it is not the Attorney General. Will someone point to a law officer or to an administrator who is going to do it except the Attorney General?" The Senate rejected Ervin's amendment, 25–64. Only five southern Democrats, none from the Deep South, voted with the majority.[26]

The vote was significant. It was an overwhelming endorsement by the Senate of the bill's toughest and most important provision. Ervin's crushing defeat meant that the southerners would have almost no hope of making substantive inroads into the bill. The absurd arguments that some of them made against the bill only worsened their dilemma. "I make the statement," Strom Thurmond solemnly declared to the Senate on May 3, "that no one in South Carolina is unconstitutionally denied the right to vote. There have been no valid complaints by anyone." Thurmond then claimed that the bill would result in "a totalitarian state in which there will be despotism and tyranny." James Eastland saw similar consequences if Congress enacted the bill. "This bill is the worst kind of tyranny," he said on May 6. "This bill and the civil rights bill passed last year are the most far-reaching acts in the history of this country. These bills are designed to destroy the culture and the civilization of a great people . . . Some say that this bill furthers democracy. The cold facts are that we are watching the sun set on human liberty and individual freedom in this country."[27]

Little that the southerners could say, however, would hold much sway in the Senate in 1965. Although most of them would vote against Kennedy's poll tax amendment, the alternative was hardly more to their liking. After all, the issue was not whether Congress should completely abolish the poll tax. The only question was how it would do so. The irony of the southerners' situation—rejecting an outright ban in favor of an aggressive, congressionally mandated court challenge—did not escape Paul Douglas. On May 10 he wryly noted that many southerners "who would support the Mansfield-Dirksen position" were the same senators "who, in the past, have chided the Court for usurping legislative functions." These southerners, Douglas said, "are now saying that we should leave this legislative duty to the courts."[28]

On May 11, with all but five southern Democrats voting with the leadership, the Senate rejected the Kennedy-Javits poll tax amendment, 45–49. Although Martin Luther King decried the Senate vote as "an insult and blasphemy," the matter was not yet resolved. The provision was still alive in the House. The following day the House Judiciary Committee reported a voting rights bill that included a ban on the poll tax as a voting requirement. A week later Mansfield and Dirksen moved to mollify the liberals by sponsoring an amendment, declaring that poll taxes did infringe on the constitutional right to vote. While still hoping that the final bill would contain an outright ban, Kennedy accepted the amendment. He admitted that "it does strengthen the poll tax section of the bill [and] will make the task of the Attorney General that much easier in the suits he is directed to bring." The amendment passed, 69–20.

In the Senate, at least, the way seemed clear to final passage. Yet southerners remained intransigent. Although not quite engaged in a full-fledged filibuster, they were determined to press ahead with scores of amendments—and they would take their time doing it.[29]

On three occasions, Mansfield requested unanimous consent to speed up debate on the bill by imposing a one-hour time limit on each amendment. Each time Ellender objected. With seventy-one amendments pending or awaiting introduction, Dirksen became exasperated. "There are mountainous pieces of legislation still to come," he complained after the Senate rebuffed Mansfield's first request on May 12. His colleagues, he added, should begin preparing for a long session. In fact, he said sarcastically, senators "better start buying Christmas presents." By the time of his third request on May 19, Mansfield announced his intention to move forcefully to end debate. On May 21 he filed a cloture motion signed by thirty-eight senators. A vote was set for the following week.[30]

On May 25, after rejecting more than a dozen weakening amendments offered by Ervin and Stennis, the Senate held a decidedly anticlimactic vote. Senators imposed cloture by a 70–30 margin. The feckless filibuster was over. It was the twenty-fifth day of debate and only the second time in the Senate's history that a filibuster of a civil rights bill had been stopped. Both had occurred within a year's time. Once cloture was assured, the southern opposition collapsed. "The way things are," said Ervin, one of the few southerners who had shown any enthusiasm for the debate, "I don't think I could even get a denunciation of the Crucifixion in the bill." A recuperated Russell, who had returned to the Senate on May 24, summed up the sentiment among southerners when he told *Time*, "If there is anything I could do, I would do it. But I assume the die is cast." [31]

The next day, facing little opposition from the southerners, the Senate voted, 77–19, to send the voting rights bill to the House. Thirty Republicans joined forty-seven Democrats in support of the bill, but the South gave little ground. Three moderate southerners who had seemed ready to break with their diehard colleagues—Democratic whip Russell Long, former whip George Smathers, and J. William Fulbright—remained securely within the fold of the southern bloc. Only five marginal southerners— Ross Bass and Albert Gore of Tennessee, Fred Harris and Mike Monroney of Oklahoma, and Ralph Yarborough of Texas—supported the bill. [32]

The House bill varied only slightly from the Senate-passed version, but there was one important difference: Liberals on the Judiciary Committee managed to restore the poll tax ban that the Senate had narrowly rejected. Although the committee formally reported the bill to the House on June 1, Rules Committee chairman Howard Smith promptly applied the brakes and delayed consideration of the bill for a month. When the House debate finally began on July 6, two prominent Republicans—Minority Leader Gerald Ford and Judiciary member William McCulloch—sparked what journalist David Broder called "a major battle for political credit" among blacks and civil rights activists. Ford and McCulloch offered a much weaker substitute bill that did not ban the poll tax. It also replaced the automatic trigger for voting examiners with a milder provision authorizing examiners only after the attorney general received twenty-five or more complaints. Furthermore, the Republican measure did not ban literacy tests in states with low voting records, nor did it include the committee provision requiring a Washington court to approve all voting laws passed by the delinquent states. After House members rejected the Republican bill, 215–166, Johnson declared that the substitute "would have seriously damaged and diluted the guarantee of the right to vote for all Americans." In an angry response, Ford and McCulloch said that Johnson's past opposition to civil rights qualified him as a "Lyndon-come-lately" on the issue. "Lyndon Johnson," they said, "has traveled a crooked path" to become an advocate of civil rights legislation.[33]

While moderates and conservatives had found the Republican amendment an attractive alternative to the administration bill, other House members were in no mood for the kind of protracted, bruising battle with the Senate that the Ford-McCulloch substitute threatened. Near-unanimous Republican support for the substitute bill had seemed assured until a July 7 speech by Virginia Democrat William Tuck, who argued that civil rights opponents should support the Republican bill. Fearing that the public would interpret their votes for the Ford-McCulloch bill as a vote against voting rights, at least fifteen Republicans threw their support to the Judiciary Committee bill. On July 9 the House overwhelmingly passed the voting rights bill—including the poll tax ban—by a vote of 333–85. In all, thirty-six southerners (thirty-three Democrats and three Republicans) supported the bill, including a former opponent of civil rights, Majority Whip Hale Boggs of Louisiana.[34]

House and Senate conferees began their first meeting in an atmosphere of optimism. The only significant difference between the two bills was the poll tax question. But proposals by Dirksen and Celler to strengthen the Senate's poll tax provision did not satisfy House liberals. Meanwhile some House Republican conferees, hoping that the poll tax question would bring down the entire bill, were even less inclined to compromise. It was just this possibility of a bill-killing deadlock that brought liberals and civil rights leaders like Martin Luther King to their senses.

At first, King and his allies derided the Senate bill as a sellout because of its weaker poll tax provision. Johnson had little patience for what he regarded as unrealistic dogma that prevented responsible compromise. "Now the smart thing to do," he told King by phone on July 7, "would be to get some language that [will] . . . get this bill passed and start registering our people and get them ready to vote next year." Johnson challenged King to find another national leader more committed to civil rights. "I'm just fighting the battle the best that I can," he assured King. "I think I'll win it, but it's going to be close, and it's going to be dangerous."

Gradually, reality set in. King decided that disagreements over the poll tax—then employed to discriminate in only four states—were simply not serious enough to risk bringing down an otherwise strong and effective bill. "While I would have preferred that the bill eliminate the poll tax at this time—once and for all," King told Katzenbach on July 28, "it does contain an express declaration by Congress that the poll tax abridges and denies the right to vote." King expressed confidence that the Senate's poll tax provision, if vigorously pursued by the attorney general, "will operate finally to bury this iniquitous device." The next day, with King's statement in hand, Katzenbach persuaded House liberals to yield to the Senate. Senate conferees responded by dropping several provisions to which the liberals objected, including one that exempted from the bill those areas where the voting-age populations were less than 20 percent nonwhite.[35]

On August 3, House members passed the conference report on the Voting Rights Act of 1965 in a lopsided vote, 328–74. The following day, after a perfunctory debate, the Senate adopted the report, 79–18. This time, six southerners supported the bill: Smathers, Bass, Gore, Harris, Monroney, and Yarborough. Only one Republican, Strom Thurmond of South Carolina, voted no.[36]

Two days later, on August 6, a joyous Lyndon Johnson—"I would rarely see him happier," aide Joseph Califano later said—went to the Capitol to sign the Voting Rights Act of 1965.[37] Speaking in the Capitol Rotunda before the signing, Johnson seized the moment to deliver another memorable and emotional speech:

> Today is a triumph for freedom as huge as any victory that has ever been won on any battlefield. Yet to seize the meaning of this day, we must recall darker times.
>
> Three-and-a-half centuries ago the first Negroes arrived at Jamestown. They did not arrive in brave ships in search of a home for freedom. They did not mingle fear and joy, in brave expectation that in this new world anything would be possible to a man strong enough to reach for it.
>
> They came in darkness and they came in chains.
>
> And today we strike away the last major shackle of those fierce and ancient bonds. Today the Negro story and the American story fuse and blend . . .

This law covers many pages. But the heart of the act is plain. Wherever—by clear and objective standards—states and counties are using regulations, or laws, or tests to deny the right to vote, they will be struck down. If it is clear that state officials still intend to discriminate, the federal examiners will be sent in to register all eligible voters. When the prospect of discrimination is gone, the examiners will be immediately withdrawn.

Under this act, if any county anywhere in this nation does not want federal intervention it need only·open its polling places to all of its people.

Johnson told a national television audience and the assembled members of Congress that the attorney general would begin filing lawsuits the next morning. The Justice Department would challenge the constitutionality of Mississippi's poll tax and would officially begin to certify states where voting discrimination existed. By the following Monday, Johnson said, the Justice Department would begin designating "many counties where past experience clearly shows that federal action is necessary and required. And by Tuesday morning, trained federal examiners will be at work registering eligible men and women in ten to fifteen counties." On that day, he said, the Justice Department would file poll tax suits in Texas, Alabama, and Virginia.

And I pledge you that we will not delay or we will not hesitate or we will not turn aside, until Americans of every race and color and origin in this country have the same right as all others to share in the process of democracy.

But these new rights carried responsibilities, Johnson said:

Presidents and Congresses, laws and lawsuits can open the doors of the polling places, and open the doors to the wondrous rewards which await the wise use of the ballot.

But only the individual Negro, and all others who have been denied the right to vote, can really walk through those doors and can use that right and can transform the vote into an instrument of justice and fulfillment.

So, let me now say to every Negro in this country: You must register. You must vote. You must learn, so your choice advances your interest and the interest of our beloved nation. Your future, and your children's future, depend on it, and I don't believe that you are going to let them down.

Johnson directed his closing words to the nation at large:

The central fact of American civilization—one so hard for others to understand—is that freedom and justice and the dignity of man are not just words to us. We believe in them. Under all the growth and the tumult and abundance, we believe. And so, as long as some among us are oppressed—and we are part of that oppression—it must blunt our faith and sap the strength of our high purpose.

Thus, this is a victory for the freedom of the American Negro. But it is also a victory for the freedom of the American nation. And every family—across this great, entire searching land—will live stronger in liberty, will live more splendid in expectation, and will be prouder to be American because of the act that you have passed that I will sign today.[38]

19

DISILLUSIONMENT AND DEFEAT

The easy part was over. Congress had finally enacted powerful legislation to guarantee the civil and voting rights of all black Americans. Enforcing those new rights would be difficult, but not as daunting as the task of creating and nurturing an economic and social environment in which black citizens could achieve the American Dream of economic independence and prosperity.

Johnson, who had long stressed the importance of economic rights for blacks, instinctively understood this. In June, even before the voting rights bill became law, he had ordered his aides to begin planning a White House conference on civil rights—"To Fulfill These Rights"—for the following November. In a June speech at Howard University, Johnson announced plans for the conference and demonstrated the depth of his understanding of the nation's black underclass. There was, he said, "another nation" of blacks, "deprived of freedom, crippled by hatred, the door of opportunity closed to hope." Johnson declared that

> Negroes are trapped—as many whites are trapped—in inherited, gateless poverty. They lack training and skills. They are shut in slums, without decent medical care. Private and public poverty combine to cripple their capacities . . .
>
> Negro poverty is not white poverty. Many of its causes and many of its cures are the same. But there are differences—deep, corrosive, obstinate differences—radiating painful roots into the community, and into the family, and the nature of the individual.
>
> These differences are not racial differences. They are solely and simply the consequences of ancient brutality, past injustice, and present prejudice. They are anguishing to observe.

Most significant to Johnson was "the breakdown of the Negro family structure" and its dire consequences:

For this, most of all, white America must accept responsibility. It flows from centuries of oppression and persecution of the Negro man. It flows from the long years of degradation and discrimination, which have attacked his dignity and assaulted his ability to provide for his family.

This, too, is not pleasant to look upon. But it must be faced by those whose serious intent is to improve the life of all Americans.

Only a minority—less than half—of all Negro children reach the age of eighteen having lived all their lives with both of their parents . . . The family is the cornerstone of our society. More than any other force it shapes the attitude, the hopes, the ambitions, and the values of the child. And when the family collapses, it is the children that are usually damaged. When it happens on a massive scale, the community itself is crippled.[1]

Only five days after Johnson signed the Voting Rights Act, the violent, angry voice of the "other nation" of blacks was heard in Los Angeles. Six days of rioting in the city's Watts district resulted in 34 deaths, more than 856 injuries, 3,100 arrests, and $200 million in property damage. It took 15,400 California National Guardsmen and 1,000 law enforcement officers to restore peace. When the mayhem ended, entire city blocks were smoldering. An incredulous German reporter observed that the area resembled his native land "during the last months of World War II." The Watts riots were the worst racial disorder in American history. Meanwhile, in Chicago, two days of racial unrest resulted in 80 injuries and 123 arrests.[2]

A minor police incident had sparked the Watts violence, but its underlying causes ran as deep as the geologic faults that traversed the southern California landscape. "The people don't feel so bad about what happened," one rioter later explained. "They had nothing to lose. They don't have jobs, decent homes. What else could they do?" As a heckler shouted at Martin Luther King, who came to inspect the riot's aftermath: "I had a dream, I had a dream—hell, we don't need no damn dreams. We want jobs."[3]

At first Johnson reacted tentatively. "We must not let anger drown understanding," he pleaded. A frustrated public, however, demanded law and order. As long as helpless southern blacks were the victims of brutal white violence, they would enjoy public sympathy. Now that the angry demands of black rioters were drowning out the peaceful pleas of black protesters, widespread public support for civil rights was in jeopardy. In a matter of days, Johnson changed his tune. "Neither old wrongs nor new fears can ever justify arson or murder," he said in a speech. "A rioter with a Molotov cocktail in his hands is not fighting for civil rights any more than a Klansman with a sheet on his back and a mask on his face." Both, Johnson said, were "lawbreakers." Even as he condemned the violence, Johnson remained hopeful that his vision of a just American society would prevail. "In twenty fields or more, we have passed—and we will pass—far-reaching programs . . . that are rich in hope and that will lead us to a better day." Pounding the lectern, Johnson cried, "And we shall overcome, and I am enlisted for the duration." [4]

In 1964 and 1965, Johnson had easily mustered a broad, bipartisan consensus to pass laws attacking what Harry McPherson called "observable cruelties"—voting and job discrimination and denied access to public facilities and accommodations. By 1965, however, the civil rights movement that Johnson had known had turned into something more volatile and dangerous. As McPherson told Johnson in June 1965, black leaders showed "more interest in discovering fresh fields for conquest than in making use of the franchise." Civil rights leaders marched "victoriously" out of the South toward new battlegrounds—the poverty-stricken tinderboxes that were the ghettos of large northern cities. [5]

The new civil rights movement trained its eye on America's largely unobservable cruelties: poverty, joblessness, inadequate education, and poor nutrition and health care. Martin Luther King, still a giant of the movement, was challenged on his left flank by more militant leaders such as Malcolm X (assassinated in early 1965), Elijah Muhammad, Floyd McKissick, and Stokely Carmichael. Each was better attuned than King to the frustrations and rage of young urban blacks. The ascendancy of these new leaders, coupled with the success of the civil rights and voting rights acts, presented King and his movement with what one civil rights historian termed "the crisis of victory." King's movement, Adam Fairclough observed, "had no program or plan for translating the notional equality of the law into the social actuality of shared wealth and power." [6]

The result was that the almost magical convergence of public support and congressional will on civil rights would never be so easily duplicated. Urban riots and growing black militancy began to chill the hearts of many northern whites, once so sympathetic to the plight of southern blacks. A Gallup poll in late 1966 showed that more than half of white Americans believed that President Johnson was moving too quickly on racial integration. By 1966 a civil rights bill that prohibited racial discrimination in the sale and rental of private housing ran into trouble in the Senate after passing the House. Erstwhile civil rights supporter Everett Dirksen, insisting that the housing provision was an unconstitutional invasion of private property rights, led the Senate opposition to the bill. Twice failing to muster enough votes to break cloture, the Senate adjourned without acting on the legislation—just one year after the overwhelming passage of the Voting Rights Act. Watts and other racial unrest, McPherson later suggested, had done the damage by "justifying the worst feelings of the racists in Congress and in the press."

In the South, meanwhile, the white backlash that Johnson and others had predicted began to emerge with a vengeance. Although blacks registered in record numbers and more than 150 now held elective office, the massive registration of new white voters offset much of the blacks' anticipated voting strength. Alabama's archsegregationist governor, George Wallace, was building a broad, loyal following beyond the South. As his strength in several primaries in 1964 had proved, many northern blue-collar whites shared Wallace's vehement opposition to civil rights. In Congress, meanwhile, the midterm elections of 1966 hit the Democratic party hard. The party lost forty-seven seats in the House and four in the Senate.[7]

One Democratic victim was Paul Douglas. His distinguished Senate career ended in defeat at the hands of his youthful Republican challenger, millionaire businessman Charles Percy. Exploiting Douglas's principled support of open housing and other civil rights legislation, Percy appealed to white voters who were shocked by racial violence and fearful that their neighborhoods would be invaded and degraded by swarms of black tenants and homeowners. Refusing to modify his position on fair housing, Douglas became the only incumbent senator defeated in 1966.[8]

Despite the growing complexity and volatility of the nation's racial problems, Johnson remained persuaded that he could improve American life with an aggressive legislative agenda. "I don't think there was ever a president that was more of an activist than Johnson," Congressman Emanuel Celler declared shortly after Johnson left the White House in 1969. Like many other members of Congress, Celler believed that the nation had undergone a unique and exhausting experience during Johnson's five-year presidency. "I don't think there was any president that could have driven—I used that word advisedly—driven the Congress as hard as he did."[9]

The legislative record of Johnson's early presidency was remarkable: Johnson presented the Eighty-ninth Congress (1965–66) with 200 legislative proposals. Congress enacted an incredible 181, including laws on civil rights, voting rights, Medicare, aid to education, aid to Appalachia, clean air, water pollution control, aid to small businesses, a military pay increase, community health services, child nutrition, rent supplements, highway safety, mine safety, tire safety, and a minimum wage increase. "He would lie, beg, cheat, steal a little, threaten, intimidate," *Time* correspondent Hugh Sidey recalled. "But he never lost sight of that ultimate goal, his idea of the Great Society."[10]

In the months after Johnson signed the Voting Rights Act, the administration moved decisively to enforce the law. By early 1966, federal examiners had registered more than 100,000 blacks in Alabama, Louisiana, Mississippi, and South Carolina. More than 200,000 new voters were registered in other states and districts covered by the act. In three separate decisions in 1966, the Supreme Court rejected South Carolina's constitutional challenge of the bill's formula for triggering voting examiners; prohibited all uses of the poll tax; and affirmed the bill's provision that guaranteed the vote to non-English-speaking citizens educated in schools under the American flag.[11]

Johnson also labored to place blacks in important positions in the judiciary and in his administration. His most prominent appointment came in 1967, when he nominated Thurgood Marshall, the former NAACP lawyer and U.S. solicitor general, as an associate justice of the Supreme Court. In all, Johnson appointed eighteen blacks to the federal bench. Black appointees to his administration included Clifford Alexander, White House deputy counsel and later chairman of the Equal Employment Opportunity Commission; Robert Weaver, secretary of Housing and Urban Development; Andrew Brimmer, assistant secretary of Commerce and member of the board of governors of the Federal Reserve System; Patricia Harris, ambassador to Luxembourg; Carl Rowan, director of the United States Information Agency; and Roger Wilkins, director of the Community Relations Service.

The ease with which the president enforced the Voting Rights Act and appointed blacks to top government positions was not always replicated in the larger civil rights arena. The daunting task of implementing and enforcing the myriad provisions of the Civil Rights Act of 1964 soon became an unmanageable burden. Unfortunately for Hubert Humphrey, the tangled enforcement of civil rights laws would nearly destroy his effectiveness as vice president. Worse, it almost ruined his sixteen-year friendship with Johnson.[12]

Humphrey believed that he would establish a new standard of usefulness and influence for the vice presidency. Johnson, after all, could not help recalling the misery and isolation he himself had endured under Kennedy. He knew how a vice president's valuable talents could be, and often were, wasted. Surely, Humphrey thought, Johnson would work to create a refreshingly different relationship with his vice president.[13]

In the early days of the administration, at least, Humphrey's assumption proved correct. At Johnson's request, Humphrey examined the federal government's civil rights enforcement efforts and advised the president to consolidate them under one umbrella. Johnson agreed. In February the president signed an executive order creating a new White House entity, the President's Council on Equal Opportunity. The vice president would chair the council and coordinate the administration's civil rights and antidiscrimination policies.[14]

Just as Humphrey appeared to have secured a vital role on Johnson's team, he fumbled the ball. In February 1965 he lost Johnson's confidence in an embarrassing disagreement over the president's decision to launch a sustained bombing of military targets in North Vietnam after Viet Cong forces assaulted a U.S. military compound, killing nine Americans and wounding seventy-six others. As Johnson prepared to drastically escalate U.S. involvement in the Southeast Asian conflict, he convened the National Security Council to discuss the decision. Believing he had the support of Secretary of State Dean Rusk and Secretary of Defense Robert McNamara, Humphrey spoke up. He opposed escalating the war. And he strongly urged Johnson to delay his decision. Rusk and McNamara, however, failed to voice their support of the vice president. Not only was Humphrey isolated in his opposition to the president's decision, but he had broken with Johnson in the presence of others. Johnson was furious with what he believed to be Humphrey's open betrayal. The consequences were severe. "He was frozen out," recalled aide Ted Van Dyk, "really sent to purgatory for a full year." While he could not prohibit Humphrey from attending National Security Council meetings, Johnson began to exclude him from other informal gatherings where he made the most important foreign policy decisions.[15]

Although Humphrey was demoralized, at least he had civil rights responsibilities—thus far, the central issue of the Johnson administration—to occupy his time. Yet in August, doubting Humphrey's determination to forcefully implement the 1964 law, Johnson cruelly stripped Humphrey of those responsibilities. Johnson "knew he had the guts, the toughness, and ability to endure the pain that a civil rights revolution would inflict," domestic policy adviser Joseph Califano explained, but the president "wasn't sure that Humphrey did." Attorney General Katzenbach believed, however, that Johnson's motivation was simply an outgrowth of his personality. "He wanted to get all the credit himself," Katzenbach said later.[16]

Almost before Humphrey knew what had happened, Johnson summarily abolished the two committees that Humphrey chaired—the Committee on Equal Employment and the Council on Equal Opportunity. Johnson transferred responsibility for enforcing the prohibition of discrimination in federally funded programs to the Justice Department. He shifted other enforcement activities to appropriate departments or agencies. To the press and the public, the whole thing was Humphrey's idea. Johnson even instructed Califano to draft a memorandum recommending the changes— and ordered him to obtain Humphrey's reluctant signature. "Johnson was really a sadist," said Humphrey's friend Edgar Berman, adding that "it was a little masochistic of Humphrey to take this." Had Humphrey enjoyed a better relationship with Johnson at the time, he might have averted what Califano viewed as a castration. Instead, aide John Stewart said, "Humphrey was left standing around looking like a damn fool." Van Dyk and Katzenbach maintained that Humphrey could have successfully challenged Johnson's decision but lacked the courage or fortitude. "Humphrey, fatally, never stood up to him," Van Dyk said.[17]

Humphrey endured other affronts. Johnson fumed whenever Humphrey received favorable press coverage. Johnson repeatedly refused Humphrey's requests to take reporters with him when he traveled. He insisted on personally approving the manifest of Humphrey's plane before each trip. Johnson blamed most leaks from the White House on Humphrey. "That goddam Humphrey," Johnson protested to his staff, "he'll say anything to anybody." Van Dyk and others even suspected that Johnson tapped Humphrey's office phones, a consequence of the president's doubts about Humphrey's discretion. "We were never fully trusted," Van Dyk said.[18]

Humphrey never complained to Johnson over these and other indignities. "Humphrey found it very difficult to stand up and really let fly his opinions, if they were opposed to those of Johnson," Harry McPherson observed. "In a nose-to-nose encounter, he was simply outmatched." But, as McPherson quickly added, "so was everybody else, for that matter. Very few men in our time have been able to stand up and face down Lyndon Johnson." Walter Heller, a friend of Humphrey and chairman of Johnson's Council of Economic Advisors, blanched at Johnson's casual abuse of Humphrey. "LBJ treated him like a staff sergeant might treat a private. I was just appalled. I was embarrassed."[19]

Humphrey's banishment from the center of civil rights enforcement did not, in itself, hinder the effective administration of the Civil Rights Act's fair employment provisions. It can be argued that Humphrey—a poor administrator served by a weak staff—could never have effectively coordinated and directed the many-faceted aspects of civil rights that Johnson initially placed at his command. Yet the subsequent enforcement arrangement devised by Johnson, Califano, and other White House and Justice Department officials was far from exemplary. Civil rights enforcement was disassembled like an automobile engine; its interlocking parts were distributed among various government departments and commissions. For example, the White House gave responsibility for federal employment practices to the Civil Service Commission but then handed the oversight of contract compliance to the Labor Department. Meanwhile, the President's Committee for Equal Opportunity in Housing, the Community Relations Service, and the U.S. Civil Rights Commission all fell into various states of disuse or outright irrelevance.[20]

Almost a year after passage of the Civil Rights Act, Johnson—now preoccupied with the Vietnam War, foreign affairs, and various domestic issues—had not named a chairman for the Equal Opportunity Employment Commission. The commission foundered before it set sail. Johnson's eventual nominee, Franklin D. Roosevelt Jr., was a monumental disappointment. Uninterested and ineffectual, Roosevelt devoted more time to yachting than to the important business of enforcing the nation's fair employment laws. A painfully long search for his successor followed his resignation in the spring of 1966. By the end of its first year, an ineffective, overworked, and underfunded EEOC had received almost nine thousand fair employment complaints and strained under the weight of a six-month backlog of three thousand cases.[21]

In 1966 Johnson finally brought Humphrey out of the White House deep freeze and bestowed on him the dubious honor of being lead spokesman for the administration's controversial Vietnam policy. To biographer Carl Solberg, the period was "the most startling chapter in Humphrey's life." In February, on a fourteen-day trip to nine Asian countries, including South Vietnam, Humphrey abruptly changed his view of the war and overcame his previous doubts about U.S. involvement. By the time he returned to the warmth of Johnson's embrace, Humphrey had become one of the loudest, most enthusiastic supporters of the president's war policies.[22]

Having discovered that the path to Johnson's favor went through Vietnam, Humphrey went overboard in his support of the war. "We went through almost a full year from mid '66 to mid '67 in which he would make the most outrageous, off-the-cuff statements," said Van Dyk. "It was almost as if we were going to stop the yellow communist horde in San Francisco." Suddenly Humphrey found himself more in agreement with belligerents such as Russell Long, Strom Thurmond, and Richard Russell than with his old liberal allies. His abrupt emergence as a hawk shocked many of his friends. "I never expected," Oregon's Wayne Morse remarked, "my vice president to make this plea for war." A group of liberal writers declared that Humphrey had "betrayed the liberal movement."[23]

As much as Vietnam reinvigorated Humphrey as vice president, it eventually destroyed Johnson's effectiveness as president. Increasingly distracted by America's deadly descent into the morass of Southeast Asia, Johnson left much of his domestic program open to attacks by conservatives, many of whom—ironically—strongly supported his Vietnam policy. By the end of 1968, conservatives in Congress would scale back Johnson's poverty, rent supplement, and model cities programs and impose stringent spending restraints on much of the budget's domestic side.[24]

In March 1968, with the Vietnam War dividing the nation and steadily eroding the president's popularity, Johnson abruptly announced that he would not seek reelection. Johnson hoped that his decision would begin a healing process for the nation. Four days later an assassin's bullet killed Martin Luther King, who had flown to Memphis to support a labor strike by the city's sanitation workers. King's death touched off an enormous wave of riots in at least 125 cities. The worst was in Washington, D.C., where ten people died in violence sparked by the death of America's best-known proponent of nonviolence.

Humphrey announced for the Democratic nomination on April 27, declaring that his candidacy would embody "the politics of happiness, the politics of purpose, and the politics of joy." Critics, and even a few supporters, ridiculed that ebullient, cheery rhetoric at a time when war, violent protest, and assassination were tearing the nation apart. But joy and optimism remained the center of Humphrey's political philosophy, even though the grueling campaign would test his temperament as never before.[25]

In June, Humphrey became the leading, perhaps the presumptive, nominee after Robert Kennedy, celebrating victory in the California primary, was assassinated at the Ambassador Hotel in Los Angeles. With Kennedy's death, prominent liberals and labor leaders gravitated toward Humphrey with one important reservation—many Americans still viewed him as the most outspoken advocate of Johnson's Vietnam war policy. Although he eventually captured the nomination at a riot-plagued convention in Chicago, Humphrey did little to give voters an idea of how his views on the unpopular war differed from Johnson's. He offered only an occasional flimsy promise of future independence from his president. Ultimately, Vietnam was a heavy burden for Humphrey's campaign to bear. Republican nominee Richard Nixon narrowly won the presidency over Humphrey and independent George Wallace.[26]

Only four years earlier, Johnson had won in the largest landslide in presidential history. Now the American electorate turned its back on his would-be successor. Fifty-seven percent of voters cast ballots for Nixon or Wallace. Viewed in that light, the election was a deafening repudiation of Lyndon Johnson's administration. The dissolution of the solid Democratic South—which had begun in 1948 after Humphrey's civil rights platform plank sent many southerners into the arms of Strom Thurmond and the Dixiecrats—was now complete. How ironic that Humphrey, the ideological and legislative father of the Civil Rights Act of 1964, would fall victim to the very forces that he had unleashed twenty years earlier. Analyzing the returns in the South with astonishing prescience, journalist Theodore White saw nothing but doom and despair for the Democrats. "If the trend line continues, the Democratic Party may disappear as a national party which can rouse loyalties in every section of the nation," White wrote in *The Making of the President, 1968.* "If the Democrats shrink to a ghetto vote in the South, they could become a party dominated by Northern labor unions, big-city minority blocs, and ideologues who control the new campus proletariat."[27]

On election night, at least, Humphrey's "politics of joy" became the politics of despair. "Edgar," he said to his close friend Edgar Berman in the early morning hours of November 6, "I let so many people down." Now, he confessed, he understood how two-time Democratic nominee Adlai Stevenson must have suffered. "But, Jesus," he sighed, "at least Stevenson lost to Eisenhower. I lost to Nixon."[28]

Over the objections of a weakened southern bloc, Congress enacted the Civil Rights Act of 1968 in April. It was, Russell said, "another in a long line of legislation designed to apply almost exclusively to the South." Although the Senate had refused to end a southern-led filibuster in three successive votes in February and March, a compromise between liberals and Republican leader Dirksen led to a narrow vote for cloture on March 4.

The most important section of the bill, and the major obstacle for southern conservatives, was its open housing provision. When the law was fully in effect by 1970, the federal government would prohibit discrimination in the sale or rental of about 80 percent of all housing units. Only private homeowners who sold their dwellings without the services of a real estate agent were exempted from the law. The act also included criminal penalties for those who injured or interfered with someone exercising a specified civil right: voting, jury duty, participation in a government program, school or college attendance, or the enjoyment of a public accommodation. The bill's major nod to southern conservatives, sponsored by Thurmond, was its anti-rioting provisions, which imposed criminal penalties for those who used interstate commerce, including the telephone, to incite or participate in a riot. Throughout the debate, Russell was only a minor figure. North Carolina's Sam Ervin led the southern opposition by offering an unsuccessful substitute amendment to the housing provision.

Still opposed to civil rights legislation, the seventy-year-old Russell had lost his enthusiasm for the fight. It was futile, he believed, to wage another bruising, all-out battle against the bill's almost-inevitable passage. He understood that most Republicans, eager to recapture the White House in the fall election, would support whatever compromise Minority Leader Dirksen might negotiate with the liberals. Once that compromise was reached, the small band of southerners could do little beyond advancing a handful of anti-rioting amendments.[29]

For Russell, still chairman of the Armed Services Committee, the most pressing issue in his world became Johnson's disastrous Vietnam war policy. Since 1954 Russell had strenuously opposed U.S. involvement in the former French Indo-China, convinced "that we would be bogged down in the jungle fighting the Chinese in their kind of war for the next 25 years."

Once the war was on, Russell supported his president—although he urged Johnson to abandon his gradual approach to the conflict in favor of a massive military effort aimed at a quick resolution.[30]

Russell delivered that advice to Johnson repeatedly: Win the war or get out! But his influence with the president was outweighed by that of Johnson's military advisers, chiefly Defense Secretary Robert McNamara. "I know from experience," Russell wrote, "that when my advice is in conflict with McNamara's, it is no longer considered." To one of his sisters, Russell complained that Johnson "won't pay any attention to me." Unable to affect the outcome of the conflict, Russell—as de facto chairman of the Appropriations Committee—devoted himself to ensuring the war's proper funding. In time Russell's disillusionment over Johnson's embrace of civil rights only exacerbated his disgust over Johnson's war policies. According to aides, friends, and family, Russell became increasingly disenchanted with his old friend and protégé throughout the 1960s. At the heart of that disappointment was Johnson's passionate embrace of civil rights, which culminated in 1965 when Johnson proclaimed, "We shall overcome!"

Russell told aides that Johnson had "stultified his convictions" on civil rights. Had he believed that Johnson's support for civil rights was the result of a genuine change of heart, he might have accepted the transformation. But, as Russell's old friend Luke Austin recalled, Russell maintained that "Johnson did this for political gain." (Russell must have forgotten that he helped Johnson enact the Civil Rights Act of 1957 precisely for the political purpose of helping his protégé win the Democratic presidential nomination.) Despite their many years of friendship, civil rights became a stumbling block in their relationship. Russell never told Johnson of his disenchantment. There was never so much as an argument over civil rights. Instead, Russell's affection for Johnson was gradually supplanted by his deep disappointment over the president's approach to civil rights, the Great Society, and the Vietnam War. Nonetheless, Johnson apparently perceived Russell's disillusionment. According to Sam Ervin, Johnson once confessed to Russell, "I know I have been a disappointment to you." Russell, said Ervin, "didn't know what to say."[31]

Russell's discontent manifested itself in the manner he began withdrawing from Johnson toward the end of his presidency. Russell grew to dread his private visits with the president, complaining to aides that during private meetings Johnson often cried. "He just couldn't stand to be subjected to that kind of emotionalism," his press secretary, Powell Moore, recalled.

When he could not avoid an Oval Office meeting with Johnson, Russell often invited a colleague, usually John Stennis, to accompany him.[32]

Angered by something Johnson did or said, or disgusted with Johnson's refusal to heed his advice, Russell sometimes refused to speak to his old friend. "There were times when he just wouldn't take phone calls from Johnson," Proctor Jones recalled, explaining that Russell instructed his receptionist to tell the White House that he was out of his office.

Nothing, however, hastened the disintegration of Russell's friendship with Johnson more than a personal dispute that erupted in February 1968. The rift began innocently when Russell recommended an old family friend, Alexander Lawrence of Savannah, for nomination to the federal bench from Georgia's Southern District. The sixty-two-year-old Lawrence had sound professional credentials. A practicing lawyer for thirty-seven years, he was the former president of the Georgia Bar Association, current president of the Georgia Historical Society, and author of several books. But Lawrence's most useful credential was his friendship with Russell—or so it seemed.[33]

Trouble developed shortly after Russell sent his recommendation to Johnson. A speech that Lawrence had delivered to a women's group in November 1958 quickly returned to haunt him. In that speech, which had so impressed Russell that he later inserted it into the *Congressional Record*, Lawrence attacked the justices of the Supreme Court as threats to liberty for usurping their constitutional authority in school desegregation and other cases. Black and white civil rights activists in Georgia seized upon the speech as evidence of Lawrence's unwillingness to uphold the Constitution in civil rights cases. Said two Georgia NAACP officials in early April, "Mr. Lawrence clearly demonstrated his inability to accept or interpret the Constitution and Supreme Court decisions which are the law of the land." They urged Russell not to "unleash Mr. Lawrence on South Georgia." Concerned that the opposition to Lawrence might influence Attorney General Ramsey Clark's recommendation, Russell went directly to Johnson on May 4. He urged the president to send the nomination promptly to the Senate.[34]

The situation placed Johnson in a quandary. He had given his attorney general wide latitude in the nomination process; moreover, he did not wish to offend civil rights groups by nominating someone who might undermine the enforcement of civil rights laws in Georgia. "The president didn't want to cause any problem," recalled White House aide Larry Temple, "but he also valued the judgment and friendship of Senator Russell." According to Temple, Johnson told Clark, "If we come to the final conclusion that we can't appoint him, then we'll come to that conclusion. We'll cross that bridge. But if there's any way at all that we can posture this man in a way that he can be appointed without hampering the judiciary, without doing anything to undermine the judiciary, I want to do it. I want to appoint this man." Doubtful that Lawrence's segregationist reputation could be rehabilitated, Clark continued his investigation. Johnson, meanwhile, quietly met with the chairman of the American Bar Association committee that reviewed judicial nominees. He made an unusual request, asking the chairman to personally investigate Lawrence's qualifications.[35]

On May 11 Russell's fears were realized. Clark informed him that he would oppose Lawrence's nomination. "To say that I was surprised, distressed and disappointed when the Attorney General told me he would not recommend Mr. Lawrence is expressing it mildly," Russell wrote in a four-page letter to Johnson on May 20. Lawrence was no racist, Russell argued. In fact, he said, Lawrence had vigorously attacked the Ku Klux Klan in 1950 when he headed the Georgia Bar Association. The opposition to Lawrence, Russell explained, came from "the extreme left." Then Russell made a rare personal appeal: Rejecting Lawrence "would, of course, be extremely embarrassing to me" because the recommendation "has been publicized and discussed over the entire state." As Russell reminded Johnson, "I have never made a personal appeal to you for a presidential appointment since you have occupied the exalted position of president of the United States." Now he was. He awaited Johnson's decision.[36]

By July, after a month of inaction on the nomination, Russell's hope turned to disgust. Clark's position, Russell wrote his friend Judge Griffin Bell of the Fifth Circuit Court of Appeals, "is unreasonable to the point of being vicious." As for the president, Russell said, "I have never been as disappointed in a man as I am in Johnson for being frightened by the prospect" of opposition from Georgia's civil rights activists. By now the controversy over Lawrence threatened not only Russell's friendship with Johnson, but the future of Johnson's two nominees to the Supreme Court.[37]

On June 13 Earl Warren resigned as chief justice. Johnson quickly nominated a reliable liberal, his old friend Associate Justice Abe Fortas. He submitted the name of another longtime friend to fill the vacancy created by the elevation of Fortas—Homer Thornberry, a judge on the Fifth Circuit Court of Appeals and a former Texas congressman. Anticipating a certain amount of southern and conservative opposition to Fortas, Johnson obtained what he thought were commitments of support from Russell and Everett Dirksen.

But now Russell had second thoughts about his commitment to Johnson. Could it be, Russell wondered, that Johnson was holding up the Lawrence nomination as a form of blackmail to ensure his support for Fortas and Thornberry? On July 1 Russell sent Johnson an unusually spiteful letter reminding him that his recommendation of Lawrence was now more than four and a half months old. "From our conversations," Russell said, he was convinced that despite the attorney general's opposition, "you would name Mr. Lawrence." Then he added:

> To be perfectly frank, even after so many years in the Senate, I was so naïve I had not even suspected that this man's nomination was being withheld from the Senate due to the changes expected on the Supreme Court of the United States until after you sent in the nominations of Fortas and Thornberry while still holding the recommendations for the nomination of Mr. Lawrence either in your office or in the Department of Justice.
>
> Whether it is intended or not, this places me in the position where, if I support your nominees for the Supreme Court, it will appear that I have done so out of my fears that you would not nominate Mr. Lawrence.

Johnson, he suggested, was treating him "as a child or a patronage-seeking ward heeler." He now advised Johnson "that in view of the long delay in handling and the juggling of this nomination, I consider myself released from any statements that I have made to you" regarding the Supreme Court nominations. Furthermore, Russell said, "you are at liberty to deal with the recommendations as to Mr. Lawrence in any way you see fit." Russell ended the three-page letter with the overwrought assertion that Lawrence and his family "have already been humiliated beyond what decent and honorable people should be required to bear at the hands of a motley collection of fanatics, mystics and publicity seekers." Before he mailed the letter, Russell summoned his Georgia colleague, Herman Talmadge, to his office. "He read me a hell of a mean letter," recalled Talmadge, who volunteered to cosign it. Although Russell declined his offer, Talmadge assured him, "Well, it will get results."[38]

As expected, the letter shocked Johnson. Outraged, he immediately phoned Clark. "I think your foot dragging on this has destroyed one of the great friendships I've had with one of the great men that has ever served this country," he said, adding, "Ramsey, I want to go ahead and nominate him." Strangely, Johnson did not immediately contact Russell. Instead he dispatched his assistant Tom Johnson, a Georgia native whom Russell admired. Tom Johnson reported that Russell believed the president was holding Lawrence until Russell announced his support of Fortas and Thornberry. Several days later, Johnson finally phoned Russell.

"Dick," Johnson began, "I have your letter here in my hand. I don't think this letter reflects creditably upon you as a statesman. I don't think it reflects very well on me as your president. I don't think it reflects very well on our long friendship." Johnson said he would not keep the letter in his files but would return it to Russell. "I hope you destroy it." Furthermore, Johnson said, there was never a connection between the Supreme Court nominees and the Lawrence nomination. Johnson added that while he would nominate Lawrence, "it's not a quid pro quo. It wasn't when I first told you I was going to. It isn't now, and it isn't going to be." Regarding the Fortas nomination, Johnson advised, "You do whatever you want to on that, and I know it'll be the right decision."

Several weeks later, after the American Bar Association determined that Lawrence was highly qualified for the position, the White House forwarded his name to the Senate, which later confirmed him. Meanwhile, the Fortas nomination fell on hard times. Hit with accusations of financial impropriety, Fortas saw his southern and Republican support evaporate. On September 26 Russell wrote to tell Johnson that "with deep regret" he would not support Fortas. In October, facing certain defeat in the Senate, Fortas withdrew his nomination.[39]

From Russell's standpoint, the Lawrence incident destroyed his friendship with Johnson. Later that year, as Johnson prepared to leave the White House, Russell refused to join dozens of colleagues who paid tribute to the president. Only when urged by his staff did he approve a routine, lifeless statement about his old friend. About that time, Russell even refused to grant an interview to historians who were gathering reminiscences of Johnson for an ambitious oral history project sponsored by the Johnson presidential library.

Almost twenty years of friendship between two of America's most influential and talented public servants was lost in a cloud of mistrust and misunderstanding. On Johnson's part, vacillation and miscommunication were at fault. As for Russell, his pride, racial insensitivity, and an overactive imagination allowed a routine dispute to balloon to enormous proportions. For another two and a half years, until Russell's death in January 1971, Johnson tried to rebuild the remnants of their relationship. Russell rebuffed each of Johnson's attempts at reconciliation.[40]

Shortly before Johnson left town in January 1969, he traveled to Capitol Hill one last time to deliver his State of the Union address. He took a moment in the speech to praise Russell, who had just been elected president pro tempore of the Senate. He had "avoided many pitfalls," Johnson told Congress, by following Russell's "good common sense counsel." Although Russell was flattered, he refused to acknowledge Johnson's gesture. The kind remark, it seemed, had done nothing to repair their shattered friendship. As the two men parted, Russell's heart remained colder than the January night air. Their paths would never cross again.[41]

Three men—their lives inextricably intertwined over several decades by politics, friendship, and civil rights—now shared something else in common. As they approached the ends of their extraordinary political careers, each endured the pain of rejection and defeat.

Russell, his thirty-five-year fight against civil rights at an end, mourned the passing of his beloved Old South and the disappearance of the Democratic party as he knew it. Humphrey's immense satisfaction with the passage of legislation he had championed for so long was transcended by the bitter sting of his defeat at Richard Nixon's hands. And Johnson, although largely responsible for the most important social legislation of the century, left the White House in dishonor—not in the bright sunshine of human rights, but under the dark clouds of a disastrous foreign war.

Notes

INTRODUCTION

1. *Inaugural Addresses of the Presidents of the United States: From George Washington to George W. Bush* (Washington, D.C.: U.S. Government Printing Office), 101–10.

1. WE HAVE JUST STARTED OUR WORK

1. Crowe, *Getting Away with Murder*, 35–36, 50–64; Whitfield, *A Death in the Delta*, 16–17; Till-Mobley, *Death of Innocence*, 101; "The Shocking Story of Approved Killing in Mississippi," *Look*, 1/24/56.

2. *Look*, 1/24/56; Whitfield, *A Death in the Delta*, 15–23; www.wikipedia.org (Emmett Till).

3. Crowe, *Getting Away with Murder*, 63; Till-Mobley, *Death of Innocence*, 138–39.

4. Till-Mobley, *Death of Innocence*, 141. For an excellent analysis of the national media's coverage of the Till case and the Montgomery, Alabama, bus boycott, see Craig Flournoy, *Reporting the Movement in Black and White: The Emmett Till Lynching and the Montgomery Bus Boycott* (Ph.D. dissertation, LSU, 2003) (http://etd.lsu.edu/docs/available/etd-0611103–164757/unrestricted/Flournoy_dis.pdf).

5. Bennett, *Before the Mayflower*, 260.

6. Ibid.

7. Matthews and Prothro, *Negroes and the New Southern Politics*, 13–14.

8. Morison, 108; Matthews and Prothro, 15; Bennett, *Before the Mayflower*, 274.

9. Bennett, *Before the Mayflower*, 277.

10. Matthews and Prothro, *Negroes and the New Southern Politics*, 17–18.

11. Bennett, *Before the Mayflower*, 277.

12. Myrdal, *An American Dilemma*, 503; Wilkins OH, CUOHC.

13. Myrdal, *An American Dilemma*, 319, 338–39.

14. *WP*, 7/7/87.

15. Burns, *The Crosswinds of Freedom*, 321; Bennett, *Before the Mayflower*, 376; Nevins and Commager, *A Pocket History of the United States*, 534; O'Neill, *American High*, 249; Halberstam, *The Fifties*, 423.

16. Cohodas, *Strom Thurmond and the Politics of Southern Change*, 254; Pollack, *Earl Warren*, 176.

17. Bennett, *Before the Mayflower*, 376.

18. Goldman with Gallen, *Thurgood Marshall*, 112; Berman, *It Is So Ordered*, 123; Bartley and Graham, *Southern Politics and the Second Reconstruction*, 53.

19. Garrow, *Bearing the Cross*, 13, 16; Branch, *Parting the Waters*, 146.

20. Garrow, *Bearing the Cross*, 20.

21. Ibid., 24.

22. Branch, *Parting the Waters*, 162; Garrow, *Bearing the Cross*, 58.

23. Branch, *Parting the Waters*, 196.

2. TO HELL WITH THE SUPREME COURT

1. *CQ Almanac*, 1956, 51.

2. Duram, *A Moderate Among Extremists*, 54, 61.

3. O'Neill, *American High*, 253; Ambrose, *Eisenhower*, Vol. 2: *The President*, 189–92.

4. Reedy to Mann, 2/11/95.

5. *CQ Almanac*, 1956, 459; Mann, *The Walls of Jericho*, 167–75.

6. Watson, *Lion in the Lobby*, 226–27.

7. *U.S. News & World Report*, 5/28/54.

8. Cohadas, *Strom Thurmond and the Politics of Southern Change*, 283–84.

9. Fite, *Richard B. Russell, Jr., Senator from Georgia*, 333.

10. Reedy OH, LBJL; Gore, *Let the Glory Out*, 104.

11. *CR*, 3/12/56, 4460.

12. Ibid., 4461–63.

13. Ibid., 4464; LBJ statement, 3/10/56, U.S. Senate, Office Files of George Reedy, Box 423, LBJL.

14. Baker, *Wheeling and Dealing*, 70.

15. Reedy OH, LBJL; Reedy memorandum, 6/9/55, Papers of George Reedy, Box 415, LBJL; Reedy OH, LBJL; Stennis OH, LBJL.

16. Dallek, *Lone Star Rising*, 490–91; Hays OH, LBJL; HHH OH, LBJL.

3. THREE SENATORS

1. McPherson, 11/9/93, author interview.

2. Fite, *Richard B. Russell, Jr., Senator from Georgia*, 225.

3. *Time*, 5/19/52.

4. For more on Russell's presidential campaign, see Fite, *Richard B. Russell, Jr., Senator from Georgia*, 271–300, and Mann, *The Walls of Jericho*, 121–28.

5. *Minnesota History*, Fall 1978.

6. Eisele, *Almost to the Presidency*, 14–15; Humphrey, *The Education of a Public Man*, 8; Amrine, *This Is Humphrey*, 35; Solberg, *Hubert Humphrey*, 43.

7. Eisele, *Almost to the Presidency*, 50; *Time*, 1/17/49.

8. Mann, *The Walls of Jericho*, 11–13.

9. Ibid., 14–21; *The Official Report of the Democratic National Convention, Philadelphia, Pennsylvania, July 12 to July 14, inclusive 1948*, Local Democratic Political Committee of Pennsylvania, 189–210; Solberg, *Hubert Humphrey*, 17; Eisele, *Almost to the Presidency*, 68.

10. Vander Zee OH, USSHO; Kearns, *Lyndon Johnson and the American Dream*, 133.

11. Muskie OH, MHS.

12. *New Republic*, 11/14/55. For info on the LBJ/HHH relationship, see Mann, *The Walls of Jericho*, 142–46.

13. Reedy, *Lyndon B. Johnson*, 158; Miller, *Lyndon*, 534; Durr OH, Birdwell OH, LBJL.

14. From LBJ's voting rights speech to Congress, 3/15/65, found in *CQ Almanac*, 1965, 1367.

15. See Caro, *The Years of Lyndon Johnson*, Vol. 2: *Means of Ascent*.

16. *CQ*, 8/7/46, 1691–93.

17. Miller, *Lyndon*, 73.

18. Connally, *In History's Shadow*, 53; Miller, *Lyndon*, 73; Clifford and Virginia Durr OH, LBJL.

19. Fite, *Richard B. Russell, Jr., Senator from Georgia*, 268; Darden OH, LBJL.

20. For more on Johnson's rise to power in the Senate, see Caro, *The Years of Lyndon Johnson*, Vol. 3: *Master of the Senate*, and Mann, *The Walls of Jericho*.

21. Rowe OH, Long OH, McGee OH, HHH OH, LBJL; Miller, *Lyndon,* 174.

22. Shuman OH, USSHO; Jackson OH, LBJL.

23. Reedy OH, LBJL.

24. Talmadge OH, LBJL.

25. Smathers OH, USSHO.

4. GALLOPING WITH THE CROWD

1. Watson, *Lion in the Lobby,* 355.

2. Ibid., 354–55; Anderson, *Eisenhower, Brownell, and the Congress,* 134; Eisenhower, *Waging Peace, 1956–1961,* 154.

3. Minow OH, LBJL.

4. Dallek, *Lone Star Rising,* 507–8; HHH to LBJ, 9/10/56, HHH Papers, Senatorial Files, Correspondence (legislative), Box 225, MHS; Eisele, *Almost to the Presidency,* 104; Solberg, *Hubert Humphrey,* 178.

5. Undated memo, Senate Papers, Office Files of George Reedy, Box 420, LBJL; Solberg, *Hubert Humphrey,* 178.

6. Kearns, *Lyndon Johnson and the American Dream,* 147.

7. Siegel OH, LBJL; Douglas OH, LBJL; Marshall OH, LBJL; Henry OH, LBJL.

8. Safire, *Safire's Political Dictionary,* 226; White, *Citadel,* 60

9. Anderson, *Outsider in the Senate,* 144–45; Shuman OH, USSHO; *Congress and the Nation,* Vol. I, 1427.

10. *CQ,* 8/7/64, 1694; Rauh OH, MSRC; Reedy to LBJ, undated, Senate Papers, Legislative Files, 57–58, Box 291, LBJL; Reedy to LBJ, undated, U.S. Senate, 1949–61, Office Files of Solis Horwitz, Box 408, LBJL.

11. Reedy to Michael Gillette, 6/2/82, LBJL.

12. *CQ Almanac,* 1957, 557.

13. Reedy, *Lyndon Johnson,* 113.

14. *CR,* 6/18/57, 9506; Mooney OH, Jackson OH, Humphrey OH, Hagerty OH, LBJL; Smathers OH, USSHO.

15. *CQ Almanac,* 1957, 561; *CR,* 6/17/57, 9348; Shuman OH, USSHO; *CR,* 6/20/57, 9827.

16. Eisenhower, *Waging Peace, 1956–1961,* 155.

17. LBJ to Johnny Cooner, 7/10/57, U.S. Senate Papers, 1949–61, Box 289, LBJL.

18. Anderson, *Outsider in the Senate,* 146.

19. *CR,* 6/20/57, 9827; *Congress and the Nation,* Vol. I, 946–54.

20. Long OH, LBJL; Kearns, *Lyndon Johnson and the American Dream,* 149.

5. THIS IS ARMAGEDDON

1. Friedman, *Southern Justice,* 64; *Congressional Digest,* 4/57, 108, 110; *NYT,* 10/20, 10/24, 10/25, 1956; *Time,* 7/29/57; *Monroe* (La.) *Morning World,* 10/19/56.

2. U.S. Commission on Civil Rights, *With Liberty and Justice for All,* 76.

3. Miller, *Lyndon,* 206.

4. *Newsweek,* 7/15, 7/22, 1957.

5. Watson, *Lion in the Lobby,* 362.

6. Douglas, *In the Fullness of Time,* 285.

7. Ibid., 285.

8. *CR,* 7/2/57, 10771–75; *WP,* 7/3/57; *U.S. News & World Report,* 7/12/57.

9. Douglas, *In the Fullness of Time,* 288.

10. *NYT,* 7/3/57.

11. Long, author interview; Stennis OH, RBRL.

12. Transcript of RBR phone conversation with Carter Pittman, 9/2/57, RBRL; Fite, *Richard B. Russell, Jr., Senator from Georgia,* 338; *Time,* 7/22, 8/12, 1957; *Newsweek,* 7/15/57.

13. Burns, *John Kennedy,* 205; *Time,* 8/12/57; Thurmond, author interview.

14. *Richard Russell: Georgia Giant,* Cox Broadcasting, 1970.

15. *CR,* 7/12/57, 11442.

16. Eisenhower, *Waging Peace, 1956–1961,* 159.

17. Reedy to LBJ, undated, Senate Papers, Legislative Files, 1957–58, Box 291, LBJL.

18. Rowe to LBJ, 7/3/57, Office Files of George Reedy, Box 421, LBJL.

19. *CR,* 7/16/57, 11826.

20. *Newsweek,* 7/29/57; *NYT,* 7/15/57.

21. *CQ Almanac,* 1957, 562.

6. THE BEST WE COULD GET

1. Anderson, *Outsider in the Senate,* 147.

2. Anderson OH, LBJL. Most published accounts have given Johnson credit for persuading Anderson to spearhead the amendment to strike Part III. "He didn't at all," Anderson insisted.

3. *CR,* 7/26/57, 12825.

4. Reedy, author interview.

5. *Public Papers of the Presidents: Dwight D. Eisenhower, 1953–1960,* 1/1–12/31/1957, 555.

6. *CQ Almanac,* 1957, 566; *WP,* 7/19/57; White, *The Professional,* 217.

7. *CR,* 7/24/57, 12564, 12565, 7/25/57, 12714.

8. Kearns, *Lyndon Johnson and the American Dream,* 148; "Beautiful Texas," PBS, *American Experience,* 9/30/91.

9. "Beautiful Texas," PBS, *American Experience,* 9/30/91; McPherson, author interview.

10. Reedy, *Lyndon B. Johnson,* 116.

11. Ibid.

12. "Open Hearing," ABC, 6/14/57, reprinted in *CR,* 7/22/57, 12290.

13. Church OH, Tully OH, LBJL.

14. Reedy, *Lyndon B. Johnson,* 117.

15. Auerbach article reprinted in *CR,* 7/29/57, 12873–74; Auerbach OH, MHS; *The Reporter,* 9/5/57; Church OH, LBJL; Reedy OH, LBJL.

16. Evans and Novak, *Lyndon B. Johnson,* 134; Brinkley, *Dean Acheson,* 205.

17. Horwitz OH, LBJL; *CQ Almanac,* 1957, 565.

18. *The Reporter,* 9/5/57.

19. *The Reporter,* 9/5/57; *CR,* 8/1/57, 13234; *Newsweek,* 8/12/57; Evans and Novak, *Lyndon B. Johnson,* 137.

20. Church OH, LBJL; *Time,* 8/12/57; Horwitz OH, LBJL; *CR,* 7/31/57, 13153–54.

21. *Time,* 8/12/57.

22. Ibid.; *CR,* 8/1/57, 13356, 8/2/57, 13422; *Congress and the Nation,* Vol. I, 1957, 1624; *NYT,* 8/2/57.

23. *CR,* 8/12/57, 14401; *Washington Evening Star,* 8/5/57.

24. *CQ Almanac,* 1957, 564, 568; *Washington Evening Star,* 8/2, 8/5, 1957; *CR,* 8/2/57, 13485.

25. *Washington Evening Star,* 8/9/57.

26. *CR,* 8/6/57, 13698–99.

27. *CQ Almanac,* 1957, 563; Rauh OH, MSRC.

28. Eisenhower, *Waging Peace, 1956–1961,* 161; *CR,* 8/23/57, 15793; *CQ Almanac,* 1957, 568.

29. Cohodas, *Strom Thurmond and the Politics of Southern Change,* 294; *NYT,* 8/30/57.

30. Reedy OH, LBJL; *NYT,* 8/30/57; Long, author interview.

31. *NYT,* 8/30/57; *CQ Almanac,* 1957, 569.

32. Douglas, *In the Fullness of Time,* 290; *NYT,* 8/25/57; White OH, Clifford OH, LBJL.

33. Wicker OH, LBJL; Burns, *John Kennedy,* 204; Rauh OH, JFKL.

34. "Beautiful Texas," PBS, *American Experience,* 9/30/91; Marshall OH, LBJL; Wofford, author interview.

35. Anderson, *Outsider in the Senate,* 148. For more on the 1957 Civil Rights Act, see Caro, *The Years of Lyndon Johnson,* Vol. 3: *Master of the Senate,* and Mann, *The Walls of Jericho.*

7. A MEANINGLESS GESTURE

1. Ambrose, *Eisenhower,* Vol. 2: *The President,* 421.

2. Branch, *Parting the Waters,* 224. Other sources on the Little Rock crisis: Duram, *A Moderate Among Extremists,* 143–59; Ambrose, *Eisenhower,* Vol. 2: *The President,* 413–23; Bartley, *The Rise of Massive Resistance,* 251–69; *U.S. News & World Report,* 10/4/57.

3. *U.S. News & World Report,* 10/4/57.

4. Ibid., 10/4/57.

5. *Newsweek,* 10/7/57.

6. RBR speech draft, 2/17/58, Dictation Series I, RBRL.

7. Morison, *The Oxford History of the American People,* 457; RBR statements, 9/12/58, RBRL.

8. Fite, *Richard B. Russell, Jr., Senator from Georgia,* 346; *Congress and the Nation,* Vol. I, 1497–1501.

9. Dallek, *Lone Star Rising,* 538; Gould, *The Most Exclusive Club,* 226.

10. *WSJ* quoted in *Time,* 11/17/58.

11. *Dallas Morning News* quoted in *Time,* 11/17/58; RBR speech text, 2/10/59, Speech Files, RBRL; Foley, *The New Senate,* 27.

12. *CQ Almanac,* 1958, 713–15, 739–46; Foley, *The New Senate,* 25–27.

13. Clark, *Congress*, 9; Connell OH, LBJL.

14. McPherson OH, LBJL; Evans and Novak, *Lyndon B. Johnson*, 196.

15. MacNeil, *Dirksen*, 167; Bennett OH, FMOC.

16. *Business Week*, 5/2/59.

17. *Time*, 1/19/59; Fite, *Richard B. Russell, Jr., Senator from Georgia*, 347.

18. *CQ Almanac*, 1959, 213.

19. *Face the Nation*, 1/18/59, CBS News, 16, 17.

20. *Time*, 1/19/59.

21. Shuman OH, USSHO; *CQ Almanac*, 1959, 212–14; Evans and Novak, *Lyndon B. Johnson*, 200–2; Dallek, *Lone Star Rising*, 547; *Face the Nation*, 1/18/59, 18.

22. Horwitz OH, LBJL; *CQ Almanac*, 1959, 213.

23. *CR*, 2/23/59, 2814–17.

24. Proxmire OH, LBJL; McPherson, *A Political Education*, 169.

25. Shaffer, *On and Off the Floor*, 217; Foley, *The New Senate*, 31.

26. *CQ*, 6/5/59, 766; *Face the Nation*, 1/18/59, 19.

27. Dallek, *Lone Star Rising*, 549.

28. *CQ Almanac*, 1959, 291.

29. Horwitz to LBJ, 2/16/59, U.S. Senate, 49–61, Office Files of Solis Horwitz, Box 408, LBJL.

30. NAACP press release, 1/22/59, Legislative Files, Senate Papers, Files of Solis Horwitz, Box 408, LBJL.

31. *CQ Almanac*, 1959, 291.

32. Ibid., 291.

33. *CQ*, 2/13/59, 277; *CQ Almanac*, 1959, 292.

34. *CQ*, 4/24/59, 569, 4/6/60, 757–58.

35. United States Commission on Civil Rights, *1959 Report of the United States Commission on Civil Rights*.

36. Ibid., 9/18/59, 1282; *CQ Almanac*, 1959, 292; *CR*, 2/15/60, 2477; Chappell, *Inside Agitators*, 171.

37. Russell speech excerpts, Dawson (Ga.) Lions Club, 12/10/59, RBRL.

38. Miller, *Lyndon*, 227; Branch, *Parting the Waters*, 271–75; Bennett, *Before the Mayflower*, 383–84.

39. Branch, *Parting the Waters*, 272.

8. A VICTORY FOR THE OLD SOUTH

1. Miller, *Lyndon*, 226.

2. RBR speech text, 2/8/60, Speech Files, RBRL.

3. Miller, *Lyndon*, 227.

4. RBR speech text, 2/9/60, Speech Files, RBRL.

5. *CQ*, 2/19/60, 255.

6. *CR*, 2/15/60, 2444.

7. Ibid., 2470.

8. McPherson, author interview.

9. *CR*, 2/15/60, 2470, 2472.

10. Ibid., 2471.

11. Siegel to LBJ, 2/2/60, Papers of the Democratic Leader, Box 374, LBJL.

12. Talmadge, *Talmadge*, 187; RBR speech text, 2/9/60, Speech Files, RBRL; *CQ Almanac*, 1960, 197.

13. *CQ Almanac*, 1960, 198; *CR*, 2/17/60, 2727.

14. *CR*, 2/23/60, 3220.

15. Ibid.

16. Ibid., 2/26/60, 3575, 3580.

17. Talmadge, *Talmadge*, 185; Talmadge, author interview.

18. Talmadge, author interview; Ervin OH, RBRL.

19. Talmadge, *Talmadge*, 185.

20. Javits, *Javits*, 339; *WP*, 3/3/60.

21. Ervin OH, RBRL; Talmadge, author interview; Sparkman OH, RBRL; Shuman OH, USSHO.

22. Miller, *Lyndon*, 228.

23. *CQ Almanac*, 1960, 198.

24. Ervin OH, RBRL; *NYT*, 3/6/60.

25. *CR*, 3/8/60, 4934, 3/10/60, 5114, 5118; *CQ Almanac*, 1960, 199.

26. *NYT*, 3/11/60; *CR*, 3/10/60, 5182.

27. *NYT*, 3/5/60.

28. *CQ Almanac*, 1960, 199.

29. *CR*, 3/24/60, 6452–55.

30. *CQ Almanac*, 1960, 200.

31. *CR*, 4/8/60, 7737; Clark, *Congress*, 14; *Time*, 4/18/60.

32. *Newsweek*, 4/11/60; *CQ Almanac*, 1960, 200.

33. RBR press release, 4/11/60, RBRL.

34. *New York Post*, 3/11/60.

9. GO GET MY LONG RIFLE

1. McPherson, *A Political Education*, 172; Shuman OH, USSHO.

2. Freeman OH, LBJL.

3. Miller, *Lyndon*, 240.

4. Connally, *In History's Shadow*, 161.

5. Wofford, *Of Kennedys and Kings*, 47; *CQ*, 5/13/60, 849.

6. Wofford, *Of Kennedys and Kings*, 47.

7. *CQ*, 7/15/60, 1248.

8. Rauh OH, MSRC.

9. *CQ*, 7/15/60, 1250; *CQ Almanac*, 1960, 773.

10. *CQ*, 7/29/60, 1352.

11. O'Donnell and Powers, *"Johnny, We Hardly Knew Ye,"* 217.

12. Ibid., 218.

13. Baker, *Wheeling and Dealing*, 126; Miller, *Lyndon*, 256.

14. McPherson OH, LBJL.

15. Harris OH, Ellington OH, LBJL.

16. Miller, *Lyndon*, 262.

17. Diggs OH, Farmer OH, LBJL.

18. Humphrey OH, LBJL; Strober and Strober, *"Let Us Begin Anew,"* 21; Viorst, *Fire in the Streets*, 238; Matusow, *The Unraveling of America*, 16.

19. Strober and Strober, *"Let Us Begin Anew,"* 20; Freeman OH, LBJL; *New Republic*, 7/25/60.

20. Fite, *Richard B. Russell, Jr., Senator from Georgia*, 376–77; RBR statement, 9/1/60, Dictation Series I, RBRL.

21. Troutman OH, RBRL.

22. Goldsmith, *Colleagues*, 80; RBR statement, 9/1/60, Dictation Series I, RBRL; Fite, *Richard B. Russell, Jr., Senator from Georgia*, 378.

23. Miller, *Lyndon*, 262.

24. *Time*, 10/24/60; *Newsweek*, 10/24, 10/31, 1960.

25. *Newsweek*, 10/24/60.

26. Evans and Novak, *Lyndon B. Johnson*, 292.

27. *Atlanta Constitution*, 10/20, 10/24, 1960; Garrow, *Bearing the Cross*, 143–45.

28. Garrow, *Bearing the Cross*, 146.

29. *Atlanta Constitution*, 10/25/60.

30. Wofford, *Of Kennedys and Kings*, 13–14.

31. Ibid., 16–17.

32. Garrow, *Bearing the Cross*, 146; Strober and Strober, *"Let Us Begin Anew,"* 35–36; Wofford, *Of Kennedys and Kings*, 19; *Atlanta Constitution*, 10/27/60.

33. Garrow, *Bearing the Cross*, 148; *Time*, 11/7/60; Wofford, *Of Kennedys and Kings*, 23; *Atlanta Constitution*, 10/28/60.

34. Eastland OH, LBJL; Halleck OH, LBJL.

35. RBR to Harvey J. Kennedy, 11/17/60, Dictation Series I, RBRL.

10. HOW DID WE LET THIS HAPPEN?

1. Miller, *Lyndon*, 273.

2. Kearns, *Lyndon Johnson and the American Dream*, 164.

3. Evans and Novak, *Lyndon B. Johnson*, 306; Baker, *Wheeling and Dealing*, 134; Shuman OH, Smathers OH, USSHO; McPherson, *A Political Education*, 183.

4. Reedy OH, Siegel OH, LBJL; Vander Zee OH, USSHO; Fulbright, author interview; Talmadge, author interview.

5. *NYT*, 1/4/61; Miller, *Lyndon*, 275–76; Evans and Novak, *Lyndon B. Johnson*, 306–7.

6. Baker, *Wheeling and Dealing*, 135; Proxmire OH, LBJL.

7. Miller, *Lyndon*, 276.

8. Baker, *Wheeling and Dealing*, 144.

9. Rowe OH, LBJL.

10. Smathers OH, USSHO; O'Donnell OH, LBJL.

11. Marshall, author interview; Kearns, *Lyndon Johnson and the American Dream*, 164; Evans and Novak, *Lyndon B. Johnson*, 314.

12. *WSJ*, 7/28/61.

13. *Life*, 9/27/68.

14. Eisele, *Almost to the Presidency*, 178.

15. McPherson OH, MHS.

16. Humphrey, *The Education of a Public Man*, 181; *WSJ*, 4/20/61.

17. *WSJ*, 4/20/61; *NYT Magazine*, 8/25/63; Gartner OH, MHS.

18. Eisele, *Almost to the Presidency*, 179, 181; *WSJ*, 4/20/61; Shuman OH, USSHO.

19. Wofford, *Of Kennedys and Kings*, 58; Wofford, author interview; Wofford OH, JFKL.

20. Wofford, *Of Kennedys and Kings*, 62–63.

21. Ibid., 98–99; Reeves, *President Kennedy*, 38–39; *CQ Almanac*, 1961, 856.

22. Goodwin, *Remembering America*, 4–5.

23. *CQ*, 1/13/61, 42; *CQ Almanac*, 1961, 392.

24. Bryant, *The Bystander*, 11.

25. *CQ Almanac*, 1961, 392; Wilkins OH, JFKL.

26. Burns OH, JFKL; *NYT*, 3/6/61.

27. Wilkins OH, LBJL.

28. Strober and Strober, *"Let Us Begin Anew,"* 277; Celler OH, JFKL; Marshall, author interview.

29. Hesburgh, author interview.

30. Schlesinger, *A Thousand Days*, 931.

31. Bryant, *The Bystander*, 193–207.

32. *CQ Almanac*, 1961, 860; Celebrezze OH, LBJL; Schlesinger, *A Thousand Days*, 933.

33. *CQ*, 2/10/61, 218.

34. Harvey, *Civil Rights During the Kennedy Administration*, 22–23; Wilkins OH, JFKL.

35. Carl Rowan in the *Star-Ledger* (Newark, NJ), 11/24/93.

36. *NYT*, 5/7/61.

37. Schlesinger, *A Thousand Days*, 934–35; *CQ Almanac*, 1961, 393.

38. *CQ*, 1/20/61, 69, 4/21/61, 668; *NYT*, 10/15/61; Marshall, author interview.

39. *CQ*, 4/21/61, 668.

40. King OH, Rauh OH, JFKL.

41. *NYT*, 10/15/61.

42. *Time*, 6/2/61.

43. *NYT*, 5/21/61.

44. *Newsweek*, 5/29/61.

45. *Time*, 6/2/61.

46. *Newsweek*, 6/5/61; *NYT*, 5/2/61; *Time*, 6/2/61.

47. Strober and Strober, *"Let Us Begin Anew,"* 294.

48. Ibid.

49. Wofford, *Of Kennedys and Kings*, 153; Wofford, author interview.

50. *Newsweek*, 6/5/61.

51. *Time*, 6/2/61.

52. Garrow, *Bearing the Cross*, 157.

53. *Time*, 6/2/61; *NYT*, 5/22/61; Garrow, *Bearing the Cross*, 158.

54. Wofford, *Of Kennedys and Kings*, 155; *Time*, 6/2/61; *Newsweek*, 6/5/61, 5/29/61; Branch, *Parting the Waters*, 412–91; Fairclough, *To Redeem the Soul of America*, 77–79.

55. *CR*, 5/22/61, 8498, 8531.

56. Ibid., 5/23/61, 8616–17, 8648.

57. *CQ Almanac*, 1961, 393; *NYT*, 9/23/61.

58. Wofford, *Of Kennedys and Kings*, 157; *CQ Almanac*, 1961, 922.

59. *CQ Almanac*, 1961, 393.

60. *CQ*, 9/22/61, 1617; *CQ Almanac*, 1961, 393–94.

61. *CQ Almanac*, 1961, 398.

11. YOU'LL NEVER GET A CIVIL RIGHTS BILL

1. *Presidential Studies Quarterly*, Fall 1991, 698; Jones, author interview.

2. Fite, *Richard B. Russell, Jr., Senator from Georgia*, 382–83.

3. *NYT*, 1/5/61; Harvey, *Civil Rights During the Kennedy Administration*, 16.

4. Darden OH, RBRL.

5. *CR*, 1/18/62, 434–35, 3/8/62, 3642.

6. Ibid., 5/29/62, 9512.

7. *CQ*, 3/16/62, 428; *CR*, 3/27/62, 5083–87.

8. *CR*, 3/16/62, 4410.

9. Ibid., 3/27/62, 5105; *CQ*, 8/31/62, 1443.

10. *CQ Almanac*, 1962, 371–75; *CR*, 5/2/62, 7607.

11. *CR*, 5/2/62, 7590.

12. *CQ Almanac*, 1962, 372.

13. Ibid., 375.

14. *CQ Almanac*, 1962, 377; *Time*, 5/18/62.

15. *CR*, 5/1/62, 7365, 5/14/62, 8294; *CQ*, 5/11/62, 790–91; *Time*, 5/18/62.

16. *CQ Almanac*, 1962, 377; Mansfield OH, JFKL.

17. Marshall OH, JFKL.

18. Harvey, *Civil Rights During the Kennedy Administration*, 37; Garrow, *Bearing the Cross*, 161.

19. *CQ*, 8/3/62, 1297.

20. *CQ Almanac*, 1962, 244–45; *Time*, 10/5/62, 10/12/62; *Newsweek*, 10/15/62; Branch, *Parting the Waters*, 649–70; Lord, *The Past That Would Not Die*, 191, 196, 207–9; Paul Johnson OH, LBJL; *USA Today*, 6/9/88; *Newark Star-Ledger*, 11/1/92; Strober and Strober, *"Let Us Begin Anew,"* 304.

21. *CR*, 9/29/62, 21282, 10/1/62, 21415; *Thomasville Times Enterprise*, 9/28/62.

22. *CQ*, 10/5/62, 1809; *NYT*, 10/3/62.

23. *Time*, 10/12/62.

24. Wofford OH, Wilkins OH, JFKL.

25. Burke Marshall OH, Sorensen OH, JFKL.

26. Robert Kennedy OH, JFKL.

27. Sorensen OH, Burke Marshall OH, JFKL.

28. Sorensen, *Kennedy*, 482; *CQ*, 11/23/62, 2203.

29. King OH, JFKL.

12. "WAIT" HAS ALWAYS MEANT "NEVER"

1. Vander Zee OH, USSHO.

2. *CQ*, 2/15/63, 190–91.

3. Ibid.

4. Clark OH, LBJL; Katzenbach OH, JFKL.

5. Reedy to LBJ, undated, Civil Rights, Confidential Memos—Reedy, Vice-Presidential Papers, LBJL.

6. Clark, *Congress*, 123; *CQ*, 2/8/63, 139.

7. *CR*, 1/23/63, 1219; *NYT*, 1/29/63.

8. McPherson, *A Political Education*, 188; *CQ*, 2/8/63, 139.

9. *Newsweek*, 8/19/63; Simon, *Public Opinion in America, 1936–1970*, 62–69.

10. *CQ*, 2/15/63, 191; Rauh OH, MSRC.

11. *CQ*, 3/8/63, 292.

12. Ibid.; Garrow, *Bearing the Cross*, 233; Rauh OH, JFKL; Wilkins OH, JFKL.

13. RBR statement, 2/28/63, RBRL; *CQ*, 3/8/63, 293.

14. *CQ*, 3/8/63, 293.

15. Smathers OH, JFKL; Solberg, *Hubert Humphrey*, 221; Watson, *Lion in the Lobby*, 544.

16. Bennett, *Before the Mayflower*, 388–89; Fairclough, *To Redeem the Soul of America*, 108.

17. *Time*, 5/10/63.

18. Garrow, *Bearing the Cross*, 237.

19. Fairclough, *To Redeem the Soul of America*, 118.

20. Garrow, *Bearing the Cross*, 239; Fairclough, *To Redeem the Soul of America*, 121.

21. Bennett, *Before the Mayflower*, 391.

22. Ibid., 392; Garrow, *Bearing the Cross*, 244–45.

23. Garrow, *Bearing the Cross*, 247; Bennett, *Before the Mayflower*, 393.

24. *Time*, 5/10/63; *Los Angeles Times*, 5/4/63; Garrow, *Bearing the Cross*, 249; *NYT*, 5/3/63; *Boston Globe*, 5/4/63.

25. *Time*, 5/10/63; *NYT*, 5/4/63.

26. *Time*, 5/17/63.

27. *Newsweek*, 5/20/63; Bennett, *Before the Mayflower*, 399.

28. *Boston Globe*, 5/4/63; *NYT*, 5/4/63; *Los Angeles Times*, 5/4/63; *Time*, 5/17/63; *Newsweek*, 5/20/63; *New York Herald Tribune*, 5/13/63.

29. *CR*, 5/21/63, 9115, 9140.

30. Garrow, *Bearing the Cross*, 251; Strober and Strober, *"Let Us Begin Anew,"* 284.

31. *Newsweek*, 5/20/63.

32. King OH, Wilkins OH, JFKL.

33. Udall OH, MSRC; *CQ*, 5/31/63, 838; Reedy to LBJ, 5/24/63, Civil Rights, Confidential Memos, Vice-Presidential Papers, LBJL; Burke Marshall OH, JFKL; Branch, *Pillar of Fire*, 88.

34. Burke Marshall OH, JFKL; Schlesinger, *Robert Kennedy and His Times*, 357; Robert Kennedy OH, JFKL; Burke Marshall, author interview.

35. Burke Marshall OH, JFKL; Glickstein OH, MSRC; Whalen and Whalen, *The Longest Debate*, 5; *WP*, 5/23/63.

36. *WP*, 5/24/63; Katzenbach OH, LBJL.

37. Burke Marshall OH, Sorensen OH, JFKL.

38. Burke Marshall OH, JFKL; *Hearings Before the Committee on Commerce, United States Senate, 88th Congress, First Session, on S. 1732, a Bill to Eliminate Discrimination in Public Accommodations Affecting Interstate Commerce* (Washington, D.C.: U.S. Government Printing Office, 1963), 1295–1300.

39. Burke Marshall OH, MSRC; RFK OH, JFKL; *CQ*, 6/21/63, 998; Berman, *A Bill Becomes a Law*, 40; Carothers, *The Public Accommodations Law of 1964*, 79.

40. Evans and Novak, *Lyndon B. Johnson*, 376.

41. LBJ speech, 5/30/63, LBJL.

13. A BILL, NOT AN ISSUE

1. Graham, *The Civil Rights Era*, 76–77.

2. Branch, *Pillar of Fire*, 92–93.

3. Burke Marshall OH, LBJL.

4. Graham, *The Civil Rights Era*, 77.

5. Transcript of LBJ/Sorensen phone conversation, 6/3/63, LBJL.

6. Sorensen, *Kennedy*, 499; Sorensen OH, RFK OH, JFKL.

7. Sorensen, *Kennedy*, 493; Burke Marshall OH, JFKL; videotape of "The Civil Rights Act of 1964: A Conference at the John F. Kennedy Library," 4/25/94, author's files.

8. *U.S. News & World Report*, 6/24/63.

9. Bennett, *Before the Mayflower*, 401–2; Branch, *Parting the Waters*, 824–25.

10. *U.S. News & World Report*, 6/24/63.

11. *NYT Magazine*, 11/20/63; *Newsweek*, 8/19/63.

12. *WSJ*, 6/19/63.

13. McGill OH, JFKL; Jones, author interview; *NYT*, 11/20/63.

14. Allen OH, Carter OH, Mudd OH, RBRL.

15. *NYT Magazine*, 10/20/63; *Newsweek*, 8/19/63.

16. Baker to Mansfield, 6/27/63, Manatos: Civil Rights, 63–65, WHCF, Aides Files, Box 6, LBJL; *CQ Almanac*, 1963, 344.

17. Whalen and Whalen, *The Longest Debate*, 13; Katzenbach OH, JFKL.

18. Cronin OH, MSRC; *CQ Almanac*, 1963, 344.

19. Katzenbach OH, JFKL; Garrow, *Bearing the Cross*, 271–72.

20. Branch, *Parting the Waters*, 839; Rauh OH, JFKL.

21. Garrow, *Bearing the Cross*, 272; RFK OH, JFKL.

22. *CQ*, 6/21/63, 999–1000.

23. Farmer OH, LBJL; Sorensen OH, JFKL.

24. Humphrey, *The Education of a Public Man*, 201–2; *CR*, 8/27/63, 15917; Rustin OH, LBJL.

25. RFK OH, JFKL; Whalen and Whalen, *The Longest Debate*, 38.

26. *CQ Almanac*, 1963, 348–49; Whalen and Whalen, *The Longest Debate*, 39.

27. *CQ Almanac*, 1963, 349; Marshall OH, MSRC.

28. *Newsweek*, 8/19/63.

29. *CQ Almanac*, 1963, 355; Allen OH, LBJL; *Hearings Before the Committee on Commerce, United States Senate, 88th Congress, First Session, on S. 1732, a Bill to Eliminate Discrimination in Public Accommodations Affecting Interstate Commerce* (Washington, D.C.: U.S. Government Printing Office, 1963), 861–66.

30. *WP*, 8/27/63.

31. McPherson OH, LBJL.

14. I WANT THAT BILL PASSED

1. Mudd OH, RBRL.

2. Leonard OH, RBRL.

3. Humphrey, *The Education of a Public Man*, 191; *Life*, 9/27/68.

4. Humphrey, *The Education of a Public Man*, 191–92.

5. *Saturday Evening Post*, 3/13/65; Riddick OH, USSHO.

6. Evans and Novak, *Lyndon B. Johnson*, 345–46; Records of the JFK Assassination, Box 85, Tapes and Transcripts of Telephone Conversations and Meetings, National Archives.

7. Notes of Troika meeting, President's Appointment File, Diary Backup, 11/25/63, Box 1, LBJL; Whalen and Whalen, *The Longest Debate*, 77; Valenti, *A Very Human President*, 117.

8. Rosenberg and Karabell, *Kennedy, Johnson, and the Quest for Justice*, 199–203; LBJ-King phone transcript, 11/25/63, Records of the JFK Assassination, Box 85, Tapes and Transcripts of Telephone Conversations and Meetings, National Archives.

9. Whalen and Whalen, *The Longest Debate*, 81.

10. Notes of Troika meeting, President's Appointment File, Diary Backup, 11/25/63, Box 1, LBJL; Burke Marshall OH, LBJL.

11. Miller, *Lyndon*, 337, 338–39; Branch, *Pillar of Fire*, 178; Humphrey, *The Education of a Public Man*, 196–97; Public Papers of the Presidents, Lyndon B. Johnson, 1963–1964, 11/27/63, 8–10; Wicker, *JFK and LBJ*, 169; Fite, *Richard B. Russell, Jr., Senator from Georgia*, 408.

12. Miller, *Lyndon*, 340; Douglas, *In the Fullness of Time*, 295.

13. Paul Johnson OH, LBJL; Wicker, *JFK and LBJ*, 175.

14. Branch, *Pillar of Fire*, 187.

15. *Washington Afro-American*, 1/19/64.

16. Heller OH, MHS; Evans and Novak, *Lyndon B. Johnson*, 351; Miller, *Lyndon*, 341.

17. LBJ-Anderson phone transcript, 11/30/63, Records of the JFK Assassination, Box 85, Tapes and Transcripts of Telephone Conversations and Meetings, National Archives; LBJ-Graham phone transcript, 12/2/63.

18. Graham, *The Civil Rights Era*, 141.

19. Whalen and Whalen, *The Longest Debate*, 91.

20. *CQ Almanac*, 1964, 344; *CQ*, 2/14/64, 293.

21. *CQ*, 2/14/64, 293.

22. Mitchell OH, LBJL.

23. Johnson, *The Vantage Point*, 157–58; *CQ*, 1/24/64, 157.

24. Kearns, *Lyndon Johnson and the American Dream*, 191.

25. Katzenbach OH, JFKL; Katzenbach OH, LBJL.

26. *Time*, 3/20/64; Manatos to O'Brien, 2/13/64, Office Files of Harry McPherson, Box 21, LBJL; Katzenbach, author interview.

27. Johnson, *The Vantage Point*, 158; Katzenbach, author interview; HHH to file, 1964, HHH Vice-Presidential Papers, Civil and Human Rights, Box 821, MHS.

28. Humphrey, *The Education of a Public Man*, 204; Miller, *Lyndon*, 368; Humphrey OH, LBJL.

29. *Meet the Press*, 3/8/64; Humphrey OH, LBJL.

30. Katzenbach remarks to "The Civil Rights Act of 1964: A Conference at the John F. Kennedy Library," 4/25/94, videotape in author's files; Wolfinger, author interview.

31. Loevy, *To End All Segregation*, 147; HHH to file, 1964, HHH Vice-Presidential Papers, Civil and Human Rights, Box 821, MHS.

32. *CR*, 2/17/63, 2882; HHH to file, 1964, HHH Vice-Presidential Papers, Civil and Human Rights, Box 821, MHS.

33. *New Republic*, 4/4/64.

34. Humphrey, *The Education of a Public Man*, 206–7.

35. Loevy, *To End All Segregation*, 144.

36. *CQ*, 6/19/64, 1205–6; *New Republic*, 4/4/65; *CR*, 4/18/64, 8369.

37. HHH Senatorial Files, Correspondence, Legislative, Box 224, MHS; Whalen and Whalen, *The Longest Debate*, 164–65; *Christian Century*, 5/13/64.

38. Hildenbrand OH, USSHO.

39. *Washington Star*, 3/15/64; RBR statement, 1/24/64, WHCF, Name File, Richard Russell, Box 344, LBJL; *Face the Nation*, 3/1/64; Talmadge, *Talmadge*, 195.

40. *NYT*, 2/23/64.

41. Humphrey, *The Education of a Public Man*, 206.

42. Long, author interview.

43. *New Republic*, 4/4/64.

44. *The Reporter*, 5/21/64; *Face the Nation*, 3/1/64.

45. *The Reporter*, 5/21/64.

46. *Washington Star*, 3/15/64; *Business Week*, 4/18/64.

47. *CQ*, 2/28/64, 385.

48. *CR*, 3/9/64, 4754; *CQ Almanac*, 1964, 356–57.

49. *CR*, 3/21/64, 5865.

50. Ibid., 3/25/64, 6429.

51. Ibid., 4/20/64, 8443.

52. Ibid., 1/29/64, 1338, 3/9/64, 4753.

53. Ibid., 3/9/64, 4744, 3/10/64, 4855. For an excellent discussion of the southerners' constitutional objections to the public accommodations section, see Carothers, *The Public Accommodations Law of 1964*, 2–10.

54. *Time*, 4/10/64; *CQ Almanac*, 1964, 357–58.

55. *Time*, 4/10/64; *CQ Almanac*, 1964, 357–58; *Time*, 4/3/64.

56. White, *The Making of the President, 1964*, 213.

15. AN IDEA WHOSE TIME HAS COME

1. *CQ*, 4/3/64, 655; *CQ Almanac*, 1964, 358; *CR*, 3/30/64, 6552–53.

2. *CQ*, 4/10/64, 682.

3. *NYT*, 4/5/64; Humphrey, *The Education of a Public Man*, 207.

4. HHH to file, 1964, HHH Vice-Presidential Papers, Civil and Human Rights, Box 821, MHS; *Time*, 4/24/64; *Newsweek*, 4/27/64; *CQ*, 4/17/64, 717.

5. HHH to file, 1964, HHH Vice-Presidential Papers, Civil and Human Rights, Box 821, MHS.

6. MacNeil, *Dirksen*, 167; Talmadge, *Talmadge*, 197; *The Reporter*, 7/16/64.

7. *WP*, 2/20/64; MacNeil, *Dirksen*, 230.

8. Whalen and Whalen, *The Longest Debate*, 155–56; Talmadge, *Talmadge*, 196.

9. Whalen and Whalen, *The Longest Debate*, 159–60; *CQ Almanac*, 1964, 359; *Time*, 4/24/64; *The Reporter*, 7/16/64.

10. *Face the Nation*, 4/19/64; *Time*, 4/24/64.

11. *CQ*, 4/17/64, 717.

12. Whalen and Whalen, *The Longest Debate*, 160.

13. Kotz, *Judgment Days*, 136–38.

14. Findlay, *Church People in the Struggle*, 55; White, *The Making of the President, 1964*, 215.

15. Whalen and Whalen, *The Longest Debate*, 165; Watson, *Lion in the Lobby*, 601; *CQ Almanac*, 1964, 360; *New Republic*, 4/64.

16. NCCC letter, 3/6/64, HHH Papers, Senatorial Files, Correspondence (Legislative), MHS; *New Republic*, 4/4/64; Findlay, *Church People in the Struggle*, 51–54.

17. Rauh OH, MSRC.

18. *America*, 5/9/64.

19. *Face the Nation*, 4/26/64.

20. *Time*, 4/24/64.

21. Ibid., 4/24; HHH-Kuchel statement, 4/15/64, HHH Papers, Senatorial Files, Correspondence (Legislative), MHS; *Face the Nation*, 3/1/64.

22. *CQ*, 5/1/64, 863.

23. *Time*, 4/24/64.

24. *CQ*, 5/1/64, 863.

25. Kearns, *Lyndon Johnson and the American Dream*, 190; Johnson, *My Brother Lyndon*, 159.

26. Rosenberg and Karabell, *Kennedy, Johnson, and the Quest for Justice*, 293.

27. Whalen and Whalen, *The Longest Debate*, 172.

28. HHH to file, 1964, HHH Vice-Presidential Papers, Civil and Human Rights, Box 821, MHS.

29. Whalen and Whalen, *The Longest Debate*, 174; *CQ Almanac*, 1964, 361–62; *Time*, 5/15/64, 5/22/64.

30. *CQ*, 5/8/64, 901.

31. *Time*, 5/22/64; *CR*, 5/12/64, 10616; *NYT*, 5/12/64.

32. *NYT*, 5/12/64; *Time*, 5/22/64.

33. *Star-Ledger* (Newark, N.J.), 10/1/92.

34. Whalen and Whalen, *The Longest Debate*, 182–83.

35. *Newsweek*, 5/25/64; *Time*, 5/22/64.

36. *CQ Almanac*, 1964, 362–65.

37. Rauh OH, MSRC; *New Republic*, 7/16/64, 5/2/64.

38. Rosenberg and Karabell, *Kennedy, Johnson, and the Quest for Justice*, 307.

39. *Time*, 5/22/64, 6/5/64; MacNeil, *Dirksen*, 236; *CR*, 5/26/64, 11943; *CQ*, 1/29/64, 1032; *CQ Almanac*, 1964, 365; *Oxford Dictionary of Quotations*, 267; *The Reporter*, 7/16/64.

40. Hildenbrand OH, USSHO; *CQ*, 5/22/64, 987.

41. Rosenberg and Karabell, *Kennedy, Johnson, and the Quest for Justice*, 308.

42. *Newsweek*, 5/25/64.

43. *CQ*, 5/29/64, 1032, 6/5/64, 1077; *Time*, 6/5/64; Whalen and Whalen, *The Longest Debate*, 190.

44. HHH to file, 1964, HHH Vice-Presidential Papers, Civil and Human Rights, Box 821, MHS.

45. *CQ Almanac*, 1964, 366–67; HHH to file, 1964, HHH Vice-Presidential Papers, Civil and Human Rights, Box 821, MHS.

46. HHH to file, 1964, HHH Vice-Presidential Papers, Civil and Human Rights, Box 821, MHS.

47. Ibid.; *Newsweek*, 6/22/64; *NYT*, 6/11/64; Rosenberg and Karabell, *Kennedy, Johnson, and the Quest for Justice*, 315–17.

48. *CQ Almanac*, 1964, 367.

49. *CR*, 6/10/64, 13308.

50. Whalen and Whalen, *The Longest Debate*, 198; *CR*, 6/10/64, 13308–9.

51. *CR*, 6/10/64, 13310.

52. Whalen and Whalen, *The Longest Debate*, 198–99; MacNeil, *Dirksen*, 236; *CQ Almanac*, 1964, 367; *Time*, 6/19/64.

53. *NYT*, 6/11/64; *Time*, 6/19/64; *Newsweek*, 6/22/64; Whalen and Whalen, *The Longest Debate*, 199.

54. *NYT*, 6/11/64; *WP*, 6/11/64; *Life*, 6/19/64.

55. *Time*, 6/19/64.

56. *CQ*, 6/12/64, 1169.

57. *CR*, 6/10/64, 13329.

58. Humphrey, *The Education of a Public Man*, 211–12; *Life*, 9/27/68.

59. *Life*, 9/27/68.

60. *CQ Almanac*, 1964, 371–72.

61. Ibid., 377; *CQ*, 7/3/64, 1331.

62. Humphrey, *The Education of a Public Man*, 210–11; *CQ*, 6/19/64, 1206; Watson, *Lion in the Lobby*, 620.

63. *Newsweek*, 6/29/64; HHH to file, 1964, HHH Vice-Presidential Papers, Civil and Human Rights, Box 821, MHS; *The Reporter*, 7/16/64.

64. Mitchell OH, LBJL; Humphrey, *The Education of a Public Man*, 211.

65. *Reader's Digest*, 12/66; LBJ to RBR, 7/23/64, WHCF, EX HU 2, Box 3, LBJL.

66. *Newsweek*, 6/29/64; *Time*, 6/26/64; Califano, *The Triumph and Tragedy of Lyndon Johnson*, 55.

67. *NYT*, 6/11/64; Shuman OH, USSHO.

68. Johnson, *The Vantage Point*, 160.

69. Eugene Williams OH, LBJL; Johnson, *The Vantage Point*, 154–55.

16. DO YOU WANT TO BE VICE PRESIDENT?

1. LBJ-Smathers phone conversation, 11/23/63, Records of the JFK Assassination, Tapes and Transcripts of Telephone Conversations and Meetings, Box 85, National Archives.

2. Humphrey, *The Education of a Public Man*, 214.

3. Kampelman, *Entering New Worlds*, 150.

4. Humphrey, *The Education of a Public Man*, 218; Eisele, *Almost to the Presidency*, 200.

5. Humphrey, *The Education of a Public Man*, 221–22; Van Dyk OH, MHS; Eisele, *Almost to the Presidency*, 204.

6. Humphrey, *The Education of a Public Man*, 218–20; *Time*, 9/4/64; Van Dyk OH, MHS.

7. Humphrey, *The Education of a Public Man*, 221.

8. *Newsweek*, 9/7/64; Miller, *Lyndon*, 387.

9. O'Donnell OH, LBJL.

10. Humphrey, *The Education of a Public Man*, 222.

11. Miller, *Lyndon*, 392; Harvey, *Black Civil Rights During the Johnson Administration*, 23; Van Dyk OH, MHS; Eisele, *Almost to the Presidency*, 212.

12. Beschloss, *Taking Charge*, 515–16.

13. Humphrey, *The Education of a Public Man*, 222–23; Miller, *Lyndon*, 392–93; Eisele, *Almost to the Presidency*, 214.

14. Rauh OH, MSRC; *New Republic*, 7/4/64.

15. *Newsweek*, 9/7/64; White, *The Making of the President, 1964*, 342–43; Humphrey, *The Education of a Public Man*, 224–26; *Christian Science Monitor*, 8/28/64.

16. *CQ*, 8/28/64, 2014–15.

17. Humphrey, *The Education of a Public Man*, 229; Van Dyk OH, MHS; Van Dyk, author interview.

18. *Public Papers of the Presidents: Lyndon B. Johnson, 1963–1964*, 1285–86; Kotz, *Judgment Days*, 224.

19. Valenti, *A Very Human President*, 207.

20. Fite, *Richard B. Russell, Jr., Senator from Georgia*, 419.

21. RBR to Carter, 9/1/64, RBRL.

22. Fite, *Richard B. Russell, Jr., Senator from Georgia*, 420–21.

17. WE ARE DEMANDING THE BALLOT

1. *CQ*, 7/10/64, 1454–55, 7/24/64, 1545, 12/18/64, 2812; *CQ Almanac*, 1964, 378; *Business Week*, 7/11/64.

2. Pollak OH, LBJL; Katzenbach, author interview.

3. *CQ*, 3/26/65, 557.

4. Ibid.; Garrow, *Protest at Selma*, 20–21; Ashmore, *Civil Rights and Wrongs*, 172.

5. Kotz, *Judgment Days*, 244.

6. Miller, *Lyndon*, 371; Katzenbach, author interview.

7. *CQ Almanac*, 1965, 538.

8. Ibid.; Garrow, *Protest at Selma*, 34.

9. Fairclough, *To Redeem the Soul of America*, 229.

10. Garrow, *Protest at Selma*, 144.

11. Fairclough, *To Redeem the Soul of America*, 230–31; *Time*, 1/29/65, 2/19/65, 2/12/65.

12. *Newsweek*, 2/8/65; *Time*, 2/26/65.

13. *CQ Almanac*, 1965, 538; *CQ*, 2/19/65, 270.

14. Fairclough, *To Redeem the Soul of America*, 238–39; *Alabama Journal* cited in *Time*, 2/26/65.

15. *Time*, 3/19/65.

16. Ibid.

17. *Newsweek*, 3/22/65.

18. Ibid.

19. *Time*, 3/19/65.

20. Shaffer, *On and Off the Floor*, 98; *Newsweek*, 3/22/65.

21. Garrow, *Protest at Selma*, 85–87; *Newsweek*, 3/22/65; *Time*, 3/19/65.

22. *Time*, 3/19/65.

23. Beschloss, *Reaching for Glory*, 222–23.

24. Garrow, *Protest at Selma*, 89–93; Johnson, *The Vantage Point*, 162.

25. *NYT*, 1/5/65; Katzenbach to O'Brien, 1/11/65, Reports on Legislation, Box 8, LBJL.

26. Evans and Novak, *Lyndon B. Johnson*, 494; Goodwin, *Remembering America*, 320; Garrow, *Protest at Selma*, 90–94; Johnson, *The Vantage Point*, 161–62; Katzenbach, author interview.

27. Johnson, *The Vantage Point*, 162; Goodwin, *Remembering America*, 320.

28. Johnson, *The Vantage Point*, 162–63; Goodwin, *Remembering America*, 321–23.

29. *Time*, 3/19/65.

30. Johnson, *The Vantage Point*, 163.

18. WE SHALL OVERCOME

1. Valenti Notes, 3/14/65, CBS Interview, "The Last Interview," Box 2, LBJL; Johnson, *The Vantage Point*, 163–64; Goodwin, *Remembering America*, 324–25.

2. *Time*, 3/26/65; Johnson, *The Vantage Point*, 164.

3. *CQ*, 3/19/65, 434–35; Pollak OH, LBJL.

4. *Newsweek*, 3/29/65; Shaffer, *On and Off the Floor*, 100.

5. *CQ Almanac*, 1965, 1365–67; Johnson, *The Vantage Point*, 165–66.

6. *CQ Almanac*, 1965, 1365–67.

7. Goodwin, *Remembering America*, 334; Garrow, *Bearing the Cross*, 408; Kearns, *Lyndon Johnson and the American Dream*, 229; Califano, *The Triumph and Tragedy of Lyndon Johnson*, 56.

8. *CQ Almanac*, 1965, 1365–67.

9. *Newsweek*, 3/29/65.

10. *Time*, 3/26/65.

11. WHCF, Name Files, Box 344, "Richard Russell," LBJL; Fite, *Richard B. Russell, Jr., Senator from Georgia*, 426.

12. *Saturday Evening Post*, 3/13/65; *WSJ*, 8/6/65.

13. Evans and Novak, *Lyndon B. Johnson*, 497; Kearns, *Lyndon Johnson and the American Dream*, 230.

14. Jones to Marvin Watson, 3/17/65, LE HU 2-7, Executive, LBJL; *Newsweek*, 5/3/65; Miller, *Lyndon*, 434.

15. Katzenbach OH, LBJL.

16. *CR*, 3/18/65, 5390, 5388; *CQ*, 3/26/65, 558; Graham, *The Civil Rights Era*, 166.

17. *CQ*, 3/26/65, 556–57; Graham, *The Civil Rights Era*, 166.

18. *Time*, 4/2/65.

19. *CQ*, 4/16/65, 685–86.

20. MacNeil, *Dirksen*, 252–53.

21. Pollak OH, LBJL; Katzenbach, author interview; *CR*, 4/21/65, 8205.

22. Katzenbach to LBJ, 5/21/65, LE HU 2-7, LBJL.

23. *CR*, 4/30/65, 9072; *CQ*, 5/7/65, 857–59; MacNeil, *Dirksen*, 255.

24. *CQ*, 5/7/65, 857, 4/30/65, 824; Pollak OH, LBJL; *CR*, 4/30/65, 9077.

25. MacNeil, *Dirksen*, 255; Katzenbach to LBJ, 5/21/65, LE HU 2-7, LBJL; *Newsweek*, 5/10/65.

26. *CR*, 5/6/65, 9805.

27. Ibid., 5/3/65, 9242–43, 5/6/65, 9830–31.

28. Ibid., 5/10/65, 10034.

29. *CQ*, 5/14/65, 899–900, 5/21/65, 962–63; *CR*, 5/19/65, 11015.

30. *CQ*, 5/21/65, 963; *CR*, 5/19/65, 11018–19, 5/21/65, 11188.

31. *Time*, 6/4/65.

32. *CQ*, 5/28/65, 1007.

33. *NYT*, 7/13/65; *CQ*, 6/4/65, 1052, 6/11/65, 1123–24, 7/2/65, 1299, 7/9/65, 1324, 7/16/65, 1361.

34. *CQ Almanac*, 1965, 561; *NYT*, 7/13/65; *CQ*, 7/16/65, 1361.

35. Beschloss, *Reaching for Glory*, 387–88; Garrow, *Protest at Selma*, 130–32; *CQ Almanac*, 1965, 562–63; Graham, *The Civil Rights Era*, 173.

36. *CQ*, 8/6/65, 1539.

37. Califano, *The Triumph and Tragedy of Lyndon Johnson*, 57.

38. LBJ speech, 8/6/65, Reports on Enrolled Legislation (PL 89-110), Box 22, LBJL; *Newsweek*, 8/16/65.

19. DISILLUSIONMENT AND DEFEAT

1. *CQ Almanac*, 1965, 571.

2. Bennett, *Before the Mayflower*, 422.

3. *Newsweek*, 8/30/65.

4. Ibid.

5. McPherson to LBJ, 6/17/65, WHCF, HU 2, Box 3, LBJL; McPherson, *A Political Education*, 343.

6. Fairclough, *To Redeem the Soul of America*, 253.

7. McPherson OH, LBJL; *CQ Almanac*, 1966, 450–51.

8. Douglas, *In the Fullness of Time*, 577–94; *CQ Almanac*, 1966, 1394–95; *Newsday*, 11/4/94.

9. Celler OH, LBJL.

10. Miller, *Lyndon*, 408.

11. Garrow, *Protest at Selma*, 185, 187; *CQ Almanac*, 1965, 564–65.

12. Memorandum: Black Appointees of the Johnson Administration; CBS Interview, "The Last Interview," Box 2, LBJL.

13. Van Dyk, author interview.

14. Solberg, *Hubert Humphrey*, 267; Humphrey, *The Education of a Public Man*, 307; *CQ Almanac*, 1965, 565–66.

15. Maclear, *The Ten Thousand Day War*, 123; Van Dyk, author interview; Van Dyk OH, Connell OH, MHS; Solberg, *Hubert Humphrey*, 274.

16. Van Dyk, author interview; Califano, *The Triumph and Tragedy of Lyndon Johnson*, 65; Katzenbach, author interview.

17. Califano, *The Triumph and Tragedy of Lyndon Johnson*, 65–69; Eisele, *Almost to the Presidency*, 236; Katzenbach and Van Dyk, author interviews.

18. Reedy, author interview; Connell OH, LBJL; Solberg, *Hubert Humphrey*, 279; Van Dyk, author interview.

19. McPherson OH, Connell OH, LBJL; Heller OH, MHS.

20. Graham, *The Civil Rights Era*, 180–86.

21. Ibid., 189–90, 201–3.

22. Solberg, *Hubert Humphrey*, 285; Eisele, *Almost to the Presidency*, 240–44.

23. Eisele, *Almost to the Presidency*, 245; Solberg, *Hubert Humphrey*, 293.

24. Kearns, *Lyndon Johnson and the American Dream*, 251–52.

25. Chester, Hodgson, and Paige, *An American Melodrama*, 145–46.

26. Eisele, *Almost to the Presidency*, 334.

27. White, *The Making of the President, 1968*, 464, 468.

28. Berman OH, MHS.

29. *CQ Almanac*, 1968, 152–62.

30. Fite, *Richard B. Russell, Jr., Senator from Georgia*, 437; *Reader's Digest*, 12/66.

31. Fite, *Richard B. Russell, Jr., Senator from Georgia*, 441, 461; Green OH, RBRL; *Atlanta Journal and Constitution Magazine*, 6/30/68; Jones, author interview; Austin OH, Lady Bird Johnson OH, Ervin OH, RBRL.

32. Moore OH, RBRL.

33. Ibid.; Jones, author interview; RBR and Talmadge to LBJ, 2/13/68, Dictation Series I, RBRL.

34. Jacksonville *Times-Union*, 4/4/68; Fite, *Richard B. Russell, Jr., Senator from Georgia*, 477–78.

35. Temple OH, RBRL.

36. Russell to LBJ, 5/20/68, Southern District Judgeship, RBRL.

37. RBR to Griffin Bell, 6/7/68, 7/2/68, Dictation Series I, RBRL.

38. Russell to LBJ, 7/1/68, Office Files of Larry Temple, Box i, LBJL; Talmadge, author interview.

39. Temple OH, RBRL; RBR to LBJ, 9/26/68, Dictation Series I, RBRL.

40. Powell Moore OH, LBJL.

41. Fite, *Richard B. Russell, Jr., Senator from Georgia*, 481.

Bibliography

LIBRARIES AND MANUSCRIPT COLLECTIONS

Columbia University Oral History Collection, Manuscript Division, Library of Congress, Washington, D.C.

Hubert H. Humphrey Collection, Minnesota Historical Society, Saint Paul, Minnesota.

Hubert H. Humphrey Oral History Project, Minnesota Historical Society, Saint Paul, Minnesota.

LBJ Library Oral History Collection, Lyndon B. Johnson Library, Austin, Texas.

"The Modern Congress in American History," Oral History Collection, Association of Former Members of Congress, Manuscript Division, Library of Congress, Washington, D.C.

Oral History Interviews, Richard B. Russell Collection, Richard B. Russell Library for Political Research and Studies, University of Georgia, Athens.

Oral History Program, John F. Kennedy Library, Boston, Massachusetts.

Papers of Lyndon B. Johnson, LBJ Library, Austin, Texas.

Ralph J. Bunche Collection, Oral History Department, Moorland-Spingarn Research Center, Howard University, Washington, D.C.

Records of the JFK Assassination, Tapes and Transcripts of Telephone Conversations and Meetings, National Archives, Washington, D.C.

Richard B. Russell Collection, Richard B. Russell Library for Political Research and Studies, University of Georgia, Athens.

Senate Staff Oral History Program, Manuscript Division, Library of Congress, Washington, D.C.

INTERVIEWS, ORAL HISTORIES, AND CORRESPONDENCE

Alexander, Clifford, 11/1/71, LBJL.
Allen, Ivan, Jr., 5/15/69, LBJL; 2/17/71, RBRL.
Anderson, Clinton P., 4/14/67, MHS; 5/20/69, LBJL.
Anderson, Eugenic Moore, 7/14/78, MHS.
Attig, Francis J., 4/5/78, USSHO.

Auerbach, Carl, 7/13/78, 7/24/78, MHS.
Austin, John Rich, 4/14/71, RBRL.
Austin, Luke, 3/13/71, RBRL.
Backstrom, Charles, 7/21/78, MHS.
Barrow, Alien E., 6/11/72, LBJL.
Bates, William M., 2/25/71, RBRL.
Bennett, Wallace, 12/1/78, FMOC.
Bentley, James Lynwood, Jr., 2/18/71, RBRL.
Berman, Edgar, 8/31/78, MHS.
Bernard, Berl, 6/17/68, JFKL.
Berry, Levette J. "Joe," 12/10/85, LBJL.
Bible, Alan Harvey, 4/30/71, RBRL.
Biemiller, Andrew, 7/25/78, MHS.
Birdwell, W. Sherman, Jr., 10/20/70, LBJL.
Boggs, Hale, 5/10/64, JFKL; 3/13/69, 3/27/69, LBJL.
Boiling, Richard, 11/1/65, JFKL; 2/27/69, LBJL.
Branton, Wiley, 1/16/69, 10/20/69, MSRC.
Brooks, David William, 3/25/71, RBRL.
Brown, Ellen, 1/3/94, author interview.
Bryant, C. Farris, 3/5/71, LBJL.
Burns, James MacGregor, 5/14/65, JFKL.
Byrd, Robert, 4/29/71, RBRL.
Calhoun, Lawton Miller, 2/26/71, RBRL.
Caplan, Marvin, 11/14/67, MSRC.
Carlton, John Thomas, 3/5/71, RBRL.
Carter, Clifton C., 10/15/68, 10/30/68, LBJL.
Carter, Hodding, 11/8/68, LBJL.
Carter, James Earl, 2/22/71, RBRL.
Case, Clifford P., 3/1/79, LBJL.
Cater, Douglass, 4/29/69, 5/26/74, LBJL.
Celebrezze, Anthony J., 1/26/71, LBJL.
Celler, Emanuel, 3/16/69, LBJL; 4/11/72, JFKL;
      4/3/78, FMOC.
Church, Frank, 5/1/69, LBJL.
Clark, Joseph, 10/2/78, FMOC.
Clark, Ramsey, 4/16/69, LBJL.
Clements, Earle, 10/24/74, 12/6/77, LBJL.
Clifford, Clark, 3/17/69, 7/2/69, LBJL; 3/24/94, author interview.
Cocke, Earl Jr., 1/28/85, RBRL.
Cohen, Wilbur, 9/4/69, MSRC.
Collins, LeRoy, 12/15/72, LBJL.

Colmer, William M., 5/5/74, LBJL.

Connell, William, 3/18/85, LBJL; 2/15/78, MHS.

Cook, Donald C., 6/30/69, LBJL.

Cronin, John, 8/18/67, MSRC.

Darden, George W. "Buddy" III, 2/12/71, RBRL.

Darden, William H., 12/6/74, RBRL; LBJL.

Davis, James, 12/3/83, LBJL.

D'Ewart, Wesley, CUOHC.

Diggs, Charles, 3/13/69, LBJL.

Dirksen, Everett M., 5/8/68, 6/30/69, LBJL.

Douglas, Paul H., 6/6/64, JFKL; 11/1/74, LBJL.

Dunahoo, R. Mark, 2/19/71, RBRL.

Durr, Virginia, 3/1/75, LBJL.

Dwoskin, Harry, 3/26/71, RBRL.

Eastland, James O., 2/19/71, LBJL; 4/21/71, RBRL.

Ellender, Allen, 8/29/67, JFKL; 6/30/69, LBJL; 4/30/71, RBRL.

Ervin, Sam J., Jr., 4/28/71, RBRL.

Farmer, James, 10/69, LBJL.

Freeman, Orville, 2/14/69, LBJL; 1/16/78, MHS.

Fulbright, J. William, 4/19/71, RBRL; 3/5/79, FMOC; 6/19/89, author interview.

Gartner, David, 6/2/78, MHS.

Glickstein, Howard, 11/10/69, MSRC.

Goldsmith, John, 3/6/71, RBRL.

Goldstein, Abe, 2/17/71, RBRL.

Gomez, Millard, 4/23/71, RBRL.

Grayson, Spence Moore, 2/25/71, RBRL.

Green, Mary Willie Russell, 7/29/73, RBRL.

Hall, Walter, 6/30/69, LBJL.

Halleck, Charles, 9/19/68, LBJL.

Hartt, Julian, 7/7/78, MHS.

Hawkins, Augustus F., 2/28/69, MSRC.

Hays, Brooks, 10/5/71, LBJL.

Heller, Walter, 8/9/78, MHS.

Henry, Aaron, 9/12/70, LBJL.

Hesburgh, Theodore, 1971, JFKL; 2/1/71, LBJL; 3/2/95, author interview.

Hildenbrand, William F., 3/20/85, USSHO.

Hill, Lister, 2/1/71, LBJL.

Horwitz, Solis, 6/9/69, LBJL.

Howard, Francis Humphrey, 2/20/78, MHS.

Humphrey, Hubert H., III, 8/17/71, 6/20/77, 6/21/77, LBJL; 1978, MHS; 4/12/94,
    author interview.

Hyneman, Charles, 8/16/78, MHS.

Jackson, Henry, 3/13/78, LBJL.

Jenkins, Walter, 9/22/83, LBJL.

Johnson, Alfred T. "Boody," 11/27/79, LBJL.

Johnson, Lady Bird, 6/28/77, RBRL.

Johnson, Paul B., 9/8/70, LBJL.

Jones, Luther, 6/13/69, LBJL.

Jones, Proctor, 11/8/93, author interview.

Kampelman, Max, 1/1/78, MHS; 2/3/94, author interview.

Katzenbach, Nicholas, 11/16/64, JFKL; 11/12/68, LBJL; 3/29/95, author interview.

Keating, Kenneth, 2/2/68, CUOHC.

Kelley, Wayne P., Jr., 3/16/71, RBRL.

Kelly, Harry, 6/20/78, MHS.

Kennedy, Robert F., 12/4/64, 12/6/64, 12/22/64, JFKL.

King, Martin Luther, Jr., 3/9/64, JFKL.

Krock, Arthur, 11/21/69, LBJL.

Lawson, Belford V., 1/11/66, JFKL.

Leonard, Earl T., 2/15/71, RBRL.

Lewis, Anthony, 7/23/70, JFKL; 4/1/94, author interview.

Long, Russell B., 4/23/71, RBRL; 2/22/77, 6/26/78, LBJL; 2/2/91, 8/28/91, 11/6/94, author interviews; 3/8/93, correspondence with author.

McGee, Gale, 2/10/69, LBJL; 6/8/79, 6/11/79, 9/17/79, FMOC.

McGill, Ralph, 1/6/66, JFKL.

McGovern, George, 7/29/78, MHS.

McPherson, Harry, 7/26/78, MHS; 11/9/93, author interview.

Magnuson, Warren, 3/14/78, LBJL.

Manatos, Mike, 7/10/69, LBJL.

Mankiewicz, Frank, 4/18/69, LBJL.

Mansfield, Mike, 6/23/64, JFKL; 12/9/93, correspondence with author.

Marshall, Burke, 6/13/64, 6/20/64, 12/4/64, 12/6/64, 12/22/64, JFKL; 10/28/68, LBJL; 2/27/70, MSRC; 6/30/94, author interview.

Marshall, Thurgood, 7/10/69, LBJL.

Martin, Louis, 5/14/69, LBJL.

Martin, Ruby G., 2/24/69, LBJL.

Minow, Newton, 3/19/71, LBJL.

Mitau, G. Theodore, 8/22/78, MHS.

Mitchell, Clarence, 12/6/68, MSRC; 4/30/69, LBJL.

Monroney, A. S. "Mike," 3/20/69, LBJL.

Mooney, Booth, 4/8/69, 3/10/77, LBJL.

Moore, Powell, 3/6/71, RBRL; 1/23/76, LBJL.

Moss, Frank, 9/20/78, FMOC.

Mudd, Roger, 3/4/71, RBRL.

Mundt, Karl, 9/21/68, LBJL.

Muskie, Edmund, 8/4/78, MHS.

Nathan, Robert, 8/31/78, MHS.

Nixon, Richard, 4/13/78, RBRL.

O'Donnell, Kenneth, 7/23/69, LBJL.

Pearson, Drew, 4/10/69, LBJL.

Peterson, Patience Russell, 9/19/73, RBRL.

Pickle, J. J. "Jake," 3/2/72, LBJL.

Pollak, Stephen, 1/30/69, LBJL.

Proxmire, William, 2/4/86, LBJL.

Raesly, Barboura, 6/16/75, RBRL.

Rauh, Joseph, 1965, JFKL; 8/28/67, MSRC; 7/30/69, LBJL; 6/22/78, MHS.

Reedy, George, 12/12/68, 12/20/68, 2/14/72, 6/7/75, 6/21/77, 5/21/82, 6/2/82 letter to Gillette, 10/27/82, 5/23–5/24/83, 8/16–8/17/83, 12/20–12/21/83, 6/22/84, LBJL; 1/7/94, author interview; 2/11/95, 2/12/95, correspondence with author.

Riddick, Floyd, 3/5/71, RBRL; 6/26/78, 2/15/79, USSHO.

Rowe, James, 9/16/69, LBJL.

Russell, Fielding, 9/5/74, RBRL.

Russell, Henry Edward "Jeb," 6/21/74, RBRL.

Rustin, Bayard, 6/17/69, LBJL.

Ryan, Ed, 7/11/78, MHS.

Saltonstall, Leverett, 1976, FMOC.

Sanders, Harold Barefoot, 11/3/69, LBJL.

Shore, William, 6/27/78, MHS.

Shuman, Howard, 6/87–10/87, USSHO.

Sidey, Hugh, 4/7/64, JFKL; 4/7/64, LBJL.

Siegel, Gerald, 5/26/69, 2/11/77, 6/17/77, LBJL.

Smathers, George, 7/10/64, JFKL; 8/89–10/89, USSHO.

Sorensen, Theodore, 5/3/64, JFKL.

Spain, Jack Holland, 4/28/71, RBRL.

Sparkman, John J., 4/28/71, RBRL; 6/9/77, LBJL.

St. Claire, Darrell, 12/16/76, USSHO.

Stacy, Ina, 4/5/71, RBRL.

Stennis, John C., 4/21/71, RBRL; 6/17/72, LBJL.

Stewart, John, 6/21/78, MHS.

Talmadge, Herman E., 3/10/66, JFKL; 7/17/69, LBJL; 4/21/71, RBRL; 1/13/95, author interview.

Tames, George, 1/13/88, USSHO.

Taylor, Hobart, 2/1/69, LBJL.

Temple, Larry, 6/12/70, 8/7/70, 8/11/70, LBJL.

Thomas, Modine, 2/10/71, 9/3/80, RBRL.

Thornberry, Homer, 12/21/70, LBJL.

Thurmond, Strom, 5/7/79, LBJL; 4/27/71, RBRL; 8/10/89, author interview.

Troutman, Robert B., Jr., 3/4/71, RBRL.

Tully, Grace, 10/1/68, LBJL.

Udall, Morris, 2/22/73, MSRC.

Underwood, Norman, 2/12/71, RBRL.

Van Dyk, Frederick "Ted," 6/21/78, MHS; 3/29/95, author interview.

Vander Zee, Rein J., 1/28/92, USSHO.

Warren, Earl, Jr., 9/21/71, LBJL.

Waters, Herbert J., 3/31/78, MHS.

Weisl, Edwin, Jr., 10/30/68, LBJL.

White, William S., 3/5/69, 3/10/69, LBJL.

Wicker, Tom, 6/16/70, LBJL.

Wilkins, Roy, 1960, CUOHC; 8/13/64, JFKL; 4/1/69, LBJL.

Williams, Eugene and Helen, 10/27/74, LBJL.

Williams, John, 5/12/79, FMOC.

Wofford, Harris, 11/29/65, JFKL; 11/10/93, author interview.

Wolfinger, Ray, 4/25/95, author interview.

Wright, Zephyr, 12/5/74, LBJL.

Young, Milton, 4/23/71, RBRL.

Young, Whitney, Jr., 6/18/69, LBJL.

Zeidman, Philip, 7/25/78, MHS.

BOOKS AND OTHER PUBLICATIONS

Abernathy, Ralph David. *And The Walls Came Tumbling Down: An Autobiography.* New York: HarperPerennial, 1989.

Adams, Sherman. *Firsthand Report: The Story of the Eisenhower Administration.* New York: Harper, 1961.

Ambrose, Stephen E. *Eisenhower.* Vol. 2, *The President.* New York: Simon & Schuster, 1984.

Amrine, Michael. *This Is Humphrey: The Story of the Senator.* New York: Doubleday, 1960.

Anderson, Clinton. *Outsider in the Senate: Senator Clinton Anderson's Memoirs.* New York: World, 1970.

Anderson, J. W. *Eisenhower, Brownell, and the Congress: The Tangled Origins of the Civil Rights Bill of 1956–1957.* University, Ala.: University of Alabama Press, 1964.

Anderson, William. *The Wild Man from Sugar Creek: The Political Career of Eugene Talmadge*. Baton Rouge: Louisiana State University Press, 1975.

Ashmore, Harry. *Civil Rights and Wrongs: A Memoir of Race and Politics, 1944–1994*. New York: Pantheon, 1994.

Baker, Bobby. *Wheeling and Dealing: Confessions of a Capitol Hill Operator*. New York: W. W. Norton, 1978.

Barnett, Richard, and Joseph Garai. *Where the States Stand on Civil Rights*. New York: Bold Face Books, 1962.

Bartley, Numan V. *The Rise of Massive Resistance: Race and Politics in the South During the 1950's*. Baton Rouge: Louisiana State University Press, 1969.

Bartley, Numan V., and Hugh D. Graham. *Southern Politics and the Second Reconstruction*. Baltimore: Johns Hopkins University Press, 1975.

Bennett, Lerone, Jr. *Before the Mayflower: A History of Black America*. New York: Penguin, 1984.

Berman, Daniel M. *A Bill Becomes a Law: Congress Enacts Civil Rights Legislation*. New York: Macmillan, 1966.

———. *It Is So Ordered: The Supreme Court Rules on School Segregation*. New York: W. W. Norton, 1966.

Berman, Edgar. *Hubert: The Triumph and Tragedy of the Humphrey I Knew*. New York: Putnam, 1979.

Berman, William C. *The Politics of Civil Rights in the Truman Administration*. Columbus: Ohio State University Press, 1970.

Bernstein, Barton J., and Allan J. Matusow. *The Truman Administration: A Documentary History*. New York: Harper & Row, 1966.

Beschloss, Michael R. *Taking Charge: The Johnson White House Tapes, 1963–1964*. New York: Simon & Schuster, 1997.

———. *Reaching for Glory: Lyndon Johnson's Secret White House Tapes, 1964–1965*. New York: Simon & Schuster, 2001.

Bowles, Chester. *Promises to Keep: My Years in Public Life, 1941–1969*. New York: Harper & Row, 1971.

Branch, Taylor. *Parting the Waters: America in the King Years, 1954–63*. New York: Simon & Schuster, 1988.

———. *Pillar of Fire: America in the King Years, 1963–65*. New York: Simon & Schuster, 1998.

———. *At Canaan's Edge: America in the King Years, 1965–68*. New York: Simon & Schuster, 2006.

Brinkley, Douglas. *Dean Acheson: The Cold War Years, 1953–71*. New Haven: Yale University Press, 1992.

Brownell, Herbert. *Advising Ike: The Memoirs of Attorney General Herbert Brownell*. Lawrence, Kans.: University Press of Kansas, 1993.

Bryant, Nick. *The Bystander: John F. Kennedy and the Struggle for Black Equality*. New York: Basic Books, 2006.

Burk, Robert Fredrick. *The Eisenhower Administration and Black Civil Rights*. Knoxville: University of Tennessee Press, 1984.

Burns, James MacGregor. *John Kennedy: A Political Profile*. New York: Harcourt, Brace, 1960.

———. *The Crosswinds of Freedom*. New York: Knopf, 1989.

Byrd, Robert C., and Mary Sharon Hall. *The Senate, 1789–1989*. Vol. I, *A Chronological Series of Addresses on the History of the Senate*. Washington, D.C.: U.S. Government Printing Office, 1989.

Califano, Joseph A., Jr. *The Triumph and Tragedy of Lyndon Johnson: The White House Years*. New York: Simon & Schuster, 1991.

Caro, Robert A. *The Years of Lyndon Johnson*. Vol. 1, *The Path to Power*. New York: Knopf, 1982.

———. *The Years of Lyndon Johnson*. Vol. 2, *Means of Ascent*. New York: Knopf, 1990.

———. *The Years of Lyndon Johnson*. Vol. 3, *Master of the Senate*. New York: Knopf, 2002.

Carothers, Leslie A. *The Public Accommodations Law of 1964: Arguments, Issues and Attitudes in a Legal Debate*. Northampton, Mass.: Smith College, 1968.

Chandler, David Leon. *The Natural Superiority of Southern Politicians: A Revisionist History*. Garden City, N.Y.: Doubleday, 1977.

Chappell, David L. *Inside Agitators: White Southerners in the Civil Rights Movement*. Baltimore: Johns Hopkins University Press, 1994.

Chester, Lewis, Godfrey Hodgson, and Bruce Paige. *An American Melodrama: The Presidential Campaign of 1968*. New York: Viking, 1969.

Clark, Joseph S. *Congress: The Sapless Branch*. New York: Harper & Row, 1964.

Clifford, Clark. *Counsel to the President: A Memoir*. New York: Random House, 1991.

Cohen, Dan. *Undefeated: The Life of Hubert Humphrey*. Minneapolis: Lerner Publications, 1978.

Cohodas, Nadine. *Strom Thurmond and the Politics of Southern Change*. New York: Simon & Schuster, 1993.

Congress and the Nation, Vol. I. Washington, D.C.: Congressional Quarterly Service, 1965.

Connally, John. *In History's Shadow: An American Odyssey*. New York: Hyperion, 1993.

Conway, Alan. *The Reconstruction of Georgia*. Minneapolis: University of Minnesota Press, 1966.

Cooper, William J., and Thomas E. Terrill. *The American South: A History*. New York: Knopf, 1990.

Cotton, Norris. *In the Senate: Amidst the Conflict and the Turmoil.* New York: Dodd, Mead & Co., 1978.

Crowe, Chris. *Getting Away with Murder: The True Story of the Emmett Till Case.* New York: Phyllis Fogelman Books, 2003.

Dabney, Dick. *A Good Man: The Life of Sam J. Ervin.* Boston: Houghton Mifflin, 1976.

Dallek, Robert. *Lone Star Rising: Lyndon Johnson and His Times, 1908–1960.* New York: Oxford, 1991.

———. *Flawed Giant: Lyndon Johnson and His Times, 1961–1973.* New York: Oxford, 1998.

———. *An Unfinished Life: John F. Kennedy, 1917–1963.* Boston: Little, Brown, 2003.

Douglas, Paul H. *In the Fullness of Time: The Memoirs of Paul H. Douglas.* New York: Harcourt Brace Jovanovich, 1972.

Dugger, Ronnie. *The Politician: The Life and Times of Lyndon Johnson—The Drive for Power, from the Frontier to Master of the Senate.* New York: Norton, 1982.

Dulles, Foster Rhea. *The Civil Rights Commission, 1957–1965.* East Lansing: Michigan State University Press, 1968.

Duram, James C. *A Moderate Among Extremists: Dwight D. Eisenhower and the School Desegregation Crisis.* Chicago: Nelson-Hall, 1981.

Eisele, Albert. *Almost to the Presidency: A Biography of Two American Politicians.* Blue Earth, Minn.: Piper, 1972.

Eisenhower, Dwight D. *Waging Peace, 1956–1961: The White House Years.* Garden City, N.Y.: Doubleday, 1965.

Engelmayer, Sheldon D., and Robert J. Wagman. *Hubert Humphrey: The Man and His Dream.* New York: Methuen, 1978.

Ervin, Sam J., Jr. *Preserving the Constitution: The Autobiography of Senator Sam J. Ervin, Jr.* Charlottesville: Michie Co., 1984.

Evans, Rowland, and Robert Novak. *Lyndon B. Johnson: The Exercise of Power.* New York: New American Library, 1966.

Face the Nation: The Collected Transcripts from the CBS Radio and Television Broadcasts. New York: Holt Information Systems, 1972.

Fairclough, Adam. *To Redeem the Soul of America: The Southern Christian Leadership Conference and Martin Luther King, Jr.* Athens: University of Georgia Press, 1987.

Findlay, James F., Jr. *Church People in the Struggle: The National Council of Churches and the Black Freedom Movement, 1950–1970.* New York: Oxford, 1993.

Fite, Gilbert C. *Richard B. Russell, Jr., Senator from Georgia.* Chapel Hill: University of North Carolina Press, 1991.

Fleming, Daniel B., Jr. *Kennedy vs. Humphrey, West Virginia, 1960: The Pivotal Battle for the Democratic Presidential Nomination.* Jefferson, N.C.: McFarland, 1992.

Foley, Michael. *The New Senate: Liberal Influence on a Conservative Institution, 1959–1972*. New Haven: Yale University Press, 1980.

Friedman, Leon. *Southern Justice*. New York: Pantheon, 1965.

Garrow, David J. *Protest at Selma: Martin Luther King, Jr., and the Voting Rights Act of 1965*. New Haven: Yale University Press, 1978.

———. *Bearing the Cross: Martin Luther King, Jr., and the Southern Christian Leadership Conference*. New York: Vintage, 1988.

Goldman, Roger, with David Gallen. *Thurgood Marshall: Justice for All*. New York: Carroll & Graf, 1992.

Goldsmith, John A. *Colleagues: Richard B. Russell and His Apprentice, Lyndon B. Johnson*. Washington, D.C.: Seven Locks Press, 1993.

Goodwin, Richard N. *Remembering America: A Voice from the Sixties*. New York: Harper & Row, 1988.

Gore, Albert. *Let the Glory Out: My South and Its Politics*. New York: Viking, 1972.

Gould, Lewis L. *The Most Exclusive Club: A History of the Modern United States Senate*. New York: Basic Books, 2005.

Graham, Hugh Davis. *The Civil Rights Era: Origins and Development of National Policy, 1960–1972*. New York: Oxford, 1990.

Greene, John Robert. *The Crusade: The Presidential Election of 1952*. Lanham, Md.: University Press of America, 1985.

Griffith, Winthrop. *Humphrey: A Candid Biography*. New York: Morrow, 1965.

Grofman, Bernard, ed. *Legacies of the 1964 Civil Rights Act*. Charlottesville: University of Virginia Press, 2000.

Halberstam, David. *The Fifties*. New York: Villard, 1993.

Harris, Fred R. *Deadlock or Decision: The U.S. Senate and the Rise of National Politics*. New York: Oxford University Press, 1993.

Harvey, James C. *Civil Rights During the Kennedy Administration*. Hattiesburg: University and College Press of Mississippi, 1971.

———. *Black Civil Rights During the Johnson Administration*. Jackson: University and College Press of Mississippi, 1973.

Hesburgh, Theodore M. *God, Country, Notre Dame*. New York: Doubleday, 1990.

Humphrey, Hubert H. *The Education of a Public Man: My Life and Politics*. Minneapolis: University of Minnesota Press, 1991.

Javits, Jacob K. *Javits: The Autobiography of a Public Man*. Boston: Houghton Mifflin, 1981.

Johnson, Lyndon. *The Vantage Point: Perspectives of the Presidency, 1963–1969*. New York: Holt, Rinehart & Winston, 1971.

Johnson, Sam Houston. *My Brother Lyndon*. New York: Cowles, 1969.

Kampelman, Max M. *Entering New Worlds: The Memoirs of a Private Man in Public Life*. New York: HarperCollins, 1991.

Kearns, Doris. *Lyndon Johnson and the American Dream*. New York: Harper & Row, 1976.

Kennedy, Stetson. *Jim Crow Guide: The Way It Was*. Boca Raton: Florida Atlantic University Press, 1990.

Kotz, Nick. *Judgment Days: Lyndon Baines Johnson, Martin Luther King, Jr., and the Laws That Changed America*. Boston: Houghton Mifflin, 2005.

Loevy, Robert D. *To End All Segregation: The Politics of the Passage of the Civil Rights Act of 1964*. Lanham, Md.: University Press of America, 1990.

Lord, Walter. *The Past That Would Not Die*. London: Hamish Hamilton, 1966.

Maclear, Michael. *The Ten Thousand Day War: Vietnam, 1945–1975*. New York: St. Martin's, 1981.

MacNeil, Neil. *Dirksen: Portrait of a Public Man*. New York: World, 1970.

McCullough, David. *Truman*. New York: Simon & Schuster, 1992.

McPherson, Harry. *A Political Education: A Journal of Life with Senators, Generals, Cabinet Members and Presidents*. Boston: Little, Brown, 1972.

Mann, Robert. *Legacy to Power: Senator Russell Long of Louisiana*. New York: Paragon House, 1992.

————. *The Walls of Jericho: Lyndon Johnson, Hubert Humphrey, Richard Russell, and the Struggle for Civil Rights*. New York: Harcourt Brace, 1996.

Martin, Harold H. *Georgia: A Bicentennial History*. New York: Norton, 1977.

Matthews, Donald R. *U.S. Senators and Their World*. New York: Vintage, 1960.

Matthews, Donald R., and James W. Prothro. *Negroes and the New Southern Politics*. New York: Harcourt, Brace & World, 1966.

Matusow, Allen J. *The Unraveling of America: A History of Liberalism in the 1960s*. New York: Harper & Row, 1984.

Miller, Merle. *Lyndon: An Oral Biography*. New York: Putnam, 1980.

Mooney, Booth. *LBJ: An Irreverent Chronicle*. New York: Thomas Y. Crowell Co., 1976.

Morison, Samuel Eliot. *The Oxford History of the American People*. New York: Mentor, 1972.

Myrdal, Gunnar. *An American Dilemma: The Negro Problem and Modern Democracy*. New York: Harper, 1944.

Nearing, Scott. *Black America*. New York: Vanguard, 1929.

Nevins, Allan, and Henry Steele Commager. *A Pocket History of the United States*. New York: Washington Square, 1986.

Nolen, Claude H. *The Negro's Image in the South: The Anatomy of White Supremacy*. Lexington: University of Kentucky Press, 1967.

O'Donnell, Kenneth P., and David F. Powers, with Joe McCarthy. *"Johnny, We Hardly Knew Ye": Memories of John Fitzgerald Kennedy*. Boston: Little, Brown, 1972.

O'Neill, William L. *American High: The Years of Confidence, 1945–1960.* New York: Free Press, 1989.

Origins and Development of Congress. Washington, D.C.: Congressional Quarterly, 1976.

Parmet, Herbert S. *JFK: The Presidency of John F. Kennedy.* New York: Dial, 1983.

Pollack, Jack Harrison. *Earl Warren: The Judge Who Changed America.* Englewood Cliffs, N.J.: Prentice-Hall, 1979.

Potter, David M. *The South and the Concurrent Majority.* Baton Rouge: Louisiana State University Press, 1972.

Public Papers of the Presidents of the United States: Dwight D. Eisenhower, 1953–1960. Washington, D.C.: U.S. Government Printing Office, 1954–61.

Public Papers of the Presidents of the United States: John F. Kennedy, 1961–1963. 3 vols. Washington, D.C.: U.S. Government Printing Office, 1962–64.

Public Papers of the Presidents of the United States: Lyndon B. Johnson, 1963–1970. 12 vols. Washington, D.C.: U.S. Government Printing Office, 1965–70.

Reedy, George E. *Lyndon B. Johnson: A Memoir.* New York: Andrews and McMeel, 1982.

———. *The U.S. Senate: Paralysis or a Search for Consensus?* New York: Crown, 1986.

Reeves, Richard. *President Kennedy: Profile of Power.* New York: Simon & Schuster, 1993.

Ripley, Randall B. *Power in the Senate.* New York: St. Martin's, 1969.

Rosenberg, Jonathan, and Zachary Karabell. *Kennedy, Johnson, and the Quest for Justice: The Civil Rights Tapes.* New York: W.W. Norton, 2003.

Ross, Irwin. *The Loneliest Campaign: The Truman Victory of 1948.* New York: New American Library, 1968.

Rowan, Carl T. *Breaking Barriers: A Memoir.* New York: HarperPerennial, 1991.

Ryskind, Allan H. *Hubert: An Unauthorized Biography of the Vice President.* New Rochelle, N.Y.: Arlington House, 1968.

Safire, William. *Safire's Political Dictionary.* New York: Random House, 1978.

Schlesinger, Arthur M., Jr. *A Thousand Days: John F. Kennedy in the White House.* Boston: Houghton Mifflin, 1965.

———. *Robert Kennedy and His Times.* Boston: Houghton Mifflin, 1978.

Shaffer, Samuel. *On and Off the Floor: Thirty Years as a Correspondent on Capitol Hill.* New York: Newsweek Books, 1980.

Simon, Rita James. *Public Opinion in America, 1936–1970.* Chicago: Rand McNally, 1974.

Solberg, Carl. *Hubert Humphrey: A Biography.* New York: W. W. Norton, 1984.

Sorensen, Theodore C. *Kennedy.* New York: Harper & Row, 1965.

Sprigle, Ray. *In the Land of Jim Crow.* New York: Simon & Schuster, 1949.

Stern, Mark. *Calculating Visions: Kennedy, Johnson, and Civil Rights.* New Brunswick, N.J.: Rutgers University Press, 1992.

Strober, Gerald S., and Deborah H. Strober. *"Let Us Begin Anew": An Oral History of the Kennedy Presidency.* New York: HarperCollins, 1993.

Talmadge, Herman E. *Talmadge: A Political Legacy, A Politician's Life.* Atlanta: Peachtree, 1987.

Till-Mobley, Mamie. *Death of Innocence: The Story of the Hate Crime That Changed America.* New York: Random House, 2003.

Understanding Congress: Research Perspectives (Papers and Commentary from "Understanding Congress: A Bicentennial Research Conference," February 9–10, 1989, Washington, D.C.). Washington, D.C.: U.S. Government Printing Office, 1991.

U.S. Commission on Civil Rights. *With Liberty and Justice for All: An Abridgement of the Report of the United States Commission on Civil Rights, 1959.* Washington, D.C.: U.S. Government Printing Office, 1959.

Valenti, Jack. *A Very Human President.* New York: W. W. Norton, 1976.

Viorst, Milton. *Fire in the Streets: America in the 1960s.* New York: Simon & Schuster, 1979.

Warren, Earl. *The Memoirs of Earl Warren.* New York: Doubleday, 1977.

Watson, Denton L. *Lion in the Lobby: Clarence Mitchell, Jr.'s Struggle for the Passage of Civil Rights Laws.* New York: Morrow, 1990.

Whalen, Charles, and Barbara Whalen. *The Longest Debate: A Legislative History of the 1964 Civil Rights Act.* Cabin John, Md.: Seven Locks Press, 1985.

White, Theodore H. *The Making of the President, 1960.* New York: Atheneum, 1961.

———. *The Making of the President, 1964.* New York: Atheneum, 1965.

———. *The Making of the President, 1968.* New York: Atheneum, 1969.

White, William S. *Citadel: The Story of the U.S. Senate.* New York: Harper & Brothers, 1957.

———. *The Professional: Lyndon B. Johnson.* Boston: Houghton Mifflin, 1964.

Whitfield, Stephen J. *A Death in the Delta: The Story of Emmett Till.* Baltimore: Johns Hopkins University Press, 1991.

Wicker, Tom. *JFK and LBJ: The Influence of Personality upon Politics.* New York: Morrow, 1968.

Wilson, Woodrow. *Congressional Government: A Study in American Politics.* Cleveland: World, 1956.

Wofford, Harris. *Of Kennedys and Kings: Making Sense of the Sixties.* New York: Farrar, Straus & Giroux, 1980.

Woodward, C. Vann. *The Strange Career of Jim Crow.* New York: Oxford, 1974.

SELECTED ARTICLES

"About That 'Political Revolt' in the South." *U.S. News & World Report,* 9/27/57, 69–70.

"Ahead of the Wind." *Time*, 11/17/58, 21–22.

"All Over? Or Just Starting?" *Time*, 9/4/64, 19-A.

"An American Tragedy." *Newsweek*, 3/22/65, 18–23.

"Another Tragic Era?" *U.S. News & World Report*, 10/4/57, 33–36, 42, 48, 50–51, 64.

"As the Senate Voted." *New Republic*, 6/20/64, 6.

"At Last, a Vote." *Time*, 5/15/64, 32.

Baker, Russell. "Humphrey: Thunder! . . . Lightning?" *NYT Magazine*, 1/11/59, 12, 34, 36, 39, 42.

———. "Master of 'The Art of the Possible.'" *NYT Magazine*, 12/1/63, 26, 130–33.

"A Barrier Falls: The U.S. Negro Moves to Vote." *Newsweek*, 8/16/65, 15–16.

Bennett, Lerone, Jr. "What Negroes Can Expect from President Lyndon Johnson." *Ebony*, 1/64, 81–83, 86–88.

Bickel, Alexander M. "After a Civil Rights Act." *New Republic*, 5/9/64, 11–15.

———. "The Voting Rights Bill Is Tough." *New Republic*, 4/3/65, 16–18.

———. "Amending the Voting Rights Bill." *New Republic*, 5/1/65, 10–11.

"Big Guns of Southern Revolt: Strategist Byrnes, Organizer Byrd, Canny Russell, Careful George." *U.S News & World Report*, 11/16/51, 46–49.

"The Bill as Amended." *New Republic*, 6/20/64, 5.

Boney, F. N. "'The Senator's Senator': Richard Brevard Russell, Jr., of Georgia." *Georgia Historical Quarterly* (Fall 1987), 477–90.

Briggs, Robert L. "A Man with Southern Connections." *New Republic*, 11/14/55, 8–9.

Busch, N. F. "Senator Russell of Georgia." *Reader's Digest*, 12/66, 150–52.

Cater, Douglass. "How the Senate Passed the Civil Rights Bill." *The Reporter*, 9/5/57, 9–13.

———. "What Makes Humphrey Run." *The Reporter*, 3/5/59, 15–20.

"The Central Point." *Time*, 3/19/65, 23–28.

"Challenge from the South." *Time*, 3/10/52, 23–24.

"Civil Rights—Backstage Drama." *Newsweek*, 8/12/57, 25–26.

"Civil Rights—Best Chance?" *Newsweek*. 7/15/57, 23–24.

"Civil Rights: Can They Satisfy Ike?" *Newsweek*, 8/19/57, 23–24.

"Civil Rights—Civil Strife?" *Newsweek*, 9/2/57, 17–19.

"Civil Rights. Now—Or Never." *Newsweek*, 8/5/57, 24–25.

"Civil Rights: Shape of Compromise." *Newsweek*, 7/29/57, 23–24.

"Civil Rights: That New Feeling." *Newsweek*, 6/1/64, 19.

"Civil Rights Bill: 'It Will Not Be Denied.'" *Newsweek*, 6/29/64, 17–18.

Clark, Joseph S. "With All Deliberate Delay: Some Thoughts on Streamlining the Senate." *New Republic*, 4/18/64, 13–15.

"Clerical Lobbyists." *America*, 5/9/64, 624.

"Close to Kingship." *Time*, 5/29/64, 22–23.

Coffin, Tris. "How Lyndon Johnson Engineered Compromise on Civil Rights Bill." *New Leader,* 8/5/57, 3–4.

Collins, Frederic W. "Senator Russell in the Last Ditch." *NYT Magazine,* 10/20/63, 16.

"Commander of the Filibuster." *U.S. News & World Report,* 3/14/60, 25.

Conn, Harry. "How Right Is Russell?" *New Republic,* 5/12/52, 9–11.

"The Controversy over Federal Civil Rights Legislation." *Congressional Digest,* 4/8/57, 99–128.

"Crack in Dike—Ike?" *Newsweek,* 5/12/52, 28–29.

"Cracking the Whip for Civil Rights." *Newsweek,* 4/13/64, 26–28, 31–32.

Crawford, Kenneth. "Second Appomattox." *Newsweek,* 5/3/65, 35.

"Crisis in Civil Rights." *Time,* 6/2/61, 14–18.

"Curtain Goes Up on Another North vs. South Debate." *U.S. News & World Report,* 7/26/57, 96–106.

"Days of Violence in the South." *Newsweek,* 5/29/61, 21–23.

"Debate in the Senate: A Meeting in Birmingham." *Time,* 4/10/64, 21–22.

"Debate on the Doctrine." *Time,* 3/11/57, 15–16.

"Dirksen Amendments." *New Republic,* 6/6/64, 3–4.

Drew, Elizabeth Brenner. "The Politics of Cloture." *New Republic,* 7/16/64, 19–23.

"The Edge of Violence." *Time,* 10/5/62, 15–17.

"Education of a Senator." *Time,* 1/17/49, 13–16.

"Electric Charges." *Time,* 3/26/65, 19–23.

"Everybody's Getting Fat." *Time,* 5/18/62, 16.

"Ev's Law." *Time,* 5/22/64, 23.

"Explosion in Alabama." *Newsweek,* 5/20/63, 25–27.

"The Final Vote." Time, 6/26/64, 17–18.

"Firebrand Senator Cools Down." *Business Week,* 6/1/63, 29–30.

"Freedom—Now." *Time,* 5/17/63, 23–25.

"'Freedom Riders' Force a Test." *Newsweek,* 6/5/61, 18–23.

"The Great Issue." *Newsweek,* 9/16/57, 33–36.

Greenfield, Meg. "The Man Who Leads the Southern Senators." *Reporter,* 5/21/64, 17–21.

"The Historic Vote: 71 to 29." *Newsweek,* 6/22/64, 25–26.

"How Senate Dean Judges Six Presidents." *U.S. News & World Report,* 2/23/70, 18.

"How the Rights Vote Was Engineered." *New Republic,* 2/29/64, 17–19.

"If a Filibuster Comes, Russell Will Be the Manager." *U.S. News & World Report,* 7/1/63, 18.

Jarman, Rufus. "The Senate's Gabbiest Freshman." *Saturday Evening Post,* 10/1/49, 30, 120–22.

"Kefauver Keeps Rolling." *Newsweek,* 5/19/52, 28.

"Kefauver's Stake." *Newsweek,* 5/5/52, 25–26.

Kempton, Murray. "Dirksen Delivers the Souls." *New Republic,* 4/2/64, 9–11.

———. "Mr. Humphrey's Conquering Hosts." *New Republic,* 4/4/64, 6–8.

Kiker, Douglas. "Russell of Georgia: The Old Guard at Its Shrewdest." *Harper's Magazine,* 9/66, 101–104.

Kopkind, Andrew. "Birth of a Bill: The Labored Progress of Voting Rights." *New Republic,* 5/15/65, 11–13.

"LBJ—Half the Way." *New Republic,* 7/25/60, 5.

"LBJ: 'I Ask for a Mandate to Begin.'" *Newsweek,* 9/7/64, 16–22.

Leuchtenburg, William E. "The Old Cowhand from Dixie." *Atlantic Monthly,* 12/92, 92–97, 100.

Lindley, Ernest K. "Statesmanlike." *Newsweek,* 8/12/57, 35.

Lisagor, Peter. "Ask Not 'What Became of Hubert Humphrey?'" *NYT Magazine,* 7/25/65, 6–7, 42–47.

Lloyd, David Demarest. "Figuring the Early Odds on the Democratic Candidates." *The Reporter,* 1/23/58, 24–29.

Manfred, Frederick. "Hubert Horatio Humphrey: A Memoir." *Minnesota History* (Fall 1978), 87–101.

"A Man Who Takes His Time." *Time,* 4/25/60, 20–24.

Martin, Harold H. "The Man Behind the Brass." *Saturday Evening Post,* 6/2/51, 22–23, 42, 45, 47.

"The Minuet." *Newsweek,* 6/15/64, 30, 35.

"Mississippi: The Sound and the Fury." *Newsweek,* 10/15/62, 23–29.

"Mississippi versus the United States." *Newsweek,* 10/8/62, 32–37.

Oberdorfer, Don. "Filibuster's Best Friend." *Saturday Evening Post,* 3/13/65, 90.

"One-Man Show." *Time,* 1/19/59, 15–16.

Peterson, Evelyn. "Sen. Humphrey Goes to Washington." *Pathfinder,* 1/26/49, 28–31.

"Political Leaders and Editors Size Up the Little Rock Crisis." *U.S. News & World Report,* 10/4/57, 58–61.

"Politics—The Impact: Losses, Gains, Outlook." *Newsweek,* 10/7/57, 28–29.

"Protest on Route 80." *Time,* 4/2/65, 21–22.

"Pulling Lightning." *Newsweek,* 5/25/64, 33.

"Quizzing Russell." *U.S. News & World Report,* 6/13/52, 54–62.

"Rearguard Commander." *Time,* 7/22/57, 12.

"Richard Russell, RIP." *National Review,* 2/9/71, 129.

"A Round for the South." *Time,* 7/22/57, 12–13.

Rovere, Richard H. "Letter from Washington." *New Yorker,* 8/31/57, 72–82.

"Russell Defends Filibuster." *NYT Magazine,* 3/15/64, 20.

"Russell Sounds Call for Civil-Rights Fight." *U.S. News & World Report,* 2/3/64, 8.

"A Salable Piece of Work." *Time,* 6/5/64, 22.

"Senator Russell of Georgia: Does He Speak for the South?" *Newsweek*, 8/19/63, 20–24.

"Shades of Bull Connor." *Newsweek*, 2/1/65, 21–22.

Shaffer, Samuel. "Hubert Humphrey Comes on Strong." *NYT Magazine*, 8/25/63, 11, 62–63.

Shannon, William V. "Why Humphrey Gets Taken for Granted." *New Republic*, 7/4/64, 10–12.

"The Shocking Story of Approved Killing in Mississippi." *Look*, 1/24/56.

Shore, William B. "One City's Struggle Against Intolerance." *The Progressive*, 1/49, 24–26.

"South in the Saddle." *Newsweek*, 3/10/52, 27–28.

"Southern Negroes & The Vote: The Blot Is Shrinking, But It Is Still Ugly." *Time*, 7/29/57, 12.

"The South Knows Better." *The Nation*, 7/20/57, 21–22.

"The South States Its Case." *U.S. News & World Report*, 6/24/63, 78–80.

"The Starry Heavens—The Moral Issue." *Newsweek*, 3/29/65, 19–22.

Stern, Mark. "Lyndon Johnson and Richard Russell: Institutions, Ambitions and Civil Rights." *Presidential Studies Quarterly* (Fall 1991), 687–704.

"Surprising Defeat." *Time*, 8/12/57, 11–16.

"Though the Heavens Fall." *Time*, 10/12/62, 19–22.

"Truman's Won't-Run Bombshell Sets Off Democratic Campaign." *Newsweek*, 4/7/52, 29–31.

"Veteran Spokesman for the Old South." *Business Week*, 4/18/64, 28–29.

"Vicious Stuff." *Time*, 7/29/57, 13.

"Victory in Jail." *Time*, 2/12/65, 16–17.

"Warm-up for the Fight Against Civil-Rights Bill." *U.S. News & World Report*, 7/12/57, 70–75.

"When Is a Majority a Majority?" *Time*, 3/20/64, 22–26.

White, William S. "The 'Club' That Is the U.S. Senate." *NYT Magazine*, 11/7/54, 9, 30, 32–34.

———. "The Southern Democrat Now Takes Over." *NYT Magazine*, 1/9/55, 9, 34, 37–38.

———. "Democrats' Board of Directors." *NYT Magazine*, 7/10/55, 10–11.

"Why the South Took Rights Law Quietly." *Business Week*, 7/11/64, 28.

Wicker, Tom. "L.B.J. in Search of His New Frontier." *NYT Magazine*, 3/19/61, 29, 123–24.

———. "Winds of Change in the Senate." *NYT Magazine*, 9/12/65, 52–53, 119–20, 122, 124.

Wieck, Paul R. "Dirksen's Double Play." *New Republic*, 4/17/65, 13–14.

"Will South End Negro Schools?" *U.S. News & World Report*, 5/28/54, 21–25.

Index